THE WORDS OF WATTS

21-Year-Old Participant in the Riot:

"In California they tells you, 'Nigger, keep your place!'
And you say: 'What you say, white man?' And they say:
'You living in the land of opportunity . . .'"

T.V. Cameraman at Scene of Rioting:

"Hey, kid! Throw a rock! Throw one! I haven't seen
you do anything yet!"

Los Angeles Police Officer:

"I've been waiting all my life for something like this to
happen! I'm gonna make mincemeat out of some of those
mother——— while I've got the chance!"

Chief Parker, L. A. Police Department:

"Los Angeles is quiet as far as racial problems are
concerned."

—from RIVERS OF BLOOD,
YEARS OF DARKNESS

"THIS IS THE HATE
THAT HATE PRODUCED, WHITE MAN."

The 1965 Los Angeles riot, one of the most brutal and terrifying episodes in American history, is considered by many to be a turning point in race relations in the United States.

How did it begin, and why? What really happened? How will it affect America's future?

Based on more than a thousand interviews and discussions with participants; first-hand observations; and examinations of documents, records and reports (many previously unavailable to the public)—here is the complete story of an explosion of hatred that shocked the nation and the world.

RIVERS OF BLOOD,
YEARS OF DARKNESS

"A GREAT BOOK. I learned more about America and Americans—and indeed about myself—from this book than anything I have read in a long time. Including William Manchester."

—John Mack Carter, Editor,
Ladies Home Journal

RIVERS OF BLOOD, YEARS OF DARKNESS

BY ROBERT CONOT

BANTAM BOOKS · TORONTO · NEW YORK · LONDON

33461

RIVERS OF BLOOD, YEARS OF DARKNESS
A Bantam Book / published August 1967
2nd printing.................August 1967
3rd printing.................August 1967
4th printing
5th printing
6th printing
7th printing

Library of Congress Catalog Card Number: 67–23524

Published simultaneously in the United States and Canada

Bantam Books are published by Bantam Books, Inc., a subsidiary
of Grosset & Dunlap, Inc. Its trade-mark, consisting of the words
"Bantam Books" and the portrayal of a bantam, is registered in the
United States Patent Office and in other countries. Marca Registrada.
Bantam Books, Inc., 271 Madison Avenue, New York, N.Y. 10016.

PRINTED IN THE UNITED STATES OF AMERICA

"It is simple to follow the easy and familiar path of personal ambition and private gain. . . . It is easier to fall in step with the slogans of others than to march to the beat of an internal drummer—to make and stand on judgments of your own. And it is far easier to accept and stand on the past, than to fight for the answers of the future.

"Jefferson Davis once came to Boston and addressed his audience in Faneuil Hall as 'Countrymen, brethren, Democrats.' Rivers of blood and years of darkness divide that day from this. But those words echo down to this hall bringing the lesson that only as countrymen and brothers can we hope to master and subdue to the service of mankind the enormous forces which rage across the world we live in. And only in this way can we pursue our personal talents to the limits of our possibility—not as Northerners or Southerners, black or white—but as men and women in the service of the American dream."

SENATOR ROBERT F. KENNEDY
University of Mississippi
March 18, 1966

Contents

III—THE LEGACY

IV—THE BLACK PRINT OF THE NEGRO

Introduction

Had the Los Angeles riot of August, 1965, been an isolated phenomenon, it would merit only passing interest. But it is probable that future historians will regard it as significant a turning point in Negro-white relations in the United States as John Brown's raid on Harpers Ferry was in the drive against slavery.

Just as Brown's raid polarized opposing forces in the slavery struggle, the Los Angeles riot symbolized the end of the era of Negro passivity—passivity that took the form of the doctrine of nonviolence, and the acceptance of white leadership in the civil rights struggle. In Los Angeles the Negro was going on record that he would no longer turn the other cheek. That, frustrated and goaded, he would strike back, whether the response of violence was an appropriate one or no.

The Los Angeles riot placed on record that the Negro has become a power in the cities. A power that civil authorities do not have the strength to cope with when it is turned against them. A power that, by 1980, will be able to control many of the major cities of the nation.

The Los Angeles riot brought into focus the massive pattern of segregation in urban areas—a segregation so vast it dwarfs that of the South. Whereas contacts between Southern whites and Negroes were governed by the rituals of caste, the economic and population structures of the South were such as to make contact continuous and inevitable, thus furnishing areas of communication. The Negro ghettos, however, are so large that they have become cities within cities, where the races never meet. It is impossible for the white person to understand the sense of isolation the residents of the ghettos have unless he himself goes into them. Within their boundaries, he will feel himself as foreign as if he had ventured to Haiti. That this is a significant factor in the outbursts of violence is highly probable. The most residentially segregated cities of the nation are Los Angeles, Cleveland, and Chicago.

Los Angeles had its riot in the summer of 1965. Cleveland and Chicago theirs in the summer of 1966.

It is the intent of this book, in presenting as complete a history as practicable of the riot, to provide the reader with an understanding of why it took place, and what may be done to prevent its repetition. For only if the lessons of Los Angeles are studied, absorbed, and acted upon is there hope that the volatile social chemicals now in interaction in the United States may be kept under control.

I The Two Americas

1   The Stranger in the City

Marquette Frye had lived in Los Angeles for eight years, but he was still a stranger in the city. He had grown up in the coal-mining town of Hanna, Wyoming, where every one of the 625 residents was a neighbor to everyone else, and he had had a sense of belonging. Not here. Here he didn't know what he was. He didn't know what he was, because he didn't know what he could be, or what he was supposed to be. He had no plans, because it seemed to him as if he had been dumped into a dead end—a dead end with but one exit: an exit that both frightened and repelled him.

And so he was lost. Lost within his cul-de-sac, that in itself was lost amidst the labyrinths of the city.

Hanna sits astride the Continental Divide just south of what had been the great Overland Trail up the Platte and down the Sweetwater River; and the high, rolling land retains much of the flavor that had greeted the settlers. The population of Carbon County, an area about the size of Vermont, still is less than 15,000, 9,000 of whom are crowded into the city of Rawlins. For the first 13 years of his life Marquette had the great all-American boyhood of romantic legend. The fact that he was a Negro had made no impact upon him. There was a large Greek community, and they had a Mediterranean tolerance for dark-skinned people. Most of the neighbors were white. His friends were white. He would go over to their houses for dinner, and they would come and spend the night with him. They were different from him and his brothers and sisters, but it was a difference like that of brown and blond hair or gray and blue eyes.

Then, in the mid-1950's, the operation of the coal mine in Hanna, like that of many small mines from Kentucky to Washington, had begun to peter out. Wallace Frye, an Oklahoma cotton farmer who had been recruited by the United Mine Workers in 1944 when there had been a shortage of miners, had to start thinking about moving. Nor was it only a question of moving. Wallace Frye had two skills: cotton farming and coal mining. Technological changes had made a manpower surplus in both. Now, in middle age, he was cast out to become part of that vast minority army, jobless and with no real prospect of ever again being able to gain anything but marginal employment. Having relatives in Los Angeles, he decided to transport his second wife Rena, his stepson Marquette, and the other children to Southern California.

The Fryes arrived in Los Angeles in 1957. From a truly integrated community they were plunged into the heart of a ghetto, where a white face was seen more rarely than in Negro sections of the Black Belt. Wallace Frye went from job to job—service-station attendant, paper-factory worker, parking-lot attendant. Rena supplemented his income by working as a domestic. The children, who hardly knew what a policeman was, were picked up on their very first day in the city.

They had gone out to get some ice cream, when they were spotted by a truant officer. He took them home, and, when it was explained to him that they were not in school because they had just arrived, he tried to give the family an insight into the area. He warned the children that they would have to work at staying out of trouble—there was an element in the community that would do its best to draw them into it.

For no one was the transition so difficult as it was for Marquette. A thin, intelligent 13-year-old who had all of his life lived as part of a white community, he was suddenly dropped, like a character from a Jules Verne balloon, into a new environment where almost all the faces he saw were colored. In them he could see himself—yet he felt no identity with them. He felt different. He was different. And his problems began.

"Hey! How come you talks funny like that? You from Mars or somethin'?" the other kids in the junior high school, the substantial majority of whom had migrated from the South or had parents who came from the South, challenged his English. It was not difficult for them to sense that he did not feel himself part of them. They retaliated by ostracizing him.

"White boy, what happened to you? You fall in a puddle of ink and come up black?"

He was an outsider. He was lost in the impersonality of the 35-pupils-per-class school. Not knowing who he was, or where he belonged—and, even more important where he was heading—his motivation dropped off, he became like a badly tuned engine chugging desperately up a hill. He didn't make it. In his senior year at Fremont High School he became a dropout.

The first time he was picked up by the police was a month before his sixteenth birthday. He was only doing what a lot of the other kids—the ones who always seemed to have change in their pockets—bragged about doing: rifling a coin machine. Telephone booths, coin-operated laundries, soft drink machines—all are easy pickings.

At 77th St. station, the police gave him a talking to. They tried to impress upon him, as they try every year to impress upon a hundred other kids picked up for the first time, what lay ahead of him if he didn't straighten out. It is a brimstone-and-hell admonition, and sometimes it works.

Sometimes.

More often, though, it becomes a joke.

"See, they can't do nothing to you!" the other kids told him after he'd been released. "The law don't allow 'em to!"

This is patently untrue, but it is believed by many, because few juveniles are ever filed on for first offenses; or even for second or third.

The fact that he'd gotten into trouble with the law brought Marquette a measure of acceptance from many of his schoolmates. The law is white. The law was against him. So Marquette had to be true black after all.

In March of the next year, 1961, he was caught taking wine, cigars, and chewing gum from a grocery store. This time a juvenile court hearing was set, and he went before the judge on May 18. The case was continued, pending the filing of a probation report.

Five days later he and some other kids, including several girls, were hanging around outside a laundromat when an older man began egging them on. Very soon Marquette found himself dared into snatching a purse, containing $18, from a woman doing her laundry. The man took the purse, and Marquette was in the process of making his escape, when the police came and collared the girls he had been with. Gallantly he returned, and gave himself up. On June 15 he was placed in the custody of the L.A. County Probation Department and sent to a forestry camp.

He stayed there two years, until he was 19 years old. Then he was released on parole. For five months thereafter he worked as a pickup and delivery man for an auto dealer. But he wasn't satisfied. He wanted something better.

"A man may be willing to swallow his pride and eat humble pie if he thinks it's going to get him somewhere," he says. "But what's the use of going hat in hand if it doesn't get you nowhere no way?"

For the next 18 months he worked only desultorily. When he is in his element he has a jaunty, Sammy Davis-like way about him that often charms people and makes them laugh. Emphasizing a point, he will take quick, small dancing steps back and forth, using his hands as if he were sparring, putting his whole body into the conversation. He has a collegiate sophistication, smoking a pipe and wearing fashionable clothes. When he puts on his wrap-around sunglasses, he looks like a swinger. Within his own age group he is popular. Yet with the anomalies and inconsistencies of a socio-economic structure dominated by whites—a white world which resembled not at all that in which he had grown up—he did not know how to cope. It was always a white man to whom he had to go looking for a job; a white man who would inspect and interrogate him as if he were a piece of material for sale. Under those conditions, he always went on the defensive. He was made to feel, as he said, "like nothing but a piece of shit."

On Wednesday, August 11, 1965, he had slept late. He had slept late because he often stayed out late at night, and there wasn't any point in getting up early. When he did get up the room was already stuffy from the sun's rays richocheting off the windows. Until a few days before it had been one of the city's really cool summers, with the temperature scarcely rising above 80. But on Monday the heat wave had descended, smothering, like a brooding hen onto an egg; and from mid-morning until late afternoon south-central Los Angeles simmered in 95-degree temperatures beneath a yellow-gray coverlet of smog. As Marquette splashed water onto his face and pulled on his slim, Italian-style pants, he decided he would accompany two of his friends, Pete and Milton, to court in Inglewood where, that afternoon, Milton was scheduled to appear for preliminary hearing on a burglary charge.

All in all, Marquette thought, things weren't too bad. Since getting out of the camp he had kept his nose clean. On July 3 he had successfully completed his two years of probation. Now, for the first time in five years, he was out from under the gun. Then, too, his stepbrother, Ronald, a year older than he, had arrived from Wyoming on Monday, and yesterday evening he had taken him around the neighborhood to introduce him to a few girls. They had had a good time partying.

Yet, one way or another, there were always problems. He hadn't had a job for months; and his girl friend, Gloria, had just told him she was pregnant.

He had his mother's gray-white 1955 Buick; and, after the hearing, he decided to go home and pick up Ronald before going over to Milton's house. It was 5 o'clock, and the breeze sucked seaward from the mountains was beginning to wipe away the pollution like grime from a dirty window. Still, the heat hadn't abated much, and it was a real pleasure when he and Ronald got over to Milton's place and were able to relax with cooling screwdrivers—vodka and orange juice.

The girls they were expecting didn't show up, so they just sat and talked. They had three or four drinks. A few minutes before 7 o'clock, when Marquette decided they'd better head home for dinner, he'd had just enough vodka to make him feel as if the world was a good place to live in after all.

He drove with verve. Slightly too fast, and not altogether in conformity with traffic regulations. As he turned north from El Segundo onto Avalon Blvd., a Negro, driving a pickup truck and waiting for the light to change, thought his behavior erratic. Coincidentally, just before the light turned green, a California Highway Patrol motorcycle officer pulled up. The truck driver, leaning from the cab, shouted to him that there seemed to be something the matter with the driver of a Buick heading north on Avalon. In response to the officer's query, he said that he "looked like he might be drunk or something."

Officer Lee Minikus gave him an informal salute in acknowledgment, gunned the cycle, and swung up Avalon Blvd. after the Buick, which was already a couple of blocks ahead.

At 65 miles an hour Minikus sped up the broad, heavily traveled street. To his right was an undeveloped area of open fields and small manufacturing plants, to his left junkyards and small businesses. Crossing 120th St. the roadway narrowed; there were stores, a café, a laundry, a beauty parlor, a neighborhood grocery featuring accounting and income-tax services. A couple of blocks farther north the neighborhood became mainly residential, consisting of recently built two-story apartment houses, interspersed here and there with old dwellings dating back to a time when the area had been used for truck farms. Lining the side streets were neat, single-family residences with well-kept lawns and plots of flowers—differing little, if at all, from other middle-class suburban neighborhoods.

As Marquette drove past 117th St., Ronald became aware of the sharp red light reflected in the rear-view mirror. He called his brother's attention to it. Marquette slowed down, then brought the car to a halt against the curb a half block north of 116th Place, stopping a few feet behind a car already parked. It just so happened that he was only a block from home—he had been planning to make a left turn onto 116th St., then left again onto Towne, which parallels Avalon.

It was just a minute or two after 7 o'clock.

At that moment, highway patrol Officer Bob Lewis, Lee Minikus's partner, was cruising on his cycle near the Harbor Freeway, six blocks to the west. Officer Wayne Wilson sat astride his cycle, watching for speeders, at an El Segundo intersection. And Officer Larry Bennett, in a CHP car, was patrolling in unincorporated county territory in the vicinity of Athens Park.

At Avalon Blvd. and 118th St., a location that Officer Minikus had just passed, Walter Gaines was working late in his barbershop. Mr. Gaines had worked long hours all of his life in order to support his closely knit family—a wife and seven children. Although he had spent most of his 40-odd years in Stockton, in the north-central part of the state, he had decided to move to Los Angeles seven years before, because Los Angeles had a barbering college, and the Stockton area, at that time, had not. Knowing that he could not afford to send his children through college, he had been determined that each of them would have a trade before he left home. So, in their early teens, while still attending high school, boys and girls alike, off he sent them to barbering school. Each of them, by the time he received his high-school diploma, also had his barbering license.

Two of his daughters were working in the shop. The younger, Joyce Ann, who would be 21 in December, had been in the shop with him until after 6 o'clock, when she had decided to go to Vergie Nash's beauty parlor, a block down on Avalon, to have her hair set.

When Marquette opened the door of the car and stepped out, he wasn't really concerned. He knew the psychology of police officers, and he was confident he would be able to handle the situation. "Mostly when an officer stops you, he'll come up to you harshly, you know. This isn't because the officer is trying to be mean to you, but because he's trying to find out what type of person you are. I mean, if you're going to be an asshole, you know he's going to treat you as such."

These were his thoughts; and he was determined that he would disarm the officer by his friendly manner.

Lee Minikus, putting down the kickstand on the cycle and taking off his gloves, saw a smiling, jaunty Marquette Frye approaching him. Marquette had on a stingy brimmed hat; pointed, Italian-style shoes; narrow, cuffless trousers; and a tailored sport shirt: they accentuated his slenderness, and made him look as if he might have stepped out of a production of *Anna Lucasta*. Minikus, on the other hand, with his boots and baggy-hipped riding trousers, his waist encircled by his gun belt, his head and face virtually hidden by the white and black crash helmet and the dark goggles covering his eyes, had the impersonality of a comic strip Batman.

Beneath this exterior he was, in actuality, a rather good-natured man with sandy red hair, a windburned face, and a prominent nose. Like so many other officers, after a hitch in the service and a brief stint at a sedentary job, he had chosen the highway patrol as a means of escaping the eight-to-five office routine. In his middle thirties, married and with three children, he had been with the CHP almost 10 years.

"Can I see your driver's license, please?" he asked Marquette.

"Well, as it happens, you see, I was down at the New Pike in Long Beach a few days ago, and it fell out of my pocket, or some fellow could have taken it. You know how it is. I lost it, and I just haven't had time to get me a new one."

It was the truth. He had lost his driver's license. But it didn't improve the situation.

"You know you were going 50 miles an hour in a 35-mile zone?" Minikus continued.

"Aw, officer. That old car wouldn't do more than 35 if you shoved it off a cliff!" Marquette laughed.

Marquette had come right up to him. Minikus, smelling his breath, asked, "Have you been drinking?"

"Well, you see," Marquette replied, "my brother, he's been in the service, and he just came in from Wyoming. So we

went over to these girls and we were sort of having a party
—and I had two or three screwdrivers. But I'm not drunk,
officer, if that's what you mean."

In recent years, different jurisdictions have adopted a number of different tests in order to determine whether a person
is intoxicated. The California Highway Patrol has chosen to
retain the field sobriety test, a method of making the determination based on the person's physical behavior. This places
a considerable burden on the officer's judgment. After checking the vehicle registration—which noted that the car belonged to Rena Frye, of 11620 Towne Ave.—and asking
Marquette his name, Minikus ordered him to walk a straight
line along the sidewalk, where a dirt strip divides the pavement from the curbing.

Marquette did as he was ordered. And did it rather successfully, *he* thought. "Now, would you like me to walk it backward?" he asked.

"No. Just stand there. Close your eyes. Put your finger to
your nose." Minikus went on to the next test.

After Marquette's performance on that and one further test,
Minikus decided that he had a 502—a drunk driver—on his
hands. He went to the motorcycle, unhooked the radio mike,
and called for his partner, Bob Lewis. He also asked for a
transportation car to take Marquette to jail.

Returning to Marquette, Minikus began filling out a ticket.
Since Marquette had no driver's license, it was necessary to
ask him for all of the information—his birth date, address,
the color of his eyes, the color of his hair.

"It's black, man!" Marquette replied. "I'm black all over,
can't you see!" He was still jovial, doing a little jig.

"You're a real comedian, aren't you?" Minikus said good-
humoredly.

While Marquette was taking his tests, people had begun to
be attracted by his antics. A good many of them had been
sitting on their steps or out on the lawns, and some had
been congregating at the Oasis Shoeshine Stand, a hangout
for Muslims, down toward Imperial Highway. A couple of
dozen of them now stood around, watching the proceedings,
laughing, talking among themselves, now and then making
some jocose remark to Marquette or Minikus. It was a pleasant evening, a half hour before sunset.

Walking home from the store, Rosalie Sanders and her
daughter Pearlie noticed the gathering. Marquette Frye had

dated Pearlie, who was now married, some years before, and Rosie, as Rosalie was known, considered herself a friend of the Frye family.

"Isn't that Marquette standing there with that officer?" she asked Pearlie.

Pearlie, looking over in the indicated direction, replied that she believed it was.

Threading her way among the people, Rosie asked one of the bystanders what was going on. He answered that it looked like the boy had had a little too much to drink, and that they were going to take him to jail.

Alarmed, Rosie set out to tell Rena Frye. On the east side of Avalon Blvd., where the action was taking place, one apartment house runs lengthwise along the street, presenting its façade to the sidewalk. To the west, however, the apartment houses are aligned perpendicular to the boulevard, so that it is possible to walk between them and reach the next row of apartments facing on Towne Ave. It would take Rosie a minute, at the most, to get to the Frye apartment.

Marquette, in the meantime, although still in good humor, was becoming concerned. Minikus continued writing the ticket. Another motorcycle officer pulled up.

"Officer, you don't have to give me a ticket or take me to jail," Marquette said, talking with his hands, and using his whole body for emphasis, the way he always did when he became excited. "I live here, half a block, right around the corner. You can let my brother Ronny drive the car home, and let me walk home. I'd appreciate it, because I done came from El Segundo and Wilmington, you know, and being a half block away from home, you could, you know, let me get by with that." Having said his piece, he started to wander off.

Officer Bob Lewis had parked his cycle. "What have you got?" he inquired of Minikus.

"A deuce!" he replied, using police slang for 502.

"Who's the one under arrest?" Lewis asked, as there were now several persons within a few feet radius of the motorbike.

Minikus pointed to Marquette, who, seeing he was the subject of discussion, returned.

"Man, I'm not drunk," Marquette said. "Can't you see I'm a good fellow who wouldn't diddledybop nobody?" Still trying to make light of it, he put one hand on Minikus's cycle.

"Get your hands off that bike!" Lewis ordered.

"Now, you don't have to do me like that," Marquette replied, feeling unjustly chastened.

Although beneath their regalia it would have been difficult to tell them apart, and both had had much the same experience on the highway patrol, in personality and looks Lewis was quite different from Minikus. An extrovert, with short-cropped light hair and a full-fleshed face, Lewis laughs easily, likes his good time, and, since divorcing his wife, has had a sharp eye for the girls. After spending seven years in the southeast Los Angeles sector, he had, in 1964, been transferred to Lake Tahoe. A few months at the California-Nevada resort had convinced him that, with nighclubs and casinos all around, the cost of living was too high. So he had asked for, and received, a transfer back to Los Angeles.

Ronald, during this time, had not stirred from the front seat of the car. He was 22 years old, the youngest of four children of Wallace Frye's previous marriage to Mary Etta Riggs. Born in Arkansas, he had been raised in Superior, Wyo., where his mother had remarried after the divorce. In 1961, following graduation from high school, he had joined the air force, becoming a mechanic and reaching the rank of airman second class. Discharged in June, he had come to Los Angeles, hoping to enroll in IBM School. Slow-spoken and quite handsome, his temperament was the opposite of Marquette's mercurial one. He figured that, whatever trouble Marquette was in, it would be better to let him work out of it by himself.

"Do you want to store the vehicle?" Lewis asked Minikus. It is standard procedure to have a car put in storage when the driver is unable to operate it, since, if it is left on the street there is danger of its being stripped.

Minikus replied in the affirmative. Lewis started walking back toward his cycle to get a storage report form. As he did, the transportation car, driven by Officer Bennett, arrived. Almost simultaneously, a truck from the South East Tow Co. in Compton, three miles away, appeared.

The driver, Joseph Lee Gabel, inquired as to which vehicle was involved. Lewis indicated to him that he was to take the Buick.

As Ronald saw the tow truck stop, then back around the parked car with apparent intent to hook onto the Buick, he decided that he'd better intervene. He went back to the motorcycle, identified himself to Minikus, told him he was Marquette's brother, and asked him if he could take the car. Minikus wanted to know if he had identification, and Ronald pulled out his wallet to show him his driver's license.

That was when Rena, wearing a loose shift, her hair in disarray, came hurrying across the street. The past spring she had had a major operation, from which she was only now fully recovering.

Seeing the tow truck operator unwinding the hook, she went up to him, and, out of breath, asked him what was going on. When he replied that he was going to tow the car away, she remonstrated with him, telling him it was hers.

"Lady, I got nothing to do with it," he answered. "You'd better talk to them officers."

Catching sight of Ronald conversing with Minikus, she went back to where they were standing. Having had the foresight to bring her driver's license along, she showed it to Minikus. Since it checked with the registration of the car, he agreed, after momentary consultation with Lewis, that she could take the Buick. Walking forward, he informed Gabel that they were making out a "no hold" on the vehicle, and that he wouldn't be needed.

Observing his mother arrive on the scene, Marquette had moved around one of the trees and toward the wall of the apartment house, some 15 feet from the curb. A couple of the men were kidding him about going to jail. From his euphoric mood he was plunging into despair. After two years of watching his step and not getting into any trouble, here he was in a mess again. Nothing ever seemed to go right for him. Nothing.

The crowd continued to swell. One lane of the street was blocked. Cars were slowing down, their occupants craning their necks. Some of the drivers parked and joined the onlookers, more than 30 of whom were now gathered on the east side in the vicinity of the vehicles, with another 15 or 20 watching from across the boulevard.

One of the spectators had engaged Minikus in conversation. Lewis was replacing the storage forms in the cycle box. Bennett had alighted from the patrol car to join them. Rena was walking over toward Marquette.

"Let me have the keys to the car," she said to him. "You know better than to drive after you've been drinking."

"Momma, I'm not going to jail. I'm *not* drunk and I am *not* going to jail." He pulled away from her.

The noise the people were making was increasing. As Lewis straightened up from the cycle he thought, for a moment, that Marquette had disappeared. Then he spotted him by the building, and called to Minikus, "We're going to have to get Frye out of that crowd!"

They started toward Marquette, whose unhappiness was increasing. As he spoke to his mother, his voice broke. He was almost crying. Spotting the officers, he started backing away, his feet shuffling, his arms waving.

"Come on, Marquette, you're coming with us." Minikus reached toward him.

Marquette slapped his hand away. "I'm not going to no sonofabitching jail!" he cried out. "I haven't did anything to be taken to jail."

"Go with them and make it easy on yourself," Rena said, caught between him and the officers.

All the old anger, the old frustration, welled up within Marquette. What right had they to treat him like this?

"You motherfucking white cops, you're not taking me anywhere!" he screamed, whipping his body about as if he were half boxer, half dancer.

There was a growl from the crowd, now about 100 in number. Many had just arrived, and, not having witnessed the beginning of the incident, had little knowledge of what the dispute was about. Marquette's defiance struck a responsive chord. The officers were white; they were outsiders; and, most of all, they were police. Years of reciprocal distrust, reciprocal contempt, and reciprocal insults had created a situation in which the residents assumed every officer to be in the wrong until he had proven himself right, just as the officers assumed every Negro guilty until he had proven his innocence. The people began to close in on the three highway patrolmen. What, a few minutes before, had seemed to be an entirely innocuous situation, was taking on an ugly tenor.

Lewis returned quickly to the motorcycle to broadcast a Code 1199—Officer Needs Help!—over the radio. Minikus retrieved the riot baton from Lewis's motorcycle, and Bennett got his shotgun from the patrol car. Together Minikus and Bennett advanced on the crowd, pushing the people back.

In the vicinity, when the Code 1199 call went out, were

motorcycle Officers Wayne Wilson and Veale J. Fondville of the highway patrol. Turning on their red lights, and with their sirens screaming, they headed for Avalon and 116th Place.

Minikus and Bennett were once more within striking distance of Marquette. While Bennett used the shotgun to keep spectators at bay, Minikus tried to duck beneath Marquette's flailing arms in order to grab him from behind.

"Hit those blue-eyed bastards!" a voice yelled.

Marquette and Minikus came into contact. Marquette, grabbing for the riot baton, got one hand on it—there was a brief scuffle before Minikus was able to regain control of it.

"Go ahead, you motherfuckers! Why don't you kill me? You'll have to kill me before you take me to jail!" Marquette shouted, dancing away from Minikus. At that moment, it would have been easy enough for Marquette to escape into the crowd, but he made no effort to do so.

Nearby, Ronald, involved despite himself, concerned about Marquette being hurt, was remonstrating with Lewis.

"You'll have to stay out of the way!" Lewis tried to brush past him.

"But he's my brother!" Ronald pleaded.

Officer Wilson, as he arrived on the scene, riot baton in hand even before he had the kickstand of the motorcycle down, was confronted by an image of blurred chaos. A chunky man, about 40, with a reddish face and short-cropped hair, he went into action with no more opportunity to assess the situation than those Negro spectators who had arrived late and assumed from what they saw that there was violent conflict between Marquette and the officers.

Wilson glimpsed the crowd—grown to perhaps 150, but seeming larger and more menacing because of the noise and the narrow confines of the action. He heard them shouting. He was well aware of their hostility. Close by he saw one officer in what appeared to be a dispute with a Negro youth. A few feet farther off, there was a fight between another Negro and an officer.

Rushing toward Ronald and Lewis, and without speaking to either, Wilson jabbed the riot baton into the pit of Ronald's stomach. As Ronald doubled over, he jabbed again. Ronald rolled to the ground.

With one adversary dispatched, it was but a half dozen steps to where Marquette was fending off Minikus. Wilson swung the baton. He caught Marquette with a glancing blow to the forehead, above the left eye. As Marquette turned instinctively to meet him, Wilson jabbed him hard in the stomach. Marquette doubled over. Instantly Minikus caught his head in a vise, and, with the fight gone out of him, had no trouble leading him to the patrol car. Throwing him across the front seat, Minikus pulled Marquette's arms behind him, and, bending over him, started to handcuff his wrists.

Rena Frye, distraught at having seen both Ronald and Marquette struck down, believed the latter to be under further attack in the police car. Rushing to his aid and trying to pull Minikus away, she, a foot shorter than the officer, sprawled awkwardly across his back. As she pulled at him she suddenly felt herself lifted up. Struggling, the back of Minikus's shirt bunched in her fist, she was torn away by Officer Fondville. Off balance, a strip of the ripped shirt in her hand, she stumbled onto the back of Officer Wilson. Both momentarily went to the ground.

Straightening up, Rena was grabbed by Fondville. Bending her over the trunk of the car, he forced her arms behind her, handcuffed her, and placed her in the rear seat.

"Put your legs inside," he ordered her.

"I wouldn't do anything for you, you white Southern bastard!" she spat at him, tears streaming down her face.

Ronald objected: "What are you arresting her for?"

Getting no answer, he became more insistent. A moment later he received his reply. Handcuffed, he too was placed inside the car.

The Negro crowd, continuing to swell, incensed by the altercation, pressed in. There were isolated shouts of: "Come on, let's get them!" "Leave the old lady alone!" "We've got no rights at all—it's just like Selma!" "Those white motherfuckers got no cause to do that!"

More highway patrol officers were arriving. With riot batons and shotguns, they kept the people back from the car.

In the front seat, Minikus had finished handcuffing Marquette. Pulling him upright on the seat, he was closing the door when Marquette, cursing, lashed out with his foot. He caught the door sharply, swinging it open, and partially springing it. As he did, one of the newly arrived officers, Taylor, kicked his feet back inside of the car, then helped Minikus cuff Marquette's legs together.

The sound of sirens was exploding from all directions as Los Angeles police sped to the scene to assist. As Sgt. V. Nicholson of the highway patrol arrived, it became evident to him that the cars converging at high speed were in danger of crashing into each other. Since the situation appeared now to be under control, he went on the radio to order the units to veer off.

Responding to the lure of the sirens, hundreds of people flocked to the area. Four blocks south of 116th Place, at Virgie Nash's beauty parlor, Joyce Ann Gaines and Joan Nash, Virgie's daughter, were unable to suppress their curiosity. Despite the fact that Joyce Ann had a headful of pink curlers and was wearing a green barber's smock to protect her white capris, they ventured into the street. As they kept asking people what was happening, and received vague, or unknowing answers in reply, they drifted farther and farther to the north, until, finally they came upon the scene shortly before 7:30 p.m.—just as all of the Fryes had been hustled into the police car.

Joyce Ann Gaines, a sociology student at Compton Junior College, is a slender, eye-catchingly attractive girl with light brown hair and a matching complexion; even the fact that she was walking around with her hair up in curlers could not hide this attractiveness. As she made her way toward the front of the crowd and asked what had happened, people were quick to tell her, "The boy in the front seat, he was already bleeding and handcuffed, and one of the cops kicked him!"

That lady in back—they jerked her around till she was screaming with the pain!"

"With all those cops, you'd think they were fighting in Vietnam!"

"We can't even go peaceful in our own way. It's just like the South!"

Joe Gabel, under the direction of Minikus, was once more hitching the Buick onto his tow truck when Jimmy Ticey walked up to him. The Ticey brothers operate the T and T Wrecking Yard twenty blocks to the south on Avalon Blvd., and Jimmy, drawn like the others by the sirens, had arrived two or three minutes before.

"Why," he asked Gabel, "are you impounding this boy's car? I mean, being legally parked, why are you all impounding?"

"What's it to you?" An officer snapped back at him. "You want to get yourself in trouble?"

"No. No." Ticey shrugged. "It's nothing to me."

He walked off, and, caught up in the agitation of the crowd, was pushed toward the spot where Joyce Ann Gaines was standing. Among the police he noticed an officer he knew, Bill Davis. Davis, because of his size—six feet five inches, and 235 pounds—stood out clearly from the rest. The residents of the area called him "Wild Bill."

Traffic on Avalon Blvd. had come to a halt. A half block to the south, one of the well-worn red buses of the South Los Angeles Transportation Co.—a subsidiary concern servicing the area, since the city does not feel it worthwhile to send its buses that far out—had had to stop. Behind it a number of cars and trucks were stacking up. The sun had disappeared into the haze of the Pacific Ocean, leaving only a few red reflections in a sky that was rapidly darkening. Driven by Bennett, the CHP car with the Fryes pulled away from the curb. Behind it, the tow truck, with the Buick hanging from its winch like a slaughtered animal, was escorted from the scene.

The police prepared to withdraw. There was the throaty sound of motorcycle engines being kicked into life as the officers separated themselves from the crowd and waited for the signal to be given to leave.

"Come on," Joan Nash said to Joyce Gaines. "Let's get back. I've got customers waiting for me."

Officers Vaughan and Taylor of the highway patrol were on their cycles, their backs half turned to the people. There were taunts from the crowd:

"Look at the yellow-bellies run!"

"Stay a while. We'll make it interesting for you mothers!"

The officers ignored the taunts. Then, suddenly, Vaughan felt something sting the back of his neck. Instinctively slapping his hand to the area, his fingers came off wet. Whirling around he saw, disappearing among the people, the back of a girl with pink curlers in her hair.

"Goddam! She spit on me!" he exclaimed to Sgt. Nicholson, who was sitting on a cycle a few feet away. Nicholson, and his partner, Gilbert, jumped off their bikes and plunged into the crowd after the girl.

"Let it go! It's not worth it!" another officer called out. But it was too late. The two highway patrolmen had been swallowed up by the people.

Within seconds the other officers dismounted to go to their assistance. At the point where they disappeared into the crowd a seething agitation began. Officer Pattee, fearful, broadcast a new Code 1199—Officer Needs Help!—call. The first cars that had left the scene, already a block or two away, swung back. Several new units, including some from the Sheriff's Department, raced to respond.

"Hey, pink lady!" someone called to Joyce Ann Gaines as she made her way through the crowd. They kidded her about the curlers in her hair, and she laughed. Then with startling suddenness, an arm snaked itself about the lower part of her face; she felt herself pulled backward.

"Who's that? What are you doing?" she giggled, thinking it was someone playing a joke. Dragged backward, trying to turn her head, she started to lose her balance and instinctively put out her arms to support herself.

Officer Gilbert, certain in his own mind after Vaughan's indication that the girl had spit on a fellow officer, was determined to bring her out of the crowd. Joan Nash grabbed Joyce Ann's extended arm and hung on. Pulled in opposite directions, Joyce Ann, struggling, called for help.

"She hasn't did a thing, and look at what they're doing to her!" Joan cried.

Jimmy Ticey, going to Joan Nash's aid, attempted to wrest Joyce Gaines away from Gilbert.

Other officers became involved in the melee.

"Wild Bill! Help us! Look at what they're doing to her. Don't let 'em do that to her, Wild Bill!" Jimmy Ticey shouted to Off. Davis.

Several patrolmen, not knowing to whom Ticey was calling, presumed he was exhorting others in the crowd to help Joyce Ann Gaines resist arrest. They jumped on him, pinioning his arms.

An officer, shorter than the others, broke Joan Nash's hold on her friend. He drew back his baton, threatening her.

"Go ahead, I dare you to hit me!" she screamed. "I dare you to hit me, 'cause I haven't did a thing!"

"You leave my sister alone!" Janet Nash hurled at him.

Gilbert, not for one moment releasing his hold on Joyce Ann, the elbow of his arm clamped tightly across her chin, half walked, half dragged her backward out into the street.

As she struggled and kicked, the pink curlers in her hair loosened and were scattered about the pavement. Bent backward, wearing the barber's smock, she took on a pregnant appearance. Away from the crowd, out as she was in the arena of the street, hundreds of people could see her.

"Look at what they're doing to that pregnant girl!" a woman shouted.

"Oh those motherfuckers!" an anguished voice cried out.

One Negro officer, Ronald Farwell, of the Los Angeles police was among those attempting to contain the crowd. "What kind of a brother are you, when you let them do that to a girl?" he was castigated and cursed.

As Sgt. Nicholson was handcuffing Jimmy Ticey, the latter was still calling out to "Wild Bill" for help. Davis came over and told him to calm down.

"Just go quietly, and you'll be all right," he promised him.

Lee Castruita, of the LAPD, had been one of those leaving the scene when another officer had called out: "There they go again!" Returning, he found himself rushing to the assistance of Officer Gilbert. As Gilbert held Joyce Gaines, Castruita handcuffed her, then started walking her toward his patrol car. Despite the handcuffs, she was more than he could handle.

"Someone give me a hand!" Castruita called out, and Los Angeles police officer Harvey Eubank ran to help him.

Together they walked the girl to Castruita's patrol car, only to discover it immovably jammed between several others. Continuing along the line of police cars, they found one at the end that had the key in the ignition. Placing Joyce Ann in the car, the officers jumped in. Unable to turn the auto around, Castruita backed it rapidly two blocks north on Avalon Blvd., to the intersection of Imperial. Here he swung into a service station and made his turn.

"Help me! Help me! Don't let the bastards take me to jail!" Joyce Gaines called out. Her resentment flaring, she bombarded the officers with invectives.

Returning to his patrol car, LAPD Officer C. A. Willig of the 77th St. division discovered that it had been stolen.

Heading north on Avalon toward the 77th St. station, Castruita and Eubank heard on the radio that they were driving a stolen car.

"Be quiet!" Castruita snapped at Joyce Gaines. He had unhooked the radio mike, and was attempting to report that he was transporting a prisoner to the station in Willig's car. "Can't you see I'm trying to broadcast?"

"I don't have to be quiet—I don't give a good goddam if you ever broadcast!" she cried, starting a shouting match between her and the officers.

Several blocks farther on, Castruita hailed a police car heading in the opposite direction. He asked them to call the station and report he was bringing in a prisoner.

Eubank got out and exchanged places with the passenger officer in the other car. The exchange between Joyce Ann and the new officer became even more acerbic.

"Why? Why? Why," she shouted, "are you doing this to me? What have I done?" She leaned forward awkwardly in the seat, trying to get an answer out of Castruita.

The new officer pulled her back. She lashed out at him with her foot.

"If you try that once more, I'll give you a kick that'll push your teeth down your throat!" he snapped.

"I'd look right stupid trying to kick you with these handcuffs on me!" she retorted, falling silent for the remainder of the five-minute ride to the station.

Along the two-block stretch of Avalon Blvd., decades of distrust, of resentment, of antipathy, of pride ground into the dust had found a focal point in the arrest of Joyce Ann Gaines. In the manner with which the police had handled the girl the people saw, or thought they saw, the contempt of the white man for the Negro. They felt, collectively, his heel grinding in their faces. They were stricken once more by the sting of his power.

"Goddam!" a woman called out. "Goddam! They'd never treat a white woman like that!"

"What kind of men are you, anyways?" another challenged. "What kind of men are you, anyways, to let them do that to our people?"

"It's a shame! It's a pitiful, crying shame!"

"Blue-eyed white devils! We is going to get you! Oh, shit! We is going to get you!"

"Motherfuckers!" It came from all sides of the crowd. "Motherfuckers!"

The police officers, although they had long worked in a culture of antagonism, had never seen hatred of such intensity. Sgt. Richard Rankin—a sergeant of two weeks' standing—of the 77th St. police station was the senior city police officer on the scene. To him it seemed, and rightly so, that the continued presence of the officers could only incite the crowd further; that it would only lead to one incident after another, each bigger than the one before. Over the loud-speaker mounted on his patrol car he ordered his men to re-form and withdraw. Once more they began disengaging themselves from the crowd.

Gabriel Pope had made his way to the scene from the corner of Imperial and Avalon Blvd. at about 7:15. For the past 30 minutes, a two-thirds empty pop bottle in his hand, he had been wandering back and forth between 116th Place and the rose-lavender painted church at the corner of 116th St. and Avalon. Strongly built, just slightly over six feet tall, he had been born in Los Angeles in 1946, the fourth child of Sam and Tessie Pope. Sam and Tessie had both been raised in Woodville, Miss. In 1942, shortly after the begin-ning of the war, Sam Pope had gone to work in the Arm-strong Rubber Co. plant in Natchez. Two years later he had moved his parents and his family to the West Coast, where, in the same job, the money was better. By the time Gabriel was born, however, returning veterans had begun to press Sam Pope for his job, and, under the pressure, his marriage had started showing cracks.

When Sam picked up Tessie at the hospital after she had given birth to Gabriel, they had stopped off at his parents' place to show them the child.

"What a beautiful baby!" his mother had exclaimed. "I'd like to have another beautiful baby like that myself!"

Two weeks later Tessie had returned with the baby and its accoutrements. She hadn't seen Sam for 10 days, and three children were enough for her to take care of, she said. So, since Sam's mother liked the baby so much, she might as well have it for a while.

Gabriel stayed with his paternal grandparents for the next eight years. For him, they became his parents. He saw his father every two or three months, and his mother even less frequently. Then, in 1954, his grandmother died. His grand-father, past 75, was not able to take care of himself, much less an 8-year-old boy.

Gabe, as everyone called him, returned to live with his mother.

In the intervening years she had had three more children, the last two by Thomas Wicket, the man who was living with

her, and whom Gabe was instructed was his stepfather. He
wasn't really, his brothers and sisters told him. Their mother
made a big to-do about how they were married, but that was
just for show.

For Gabe, his life collapsed. He was a stranger in his own
family. Though his older sister tried to be kind to him, the
others ignored him. The apartment had only two bedrooms.
His mother and stepfather slept in one; four of the children
in the second; Gabe and the youngest of his stepbrothers
shared the couch in the living room. At his grandparents he
had not only had his own bed, but his own room. He felt as
if he were an orphan.

He moped. He didn't eat. He picked fights with the other
children. He generated conflict between Thomas Wicket and
his mother.

After two months, Tessie took Gabe aside. She suggested
that he wasn't happy living with them. Gabe agreed. Wouldn't
he, Tessie asked, like it better going to live with his grandparents? Gabe thought she was asking if he would like to
return to his grandfather's house, and his heart leaped with
joy. Yes, he said, he would like that.

Two days later, to his bewilderment, he was placed on a
bus headed for Woodville, Miss. He was going to be making
his home with Oss and Millie Davis, Tessie's parents.

Oss Davis was in his middle fifties. He had worked hard
all of his life. He had kept his place. He owned his own
farm of 30 acres between Woodville and Centreville. Maybe
the house he lived in wasn't much, but it had electricity,
and he'd never in all his life lived in a place that had indoor
plumbing, so, as he said, he didn't think he would care for
it anyhow. He grew cotton and corn, he raised pigs and
chickens, and he had his own cow for milk. His proudest
possession was a 1937 Ford from which parts kept dropping
off like dry scales from a fish. The fewer parts it had, the
better it seemed to run.

When he received the telegram that his grandson was coming to visit, he was perplexed, but he didn't let it worry him.
He and Millie had brought eight children into the world.
Three of them had died before they were a year old, and
four had survived to adulthood. He believed he had raised
them right—they had gone to church every Wednesday evening, and twice on Sundays. He knew, though, that in a lot

of ways they thought different from him, and, as he said, he was suspicioning that all wasn't right with Tessie.

Bewildered as he was, Gabe didn't put up much of a fight against Oss at first. What he missed most of all was television, and what he hated most were the seemingly endless sessions in church. When he saw Oss go out and chop off the head of a chicken, or, at pig-killing time, string the pig up upside down and then slit its throat, he was, initially, shocked and nauseated. But soon he got used to it, and would be no more squeamish about wielding an ax than Oss. What he couldn't get used to were Oss's constant warnings about being careful, his admonitions that a boy must know his place. When Oss really got going on the subject he would tell of the time that "one of them ungodly niggers" had stirred up the white community, and they had hung him up by his heels from a tree and taken turns shooting at him. Every time a shot had hit him he'd twitched and hollered for mercy, but it hadn't done him any good, because he didn't know his God.

Gabe had asked Oss what God had had to do with it. Oss, drawing back his hand as if to slap him, had warned him not to sass him. Gabe knew then that, despite all of his pretensions, Oss lived in fear. And he saw him as less than a man.

By the time he was 13 years old, there was rebellion in Gabe's heart. There was no longer much that Oss could do to handle him. White people whom Oss had known all of his life shook their heads and counseled him to do something about that boy. Oss tried. But the more he tried, the more recalcitrant Gabe seemed to become.

The final straw had come the next year, when Gabe was 14. He was standing in line in the post office in Woodville when a white man had come up and said, "Let me get by, boy, I'm in a hurry!"

"Man, I'm just as much in a hurry as you is," Gabe had replied, and stood his ground.

In the ensuing altercation, the white man had shoved Gabe. Gabe had shoved him back! It had been a scandal.

"We kaint keap him no more," Oss had written to Tessie. "We is feared for his sake, and our too."

Six years after he had left, Gabriel Pope returned to Los Angeles. He was big for his age. He had been toughened on the farm. And he had a cockiness that made others wary of him.

His mother was now living in the Jordan Downs Housing Project in Watts. Thomas Wicket, although he still came around periodically, was no longer living with her, and she hadn't had any real contact for years with Sam Pope. All of her children by Pope were being supported by the Bureau of Public Assistance, and Gabe was simply added to the list.

He enrolled in Edwin Markham Junior High School, and the next year he was passed, not graduated, on to Jordan High. He wasn't graduated, since he obviously lacked qualifications. But, since he was 15, he was out of place and a disturbing influence in the junior high school. They had to do something with him. So they gave him to Jordan.

When he went to Jordan, Gabe decided that he would do well. This determination quickly went to pieces when he discovered the books he was given might just as well have been printed in Chinese. He couldn't read them. Most of what his teachers said in class, about mathematics and English, seemed gibberish. He sat there bored. He gave his teachers a hard time. He flirted outrageously with the girls. He got into trashcan fights and threw food across the tables in the cafeteria. He became quickly identified as a hardhead. His counselor tried at first to work with him, but there was no communication between them. To the counselor, who had four times the load he should have, Gabe fell into a pattern. He was one of those tough cases that, lacking the wherewithal, just had to be shrugged off.

Gabe failed 10B twice, and then was passed on to 10A. It was the only practical thing to do with him. If all those failing were forced to repeat the same grades endlessly, the schools would soon be so clogged as to collapse the entire educational structure. Anyone who keeps his nose clean has a reasonable opportunity of, sooner or later, being pushed out at the top by the mass of new students coming in at the bottom. Whether he knows anything or not is irrelevant.

Gabe didn't keep his nose clean. He ditched classes whenever he felt like it, and he was suspended several times. He decided that, if he were going to continue going to school, he had to have better clothes. Clothes are the symbol of status. And status is the most important thing in the school.

He began working at a car wash on weekends. It was mean and dirty work, and it paid only $1 an hour. More often than not he had to fight to keep the man from cheating him even out of some of that.

Still, he now had $15 to $20 a week he could call his own. He bought himself some jazzy slacks and sport shirts, and a coat. He could take out a girl, and not feel like dirt. It really perked him up.

That lasted for five months. Then his mother inadvertently let it slip to the social worker that Gabriel had a job, and the next month he was deducted from the check. His mother told him he would have to give her money with which to buy him food—so there he was, working for nothing. He really hated his mother for being so stupid.

He quit his job. That created more problems with the BPA. The next fall his counselor at Jordan suggested that perhaps he might be happier with a work-study program, in which he would have a job and go to school only part time. He agreed, and found a job in an auto wrecking yard. He went to classes in the evening a couple of times, and then didn't bother to return. Once there was a question as to why he wasn't attending, but it was a perfunctory one. There were too many other problems for school officials to be worrying about Gabriel Pope.

He worked desultorily. He would hold a job for a few months, then something would happen and he would be out of work for an equal period of time. He'd hustle at pool halls; he'd do odd jobs for one of the numerous bookies in the area; if things got really bad, he'd go out with the gang and clout some cars.

Before he was 18 he'd been stopped and questioned by the police twice, both times for curfew violation. Los Angeles has an ordinance prohibiting any person below the age of 18 from being on the street after 10 p.m. unless accompanied by a near relative. From a practical standpoint the ordinance is difficult to enforce, and on Friday and Saturday nights Hollywood Blvd. is jammed with teenagers that the police ignore as long as they behave themselves. In the high crime area of southeast Los Angeles, however, anything that moves at night is liable to be stopped, and the ordinance provides a handy catch-all.

In the summer of 1964 Gabe was working 103rd St. in Watts, peddling bennies, red devils, and some of the numerous other pick-me-up, lay-you-down drugs for which the middle-class American has little trouble getting his doctor to write a prescription, but for which the less affluent society is willing to pay a premium. Every so often he would run into the well-dressed, quiet-spoken representative of the Muslims who stood in front of the Food Giant Market, selling *Muhammad Speaks*. Gabriel would sometimes stop to needle him: "They turned you paper boys into real dudes, ain't they? I bet you wears a coat and tie when you takes your bath!"

The Muslim, in turn, would say to him, "You are letting *the man*[1] twist you around his little finger. Here you is, penny picking, and putting yourself right where he wants you, like a mouse tickling a cat's whiskers. Pretty soon that cat's gonna jump, and you're gonna be in jail, which is where he wants to see you. Listen to us, brother. Live up to your heritage. Don't let *the man* degrade you!"

Gabe did not believe in the Muslims. His thinking was that all the preachers were out only to feather their own nests, and he couldn't see that the Muslims were much different.

But he did think about what the Muslim had said. Right about the same time he began going steady with Lada Young, whom he'd met that spring. Lada had finished high school. She was working as a waitress and was going to secretarial school during the daytime. He liked her and kept asking her, "What for are you doing all this? You know nothing's never going to happen." But she refused to believe that. She said she would make it happen.

He would say, "Shit, you don't know what you talking about!" But he had doubts about his own convictions.

Then a couple of the other peddlers in the neighborhood got arrested. And that thing about penny picking really started nagging him.

He found work in the tire department of an automotive center, and it turned out to be a job more to his liking than any he'd had before. In November he bought a 1956 Chevy. Spending all of his spare time working on it, scrounging parts here and there, within a couple of months he had it looking like a pretty sharp model. He felt good when he took Lada out in it; he felt good when he would see his friends on the street, and could wave to them, knowing that in their eyes he was making it.

Every so often Michael Lasky, white, a former UCLA student, and a Marxist-Leninist Communist (as he calls himself), would come by the Pastrami-dip place where the auto-

---

[1] The white man.

motive center's Negro employees went to lunch and try to organize them. He usually had a white girl carrying a few copies of the *Peking Review,* containing such statements by Mao Tse-tung as:

"On behalf of the Chinese people, I wish to take this opportunity to express our resolute support for the American Negroes in their struggle against racial discrimination and for freedom and equal rights. . . . The evil system of colonialism and imperialism grew up along with the enslavement of Negroes and the trade in Negroes, and it will surely come to its end with the thorough emancipation of the black people."

"The Martin Luther Kings, Farmers, Randolphs, Formans and all the other sell-outs such as Ferrell and Hawkins,[2] by casting their vote for the 'democracy' of the white ruling class, keep the Negroes in bondage," Lasky averred, passing out handbills urging, "Support the people's revolutionary union!"

They were polite to him, but they laughed, asking, "Is them white Chinese, or black Chinese?"

"Mr. Charley is the snarling, ugly face with the bloody fangs," Lasky declared. But Lasky himself was a Mr. Charley, and there had been too many white men before him who, protesting that they were there to help the Negro, had only made use of him. They couldn't see where Lasky was much different. They didn't believe him. They didn't trust him.

It was around Easter time that, as Gabe was driving down Central Ave. with Lada in the car, the police stopped him. They made him get out of the car and stand spreadeagled against its side as they searched him. When he protested and wanted to know what it was all about, they told him to shut up:

"We can do it here, or down at the station, buddy. Take your choice!"

After patting him down, they made Lada get out of the car also. Then they took out the seats, and threw them onto the sidewalk. After that, they did the same with the paraphernalia in the trunk. When they couldn't find any contraband, they called in on the police radio to run a make on him,

---

[2] Douglas Ferrell is a state assemblyman; Gus Hawkins a congressman. Both are Negroes, representing the southeast Los Angeles area.

and, while waiting for a reply, filled out an FI (field iterro-
gation) slip on him. When he continued to press them as to
what it was about they said that there had been a burglary
in the area, and that his vehicle fitted the description of the
one used by the suspects. He knew that wasn't true. He knew
—in his own mind—they'd stopped him only because he had
a sharp-looking car, and they wanted to harass him.

When they got the word back on the radio, they said, "It
looks like you check out okay, Gabriel."

They handed him back his driver's license and drove off,
leaving him standing there with the car gutted and its contents piled in a heap. "Motherfuckers!" he cried in rage after
them, shaking with the fury and the helplessness of his humiliation.

Here, in August, four months later, all that old feeling
welled up in him as he watched the police pull out. All the
old feeling of being stomped into the ground, of having no
right to his own manhood, of having to crawl before the
white man. Of the white man abusing Negro women, and
the Negro man standing by in cowardly indifference—the girl
with the pink curlers could just as well have been Lada.

"It burn your soul, but what can you do?" said a woman
next to him, and her words were like a solo to the orchestra
of imprecations rising about him. Without conscious thought
of his action he darted into the street and hurled the empty
pop bottle in his hand toward the last of the departing black-
and-white cars. Striking the rear fender of Sgt. Rankin's car,
it shattered. And it was as if in that shattering the thousand
people lining the street found their own release. It was as if
in one violent contortion the bonds of restraint were snapped.
Rocks, bottles, pieces of wood and iron—whatever missiles
came to hand—were projected against the sides and windows
of the bus and automobiles that, halted for the past 20 minutes by the jammed street, unwittingly started through the
gauntlet. The people had not been able to overcome the
power of the police. But they could, and would, vent their
fury on other white people. The white people who used the
police to keep them from asserting their rights.

It was 7:45 p.m. Amidst the rending sounds of tearing
metal, splintering glass, cries of bewilderment and shouts of
triumph, the Los Angeles uprising had begun.

2   The Folly of Manual Labors

Sgt. Richard Rankin and his partner, Officer Gary Beebe, halted
the black-and-white car 11 blocks to the north, at 108th St.,
in order to assess the damage—which was minor—and call
in a report of the incident to Lt. Elbert W. Mead, the night
watch commander at the 77th St. police station. Rankin, lean,
hard-fleshed, in his early thirties, had been born and raised
in Long Beach, no more than five miles from where he was
now parked. Addicted to hunting and fishing, he had remained single after serving in the navy during the Korean
War. He was an 11-year veteran of the police force and had
received his sergeant stripes only two weeks before.

The red bus, its windows a jagged jumble of spiderwebbed
glass, pulled up alongside. Hissing the door open, the Negro
driver called to the officers, "Man! Those people down there
have gone wild!"

He was seconded by his complement of passengers, both
Negro and Caucasian. Behind the bus a half dozen autos
pulled up, their occupants swarming around the patrol car
like angry bees.

All of the police had pulled out of the immediate area of
the conflict, and Rankin was still hopeful that, with the irri-
tant removed, the people would quiet down of their own accord. It is standard policy of the LAPD to operate as inconspicuously as possible in Negro areas. There was no
doubt in Rankin's mind that he was dealing with a dangerous situation—in the past three or four years there had been
more than a dozen incidents which had had the potential of
exploding into full-scale riots. Therefore, ordering other officers to follow him, he turned off Avalon Blvd. and made
his way five blocks west on 108th St. to Clovis Ave. There,
in an empty lot behind a warehouse, he established a staging
area. After radioing for help, he decided to return to Avalon
Blvd. and 116th St. to assess the situation. "Wild Bill" Davis
as the senior officer present, was left in charge, pending the

arrival of another sergeant's car. That sergeant's car would provide the only direct link Rankin had with the staging area, since the radio equipment of the basic units allows them to communicate only with the central dispatcher. The sergeants' radios carry an extra frequency, enabling them to talk to each other as well.[1]

Driving down Central Ave., the first main artery to the east of Avalon, Sgt. Rankin, followed by two other patrol cars, turned west on 118th St. The streets of the neat, well-kept residential neighborhood were dark and empty as he passed through them. Emerging onto Avalon two blocks to the south of where the people had gathered, and pulling into the parking lot of the market at the corner, he lit a cigar. No one paid any attention to him. He watched the action of the crowd. It was aimless and desultory, with many motorists driving through unmolested, and some, sporadically, getting peppered.

After observing the people for some 15 minutes, Rankin tried to reach the Clovis staging area, but was unable to do so—the other sergeant's car had not arrived. The inadequacy of communications, which was to plague law-enforcement agencies throughout the riot, was beginning to manifest itself.

Since it appeared to Rankin that the crowd was growing larger, he decided to set up a command post at Imperial Highway, just to the north of the area of main disturbance, and he communicated this decison to Lt. Mead.

Only 13 of the more than 5,000 men on the force outranked Lt. Mead in the number of years of service. Born, like Chief Parker, in South Dakota, Mead had first come to California in the late 1920's to attend USC, some few years later receiving his law degree. Admitted to the bar, he had, in 1929, joined the police force.

At that time it had been a good department, but, within a half dozen years, under the administration of Mayor Joe Shaw and his brother Frank, it had become the most corrupt in the country. Before every promotional exam, word would go out to each man how much it would cost him to make the list—sergeancies were priced between $300 and $500, lieutenancies and captaincies higher. When Fletcher Bowron was elected mayor on a reform platform in 1940, Mead, who

---

[1] Because of the number of patrol cars out, to have car-to-car communications would result in chaos on the air waves.

was then assigned to the Hollywood division, saw his captain come in the next morning, clean out his desk, and walk out without a word. Twenty-two other captains and chiefs had gone with him. The hundred men from that era on the force today—including, before he died, Chief Parker, five deputy chiefs, six inspectors and seven captains—had had to struggle (successfully) to keep their heads out of the cesspool of corruption, and had been deeply scarred by the experience—an experience that has contributed considerably to the personality of the Los Angeles police as it exists today.

It was now nearing 9 o'clock, and Lt. Mead, after reporting on the situation and requesting help from other divisions, tried to reach Insp. Karl Lee, in over-all charge of the 77th division. Insp. Lee was away from home, attending a law class. Capt. Thomas King, head of 77th's day-to-day operations, was on vacation at Lake Arrowhead. Mead, therefore, called Lt. Frank Beeson, second in command, at his home in Whittier.

Meanwhile in his house on 119th St., 60-year-old Benjamin Peery had heard the sirens screaming up and down Avalon Blvd. and said to his wife, "The king of Siam just arrived. I think I will go out and see him!"

Like most of the others who began milling about, he had only scant knowledge of what had occurred during the arrests, and had to rely on the stories that were swirling through the crowd.

"It was just terrible! They arrested two boys and his wife, and the woman was eight days pregnant. And they leaned her over a car and beat her!"

"There was this little girl, and they choked and beat her and drug her by her hair!" The woman reached inside the pocket of her dress and pulled out a pink curler.

It was like a neighborhood fair. The temperature was 75 degrees, the humidity 67 per cent—an unusually mild and pleasant evening for Southern California where, no matter how hot the day, the nights tend to be chilly. People were sitting on their steps, on the curbs, on the walls dividing the apartment houses, on the porches of the few older residences remaining along the boulevard. They were congregating at the stores: at Richard Brice's at the corner of 117th St.; at the Bing & Yet Market on 115th; at the liquor store on the corner of Avalon and Imperial, and the small café next to it; at Jerry's Barbecue, across the street; at Vivian and Fred's Market; at the drug store; on the fringes of the Shell and Standard Oil service stations. The kids were darting everywhere. They were chasing each other, they were throwing rocks at each other—as they did, day in, day out, year after year—and when the mood hit them they would throw a rock at one of the cars that gingerly poked their way through the crowd. There were halters and shorts, bare feet and loose summer dresses, and young men bare-chested. They ate ice cream and fried pork skin, and drank beer and soda pop. Everybody was out, and everybody was talking about the police, and about how the Negro people always got the short end of the stick. And everybody agreed it was a damn crying shame!

Although they lived within a few blocks of each other, it was the first time that Timothy O'Seyre had seen Trixie Russell in over a year. They had attended Jordan High School together in 1955, but O'Seyre was one of the few in his class who had graduated. His father had worked at Douglas Aircraft Co. in Santa Monica since 1942, and the family had lived in the Willowbrook area near Avalon and Imperial since 1944—when a government project to build houses for aircraft workers in Santa Monica had resulted in such a storm of protest, because many of the workers were Negro, that it had been shifted to the southeast Los Angeles area, despite the fact that this meant the workers had to commute 12 miles each way.

The O'Seyre family had always been a stable one, and Timothy's brother Warner had graduated from the ghetto. Having attended Los Angeles State, he was teaching at Jordan High School in Watts, and, even though it meant a drive of several miles each way, he preferred to live on the west side.

Timothy had no desire to follow him, he had been *integrated* once, and the experience had left him with a bitter taste. In the air force in Japan everything on the base had been equal, and there was seldom an incident. Yet, off base, the white servicemen had managed to segregate recreation and entertainment facilities as completely as if they had been in the Deep South. They did not do it systematically, it just happened. It happened because white and Negro servicemen did not mingle off duty, and because whites would abandon facilities frequented by Negroes. Once the pattern had been established, a Negro would find himself unwelcomed by the proprietor of those places considered white—it was not a matter of prejudice; just business.

After he had been discharged, Timothy, with his father's help, had gotten a job at Douglas, where he was now a metal finisher. He was cynical about the motives of the white power structure—the Whips! The civil rights laws looked good, but they were like an array of five-gallon jugs each of which had about five drops of water in it—a thirsty man didn't care about the jugs, he wanted the water. Kids were arriving from Alabama and they had less contact with the whites here than they'd had there—if the Caucasians weren't as prejudiced in Los Angeles as they had been in Birmingham, the kids never had a chance to find out.

The kids were hemmed in in a prison created by vast distances and a public transportation system that would have made the Toonerville Trolley look good. They couldn't go outside the area, and often they couldn't even use the facilities, inadequate as they are, in it—the gangs control most of the parks, and if a boy wants to go to the park he either must join the gang or else pay protection. O'Seyre had been helping at the Non-Violent Action Committee Center just set up a few months ago on Central Ave., and it was appalling how the children flocked to the dingy little store front as if it were the Taj Mahal—they had no place else to go.

Trixie, 26, worked at Cedars of Lebanon Hospital in Hollywood as a nurse's aide. She had four children and a sometime husband. The children, ranging in age from eight to three, she left with her mother during the day. It took her almost two hours each way to go to and from work on the bus, which meant that she was home only about 11 hours out of every 24. She had been 15, and Wash, her husband, 17, when she'd gotten pregnant, and they'd both dropped out of school to get married. Wash wasn't a bad sort, but by the time he was 22 he had three children to support; and with the kind of jobs he was able to get it had been, at best, a hand-to-mouth existence—never enough money for anything but the rent and the groceries, clothes and the car—and usually not enough for those. There had been constant quarrels about money, and he'd finally taken to coming home only when he felt like it—only when he'd felt he had to have some balm for his bitterness and hurt, only when he had to have someone on whom he could take out the hate that had been, more and more, tearing him apart.

An individual, twirling a beer in his hand, walked up to Trixie and O'Seyre.

"Man!" he said. "The people is tired. They is tired getting stuck in the bucket by the police. They is tired of this molestation!"

"You are right, brother. You are right!" A woman joined them. "They have just beat on three little girls, and one of them was an expected mother!"

"It was like they took those two 14-year-old girls out of class and handcuffed them and drove them down to jail," Trixie said, referring to an incident two years before that had become a *cause célèbre* in the community. The police argument that all prisoners are handcuffed routinely, because bitter experience has taught officers that a violent teenager is just as difficult to handle as a violent adult,[2] had done nothing to assuage Negro sensitivity.

"We is worse off than Bogalusa. Like the Deacons[3] they got there, the police is afraid of them, and they don't let 'em brutalize the people no more!"

"Yeah, man, that's what we need!" A teenager standing by, agreed.

"It don't make much difference—Mississippi or California —it's all the same. They shoots the people down there for their civil rights, and here they comes up to the door, busting and shooting this poor old woman[4] right in her own house. No rights. We got no rights!"

"Like in the hospital in Hollywood," Trixie declared, "the white people, they asks me, what's wrong with you soul folk, you got all this opportunity, and all this equality, how come you ain't equal? And this nurse, she went to college five years and all that, and she moved to Altadena, and the first thing they does they dumps garbage on her lawn, and they throws rocks through her window and tells her to get the fuck out, and before she knows it they're shooting at her! So I

[2] In actuality, few juvenile girls are ever handcuffed.
[3] The Deacons for Defense. In late July, Charles Sims, president of the organization, had visited Los Angeles, and at a rally sponsored by author Louis Lomax, $7,000 had been raised.
[4] Mrs. Ella D. Carter, of 4072½ San Pedro St. Mrs. Carter awoke one night to hear a noise in the bushes outside her door, and, thinking it was a prowler, fired at him. Two plainclothes officers, who were skulking about in the mistaken impression that the house was being used for gambling, returned the fire through the door and wounded Mrs. Carter.

says what do you make of that, white man, and they shakes their head like they some kind of poodle, and make with this mumbo-jumbo like how we got to earn respect. And I says to them, look baby, what for we got to earn what you got free?"

"Shit!" a woman said. "Them Charley bastards won't even give you no water. Here it is, a hundred degrees, and the pipes as dry as a well in the Sahara! They do anything to spite the soul folk!"

Over on Central Ave., a few blocks away, the white land-lord had left 16 families in his two apartment buildings high and dry. He had disconnected the water because he had be-come fed up trying to collect rents—in the southeast area rental losses may absorb as much as 50 per cent of the po-tential gross of an apartment building. Some owners simply abandon their properties, which are immediately stripped of everything movable from toilet bowls to window frames, as if a school of mammalian piranha had swarmed over them. This particular landlord, unwilling to put up with the weeks of delay in moving a family out by court order, had decided to evict everybody *en masse* by a more direct method. It was typical of the wrongs multiplied by wrongs producing further wrongs that have created the morass of frustration and frayed tempers on both sides.

Shortly after 9 o'clock, representatives from the news media began arriving at the corner of Avalon and Imperial, and one or two radio stations started broadcasting sketchy accounts of a disturbance. At the 77th St. station, Lt. Mead ordered Lee Castruita, of Mexican origin, and Ronald Far-well, a Negro—two of the officers who had been on the scene originally—to change into civilian clothes and return to the area to act as intelligence officers. At 9:25 a rock was hurled through a window of the station wagon belonging to television station KNXT, the CBS outlet. At 9:30, Lt. Frank Beeson arrived to take command.

Sgt. Rankin had set up the police command post, consist-ing of a station wagon with map board and radio, at the broad intersection of the two principal thoroughfares, Avalon Blvd. and Imperial Highway, the latter a key east-west artery running some 40 miles from the Pacific Ocean to Yorba Linda in Orange County. In order to warn and protect motorists, Rankin sent groups of policemen to the Stanford and San Pedro intersections on Imperial. Traffic, however, was allowed to continue to flow through—the officers had no authority to order drivers not to continue, and, besides, there were no provisions for an orderly detour around the danger area.

The gaps in police communications added to the chaos. While Sgt. Rankin was broadcasting instructions for all officers to stay away from Avalon Blvd. south of Imperial, some patrol cars and motorcycle officers continued to come up the boulevard or enter into it from the side streets, driving directly into the midst of the crowd. Some made it out again, but others found themselves stuck as fast as if they had driven into a mass of molasses. Their frantic Officer Needs Help calls drew more police. So that, while one car freed itself, another would be plummeting into the trap.

It was impossible for Lt. Beeson, during the first half hour he was on the scene, to make heads or tails of the situation. Looking down Avalon Blvd. was like glancing through a telescope obscured by a mass of ants. Except for brief reports by those officers who had inadvertently trapped themselves, he had no intelligence of what was going on. (He was unaware of the mission Castruita and Farwell had been sent on by Lt. Mead, and never was able to draw any information from them.) Close to 80 officers had arrived, and they were milling about edgily, subject to taunts and an occasional rock hurled by the teenagers standing in knots on the south side of Imperial. Newspaper reporters and newsreel cameramen from television stations were wandering about.

Like kids everywhere, the kids on the scene were inspired to perform for them.

If Frank Beeson didn't know precisely what he should do, he knew—or thought he knew—the things he definitely should not. Under Chief Parker the department had become so supersensitive to possible charges of brutality that it had divested itself of the tools that could bring such charges about: it does not own police dogs; it prohibits the use of fire hoses, and, for all practical purposes, tear gas in the dispersal of crowds; it would fire on a crowd only if the people were assaulting the officers, and then only as a last resort. Beeson made sure that his men knew this—there was to be no employment of firearms.

Tall, broad-shouldered, his dark hair pushing a sharp prow down across his forehead, his eyes expressive and often troubled, Beeson is a second-generation officer, his father having served on the Los Angeles force before him. Graduating from high school in 1948, he had attended Occidental College for one year and worked as a truck driver and warehouseman before joining the navy and becoming a flight engineer. After serving for four years, he had been discharged in September of 1954, and, immediately thereafter, at the age of 24, had joined the police force. Winning his lieutenancy in the minimum time span, eight years, he is one of the new breed of officers the department prides itself on.

It is not easy to become a Los Angeles police officer. In 1964 only 7.4 per cent of those who attempted to get on the force made it. This was the breakdown:

TOOK WRITTEN EXAMINATION:	3,906
PASSED WRITTEN EXAMINATION:	2,362
PASSED PHYSICAL AGILITY EXAM:	1,720
PASSED ORAL EXAMINATION:	1,223
PASSED MEDICAL EXAMINATION:	583
PASSED PSYCHIATRIC EXAMINATION:	493
DECLINED POSITION:	170
BACKGROUND NOT ACCEPTABLE:	56
ENTERED POLICE ACADEMY:	358
GRADUATED:	291

The average score achieved by academy graduates on the general intelligence test is 107—some 7 seven points higher than the national norm, though this is not, and cannot be, an exact figure. While many officers are of superior intelligence —120 and above—there are others, of course, whose score is below 100. Of the 5,000 officers, approximately 1,000 who have failed to rise above the rank of patrolman may be considered old-timers (17 or more years of service), and some of these, undoubtedly, could not make the force today.

When Frank Pinter had been assigned to the 77th St. division nine months before, his fellow officers at the Hollywood station had kidded him about being transferred to "the L.A. Congo." But, at that, they had said, it was probably better than "occupied Newton," one of the other of the three predominantly Negro divisions.

Pinter, 27, had joined the force six years before at the minimum legal age, 21. His parents had come to California from Iowa in the early 1950's, and had settled in Bellflower, one of the mushrooming residential communities between Long Beach and Los Angeles. A diligent student, and hard-working if not outstanding athlete in high school, he had, briefly, attended Cerritos Junior College. Then, through the influence of his father, a printer, he had gained entrance to the apprenticeship program in that trade. This, however, had been merely marking time—there had never been much doubt in his mind that he wanted to be a policeman.

There were things about the job that he hadn't anticipated. Though always of sober and industrious bent, there had been times when he liked to let his hair down, and he hadn't thought it a great sin to get high at parties. A policeman, however, the instructor at the academy had warned the class, couldn't afford to do that. Once he became a police officer, he was a police officer 24 hours a day. If the neighbors saw him staggering tipsily about—even if it was in his own front yard —they wouldn't say, "Look at good old so-and-so hanging one on!" But, "Look at that bum of a cop, drunk again!" It would be a reflection on the entire force.

It wasn't too long thereafter that the point had been concretely emphasized—an off-duty officer who had become involved in an altercation at a tavern had been sent packing by the department's Board of Rights.

It had become a matter of watching his every step, of suppressing his instincts in favor of what the manual prescribed. "If you go by the law, you can't be wrong," he was told. "You're not supposed to be the judge and the jury. If you see a man violating the law, it's your duty to arrest him. You can't give one man a ticket and let another one go. If there's some question about extenuating circumstances, that's what the courts are for. If you start making summary judgments on the scene, not only is this prejudicial, but people will start wondering about you—why did you let that man in the Cadillac go? What went on between you and that blonde? Remember—the law is the law, and we enforce it equally!"

Very shortly thereafter he had gotten married; and, within the space of two and a half years, he and his wife had had two children. The salary of $600 a month which had seemed quite adequate for a bachelor suddenly had seemed adequate no longer. It was not, as a matter of fact, enough to pay the installments on the two cars, the house, the furniture, the television and hi-fi, the doctor bills, the entertainment expenses and the baby sitter—after all, you can't expect a guy 23 years old just to sit around the house and watch television. He had fallen behind in his payments, his creditors had begun pressing him. One day the captain at the station had called him into the office.

It had been a fatherly chat. One of the creditors had telephoned police administration, threatening to attach Pinter's salary. The captain had pointed out that a Los Angeles police officer is expected to be responsible in all things, including the handling of his money; that he must discipline himself, and couldn't allow himself to get into debt to the point where it might reflect upon his character. The captain had offered to help him work things out—and the way things had worked out he'd had to get rid of the hi-fi and one of the cars, to quit water skiing, and to cut down on the bowling and the nights out with his wife.

He became thrifty, and becoming thrifty had begun to watch for waste elsewhere, especially in government. If, with his limited means, he had to pay taxes, he wanted the government to be as careful with money as he himself had to be. Since it was necessary for him to discipline himself, he began to become less and less indulgent of others who showed lack of discipline. Since his world was an orderly and sober one, he more and more resented those people who would disturb it—he instinctively felt threatened by anyone who was trying to rock the boat.

In the locker room on the first night he had reported to the 77th St. station, one of the officers, walking out, had commented, to no one in particular, "L.S.M.F.T."

"L.S.M.F.T.?" Pinter had looked questioningly at his partner.

"Let's shoot a motherfucker tonight! Got your nigger-knocker[5] all shined up?"

He had been taken aback by the unabashed display of antagonism toward the Negroes. Before joining the force his attitude had been entirely neutral. There had been a few Negroes in school—a couple of them had played with him on the baseball team—and he had always gotten along with them. Otherwise he'd had little contact with minorities, and this contact had not increased in the areas of his first two assignments on the force, Highland Park and Hollywood, both predominantly white. That, however, had not kept him from learning, in numerous conversations with fellow officers, that Negroes are responsible for more than 60 per cent of

[5] Riot baton, or night stick.

all crimes of violence; that in any encounter with a Negro there is always more danger than in a like encounter with a Caucasian; that the Negroes and their left-wing allies are the agitators and the underminers of the American system. He had heard many stories of experiences fellow officers had had with Negroes, and, subtly, he had developed his own prejudices. Yet he had continued to believe that it was his duty to suppress these prejudices, and to enforce the law equally.

The casual way in which the officer had called, "L.S.M.-F.T.," as he walked out, had shocked him.

Yet what he encountered on the streets of the 77th division had so appalled him that two weeks later he had been able to shrug at such expressions as "nigger knockers" and "nigger hatcheries," the latter referring to the housing projects and the rate of reproduction therein. But nothing had prepared him for the licentiousness, the idleness, the lack of morality he met everywhere. Nothing had prepared him for the anxiety generated by the knowledge that violence was always simmering just beneath the surface, that there was no way of anticipating when it would explode. Nothing had prepared him for the uninhibited sexual activities of the people, the profanity employed without embarrassment by the women as well as the men, the manner of their beating and cutting on each other: men on men, women on women, women on men, and—what according to his upbringing was almost unbelievable—men on women. Nothing had prepared him for the way in which they threw their money around with, apparently, no thought of tomorrow. Nothing had prepared him for the manner in which they challenged his right to hold them responsible for infractions of the law. . . .

"Look, man, what I do? I made a little turn around the corner, right? Now, there wasn't no traffic, there wasn't no people. . . ."

"You saw the stop sign?"

"Sure, man, I saw that sign, but . . ."

"When there's a stop sign, the law says you stop!"

"But, man, like that's 11 o'clock in the morning, when you got all those cars whooming by, not 11 o'clock at night! You show me, now you come here and show me," he had tugged at his sleeve, "how I could hurt anybody making it round that corner? Why, if there'd been a flea there and he'd hopped, I'd have stop for him!"

He could only tell the man what he himself had been told:

it wasn't the police officer's place to make judgments on the law ("But you *is* the law!" the man had cried out), that's what the judge is for, and if he, the man, thought there were extenuating circumstances, then he could tell them to the judge. Yet the man would continue the debate long after he could see that it was pointless, he would continue it to physically exhausting lengths; and, finally, when he could no longer procrastinate signing the ticket, the wheedling, complaisant mask on his face would fall away, and with eyes full of hate he would spit out, "Why don't you motherfuckers get the hell out of here and stop harassing the poor people?"

Pinter recognized that the people—at least a majority of those with whom he came into contact—were so diametrically different from his concepts of decency and morality, so different in character from himself, that he would clash with them no matter what the color of their skin, no matter, even, that he was or was not a policeman. And, as an officer sworn to uphold the law, the gulf was so wide—it seemed to him—that it could never be bridged; the Negroes' antipathy toward the police so pervasive it was always in the air. It is an antipathy that, for the officer, makes going to work like going into battle, and every day that he can go without a major incident is worthy of a sigh of thanksgiving.

"Hey, fuzz! The way you look your mother was a monkey's whore!" a 15-year-old boy screamed at Pinter. His remark was followed by a chorus of taunts from the kids congregating at the Shell station, laughing, jumping up and down, daring the officers to come and get them.

"They've already stripped all the bark off my family tree," Pinter commented to the officer standing next to him. "Looks like they're getting ready to start chopping on the trunk!"

"For a bunch that keeps hollering about civil rights, they don't look so civil to me!" he retorted.

There were mutterings among the officers: "What are we standing around for?" "Let's move these black bastards out of here!" "Knock a few heads together and teach 'em a lesson!"

Beeson, sensitive to the frustration and tension of his men, felt them as intensely as they. But, unlike them, he carried the whole weight of the department on his shoulders; every action, or nonaction, of his was going to be subjected to minute scrutiny. Still lacking firsthand information as to the situation on Avalon to the south, he decided—according to the instructions in the technical manual, and against Sgt. Rankin's advice—to send a motorcycle officer to scout the area. Zooming off, the officer returned a few minutes later, the cycle dented, his arm blue and swelling, to report that the people were still throwing rocks.

"We went by the manual," Lt. Mead said later, "and our biggest mistake was that we didn't stuff it in the incinerator!"

Beeson made up his mind. He would have to take action to reassert the authority of the police. The kids, seeing the officers standing, doing nothing except ward off rocks and push back those individuals who encroached upon the intersection, were growing bolder, more vociferous. Newsmen, filming the scene, encouraged each of the youths to try to become the star of the action. It was 10:10 when, forming two squads of 10 men each, keeping the other 60 in reserve, Beeson moved against the crowd on the south side of Imperial Highway. Released from their passive role, the officers took to the task with gusto—they pushed the kids back across the apron of the service station; they made them run, and, where there was resistance, or a reluctance to move quickly enough, they used their batons effectively. Here and there brief scuffles erupted, a few people were thrown to the ground and their arms locked behind them. In 10 minutes it was all over. The policemen, some panting from the exertion, returned to their own lines, bringing a dozen or so of the more unruly with them. There was a temporary lull; a temporary clearing of people from the intersection. Then, like water making its way through sandy soil, they seeped back. And they were angrier than before.

"Three for one! Three for one!" they began the Muslim chant that set the officers' teeth on edge.

At the gasoline stations along the highway an incongruous air of normalcy prevailed. Motorists of both races were stopping unmolested, having their gas tanks filled and windshields wiped, and driving off again. One white driver pulled into the Standard Station and the kids looked at him curiously as he stood by his car as it was serviced, the attendant assiduously wiping the windshield. The driver climbed back into the car, pulled out of the station, and wham!—a rock slammed against the clean glass, splintering it.

The kids were convulsed with laughter.

In front of the café on the east side of Avalon a knot of people had gathered. They were linked by their intensity.

Suddenly, a cheer erupted from them—from the transistor radio over which they were bent Vince Scully was giving the word that Maury Wills was sliding across home plate with the game's only run as Don Drysdale and the Dodgers beat the New York Mets 1 to 0.

A moment later and the same group was scattering—driven before two squads of white-helmeted, baton-bearing policemen, their boots rhythmically beating the pavement as they dog-trotted down Avalon. An imploring Officer Needs Help call had been issued from a car trapped at 116th St. Frank Pinter, in the van, could see its headlights scurrying back and forth in small sweeps like the eyes of a trapped rabbit, then come completely to rest as youths swarmed over it, beating on the windows with their fists, jumping up and down on the trunk, rocking the body back and forth. There were shouts and curses as the wave of officers smashed into them, grabbed those they could, and cleared the rest away from the car.

3   Color the Monster White

Cotter Williams, at 15½, was a well-proportioned five feet ten inches tall, but a mass of hair standing a full three inches straight up on his head made him look taller. He and his friend, Dandy Briggs, had been at the movies, and Cotter had taken a foot-long stick sharpened to a fine point with him. Sometimes, during a show, everything would quiet down on the screen, there wouldn't be any talk or music, and then you could hear the rats scurrying between the seats. It was always great fun when one of them brushed against a girl's leg and she screamed. Tonight, Cotter had determined he would spear himself a rat, and he was bitterly disappointed that he had failed.

The show was over and, as they walked, Cotter twirled the sharpened end of the stick against the palm of his hand—he felt frustrated. Feeling frustrated, he thought of his sister, Baby Doe, a year older than he. She'd gone and had her hair straightened and bleached and was walking the streets—and, from what he could see, she was doing all right. Every couple of weeks, if he hit her right, she might even give him $2 or $3.

He liked Baby Doe. She wasn't really his sister, only his half-sister; her father had been somebody named Simmons. Cotter had seen his own father, Allys Williams, only once, about 10 years before, and he couldn't remember anything about him. Allys Williams had been born near Camp Ruby in eastern Texas, and it was there that he'd spent the first 20-odd years of his life, gotten married, and fathered his first son, Tommy. But in Camp Ruby there had been no way he could make it, so in 1947, when Tommy was one year old, he had told Sara, his wife, that he was heading for Chicago, and would send for her as soon as he got settled. A year had gone by and Sara had heard nothing from him—not that she'd expected any letters: Allys could sign his name, but, beyond that, he could hardly read, much less write. So she had waited. Working for a white family in Jasper, she had made $1.75 a day, and the lady had complained about having to pay so much, saying that before the war, which shook everything up, a nigger had considered herself lucky if she got a dollar. Almost another year had passed when this fellow Simmons, whom Sara had known casually, had said that he was driving to California and would be willing to take her and Tommy along. Sara had a sister who'd moved to Los Angeles, so she'd decided to take Simmons up on it. Leaving word with Allys's mother as to where she was going, she'd taken off.

Baby Doe was just one of those things that had happened on the trip, and, when Allys had finally caught up, Sara had been in Los Angeles County General Hospital, having the baby. Allys hadn't said much about it, and they'd tried living together for a few months, but there had been too many distractions. Los Angeles wasn't like Camp Ruby, it was so much more complicated that she hadn't even wanted to think about it. In Camp Ruby it had seemed all right if you didn't do anything more than go to bed together at night; in California you had to have more than that to make a marriage work. The only job Allys had been able to find was as a night janitor—and he had been lucky to get that. He would get off at 2:30 in the morning, and sometimes he wouldn't show up until 7—so he and Sara had been accusing each other, and fighting, and one time he had thrown a bottle at her and cut her ear so that she had to have 10 stitches taken. Then there had been a burglary at the place Allys worked, and the police had been suspicious of him. It turned out that Allys had spent six months in jail in Chicago for a burglary there, so that had cinched it. He had been arrested. Ultimately, at the trial, he had been cleared, but that was more than three months later, three months that he'd spent in jail because he couldn't raise the $2,500 bail. After that, it was kind of understood that he wouldn't come home again.

In the meantime, Cotter had been born. Sara had applied for public assistance; and, about six months later, after a lot of legal things she couldn't understand, she'd started receiving a check for $125 monthly. In 1951 she'd begun renting half of a small, white duplex from a Mr. Browning, who lived in the other half.

Mr. Browning was a short man, in his early fifties, a bachelor, and the way things had started out, he'd taken an interest in the kids, and brought them candy and small, inexpensive toys. A carpenter by trade, he had, of course, never been able to gain admittance to the carpenter's union because of his color, and so had been barred from the well-paying jobs on the big construction projects. Nevertheless, over the years he had built up his own clientele among the white residents of Westchester and Inglewood, and he worked steadily, making between $2 and $2.50 an hour. Living frugally, he had bought some property, had a little money in the bank, and, in middle-class terminology, was a credit to the community.

So had begun the golden years for Cotter Williams. Although "Uncle Browning" had always kept his separate apartment and never lived with Sara, he was the only father Cotter and the other children ever knew. He would drive them to the beach, make sure that they had the proper clothes to wear, and take an interest in their school work. He had refurbished the apartment, and seen to it that Sara didn't overextend herself in the things she bought. In 1955 Sara had borne him a son, Quentin, and a little less than two years later Doris Elizabeth had come along. It had been during this time that, due to the tensions and frictions generated by the

social worker from the BPA—who was only doing her job—
the relationship had started to deteriorate.

When Quentin was born and the surprised social worker
had seen him for the first time on her regular, semiannual
home visit, she had asked Sara if it was her child, and Sara
had replied that it was Mr. Browning's child. The social
worker had wanted to know all about Mr. Browning, and
told Sara that she would have to bring Mr. Browning in to
the office. This had made Mr. Browning uneasy; but he had
gone. The social worker had told him and Sara that there
were now all sorts of complications, and since they were living together . . .

But, Mr. Browning had said, they were not living together.
The social worker had scratched her head and said this
seemed to be a matter of legal technicalities, and she would
have to consult her superior about whether Mr. Browning
was or was not living with Sara Williams. In the meantime,
was Mr. Browning prepared to support Quentin?

Mr. Browning had said Yes, he was fully prepared to do so.

How much, the social worker had asked, was Mr. Browning contributing to the support of Sara, and Mr. Browning
had said that, since they were not living together, he wasn't
contributing anything, but that he did have dinner with her
several times a week, and paid her for preparing the food.

Then, the social worker had continued, wasn't it true that
Mr. Browning had given Mrs. Williams a television set and
refurbished her apartment, and Mr. Browning had said Yes,
that was true, but he had done so only in his role of landlord.

Did they, perhaps, the social worker had inquired, have
intentions of getting married?

Sara had replied that she had been thinking about getting
a divorce from Allys Williams, but the lawyer had told her
it would cost $500 or $600, and, besides, she had no idea
where Allys was.

Yes, the social worker had agreed, the district attorney's
office had been looking for Allys for three years on a failure-
to-provide warrant for not contributing to the support of
Cotter and Tommy, and they hadn't had much luck finding
him either.

Things had remained that way until after the birth of Doris
Elizabeth, when the new social worker had told Sara that
she would have to settle her relationship with Mr. Browning

one way or the other. Shortly thereafter, a special investigator had come knocking on Sara's door at 12:30 one night and insisted on searching the apartment. Despite the fact that he hadn't found Mr. Browning there, the social worker had said later that she would have to make the assumption that Sara and Mr. Browning were living together, and that Sara, therefore, would have to be cut from the relief rolls.

Cotter, then eight, hadn't been aware of what the fuss was about; all he had known was that Mr. Browning and his mother were bickering where before they'd always gotten along. Cotter had asked Tommy, who was then 12, about it, and Tommy had said that the white people were mad because their mother had had another baby, and when Cotter had asked why it should make a difference to the white people one way or the other, Tommy had shrugged and said he guessed that the white man just didn't like colored folk in general. This had worried Cotter. The only whites he had ever known were the man in the store at the corner, and the teachers in school. Every time he looked at them, he had wondered—he couldn't ask them, of course—why it was they didn't like colored folk?

One day two and a half years after the birth of Doris Elizabeth, Sara had told Cotter to get his things together, they were moving. Cotter had asked where they and Mr. Browning were moving, and Sara had told him not to be so stupid, Mr. Browning wasn't moving anywhere. When that had sunk in on Cotter he had cried and cried. That hadn't made any difference, of course; a couple of days later there they were in the Jordan Downs Housing Project. They had three bedrooms, which was one more than they'd had before, and everything was neat and clean, but to Cotter it had seemed foreign and cold. A few days later he had run away. For two days he had slept in a shack. On the second morning when he had awakened he had seen two enormous pair of black boots. It had been the most frightening moment of his life. The two giant-sized policemen had taken him to the station, and chided him for running away from his mother, who surely loved him. As he had crouched there on the hard chair in the station, it had been the first time he had ever been alone in the white world; as he thought about what Tommy had said, his heart thumped as it never had before. When his mother finally had come for him, and it turned out he was able to escape from the white world alive, he had known that it was something he wanted to avoid. He didn't understand it. It frightened him.

He hated it.

About a year after they moved to the housing project his mother had introduced him and the other children to King Cowper, a dark, big man not more than 25. They had grown used to seeing him around the house five or six days every month, but had never learned much about him. When King and Sara had split up, he had left behind John Kennedy Cowper, who was born in 1963. The other children felt no relationship to him and ignored him, except for Doris Elizabeth, who thought he was cute and pretended he was her doll.

Now, coming abreast of a taco and hamburger stand, Cotter and Dandy decided to get something to eat. Dandy was uneasy because they were on the fringe of Gladiator territory, and you never knew when a bunch was going to come up and start challenging you. Dandy ran with the Slausons, and any time the Gladiators could catch a Slauson they'd just as soon as not bloody him up. The Slausons, centered on Fremont High School, had the reputation of being the biggest of the gangs, with, possibly, as many as 500 members, although, in truth, they were not so much one gang as a loose confederation of several neighborhood groups. Dandy had gone to war with the Slausons only once—that was after the Gladiators had come and crashed a party—and, that time, there had been only about 20 of them. They'd driven over to 54th St., where the Gladiators congregated, but they hadn't been able to find any action, so they'd taken their revenge by busting open a half dozen coin telephones in the Gladiator territory.

As Cotter waited for his taco he continued twirling the sharpened stick—he wouldn't mind a little set-to as long as he had himself some good protection like that.

"Hey," he said to Dandy, "d'you hear where that old white bastard on Manchester blew up one of the blood?"

Dandy had heard of it. The man was 87-year-old Oliver Cromwell Edwards, one of the few white residents, almost all in their sixties or older, who had refused to pull out of the area. A recluse, he was senile and dying, and constantly being badgered by rock-throwing kids who considered his place "the haunted house." Finally, his mind had snapped, and he had blasted one of his tormentors to bits with a shotgun.

"Shit!" said Cotter, who had on occasion when he was younger thrown rocks at the house himself, "they shouldn't have took him to jail. Now there's no place for nobody to have fun!"

When the man handed the tacos across the counter, he asked them if they'd heard there was a rumble going on with the police down at Avalon and Imperial. Cotter said No, he hadn't; what was it all about? Just as the man started to say he didn't know, he'd only heard it on the radio, this car pulled up. Three guys got out, and Dandy started to tense. But, it turned out, they were Businessmen from up at South Park. Dandy, who'd lived near there, knew the driver, and they all started talking about the action. Cotter remarked that he'd sure like to go see for himself. Okay, said the driver, he'd wheel them down.

4   You Can't Talk to *The Man!*

When Deputy Chief of Police Roger Murdock, head of the 2,700-man patrol bureau and a veteran of 34 years on the force, arrived on the scene it was 11 o'clock. Murdock had been called at home and informed of the disturbance. At the time he had been preparing to go to the Harvey Aluminum Plant at 190th St. and Normandie Ave., about five miles to the southwest of Avalon and Imperial, and at first he had assumed that the call related to the strike of employees there against the company. In the past few weeks there had been several outbursts of violence, as a result of which the sheriff had stationed 200 men nearby. These men would be instantly available to supplement the Los Angeles police at Avalon and Imperial—should Murdock ask for them.

It was a confused panorama Murdock witnessed at Avalon and Imperial. Several Negroes, both men and women, were being hustled into police cars to be transported to the 77th St. station. At the northwest corner of the intersection a score of motorcycles were herded together like horses in a corral. A barbershop behind them had had its window smashed by a rock aimed at the officers. Here and there newsmen were wandering about, interviewing people, trying to piece together a coherent story from the many bits of sometimes unrelated, sometimes contradictory information. As the violence seemed to be mostly verbal in nature, some were wondering whether it wasn't all a big flap about nothing.

A brief flareup occurred at the service station as a squad charged in to clear away the crowd.

"Close up! Goddammit! Close this place up!" an officer shouted at the attendant, who replied that the station stayed open 24 hours a day, and he couldn't close it without the owner's permission.

A couple of rocks came flying, one clanging against the metal of a pump.

"Say, man," the attendant addressed himself to the officer, "could you back your people out of here, like, when you're here they keeps throwing rocks, and I don't want to get no glass busted!"

His suggestion was not well received.

"Hey, kid! Throw a rock! Throw one!" A cameraman, standing right beside Lt. Beeson shouted across the street, simultaneously aiming his camera to catch the action. "I haven't seen you do anything yet!"

"And you haven't seen me do anything yet, either!" Beeson stormed at him. "If you don't shut up I'm going to punch you right on the nose!" Momentarily he forgot what shock it would be for the white community to see a white police lieutenant punching a white photographer on the nose at a Negro riot.

Twenty-nine persons had been arrested, and, because of the officers necessary to transport them to the station, the force in the field was down to about 70 men.

On Avalon, not far from the intersection, is a shoeshine stand operated by the Muslim brotherhood. Forty or 50 persons were there, formed in a semicircle around a woman in a flowered print dress. Crying, she had her arm around an 8-year-old boy, also crying. His knees and arms were skinned and he had a swollen eye.

"Look what they do to my baby!" she cried. "They knock

him down and stomp on him! They try to kill him—and he
only a baby!"

"I gonna get myself one of those motherfuckers!" a man,
spitting blood from his mouth, averred. "Sonofabitch come
up to me and hit me right square in the mouth with his
stick. That don't set right with me!"

"See!" one of the Muslim brothers said in a low tone of
voice. "We been telling you. You can't talk to *the man*. He
don't want to hear what you got to say!"

A husky, good-looking boy, six feet two inches tall,
rounded the corner. He carried a two-by-four board with a
nail imbedded in it. Suspended from the nail by a piece of
rope was a half-brick, which he twirled above his head. It
was a wicked weapon. People jumped out of the way.

"Hey, boy! Watch where you throws that thing!"

"I'm gonna lowbridge me one o' those motherfuckers!" he
said jauntily.

Garban Tivoli Godrick had been born 17 years before to
Martha Godrick three days before her fourteenth birthday.
He had never lived with his mother, and once when he had
asked his grandmother who his father was, she had told him
that she didn't know; that he shouldn't concern himself with
it; that it was none of his business. He had been raised by
his greatuncle. He had been a good student. He had given
no one trouble until shortly before he was 12 years old.

That was when he'd started wondering. The fact that no
one would answer him had only made him wonder more.
His greatuncle was getting on in years and was retired from
the Department of Water and Power—all he did was watch
television and mix with the preaching people. So G. T. had
started cutting out and running with the Rocket Men—it
was just a block gang, 15 or 20 kids, but it had given him
an identity he couldn't find elsewhere. The police had started
picking him up—curfew violations, suspicion, things like that
—and the only thing his greatuncle had been able to think
of was to whip him. The Rocket Men had had their own
girls, whom they called the Rockettes, and when G. T. was
just about 15 he got one of them pregnant. She was 13, so
her family said he'd raped her. He couldn't prove different,
and his greatuncle told the judge that G. T. had gotten too
big for him to whip and he didn't know what else he could
do with him, so the judge had placed him under the au-

thority of the L.A. County Probation Department, which had sent him to one of its camps. He was there eight months. When his grandmother said she would be willing to assume responsibility for him, the probation department had released him to her.

His grandmother, Willow Godrick, had come into a little money, and was the proprietess of a pool hall. She told G. T. that he would have to earn his keep. She set him to racking balls, which, if he was lucky, earned him 50¢ a night in tips. At Camp Afflerbaugh he had, for the first time in three years, taken an interest in his studies, and had, for all practical purposes, compressed two years of junior high school into eight months.

After his release he had enrolled as a freshman at Jordan High School. Jordan hadn't wanted to take him, and it was only the pressure the probation officer had brought to bear that had gotten him in.

He hadn't done well. There was too much conflict—his grandmother wouldn't give him money for clothes, or haircuts, or any personal necessities, so he started hustling. In class his mind kept drifting back to the pool tables, to the quick, silent run of the ball across the table, the satisfying click and pure thud of the right ball driven into the right pocket. Even so, he might have coped with that if it hadn't been for his reversion to an unfortunate lack of control.

At night, he wet his bed. He didn't do it all the time—he hadn't done it once in camp—but there were periods of three or four months when he couldn't seem to do anything about it. Two weeks after he'd started again, his grandmother, for whom this was a new experience since she had very seldom seen him when he was younger, told him he was a no-good parcel just like his father and she wasn't going to have anybody pissing up her beds. She told him to get out!

"Before I goes," he had demanded, "tell me who my father was."

"He was your grandfather!"

While that was sinking in on him, she had changed her mind. She couldn't put her own flesh and blood out in the street, no matter what kind of an animal he was, she had said. He could sleep in the pool hall; on the floor! God help him if she found him on a table. If she discovered one little piss mark on one of the tables, she'd have the police come and pick him up!

On the floor of the pool hall he had slept. And he had smelled. It hadn't been long before no one could stand to be near him. He was called into the office of the principal, and, since he couldn't explain why he should be going to school in the condition he was in, it was assumed that it was deliberate. He was suspended. Likely as not that would have been the end of G. T.'s schooling, if it hadn't been for Prentiss Tighe.

Tighe was one of those remarkable persons who, no matter how often or how hard they are hit, refuse to buckle. His father was serving a life term in the Georgia State Penitentiary as an habitual criminal—he had been convicted once for burglary and twice for assault with a deadly weapon; since both assaults had been on white men, the judgment could hardly have been otherwise—and his mother was a tubercular who had died when he was 12. The only relative he had known of was an older half-brother who lived in Los Angeles, so at the age of 12 he had started out for California from Waycross, Ga., with $6 and an address written on a tattered envelope.

He had not arrived until he was 13 years old. But he had arrived. His half-brother, who was barely aware of his existence, had not been overjoyed to see him. Prentiss had lived in his house for three years, each year more difficult than the one before. He had stuck it out because he was determined that he wasn't going to knuckle under; that he wasn't going to let the system beat him. Even if he had to do it in hell, he was going to finish school.

Prentiss was not by any means brilliant—he made mostly C's—but he had one great asset that he worked and worked to perfect: he could make a basketball perform as if it were a trained seal. And he had known that with that asset, if he could hang on until he graduated from high school, there would be a lot of people willing to give him a boost.

Before Prentiss started his senior year, his half-brother had kicked him out—literally kicked him out onto the street one night with his suitcase and his basketball, and even less money than he'd left Georgia with five years before. Prentiss had moved his things into a garage that had been condemned and abandoned a half dozen years before. He had cleaned out the rats and built a bed from the rusted frame of an auto. He had gone to work as a busboy in a café where, even though he was paid practically nothing, he could always get something to eat. He had gone back to school as if nothing had happened. And he had kept his hands on the basketball as if it were the Holy Grail.

Tighe had gotten to know G. T. and taken a liking to him. They had played basketball together in the summer league, and G. T., big and strong and still growing, was so clumsy when he first started out that one time when he went high to stuff the ball through the hoop he forgot to let go of it. But G. T. had learned and gotten better, and Prentiss Tighe had become the only friend he had ever had.

When G. T. was suspended it was only Prentiss who had gotten the truth out of him. And when he had gotten the truth out of him, he had told him that he could move into the garage with him. For the four months that they lived together, G. T. had done well; very well. His counselor at Jordan had thought that the suspension had really sobered him up.

But then, at mid-year—early in 1965—Prentiss had graduated. He had received a scholarship to a midwestern university, and left. When he left, all the order he had put into G. T.'s life had left with him. G. T. had inherited the garage. But he didn't have the vision of a goal that Prentiss had. All he was concerned with was making it from day to day. And for making it from day to day, what they were teaching at school didn't seem pertinent.

Like Prentiss, G. T. had needed money to live on. He got it by hustling at the pool hall—he could shoot a pretty fair game himself now—and, having made some connections, by pushing marijuana. Right across from school was a lunch stand, and there he could usually make a quick sale. A matchbox went for $7. But, more often than not, he would sell single joints for 50¢ apiece. The day he turned 17 the cops had picked him up, but he'd seen them coming and managed to dump the stuff, so they'd had to let him go.

"Yeah, man!" G. T. said, testing the rope on the sling. "I'm ready for them fuzz when they come again!" Garban Tivoli Godrick was not really angry at the police. Having smoked a couple of marijuana cigarettes he was simply feeling high, he was feeling that he could meet the police on equal footing. And he wanted to prove it!

5   In Defiance of the Whips

Shortly after 10:30 p.m., Leon Smith, a consultant on the
staff of the L.A. County Human Relations Commission, was
at his home in the Baldwin Hills section, preparing to go to
a party, when he received a call from John Buggs, the executive director of the commission. Buggs had heard on television about the disturbance, and he suggested to Smith that
they drive down to see what it was about.

Smith arrived at the scene at approximately 11:15 p.m.
There was a certain unreality about the brightly lit intersection—photographers, radio reporters with tape recorders, and
television newsreel cameramen wandering about—as if it
were a motion picture set. The police were lined up on one
side, the crowd on the other. Then, as if an invisible director
shouted, "Action!" a few rocks would arc from the back
ranks of the people, the police would charge, the people in
front would be scattered. The officers would try to catch the
rock throwers, but the boys were too fleet for the law. One
officer rounded a corner by the gas station in pursuit of a
group of teenagers and returned herding two captives—both
12-year-old girls.

Within a few minutes of his arrival, Smith met John Buggs
and Herbert Carter, another member of the Human Relations staff. After discussing it briefly, they decided to ask
the police to block off Imperial Highway, so as to prevent
cars from coming through and providing targets for the rock
throwers.

Lt. Beeson, when they approached him, told them that
was impossible; that he had no authority to block a public
thoroughfare. It seemed to Beeson that it was the police,
who, by their presence, were inciting the crowd. If the police
were to remove themselves, he thought, the people might
disperse and go home of their own accord. He discussed the
matter with Deputy Chief Murdock, and Murdock agreed
with him.

"You'd better pack your gear," Beeson told a newsreel camerman. "We're pulling out."

"You can do what you want. I'm staying!" the newsman replied.

"They're likely to start getting rough on you—once we're gone!"

"Are you kidding?" the newsman was conscious of his status. "They wouldn't dare!"

It was nearly midnight as the officers began to withdraw.

"Hey, man! Whitey's running!"

"The motherfuckers are scared!"

The word raced down the street. The police were leaving. The Negro people had driven them out. The Negro people had won a victory over their persecutors. The feeling was heady. It demanded, somehow, a further display of new-found power. The youths surged forward across Imperial Blvd.

When Cotter Williams and Dandy Briggs piled out of the car on Avalon Blvd. just north of Imperial, the last patrol car was disappearing down the highway toward the Harbor Freeway—the corner was like the eye of a storm.

"Shit! We missed it!" said Cotter.

Despite the lull, John Buggs and his aides were apprehensive.

"They never learn," complained Smith, referring to the police. "They can have one close call after another, and they still keep going about things in the same way!"

Almost precisely one year before, on July 31, 1964, in Watts, two miles to the northeast, a situation had developed at least as tense and perhaps more so than that here. A Negro had held up a service station in Downey, a nearby community, and shot the attendant, who in his dying moments had scrawled out the car's license number. When the car had been discovered by the police on 103rd St., the main thoroughfare through Watts, the driver had refused to halt. The officers had chased him, fired several shots, and finally had run him down, fatally wounded, at the corner of Grape St., just across from the Jordan Downs Housing Project. As the people had poured out of the apartments they had seen the crashed car, the driver bloody and dying on the pavement, the police with their guns standing around—they had assumed that the driver had been shot because he was black and the officers were white. They had known nothing of the other shooting, and there had been, in effect, no way they could learn of it, because there was no communication between them and the officers. It was this incident that had led the South Central Welfare Planning Council to set up the Task Force Committee for the Prevention of Riots. The committee had met several times and solicited the cooperation of the police department, which had not been forthcoming. It was not, Chief Parker believed, the business of the police to engage in sociology.

One of the newsmen had his white Buick parked in the service station. He decided it was time to leave. Several youths were leaning against the fenders. Others were encamped on the back bumper. Perhaps a score, including Cotter and Dandy, were in the general vicinity. None of them bothered him as he unlocked the door on the driver's side, climbed in, and turned on the ignition.

As the engine caught and raced he expected them to get out of the way. They did not move.

"Come on!" He stuck his head out of the window. "I've got business!"

"You gonna write the true story? You gonna put the truth in the paper?"

"Don't you worry about that? Hey you—!" he yelled at the kids in back. "Get off of there!"

They replied by bouncing the car up and down on its springs.

"Say please, Whitey!" they taunted him. "You on our set now!"

"Hey, boy!" Briggs came up to the window, throwing the word "boy" at the newsman with relish. "What you give us if we move?"

"I'll give you a kick in the—! You don't get out of the way, I'll call the police!"

"Man, them police can't help you! They running shitass scared! We the boss here now! You gotta talk to us. And you gotta talk nice like, Charley!"

A half dozen kids on either side of the car began rocking it from side to side.

"I'll talk the only language you hoodlums understand!" The newsman opened the door of the car and jumped out. As he headed for a phone booth a few feet away, he was suddenly surrounded by an arena of dark, angry young faces.

"Listen, you white motherfucker! We've had enough of

your shit!" An older man had him by the shirt. "We are not gonna have no more of it. We are tired of getting beat down. And we are ready, baby, you can say we are ready, to fight!"

"You apologize. You talk to us decent!" Cotter shouted.

"I'll talk to you hoodlums like . . ."

A fist crashed into his face. He fell backward to the ground. They jumped on him then—Cotter, G. T. and Briggs, all the kids who had been standing around. They vented their anger on the white newsman who, like the white man's police, was the representative of the white power structure—the Whips!—who had for 300 years held them in slavery and suppression. They held him down, rubbing his face into the concrete, while the women laughed and egged them on.

Carter, Leon Smith, Buggs and Robert Hall, a husky, mustachioed member of the Non-Violent Action Committee, jumped in, and pulled them off. Yet the brief swirl had been like an agitation in a body of water, particle rubbing against particle and setting the whole mass in motion.

Nicholas Beck, a reporter for UPI, was standing in a telephone booth nearby. Stones began to rain against it, slivers of glass flying through the booth. Hanging up abruptly, he stepped out—right into the path of a fist that smashed into his face, breaking his glasses. Repeated blows sent him buckling to the ground. Only the intervention of Hall and the Human Relations people saved him from further attack.

"Why you want to stop us when they been beating on us for years?" one of the youths complained.

Darrel Hirsch, an engineer, his wife and 6-year-old daughter were out driving. They stopped for the light at the intersection. Suddenly, from every direction, bottles, planks, rocks rained toward them, a knife blade stabbed through the top of the convertible. Figures darting toward the center of the street released their missiles, then darted back. An open-topped Volkswagen caught in the barrage scurried about, twisted into a U-turn, and was sent screaming down the highway in the direction from which it had come.

Garban Tivoli Godrick waited. He waited for the biggest, newest, shiniest car that, reflexively, halted for the red light at the intersection. And when he had the one he wanted, he made a run for it, he swung the brick tied to the two-by-four, he let it fly against the windshield right in front of the driver's face. In the explosion of the glass into a thousand cracks it was as if the white face disintegrated.

G. T. ran back to the curb. He hadn't felt so good—he had never felt so good! He was flushed with excitement. He turned to a woman who was standing there, watching.

"Man, you know that hurt! That hurt when you get a big new shiny car all busted up! You gets busted in the mouth, you gets beat on, and you heals up again—that don't hurt so much! But you get a big car like that, a big car like you all proud of, and you gets that busted—that hurt! That hurt real bad!"

Herbert Carter decided to move his car to prevent its being damaged. He drove it two blocks, started to walk back, and spotted a police car driving slowly away from the area. Flagging it down, he pleaded with the officers: "You've got to block off that intersection! There are people getting hurt!"

"I'm sorry. We don't have any authority to do that," was the reply.

"Well, dammit, you'd better get authority, then!" Carter exploded.

The intersection glistened with debris. It was like a garden of glass and metal and rock tinted with oil slicks, seeded with abandoned hubcaps, a rear-view mirror, and other accessories. It was midnight—the change of shifts at the factories. Workers, driving to and fro, came into the intersection. A few were attacked. Others escaped unscathed. There was no real pattern, no determining factor—Negroes as well as whites were bombarded. Timothy O'Seyre, at the corner of 119th St. and Avalon, tried to flag down drivers to detour them around the area, but he didn't have much luck. There was little light—the city has been noticeably parsimonious in installing street lighting in Negro areas and whole neighborhoods remain as dark as the bayous of Louisiana— and no man, white or black, was going to stop for a Negro frantically waving at them in the middle of the night.

It was newsmen, however, who were the primary target. A plump photographer, camera in hand, two other cameras dangling from his neck and bouncing up and down as he ran, was pursued down the middle of the street by a pack of kids—they laughed at him and let him go.

"Run, Whitey!" they shouted.

On their transistor radios, the people in the street could hear the news broadcasts saying that a riot was in progress, that Negroes were attacking the police. They were angry with the newsmen for not saying why there was this riot, what the grievances of the people were, how it had all started.

The white reporters couldn't understand it. In Western culture the newspaperman is, generally, cast in an aura of glamor, he has the prerogatives and immunities of a priest or a doctor, he feels himself secure from intentional attack. Anyone who violates these mores, in his thinking, must be more than slightly mad. He is not aware—because his awareness has never been stimulated by any degree of personal contact—that because of his quasi-official status the Negroes identify him with the police. They identify him with the white press which, in their mind, ignores Negroes except when they commit crimes, slants what stories it does print, and systematically works with the Whips to keep the lid clamped on.

The newsman thought he was a hero. The black man thought he was a villain.

The most imposing symbol of the press was a station wagon—the mobile unit of television station KNXT. It was captured by the kids; brought to the intersection, looted, rocked back and forth until—as a shout erupted—it toppled onto its side. A small pool of gasoline began to form by the spout to the gas tank, its smell pervasive in the air.

Dandy Briggs, 19 years of age, stood by the car and lit a cigarette. He walked with a slight limp—his left leg was shorter than his right. When he was 13 years old he'd been hit by a car like a lot of other kids in the southeast Los Angeles area are hit by cars because they are always out, playing in the streets. Because here more cars and more kids come together than probably anywhere else in the world, because the kids have little supervision, because they never think about consequences and so get careless, because the drivers are lulled into a false sense of security and high speeds by the unobstructed, often wide streets.

When Briggs had been hit he had only been in Los Angeles six months. He'd come to California with his family from Midnight, Miss., and the school people had put him in the sixth grade. Yet as he'd looked up at the car that had hit him he hadn't been able to read the license plate—he'd never learned to read well enough. His first impression as the initial shock had subsided had been of the white man. There he was, standing, wringing his hands, the people from the neighborhood cursing him. And things had really been getting tense before the police arrived.

When they came, the people had wanted them to take Briggs to the hospital. But they had said they couldn't do that; it was against the law. They had radioed for an ambulance. In that area, however, it often takes time for an ambulance to arrive—the distances are great, the profits low—and there hadn't been one available right away. Then it had turned out that where the accident had occurred wasn't in the city but about 100 feet across the line in the county, so the ambulance service which had a contract with the city couldn't come and pick Briggs up, and another ambulance service, operating in county territory, had had to be called. Dandy had lain there for more than an hour. His mother had become hysterical; his brothers and sisters screamed that the man had killed Briggs! The people had grown angrier and angrier. They hadn't been able to understand why the police didn't take Briggs to the hospital, they hadn't been able to understand why the ambulance didn't come, they hadn't been able to understand the sophistication and subtleties of the white man's law that made all these things difficult. They *had* known that the police represented that law, so there had been a lot of expressions of opinion that no white housewife would ever hear, and before an ambulance finally had arrived it had taken four more police cars to control the crowd.

Briggs remembered that. He remembered it was the white man who had given him the pain and the limp. He remembered a lot of other things about the white man, too, things that were all jumbled in his mind. About how, when he was 11 years old, his father had taken him and his three brothers to the white man's place to pick fruit, and his father was supposed to get 75¢ an hour and the kids 35¢. They'd worked all day, they'd worked 12 hours as hard as they could because their father had said that's what they should do, they should show the man they were good workers and then he'd hire them again.

When reckoning time had come the man had done a lot of figuring and then said that they'd earned $16.75, and Dandy's father, who couldn't figure, said that didn't seem an awful lot of money for four people working all day, so the man had gotten very upset and asked, "Nigger, are you accusing me of cheating you?"

And Dandy's father had had to say, "No, sir!"

Though he had known that he was cheating, and all the kids had known that he was—and what was worse they had known he knew they knew—they had known it wasn't the money that made that much difference. He was only doing it because he wanted to show them who was smarter, who was the boss.

That was what they'd come to California to get away from, and when they'd gotten here his father had bought an old clunker of a car that really shouldn't have been on the road, but which he had to have to get to work. They hadn't been in Los Angeles two months when the police in South Pasadena had stopped them one Sunday as they were out driving, had stopped them only because it seemed strange to them that a Negro should be driving in South Pasadena. The police had made his father get out and spreadeagle himself against the side of the car to be searched. After they'd checked his driver's license and asked him where he was from, one officer who was at least 15 years younger than he had said to him, "Well, Billy, this is not like Mississippi. You're going to have to behave yourself here!"

And the other officer had chimed in, "That's right, Billy, we don't play no favorites. You act right with us, and we'll act right with you!"

And Bill Briggs hadn't been able to answer them any more than he'd been able to answer the man in Mississippi. And Dandy, who had seen his humiliation, who had felt his humiliation, had thought different. He had thought it was just like Mississippi.

He had thought it was just like Mississippi when he, with a group from school, was taken to the beach, and the lifeguard had told the counselor he would have to keep all of them in one section. The lifeguard had explained that it was for their own safety, that he wouldn't be able to watch everyone if they ran all over the place. But Dandy had noticed that it was only the colored kids he was so worried about, that there *were* white kids running around all over the place—so presumably he was letting *them* drown as they pleased.

He had thought it was just like Mississippi when, the summer before, he and some other Negro kids had gotten a job distributing free samples, and they had been driven to one of the all-white communities in Orange County. When lunch time had come they'd stopped in a coffee shop to have something to eat. They had had to wait and wait while the waitress assigned to their table served other customers who had arrived ten minutes and more after they. Finally they had said something; there had been a flareup; the manager had come and told them that, if they would quiet down, he would see that they were served. They had been served. As they were getting ready to leave a couple of policemen had come in for their lunch. The waitress, they noticed, had started talking to them and nodding over in their direction. That afternoon, after they'd gone out again, the police had started following them. After an hour the police had picked them up and charged them with soliciting without a license, although they hadn't been soliciting at all. They had been taken to the station. After a half hour they had been released without any charges being filed.

The officer had told them, "We just don't want you niggers messing up here like you've been messing up every place else."

Dandy finished lighting the cigarette. He kept seeing all those white faces. He kept hearing the words—nigger . . . cheating . . . Billy . . . not like Mississippi . . . nigger . . . messing up . . . nigger—he looked down and the match was burning itself out in his fingers; he smelled the gasoline and he saw the spreading pool. He took a piece of paper, and touched a match to it.

The fire caught on slowly. But, once it got going, it suddenly leaped high, it reached out so fiercely that the people had to jump back. There was the stench of rubber, of blistering paint, of crumbling plastic.

A woman standing nearby began to clap her hands—a rhythmic clapping like the beat of a drum.

6   "Tell Mr. Hoffa to Go to Hell!"

At midnight, Kenneth Hahn, one of the five members of the L.A. County Board of Supervisors, received a call from Undersheriff James Downey. (Sheriff Peter Pitchess was on vacation in Canada.) Downey told Hahn that the sheriff's department had received a request that the 200 deputies at the Harvey Aluminum Plant be put on a standby alert in case they were needed, and that a potential riot situation seemed to be developing in his district.

Hahn, a scholarly looking, bespectacled man in his early forties, telephoned his deputy, Phil Pennington. Together they drove out, eastward, on Imperial Highway. They passed over the freeway, they crossed Broadway—they saw nothing. The neighborhood appeared as quiet as Hahn had ever seen it. At San Pedro they stopped for the light.

"Looks like we got out of bed for nothing," Hahn remarked.

They continued the long block toward Avalon, they crossed the railroad tracks. Nearby a lone Negro boy peered into the car, saw the white faces, made a sweeping curve of arm and thumb in downward motion—suddenly the street was aswarm, people were running this way and that, the pavement was littered with debris. It appeared to Hahn as if there had been a traffic accident.

As they slowed down, kids poured from between buildings, from behind cars, there were shouts, a hailstone clatter against the metal of the car, then the sharp crack of glass —Hahn felt a small trickle of blood on the side of his neck. Pennington—who had a cut on his leg that he didn't notice until an hour later—accelerated, the tires ground against and spun on the debris. Three blocks farther on, where the highway makes a jog toward the south, a sheriff's car was parked—here, again, there was not the least sign of disturbance. Pennington braked sharply.

Hahn jumped out and went to talk to the officers. He was disturbed. He had seen no police officers. He wanted to know why traffic was not being halted. The sheriff's men explained that no request had, as yet, been made for aid by the police department—they could not act unless such a request came. Looking at the blood on Hahn's neck they suggested he might need first aid.

A Negro couple, Mr. and Mrs. C. Brantley, lived in the house in front of which Pennington had parked, and Mrs. Brantley, upon Hahn's appearance, treated the cut. Using the telephone, Hahn called Lt. Mead at the 77th police station, and told him to get the police back into the area. That done, he and the others formed a human chain across the highway to block the westward flow of traffic.

Lt. Beeson and Sgt. Rankin had stopped their patrol cars on Imperial Highway just before reaching the on-ramp to the Harbor Freeway. It was only a few minutes before the first civilian car pulled up—windshield cracked, windows broken—then, during the next half hour, one after another they arrived, about a dozen in all. Some of the people were angry; some were laughing—they had never experienced anything like it, there was something comical in the illogic of the attacks; some had come through unscathed; some were bleeding from glass cuts. Over Sgt. Rankin's radio crackled the order for all officers to return to Avalon and Imperial. Rankin looked at his partner, and had a sinking sensation. He didn't want to go back into that hate.

It was midnight when Gabriel Pope picked up his girl, Lada Young, at the restaurant on the west side where she worked. He told her about the arrests of the Fryes and Joyce Ann Gaines, and how he'd gotten so mad that he'd thrown a bottle at the police car as it was leaving. After that, he'd mostly just wandered around, talking to the people, all of them airing their grievances.

"It was like we was getting together, you know, talking about things, and we was getting this big picture about how things was. And you knows it, and you knows Mr. Charley is laughing at you, and it's bad. In Mississippi they comes at you, and they says: 'Nigger, keep your place!' So you keeps your place, and you say: 'You wait, white man, you wait; the day is gonna come!'

"In California they tells you, 'Nigger, keep your place!' And you say: 'What you say, white man?' And they say: 'You living in the land of opportunity, Mr. Pope!' So you don't know what to think—you turns around and walks off. Then it come: 'Boy, just don't you get outa line, or I'll bust your head!' So you make for him—and there he is: standing, smiling. That's what bust you all up inside—the high-pockrassy!"

Lada wanted to correct the mispronunciation, but she let it go. Three-fourths of the people mispronounced, three-fourths spoke idiomatically—even some of those who knew better. It was like a revolt against Caucasian standards, against the standards that the middle-class Negro, who had abandoned the area, had adopted. Lada herself came from

one of the older, more established families—her parents
didn't think too much of her going out with Gabriel, who
was considerably darker in hue than she, and who came
from one of those families who, her mother complained,
had ruined the area.

Lada had graduated the year before from Jordan High
School, where she had been in the academically enriched
program. The A.E. program, as it is called, is a euphemism
—in West Los Angeles, or any other middle-class Caucasian
neighborhood, it is the standard college preparatory program. At Jordan, only the top 18 per cent are enrolled in it.

Only the top 18 per cent are enrolled, because, of the
2,035 students, 855 have scored 80 or below on their IQ
tests. (Psychologists, generally, accept a score of 75 as that
below which persons fall in the feeble-minded category. IQ
tests, of course, measure not only mental capacity but the
mental level—the degree to which the innate capacity has
been developed.) Sixty per cent of the enrollees come from
homes which receive some welfare aid. One hundred and
twenty-five are returnees from the California Youth Authority and L.A. County Probation Department camps, meaning
that they have been in serious, and, quite likely, repetitive
trouble.

Lada's classes in the A.E. program—mathematics, alge-
bra, English, science, business education, etc.—had been
quite small, many with no more than 20 students, and Los
Angeles city school authorities like to point out that the
average class size at Jordan is 28.4, lower than that of most
high schools in white districts. The A.E. classes are not the
only ones kept small. Some of the numerous other special
classes are even smaller. Those for mentally retarded are
limited to 18; basic reading classes—which, in actuality, are
elementary classes conducted at a high school level—to 20;
reading improvement classes to 25.

Hence, in order to attain an average of 28.4, it is not unusual for the *standard* class to have 35 or more pupils.

As a result, the school has the highest dropout and lowest attendance rate in the system. Since allocation of many
funds is based upon average attendance, this means that
there is less money available for cultural and extracurricular
activities than at other schools. This leads to a deterioration
of morale and further dropouts. Lada had played in the
band, but there had been no uniforms. Only because another,

all-white school, had donated uniforms, had Jordan had a band that year.

The school did not have an auditorium. That had been condemned, and was in the process of being rebuilt. Much of its lighting—as in the metal shop, graphic arts, drafting room, etc.—is reminiscent of the gaslight era. There is not nearly enough equipment to meet the needs—when Gabriel had wanted to get into the auto shop, he had discovered that he couldn't, because there weren't enough tools to go around.

Just getting to and from school could often be a problem for girls having to run the gauntlet of the aging dropouts hanging around at the lunch stand across from the entrance and at the fringes of the Jordan Downs Housing Project next to the school. On more than one occasion Lada had been propositioned by pimps. It was during one of these incidents when a dude, who had been scoring and was high from the weed, had gotten real nasty and insistent with her, that Gabriel Pope had come to her rescue. He could just as well, like the others standing around, have laughed and waited for her to work her own, way out. But he had stepped in, hit the dude a couple of licks, and told him to split.

Gabe had been pushing, then, and whenever there'd be a party, or the team had won a big victory, business would be good, because it was considered real lame if you didn't get high. Lada hadn't disapproved of him, but she'd never taken him up on any of his offers of marijuana or bennies, and had told him she wouldn't go out with him unless he stopped pushing. It was a practical consideration on her part—she didn't want to get involved with the police.

If Gabriel had been stupid, Lada never would have started going with him. But Gabriel, although he was, for all practical purposes, uneducated, had intelligence. What's more, his soul hadn't died in him. Unlike so many of the others, he could still feel—he could feel his own hurt and he could feel the hurt of others. Because he remained sensitive, because his emotions hadn't all died and encrusted him in their scales as they had a good proportion of the other kids, his encounters with the police were especially dangerous. Every time Lada caught sight of a squad car it was as if someone put a knife to her throat.

She had planned to go on to college; junior college, at least. But, during her last semester in high school, her father had lost his job driving a delivery truck for a record company—the company had relocated in the East—and money had started getting tight. Roy Young had never been able to get any of the big-paying jobs, such as driving long-haul or beer delivery trucks, because the Teamsters excluded Negroes from these. A few years ago he had helped the Urban League organize a boycott of Anheuser Busch because the company did not use Negro drivers, but it had, ultimately, turned into a fiasco. The brewery had indicated its willingness to employ Negroes, but the union local had balked—three times meetings had been set with union officials, and each time they had failed to appear. Joe Louis had been sent to get a letter from Jimmy Hoffa, and the local had replied, "Tell Mr. Hoffa to go to hell!"

That had been the end of it. The national had backed off. An attorney for the union had said, "So let's admit it. The teamsters discriminate. So what?" The boycott had fallen apart. There are still no Negroes driving the beer trucks.

Roy Young, with overtime, had often made more than $150 a week. His wife, Cora, who worked as a domestic in Beverly Hills, making $12 a day, had brought home another $60, so they had lived quite comfortably. They were buying a house; they had a new car; the furniture was in good condition, and there was a new combination stereo-color tv set in the living room. With all those payments to be made, money had started getting tight, when, after a couple of months, Roy hadn't been able to get another truck driving job. The material things that Roy and Cora had were the ones that gave them their self-respect, that showed that they had gotten somewhere in the world, that enabled Roy, when he went out driving in his Buick, to look the white man in the eye. To lose any of them—and the interest they were paying ranged from 14 per cent on the car to 24 per cent on the tv set—would have killed Roy and Cora.

So he worked as a parking-lot attendant in the daytime, and at night had a job as a janitorial trainee. Cora went out to Beverly Hills six times a week instead of five, and when the people out there saw Roy dropping her off in the Buick they smiled and felt happy that the Negroes were doing so well. Lada's brother, who was a marine in Vietnam, sent home money. And Lada, who could have gone to junior college free, went out looking for work instead, because she felt that she ought to contribute.

(In Beverly Hills, the white liberal shook his head when Cora revealed Lada had decided not to go on to college. He couldn't understand why, when it would cost her nothing, she didn't want to do it. He knew that, from Jordan, only about a fourth of the graduates continue on to junior college, while in most white districts the percentage is double or higher, and the apparent lack of ambition in the Negro concerned him.)

Lada had not been particularly apprehensive when she had gone job hunting. She had always had a good relationship with the white teachers at Jordan—where the faculty is about half white, half Negro—and, although she had never had a great deal of contact with Caucasians, she was not afraid of them. The first job she had applied for was as service representative for the telephone company. She had passed the test with flying colors, and had been referred to an office in the southeast area, near her home.

She had gone to the office at the appointed hour for her interview with the supervisor of the telephone service bureau, a gentle appearing, graying lady. Lada had smiled at her and thought that she would have no trouble establishing a rapport. She had been shocked by the hostility in the voice opposite her, by the impeaching quality of the questions.

"I'm afraid you won't do. You distinctly lack the qualifications necessary for public contact work," the supervisor had told her. On the referral sheet she had written: "Miss Young's voice tone and speech habits would preclude my accepting her. She has a decided drawl, she drops her r's and slurs her words together in a manner that would cause considerable difficulty in this type of work."

Lada had been shocked. She had accepted the supervisor's evaluation of herself, and wondered how she could have been so unaware of her faults. It had shattered her confidence, so much so that she had not been able to get herself to do anything for the next few days, and finally had called her old counselor at Jordan to ask for advice. The counselor's advice had, momentarily, astonished her: "Forget it!" She had not been the first. Although the office in question serves a largely Negro area, only one of the 29 service representatives there was a Negro.

When she had gone to answer an advertisement for reservation clerks, the interviewer had told her that, he was sorry, a mistake had been made. There had been only one opening, and that had been filled. Suspicious, she had decided to wait outside the office. An hour had passed, a white girl had come, gone in. She had emerged 20 minutes later.

"Did you get the job?" Lada had asked her.

"Oh, sure," she'd replied. "It's a snap. The guy even asked me if I knew of anybody else. They've got a lot of openings!"

Answering an ad for file clerk trainee, she had been told that it required experience. When she expressed surprise that a trainee should have to have experience, the story had changed: the training program had been temporarily discontinued. But, as she looked in the classified section of the newspaper, the ad had continued to run, week after week.

She had begun to check around. She wanted to take the civil service test, but most of the jobs required secretarial training. The summer of 1964 had been half over, and she had gotten nowhere. So she had decided to go to work as a waitress, and think things over. Thinking things over, she had become determined that she was not going to let the system beat her, she was not going to let it keep her down at the level it had kept her parents. In the fall, while continuing to work, she had enrolled in business school.

Gabriel drove back to Avalon and Imperial. Lada asked him what good the rock throwing had done? He said that, well, baby, it had gotten rid of the police. It had gotten rid of the police who were stooling for the white people in Bel Air and Anaheim, and maybe now the white man would know that the black people meant business. That they were tired of him; tired of hearing him talk out of both sides of his mouth.

When they got back to the corner, a shiny red fire truck was standing there, the firemen dousing the last embers in the KNXT station wagon and warily keeping an eye on the crowd, from which rocks spurted occasionally. As Lada looked around and saw what the kids were doing, how they were busting up the cars that were coming through, she asked Gabriel if that's how they intended to get the message through to the white man, throwing rocks at women and children? Gabriel replied that the white people had been doing the same thing to the Negroes for hundreds of years. Lada said that didn't necessarily make it right. So Gabriel agreed to try and talk to the kids. He went down the line; he came upon Garban Tivoli Godrick, who was tightening the rope on his sling. And G. T., who knew Gabriel from the pool hall and the other joints, started to tell him about his exploits, how they were giving Whitey hell! And Gabriel told him, "Cool it, baby. We've made our point!"

Cleo Ticey had been wandering about the area, talking, drinking, listening—"because I wanted to tell somebody what happened because I was watching and seeing but I never could get nobody to listen to see what happened"—ever since the police had taken his brother Jimmy to the station for calling to "Wild Bill" to help Joyce Ann Gaines.[1] His younger brother, Avan, 23, was out there, throwing rocks at cars, and once in a while Cleo caught sight of him. Avan was out there in the intersection, his hands full of rocks, when the sirens seemed to explode right in on top, the red eyes of two dozen police cars flashing down. Before anyone knew it, the white-helmeted, black-booted, blue men were into the crowd, their batons punching and swinging. Cleo saw one grab his brother, he saw him struggle, saw, hazily, the motion of a club.

And Cleo who had sworn before that "I'm not going never in my whole life ever going to see my brother hit for nothin', even if he's wrong!" started for the policeman. He started for him and was intercepted by another, who swung his club down on top of Cleo's head.

As blood spurted onto Cleo's shirt, Cleo turned to him and said, "Shit, man, nobody can hurt my head—that's impossible!"

The crowd was sprung open; the night exploded into swirling groups of officers and Negroes that merged, separated, merged again—guilty and innocent mixed inextricably. People screamed, young kids were trampled underfoot, Lada found herself carried by the moving mass to the opposite side of the street, there was thrown out of it as if into a backwater. On the apron of the service station a boy threw a rock, two officers chased and tackled him, brought him down, repeatedly began jabbing their clubs into his side to take the fight out of him.

"Please don't hit him any more," Lada cried. "You don't have to kill him!"

"You black bitch! Keep your fucking nose out of this!" One of the officers turned on her, stuck his club between her legs, gave a small twist, and down she went.

[1] See page 19.

G. T. heaved his brick, board and all, at an officer. Three others started chasing him as he headed up between two buildings. They were in full pursuit, they saw him disappear into the darkness—suddenly, as if in a slapstick movie, he was multiplied by 12. At the spot where he had disappeared a whole horde of kids rushed out, their arms pumping missiles at the police.

Timothy O'Seyre was still in the middle of the street. He had heard the sirens. The crowd started being shoved down toward him, people were running, crisscrossing, tripping, a girl in a halter had had it torn loose and was desperately trying to keep her bosom within the confines of the loosely flapping garment. As they swept the street, O'Seyre's eyes fastened on the figure of Trixie Russell's eldest boy. O'Seyre called to him. The boy didn't hear him, or hearing him, ignored him. So O'Seyre went after him. He had just caught hold of his arm when the police burst through the last remnants of the crowd and plummeted onto him.

"Get your black ass home, nigger!" one of the officers shouted at O'Seyre.

"Motherfucking cops!" the 10-year-old boy yelled back.

A score of persons were in the group in which Cotter Williams had been caught. A half dozen police were running them. A girl tripped, her legs entangled themselves in other legs; bodies spilled over each other. Policemen pulled, pushed, jabbed. Cotter was grasping his sharpened stick, half crouched, one hand balanced on top of someone's shoulder who was flat on the ground. A dark blue thigh broke through between a red dress and a pair of ragged Bermuda shorts, viciously he stabbed at it.

Rocks were flying everywhere, banging indiscriminately into all of the combatants. A boy chased by the police darted into a house, slamming the door into the officers' faces. The police kicked down the door. A motorcycle officer chasing another boy went after him like a cowboy after a dogey, corraling him on the sidewalk right by the plate glass window of the Bing & Yet Market. A brick hurtled at the officer; he ducked—down came the window like sheet ice scaling off.

In a half hour where there had been a mass of half a thousand persons there were only scattered remnants. Yet it was as if the police had cut into the heart of a cancer—cells of the malignancy were being dispersed everywhere.

Cars halting at stoplights were surrounded, rocked back and forth until the bewildered whites fled from them in terror. As soon as the occupants were gone, the cars would be overturned, set afire. Even Negroes did not escape—Bobby Bennett, an auto agency employee, had a two-by-four driven through his window.

Nor was nonprejudice a pass of safe conduct. Sam Arnold, an aircraft worker, was eastbound on Imperial when a brick bounced off his car. He stopped, backed up, and saw a lot of Negro boys. He shouted at them that there wasn't any need to do that, he was in sympathy with the civil rights cause.

"Motherfucking Whitey! You've got no business down here—get your ass out!" they yelled, renewing the barrage.

Dave is a husky, redhaired, 20-year-old Caucasian who looks like a football tackle. A junior college student, he was a member of CORE and had, the summer before, worked in the bayou country of Louisiana organizing voters and teaching in freedom schools. Trained in nonviolence, he had, several times, been set upon by whites in the South.

At 10:30 p.m. he, together with Liz, a white girl, and Wayne, a Negro, had gone into the area to look for CORE leader Robert Hall. They had been on the north side of Imperial when the police had appeared. They had seen a Negro boy riding a bicycle sent flying by an officer. Together with a group of Negroes they were making their way north on Avalon, when from an alley a cry was raised: "There's Whitey—get him!"

A couple of chunks of concrete flew at Dave. One hit him on the shoulder, another in the back. Knocked to the sidewalk, he instinctively rolled into a protective position. Several kids, rushing out, kicked at him.

Wayne tried to stop them. He told them: "They're with us!"

"Nigger!" they yelled at him. "If they're with you, then you ain't part of us. You're all white, and your skin don't make no difference!"

One of the Negroes in the group with Dave and Wayne threw a bottle at the attackers—a new melee began, black against black. Dave and Liz ran. At a street corner three blocks farther north they stopped to get their breath.

"Hey, you white bastard!" a kid yelled at them. "You better call a taxi!"

With no taxi available, they were driven out of the area by a Negro couple.

Several blocks to the south, where the Bing & Yet Market had been laid open, kids began wandering through the slash in its front, helping themselves to whatever was at hand. In the confusion there was no one to stop them. They took mostly what was immediately consumable—beer, milk, wine, ice cream, bread, candy. One boy combined cashew nuts and lobster—they were the things his mother had never been able to afford.

At least two dozen civilians, both Negro and white, had been injured seriously, countless others receiving minor cuts and bruises. Seventeen police officers were treated. But, as Deputy Chief Thomas Reddin said, by 2:30 a.m. the L.A. Police Department assumed it was all over.

7   Mothers' Day Comes Twice a Month

When Cotter Williams returned home, the rent party his mother was holding was still going on.

Sara Williams had run into money troubles. Sara Williams had run into money troubles because last mothers' day, the first of August—mothers' day in the projects comes twice a month: the first and the fifteenth, when the checks from the county arrive, and the prices automatically go up a few cents in many stores—the social worker at BPA had told her that her voucher was being temporarily withheld because a mistake had been made. Sara had protested that it wasn't her fault about the mistake, so why should she be *impoverishized* for it?

The worker had replied, "Well, Mrs. Williams, perhaps you haven't been quite truthful with us."

As usual, there was some truth on both sides. When Tommy, her eldest son, now 19, had been sent away to the California Youth Authority Camp at Paso Robles, Sara had not called the BPA to report it—she figured that was the state's business, and since the CYA had taken Tommy, the BPA should know about it. The social worker, however, hadn't discovered it until two months later. What's more, because of a clerical error, Sara had continued to receive Tommy's allotment for another two months after that. That made four months in all that had, somehow, to be repaid to the state. Additionally, there was now some question about Baby Doe: had she dropped out of school; was she still living at home; just exactly what *was* she doing?

So for Sara there had been no check on the first of August. Like everyone else in the projects, if the check didn't come, she was in trouble, bad trouble. Two or three days and then the money, all the money she had, would be gone.

The first thing she had done was pawn her sewing machine. The sewing machine she had bought in March, when she'd had that little extra money. Every mothers' day the project is overrun with salesmen, most of them white. The salesmen peddle everything from appliances like washing and sewing machines to household necessities like towels and thread. The collectors follow after them as street cleaners follow a parade.

The salesman told her that he had a once-in-a-lifetime offer on a sewing machine—his company had gotten thousands of the machines on consignment from a manufacturer on the proviso that they would sell more of them than anyone else in the world, so she, Mrs. Williams, could be the beneficiary of the fix his company had gotten itself into. The machine cost only $95, with a $25 down payment, and surely she could afford that. What's more, the company had a lesson plan, which would provide her with a lesson a month on sewing techniques for a whole year.

So Sara had gone and ordered the machine, and it had been delivered within the week. It had had a lot of little gadgets and things, and it was almost more than she'd expected. She had been really pleased with it.

On mothers' day, the first of the next month, the collector had appeared, and explained to her that, since she had made a $25 down payment, she now owed only $198.60.

There must be some mistake, she had told him, the total cost was only $95, that's what the salesman had told her.

He replied that he didn't know how the salesman could have possibly told her that; it was true that the basic cost of the machine was only $95, but the company didn't just

sell the basic machine. The package price, tax included, was
a firm $223.60. That included $60 for the attachments, and
$60, at $5 each, for the 12 lessons, which would be sent to
her every month.

Sara had become very angry and said that the salesman
had been nothing but a liar. The collector had agreed with
her. The salesman appeared not to have been quite truthful,
and the company would certainly look into it. In the meantime, however, this was the bill: $198.60.

She had asked him if she just couldn't have the machine,
and forget about all the attachments, lessons and things, and
he had replied, "Certainly not!" The company would not
sell her an inferior product. As for the lessons, she would
never be able to operate the machine properly without them,
and might even injure herself—the company could not bear
the thought of that!

So she had said she supposed, much as she liked the machine, she would have to give it back, and could she please
have her $25 returned.

That would be impossible, the collector had replied, the
$25 had signified her good faith, and she now had had the
machine almost a month. However, he was determined himself to help her, and so had managed to work out a formula
where she would have to pay only $18.83 a month for 12
months in order to buy the machine. Surely that much she
could afford. As a matter of fact, if she thought about it,
she could probably make more money sewing for other people, or letting other people sew on the machine, than she
would have to pay.

So she had bought the machine, and it had become her
"negotiable." Almost everyone has some negotiable, some
hard goods that they can pawn when the money runs out—
which it does periodically. Usually the negotiable is a sewing machine, or a camera, or a gun, or a radio, or an electric kitchen appliance—seldom a tv set. Tv sets aren't considered negotiables. They are necessities.

When the collector had come on the first of August she'd
had to tell him that she couldn't pay him, that he'd have to
come back on the fifteenth. All right, the collector had
agreed, but if she didn't have the money on the fifteenth,
"We'll have to come back and pick up our machine!"

That's when she'd taken it down to the pawnshop and gotten a $20 loan—the interest on it was $5 a month.

The $20 lasted her a week, after which she'd decided to hold the rent party. A half dozen neighbors came over to play poker, and, since she was throwing the party, she got a dime out of every kitty. Sometimes, if there was wind that somebody had come into some money, the parties got to be big things; some of the west side gamblers would drift in, and as much as $1,000 might change hands. Usually, though, the party is a neighborhood affair; and the person who throws it is obligated, afterward, to attend any rent party that one of the guests might decide to hold.

When Cotter brought the news that there had been an uprising down on Imperial against the police, they stopped playing, and wanted to know what it was all about. Cotter told them that the police had stopped and raped a pregnant mother, and that the people had gotten angry and driven them out.

(Distorted as Cotter's account was, it gained wide credence in the area because it had a certain basis in fact. The previous month, Mrs. Beverly Tate, of 855 W. 60th St., mother of two, had been out driving with a friend, Herman Overton, when they had been stopped by two police officers, William D. McLeod and Thomas B. Roberts. McLeod had said that there was a warrant outstanding against Mrs. Tate, and told Overton to go on home. After Overton had left, McLeod remarked to his partner that the girl was cute, and, leaving him, had driven her to an isolated location where, according to her, he had raped her, or, more precisely, forced her into an act of oral-genital intercourse. McLeod claimed that she had consented to the act.

(Investigators for the Internal Affairs Division of the police department chose to believe the girl. McLeod was fired and Roberts suspended for six months, and the case was turned over to the District Attorney's office for prosecution. On Friday, August 13, it was presented to the County Grand Jury.

(When the grand jury met, the city was in turmoil, and the white jurors decided to take the word of the white police officers rather than that of the Negro girl. They refused to indict. Commenting, Dist. Att. Evelle J. Younger said, "The conduct on the part of the officers was reprehensible. It is a disgusting, terrible thing. But . . . it isn't a crime unless she refused to consent."

(A month later, Mrs. Tate died under mysterious circumstances while attending a party. Although there was almost certainly no connection between her death and the previous incident, many of the people in the area have their doubts. They have their doubts because vast numbers of them never read a newspaper, and hence rely on word-of-mouth and television for knowledge of what is going on. Word-of-mouth consists of rumors with various degrees of distortion, and television has, for all practical purposes, been unaware that there are Americans whose skins are not white.

(Furthermore, the incident was hardly the first of its kind. It was practically a replay of one that had occurred on Dec. 18, 1961, when Ruth Ball charged that Officer Donald H. Miner had forced her into an act of copulation, her escort, meanwhile, being taken and held in the squad car. When Miss Ball pressed charges, Miner resigned, and the city paid her $1,200 in damages.)

"Shit, baby," said Willie Ridley, "you ain't gonna keep no police out of here. Mr. Charley, he need the police to protect him when he cheat the people. The prophet, he speak right when he say the black man never gonna get no due from the white man. The black man, he got to disintegrate hisself!" Ridley was not a Muslim, because he couldn't go for all that stuff they put on about the women and the drinking and the smoking, and, especially, the eating—like you aren't supposed to eat any kind of nuts or the large-size navy bean, only the small-size navy bean—but he often talked as if he were. He talked as if he were because the Muslim talk gives the black man dignity and power, it makes him feel like he is somebody!

"You right, brother," said Hester LaPlace, Sara's neighbor and Willie's girlfriend. "Police is the ones keeping them blond, blue-eyed Jew devils in business cheatin' us. That why they got us on welfare, so's they can get rich off of us and take all the money out to Beverly Hills!"

"Like they charge a dollar to cash a little bitty check, and you got to buy $5 worth o' stuff that don't 'mount to nothin' to boot!" another agreed.

They were consumed with bitterness against the merchants, a majority of whom are of Mexican, Oriental, or Jewish descent, reflecting the area's ethnic mixture prior to the implosive arrival of Negroes.

"You gets the rich people that lives out in Hollywood, and they buys their groceries cheaper than we cans," Hester continued, "and then they ships their second day goods down here and we poor people have to pay more than they does!"

To a large extent her complaint was justified. Many of the food stores in the area are small, mama-papa operations that are obsolete and can survive only in a poverty area, and only by squeezing out every possible cent. In 1964 a survey conducted by the Los Angeles Times-Mirror Co. showed that in the city's core—the Negro-Mexican area—of 791 stores only 39 were supermarkets, and of the remainder only 29 could be classified Class A. There are 149 Class B markets and the vast majority, 574, are Class C, the lowest rating. These stores cannot afford membership in one of the nonprofit wholesale buying associations; they lack storage space and refrigeration equipment (which means that they have to buy in small quantities); their volume of sales is low—all factors that contribute to the driving up of prices. Inferior cuts of meat are sold because they are cheaper; though, for the reasons stated above, they may be almost as expensive as better cuts sold in Caucasian areas. Bread and vegetables lie on the shelf and become stale and wilted, but must be sold because the margin of profit does not permit writing them off. Kids are constantly running in and out, knocking things off shelves, breaking them, stealing them—the loss from pilferage alone sometimes runs as high as 10 per cent. Land valuations, hence taxes, are high. The cost of fire and burglary insurance borders on the prohibitive.

As a result, it has become a dog-eat-dog world, with the merchants and the customers having nothing in common except a mutual necessity. The customer steals, and the merchant cheats. He charges up to 2½ per cent of a check's amount for cashing it because it is a service he performs and it is important that he make his nickel out of every such service, and because even welfare checks are sometimes fraudulently endorsed.

(Thousands and thousands of persons in the area, lacking drivers' licenses, have no means of personal identification whatever. Hence a merchant can often not be certain that the person cashing a welfare check is the person to whom the check was made out, and there is a small but constant stealing of checks from mail boxes. Lately, some of the more clever recipients have discovered that they can exchange checks, endorse and cash them, then claim that the checks were never received. If, when the canceled check is returned, the signature does not match that of the recipient, there is no proof that the check ever reached the recipient, and the state bounces it and makes out a new voucher. There is no loss to the state, and the over-all amount of such frauds is negligible. But the small merchant who gets stuck with even one $150 or $200 bum check a month is not a very happy fellow.)

"Shit, man," Willie Ridley said, "the ofays is out to keep us where we is, there ain't rhyme or reason they does us the way they is if they wasn't. Like Hester got her window broke, and I say that okay, baby, I fix it for you, I can get the glass for nothin'. And the big-ass project manager, he comes down, and say, 'No man, you can't do that, don't you touch nothing!' And then he get some white feller down, and charge her $5. Ain't that right, baby?"

"Not only that, but Willie, he say he paint the place up, and the man says, 'Don't nobody paint the place but me.' So then he find out that they give me $20 more on my check, and right away he raise the rent $5!"

"You know that scrawny little tree they had out front?" Sara asked. "When the kids come and run over it, the manager, he said I'd have to pay for a new one, and he charge me $12.50. And Cotter," she indicated her son, "he said I'll go out and get you a tree three times that big, and it won't cost you nothin'. But right there the next day was this Japanese man with this little twig that don't look like nothin', and they charge me $12.50!"

"Look what they do to me!" Ridley went on. "All my life I be working with metal, and then they get a little thing that runs a piece of paper through, and all of a sudden there it is, working my machine and they slap me on the shoulder and say, 'Willie, you be a good man, but we don't need you no more!' Forty-five years old and working a good 30 of them, and they say, Willie, you too old, Willie, you been deplaced! Hester, she go to the BPA for money to feed the kids, and they say you got a husband, and she say Yes, no, you know we live together five years. And they say, too bad, we got no money for you. So then they calls me in and they say: you willing to work? And I say, sure man, I work all my life. So they give me this test and they say it show I be good at hospital work, they gonna train me for hospital work, so they send me down to County General at $1.25 an hour to carry slop buckets, and I say:

What you training me for, to be a shit wiper? And they gets all upset at that. But you knows that ain't no work for a man. BPA or no BPA, I just about ready to cut loose!"

"Like Johnnie Lee say," Hester was referring to Johnnie Lee Tillmon, "the only way the soul folk ever gonna get anywheres in the white man's world is to tell him he go his way and we go our, for the only thing he want with us is the exploitation!"

Hester had recently joined *Mothers Anonymous,* an organization of women on welfare aid founded in 1963 by Johnnie Lee Tillmon, herself the mother of six. A large, buxom woman in her late thirties, born in Arkansas, she had, for 18 years worked in a laundry, her highest salary being $67 per week. Separated from her husband, she had developed arthritis, and, as a result, had started receiving welfare aid. Realizing that when her children were 18 she would no longer receive aid and would be "too old to go to school and too young for old age assistance," she had started going to school during the summer in 1962 to supplement her tenth grade—Arkansas level—education.

Training to be a cashier and manager, Mrs. Tillmon works in a small grocery store. It is a store that is this side of the European Middle Ages—but not by very many years.

Not much bigger than 150 square feet, a good portion of it is filled with a jumble of crates and other paraphernalia. Children's toys—with all-year lay-away plans for Christmas purchase—are interspersed with canned goods on the shelves. A nonrefrigerated meat case contains only some wilted lettuce and stray packages of lunch meat. The store caters mostly to kids, and, when school is out, they mill about it as if it were an amusement park.

Mrs. Tillmon, who is afraid to remarry because she doesn't hear from her husband and doesn't know whether or not he got a divorce, has little use for BPA regulations. The minute she applies for public assistance, a woman has no privacy left, she complains. "You can't see a man over two weeks or he has to take on the responsibility of a stepfather—it drives out a man and prevents you from ever getting married. You are supposed to become children and not be interested in keeping company with a man. The check is supposed to make you a hermit. Well, things have to go on, check or no check!"

Her oldest boy has one pair of school pants, which she

makes him change as soon as he arrives home. She sews well and makes her own children's clothes. "We might have to eat beans three times a week, but the kids will never drop out because they have no clothes to wear."

There are few women with the strength of character of Mrs. Tillmon, yet her lack of education and sophistication handicap her, and she is able to receive almost no help for Mothers Anonymous, the kind of grass-roots organization that could, potentially, do more than all the programs imposed from the top down. Among her goals are more emphasis on basic education so that kids don't graduate from high school unable to read, write, or spell; the fostering of on-the-job training and rehabilitation; and the dissemination of birth control information to cut down on illegitimacy.

Yet, until very recently, while children multiplied unchecked—the Negro birth rate in Los Angeles is 33.5 per 1,000 population as against 20.0 for Caucasians—social workers for the county were forbidden by fiat to discuss birth control. The Planned Parenthood Association, which wanted to open a number of clinics in the area, was refused federal funds.

"That's right!" said Willie Ridley. "The white man have lived off the sweat of the black man for 300 years, and he ain't gonna let all that nice, free labor go of his own will. He gonna have to be shown!"

"Baby, we gonna show him!" said Cotter. "We gonna meet again tomorrow night, and we gonna show him!"

8   "You Figure It Out, Buddy!"

Barney Wateridge was tense. He had been tense all evening in the integrated company at the political meeting in a private home. As the meeting was breaking up, they had heard on the radio about the riot, and it was past 1 o'clock in the morning as he swung the Chevrolet Corvette onto La

Brea Ave. With him in the car was Anita Greyson, a social worker for the BPA. A casual acquaintance, she had asked Barney for a lift, and he could hardly have refused her. But he didn't like it.

Anita was young, attractive, and white.

Though he had been moving about in Caucasian society for a number of years, Barney still felt ill at ease in the company of whites, afraid he would make some gross grammatical error, or let his manners slip. During the course of the evening he had smoked a pack and a half of cigarettes, and when they came to the all-night Thrifty Drug Store at the corner of Jefferson Blvd., he decided to stop and buy a carton. As he pulled up, he left the engine running, but automatically flipped the lights on to parking. Anita stayed in the car. When he returned, he placed the cigarettes down between the seats, backed up, and pulled out. He had almost reached Adams, four blocks farther on, when he saw the red light winking behind him.

The light jolted his stomach into a seething cauldron.

Pulling the car to the curb, he got out and walked back, meeting the officer halfway.

"Good evening, sir," the officer said courtesouly. "May I see your driver's license."

Barney pulled out his wallet, and handed him the license. The officer looked at it.

"Whose car is this?" he asked.

Had it been a white driver, the question might not have been asked, or, if it had been, would probably have been phrased as: "Is this your car?" But it had been part of Barney's reformation that he had learned to ignore the small insult; the insult that might be unintentional.

"It's mine," he replied evenly.

The officer went up to the car, bent down and shone his flashlight onto the windshield visor on the driver's side where the registration was displayed. He checked it against the license. Barney held his breath, but the officer did not even glance at Anita.

"Okay." He straightened up. "Do you know you were driving without your lights on?"

Barney didn't. He went around to the front of the car. Sure enough, he had his parking lights on, but the headlights were off.

"I'm sorry," he said. "I'd just stopped at Thrifty's, and it was so light there, I guess I hadn't noticed."

"Well, just watch it!" the officer said, starting to hand the driver's license back.

"Thank you very much, officer," Anita said, leaning across the seat toward the driver's side.

The officer looked at her; looked again at Barney. Then, without a word, he pulled back the driver's license, returned to his car, and began writing out a ticket. Barney watched him. A couple of minutes later he was back, clipboard in hand, indicating to Barney where he should sign the ticket, and when and where his court appearance was to be.

Barney looked at the ticket. It cited him for driving without his lights, and for speeding.

"Look!" he said. "I'm guilty of the lights. But I wasn't speeding."

"You must have been," the officer replied. "Otherwise, why would you be driving without your lights on?"

There was no point arguing. Barney signed. He signed and said, "What made you change your mind?"

The officer looked straight toward Anita. "You figure it out, buddy!"

When Barney got back to his apartment in the Hollywood hills, his hands were shaking. He sat in the dark, unable to sleep, smoking cigarette after cigarette. He supposed he should be proud of himself: he had kept his temper. Ten years before, he wouldn't have. Ten years before he would have lashed back, he would have hurt himself more than the white man, but he wouldn't have cared. He wouldn't have cared so long as he could have destroyed the ofay together with himself.

Barney had been born in Puerto Rico in 1937, and been taken to New York in 1943. After a while his father had cut loose, and he was left alone with his mother. He had been in the eighth grade when he'd gotten turned on to marijuana. One day he didn't feel like going to school, so he'd just hung around the block. After that, every day he'd start for school but never get there. He knew he should go, but it was just too much for him. Nobody at the school cared whether he went or not, nobody seemed even to know whether he was there. One day he'd forced himself to go back. He had gone to three classes, and it had confirmed all of his previous impressions.

He'd split again, and never returned.

He'd gotten a job paying $32.50 a week, washing dishes at a restaurant. He had a pad that he shared with another guy, and for which he paid $6 a week. It was exactly six feet by eight feet, and on one side it had a partition that went up only three fourths of the way to the ceiling. A broad had the cubicle next door, and when he was home at night he'd listen to her bringing up her tricks. Sometimes he'd knock on the wall when the guy was there and try to peddle him a couple of joints—if the guy went for it Barney would pull himself up to the top of the partition, and, hanging there, make the deal. One night when she'd been lonely, the broad had invited him over. That had turned out to be no favor, for she'd given him a dose of the clap.

He'd been 14 years old at the time.

After a while he'd gone round to visit his mother. She'd gotten pregnant again, so he'd told her he'd come home and help her around the house. That summer his father had shown up and asked him if he wanted to go to California.

Barney had gone to California. After a few months, he'd headed back East. His money had run out when he reached Joliet, Ill. He'd been there a couple of months, when a fellow he'd met, had said, "Let's go to Florida!"

To Florida they had gone. They had picked fruit, but then gotten into an altercation with the foreman, and were given a floater out of town. From Florida Barney had gone back to Chicago. From Chicago to Kansas City. From Kansas City to Arizona. He had arrived in California, stayed 10 months, then gone back East again. Four months later he had been back on the West Coast. He hitchhiked. He traveled by boxcar, truck, and barge. One time he found a bicycle, and rode it till the tires gave out. He financed himself by working at the dirty jobs nobody else wanted, making just enough money so he could quit. Wherever he went, it wouldn't take him long before he'd be able to make a connection. Once he had 40 or 50 bucks, he could buy some joints, set himself up, and start pushing. As far as he was concerned, working or pushing, they were both the same.

Finally, in 1953, when he'd come back to California, he'd moved in with his father, who was a custodian for the county, and his stepmother, who was a waitress. He had reenrolled in school, but it had been like before—there seemed no point to it. He did have a great natural talent for drawing—it ran in the family—so he'd switched to trade school. Even so, it hadn't been long before he was back peddling weed again.

He was starting to move into the big time. He and two other guys and a broad had driven down to Chihuahua to pick up weed and pills. They had 14 kilos in the car, and the border patrol had had them pegged and had shaken them down, but could find nothing. As they had arrived back in Los Angeles they had noticed that they were being followed. Barney had been let off at Manchester Playground while the others had gone to make the delivery. He was sitting there on a bench when a police car had started toward him across the grass, and he could see a plainclothes man coming from the other direction. He had had no place to go, so he'd sat there and waited.

"All right, son. Let's go," the cop had said.

"I'm not your fucking son!" he had shot back. But the cop had seemed like a decent sort, so he hadn't put up any resistance.

He'd been made a ward of the juvenile court. The L.A. County Probation Department had sent him to one of its forestry camps, where he'd worked a half day and gone to school half. For the first time in his life he had known that he would eat well every day, that he would have a clean bed to sleep in at night. For the first time in his life he had been able to identify with a group. The camp was divided into squads with names such as Seminoles and Cherokees, who competed against each other for privileges and status—and it was expected by his own peers that he would not let the group down. For the first time, if he did well, he had been rewarded with such small privileges as being named "cab boy"—the one who would ride in the cab of the truck and be a project leader. For the first time he had been able to see his own standing in comparison to the others—rankings were posted weekly on the bulletin board with such notations as "Very good work," or "Unsatisfactory—cry baby." For the first time in his life he had had the feeling that somebody knew who he was; that whatever he did, good or bad, would be recognized. That it did make a difference.

When they saw what artistic talent he had, they had let him concentrate on that. They had a workshop with a lot of materials, and an instructor who really knew what he was doing. Barney had drawn and he had painted; he had begun to live for those hours when he could sit down at his board.

One day he had been in a counseling session with three of the other kids, and the atmosphere had been charged with animosity. Usually that meant it was just a couple of hours of sparring. But this one ofay character had broken through.

"Hate me!" he'd said. "I want you to hate me. But use that hate in a constructive way, don't let it destroy you!"

They hadn't understood him at first.

"The man who has it in for you," he had gone on, "he wants to set you up. Let's say I come up to you and I call you a 'nigger,' I keep telling you you're a black bastard, until finally you can take it no longer, so you hit me. As soon as you've hit me I call the cops and we all beat on you, and then throw you in jail. You've done exactly what I wanted you to, and I've wound up getting you just where I wanted. Every time you let yourself be pushed like that, all you're doing is helping the man you hate—the white bigot. Stick a knife into somebody, and he'll yell, 'Look at those savages!' Go around peddling pot, or hustling for some gal, and you'll make him a real happy fellow, pointing out 'nigger vice.' Ditch school, and he'll be able to call you uneducated baboons!"

It had been a new approach, one that Barney had never heard before. A white man telling him to hate. It had hit him that what he was saying was right. He had listened as he had never listened before.

"The only reason the white man can hurt you is because he's got power over you. And he'll hurt you again and again, until you've worked yourself up to a point where you're independent of that power. Let's say you go in a barbershop, and the man says, 'Nigger, get out of here!' If you've got no car, if you've only got a few dollars in your pocket and it's the only shop in the neighborhood, he's really got you, hasn't he? All you can do is get mad and call him a white motherfucker—one thing leads to another, you get in a fight —and like I was saying, you wind up exactly where he wants you.

"But suppose you've got a nice fat wallet and are driving a Cadillac, and the man says, 'Nigger, get out of here!' You can look at him like the pitiable little fellow he is, drive out to Beverly Hills, and get your haircut where they like the smell of your money. So hate. Because hate is a great driving force. But let it drive you up, not down!"

That had been the turning point for Barney. That, and the fact that a Caucasian woman, an artist herself, had seen his work, been impressed with it, and decided to go to bat for him. When, after 10 months, he had been released from the probation camp, he had been able, with her help, to obtain a scholarship to Otis Art Institute. He had started working even before he graduated. In 1957 he had become employed full-time by a Negro newspaper.

The next year an advertising agency, primarily dealing with the Negro market, had hired him. Three years after that his work had become so well known and so highly regarded, that one of the larger advertising agencies had decided they could afford to overlook the color of his skin. That had been at least a partial fulfillment of the counselor's prophecy: his hate had driven him up to the point where the little white man, the fry cook who used to call him "black boy" and order him about, had lost his power over him.

That's when he'd bought the Corvette. He loved that car. Driving it, he felt not only equal, but superior; spiritually clean. It was something that the white man could not deny him, that protected him from the feeling that being black was degrading. For that was the white man's greatest triumph, that he had been able to make black synonymous with meanness and squalor. That was why the hostility always lurked just beneath the surface in Barney—it was the only way he knew how to cope with the feeling that, at best, the white man condescendingly tolerated him.

Hollywood is one of the world's better places for equality —as long as you don't live there—and Barney had had his ups and downs finding an apartment. Even after he'd found it—or, more truthfully, a Caucasian had found it for him— he had been subjected to petty harassments: his television antenna had been cut; mysterious voices had emanated from the plumbing in the middle of the night; a dead skunk floating down on a piece of rope had parked itself in front of his window.

These things had been easier to cope with than the unseen bigotry, the constant question flitting through his mind when he'd be ignored by a white neighbor; how much does he hate me?

After a couple of years he'd been beginning not to let it bother him when, one morning, at 7 o'clock, he'd gone out to find the Corvette with a flat tire. It was parked on a steep hill, and the only level place was the driveway of a house. Not thinking too much about it, he'd backed the car into the driveway, and had just gotten the front wheel off, when a woman in a bathrobe and curlers had emerged.

"What do you think you're doing there?" she had demanded.

He had explained to her that he had a flat tire; that the driveway was the only place in the vicinity where he could change it without running the risk of the jack's slipping.

"You get out of there right now!" she had screamed at him.

"I can't," he had said. "If you'll just give me a minute—!"

"I'll give you one minute. Then I'm going to call the police!"

She had gone inside the house, and slammed the door. Thirty seconds later she had reemerged.

"What are you doing? Why aren't you gone yet?"

"I'm putting the wheel on. I'm putting it on," he had tried to placate her.

"You're doing it deliberately! You're blocking my driveway, and I'm expecting some people at any minute. I'm going to call the police!"

"You'll have to call the police, then. I can't help it."

She had gone back inside the house. He was just finishing tightening the wheel nuts when she came out again.

"This is really too much! At 7 o'clock in the morning! I'm calling the police!" she had yelled.

"Call them!" He had thrown up his hands. "I'm about to leave!"

She had started for the door; then turned around. "I don't know what gives you such nerve! It must be your color!"

He had just wanted to forget it. But then he had started to think. The incident had undoubtedly given the old shrew a great deal of satisfaction. She would tell her friends about it, she would embellish it, make out that he had sassed her, and they would all cluck together in self-righteousness about the "no-good niggers!" So he had gone out, bought a box of the finest candy, had it gift-wrapped, and delivered to her house with the following note: "Thank you for allowing me to use your driveway this morning."

Outside the window of Barney's apartment the first birds were beginning to chirp. Barney lit another cigarette. He had done everything the white society considers proper. He wore Brooks Brothers suits, he had adjusted—after long struggle —his grammar to its ways, he had learned to play bridge, he was circumspect about his sex life, he practiced politeness. Yet, despite all this, he might just as well have been an untouchable in India, there were certain places he could not go, certain things he could not do—if a white girl were seen in his car, it made him fair game for any policeman.

9   Support Your Local Police!

There were a half dozen of them that gathered in Garban Tivoli Godrick's garage after raiding the shelves of the Bing & Yet Market. They ate and drank indiscriminately, mixing beer and Coca-Cola, Fritos and Hershey bars. Against one wall G. T. had pinned a picture of Sheriffs Price and Rainey of Mississippi sitting with their feet up, fat-jowled and laughing; below, in bold black letters, the caption: SUPPORT YOUR LOCAL POLICE. The kids were taking turns throwing darts at it.

"Man, I'm starting to float! I'm floatin' like I was a bird on a cloud!" a 13-year-old, who was bagging it over in one corner, exulted. He was holding a bag, a tube of glue inside, and, as he sniffed at it, the bag moved in and out like a bellows. "I'll lick 'em all!" he shouted. "I'll bust those blue-assed motherfuckers!"

Pancho Pedrally was getting to feel crazy, real crazy. He could see himself 10 feet tall, smashing all the little white cops around. Pancho wasn't his real name, but everybody had started calling him that after the spree he had gone on when he was 10 years old.

It had started in school, during lunch period. Los Angeles schools have no free lunch program, and no cafeterias in those schools in which the cafeteria isn't self-supporting.

The effect of this policy had been that in most schools in the Negro and Mexican-American areas the cafeterias have been discontinued.

Every day at noon, Pancho had to give up part of the lunch his mother fixed him to one of the bigger kids. Refusing would do no good. If he refused, they'd just beat him up, and take it all. If he had a dime, he would be able to pay them off. But he never had a dime. A dime was something his mother would give him maybe once a week.

After a while he'd gotten tired of going hungry. One Monday he had told them to go to hell, he wasn't giving up his lunch. Although he fought, they had taken it from him. Tuesday the same thing had happened. On Wednesday, when he had been challenged, he'd run home, gotten the .32 revolver his mother kept under her pillow, and come back shooting.

They'd backed off, saying, "Man, you is the boss!"

He'd made them run. He'd never had a feeling like that before, making them run! That was when he and his buddy had split from the school. After a while they'd come upon a Mexican kid riding a bike.

"Give it to me!" Pancho had said. When the kid hadn't looked like he was going to, Pancho had shot it out from under him. After that they'd taken the bike and ridden it down to the bus stop. When the bus had come, they'd climbed on. Pancho had pointed the revolver at the driver. The driver, who thought it was a toy, had laughed. Whereupon Pancho had shot one of the toy bullets right through the driver's toes.

That heist had netted him $20, which Pancho thought had been a good day's work, and would keep him in lunches for quite a while. Unfortunately, the police hadn't approved, so he'd spent a couple of weeks in juvenile hall before a judge had decided he could be returned home on probation.

"You know what we do tomorrow!" Pancho looked up from the glue bag. "We gets us a motherfucker chasing us over to the swamp, and we gets him in there, we sticks his head under till he burgle-gurgle come up with a mouthful of pollywogs! Shit, man! They never find him there!"

Pancho was referring to an abandoned cesspool, 10,000 square yards in size and approximately four feet deep, in which he and the other neighborhood kids often played.

"Yeah. You talk like big shit!" G. T. said. "I didn't see you do nothing tonight. All you do is get stupid high sniffing that stuff!"

"You wait till tomorrow. I'm gonna get me some guns."

"Yeah, man. That's what we got to do. Get us some guns!" A couple of the others agreed.

"Like wham, baby! We gets 'em like Cassius Clay!"

"Yeah, man. They don't mess round with those Muslims none!"

"You see those motherfuckers run. Man, they was running like their tail was on fire. They come down tomorrow night, we run 'em out good!"

"Yeah, man. I hear the Muslims are getting ready. Then it's gonna be real groovy!"

"Shit! We don't need no Muslims. Them's old people! A lot of old people like that ain't going to help us none. Their life's done!"

"That's right. Here they don't give a fuck. Down South they care!"

"Yeah. That's what I want to do. Go down South and dig on them Whiteys. That be real groovy!"

"Big shit! They got that Caucasian club down South like the Muslims. They digs screws into the soul people, and pulls all their flesh out!"

"And they takes little kids—chop chop!—off go their heads!"

"Yeah. But there's a lot of them big-ass people from the South come out here. They drives right down Imperial."

"You right, man. We gonna get 'em—right on Imperial!"

"M-m-motherf-f-fucking Whiteys!" A 17-year-old, holding onto a pint of whiskey, shivered, then coughed violently. "They w-w-wants to k-k-kill us all!"

(He had been sick for over a year, but had never seen a doctor. His mother kept saying she thought he was just run down, but chances were that he would become an entry in an endless file of statistics. With 18 per cent of the city's population, the Negro-Mexican areas have 28 per cent of the tuberculosis, 42 per cent of the rheumatic fever and food poisoning; 44 per cent of the dysentery; 46 per cent of venereal diseases; 40 per cent of the epilepsy; 100 per cent of the polio, brucellosis, and diphtheria.)

"Ain't nobody gonna kill me," Pancho said. "Tomorrow

night, we gonna get all the brothers down! We gonna have us a real groovy set-to!"

"Yeah. We gets the Businessmen, and the Gladiators, and the Swampmen. We rounds us up an old bunch of the Huns and the Valiants. Maybe even some of the Parks and the Del Vikings come down. And the Slausons. We gets the Slausons, and we have ourselves a real congregation!"

Pancho had started laughing. His whole body was shaking with laughter. "Crazy groovy!" he held his side. "Crazy groovy that cop with the pollywogs!"

10   "The Magnitude of This Affair Is Not as Great ..."

A few blocks away, on 115th St., two white police officers were assisting a Negro woman giving birth. It was dawn, and already the wind had started blowing from the desert— by 8 o'clock the temperature was starting to nudge up toward 80.

John Buggs, the executive director of the L.A. County Human Relations Commission, knew that this time it was serious. Over the past few years there had been other incidents that could have exploded—the riot at the zoo in Griffith Park, a melee following a track meet at Jefferson High School—but they had always dissipated themselves for lack of a focal point or issue. Last night, however, had convinced him that that focal point had been found. When he reached his office and heard from Leon Smith and Herbert Carter, who had returned to the area at 7 o'clock, that people were already beginning to reassemble, that they were saying, "I've got my stuff ready. If I'm going to die, it might as well be here as in Viet!" "Whitey been kicking my ass too long! It's on tonight!" Buggs decided it was going to take everybody's skills and efforts to avert a repetition of the previous violence.

A smallish man, with hair graying at the temples, Buggs

had been born in Georgia during the First World War, attended Dillard University in New Orleans, and received an M.A. in sociology from Fisk. Growing up in a small Southern town, Buggs recalls vividly with what hopelessness his parents had discussed lynchings that were almost routine occurrences in the 1920's and 1930's, while books such as *The Truth About Lynching and the Negro in the South,* written by a Maryland professor, Winfield H. Collins, suggested that the Negro race should be grateful for every one of its members who was lynched. In 1925 Buggs's father and brother had been clubbed and shot at by three white men because his father had not gotten out of their way quickly enough on a muddy road—the Negroes in Brunswick, Ga., could feel frustrated; but that was all.

In 1942, while he was a social science teacher in a private Athens, Ala., high school, Buggs and a friend had been stood up for two hours in the town square by 30 members of the Alabama National Guard. Cursed, threatened, spat upon, their crime had been they were smoking cigarettes during a practice blackout, and, more to the point, that they lived in the same house on the campus with the principal and his wife—who were white.

After that, Buggs had moved to Florida, becoming director of Fessenden Academy in Marion County, an experimental school operated by the American Missionary Association of the Congregational Church. In 1951 he had transported his family to Los Angeles, where he worked as a newspaper editor, social case worker, and deputy probation officer. In 1954 he had been appointed executive director of the Human Relations Commission, a post in which he has gained national recognition.

Relations between the police and Negroes, which had begun a steady decline in the mid-1950's, had started spinning dizzily toward rock bottom after a shooting incident at the Muslim Temple in April, 1962, in which one Negro had been killed and six wounded, and which had almost totally polarized the black and white communities.

While the whites had remained blissfully unaware that anyone or anything more was involved than a small, erratic minority, a mass meeting of Negroes had been held at one of the area's largest Baptist churches to protest—rightly or wrongly, for, as is usually the case in such incidents, it is probable that neither side was wholly without blame, and both tended to overreact—police brutality, and to appeal to city officials to hear their grievances. When Mayor Sam Yorty ignored them, they carried their plea first to Gov. Brown, then the UN, and, ultimately, the U.S. Commission on Civil Rights.

As a result, the California Advisory Committee to the Commission, headed by Episcopal Bishop James A. Pike, and containing among its members a former Republican national committeewoman, a former member of the Los Angeles police commission, and a municipal court judge, had scheduled hearings in Los Angeles in June.

When the committee had arrived in Los Angeles, it had been welcomed with all the fervor of a bear in a beehive. Mayor Yorty had suggested an investigation of the hearing to determine if it had been Communist-inspired.

Chief Parker had averred, "I do not believe that there is any difficult problem existing in the relationship between the Los Angeles Police Department and the Negro community."

He had stressed, instead, that, in truth, the police are the maligned minority, and that all charges of police brutality are the result of a Communist-instigated campaign to undermine law enforcement. "Too many of the people do not realize," he had said, "that they are attacking our system of justice. I think there is only one substitute for this system, and that is the totalitarian system, and they execute you and talk about you later."

John Buggs's viewpoint had been more balanced: "A situation is being created in which the claim by minority-group persons of police brutality and the counterclaim of police agencies of minority-group resistance to police authority are beginning to be self-fulfilling prophecies." What Buggs had meant was that, with persons of minority races feeling that in every encounter with police they would be treated roughly, and police officers believing that in every such encounter they would meet with resistance, "The very expectations of opposing parties will create what each expects."

Four months later, in December, Chief Parker had issued Special Order No. 33: "Mere knowledge of the constitutional guarantees of racial equality and religious liberty will not suffice. Every member . . . must recognize these principles . . . and demonstrate such recognition. . . . Officers should be especially alert to detect and prevent situations . . . conducive to racial or religious tensions.

"In his daily contact with the people the policeman shall avoid all derogatory comments. . . . Special interest shall be shown in interracial and interreligious problems. . . . A police officer must learn to distinguish between his right to hold personal opinions as a citizen and his sworn duty as an officer. . . . Any manifestation of prejudice while acting as a member of the Police Department cannot be tolerated."

Shortly thereafter, a police officer had pulled Philip Wing, a physical education teacher at Catholic Verbum Dei High School, to the side of the road. "Where the hell you going, you black nigger?" he had inquired.

In six weeks during April and May, 1964, starting with the previously mentioned incident at a track meet at Jefferson High School when police had tried to arrest a teenager for being drunk, four other incidents between police and Negroes had occurred. Reporting by some of the news media was distorted, and, generally, completely out of proportion to the size of the incident. In three of them rocks had been thrown at the police. In one the California Highway Patrol was involved.

When the city's three Negro councilmen warned that the situation was approaching the breaking point, radio station KNX, the CBS outlet, editorialized that they were "encouraging violence in the Negro community" and that they seemed to lack respect for law and order.

On May 24, 1964, Howard H. Jewel, an assistant attorney general of the state of California, felt sufficiently concerned to write a memorandum to Att. Gen. Stanley Mosk.

"Soon the 'long hot summer' will be upon us. The evidence from Los Angeles is ominous."

Jewel discussed the difference between the situations in San Francisco and Los Angeles.

"Chief Cahill of San Francisco has bent every effort to convince San Francisco and his own police department that the civil rights struggle is not between the demonstrators and the police. . . . Chief Parker, by contrast, has made it clear that the struggle *is* between the police department and the demonstrators.

". . . I believe the Chief is right when he says he can 'handle' the demonstrators. But I think he is missing the point.

"In Los Angeles if demonstrators are joined by the Negro

community at large, the policing will no longer be done by the Los Angeles Police Department, but by the State Militia. If violence erupts, millions in property damage may ensue, untold lives may be lost, and California will have received an unsurpassed injury to her reputation.

"One cannot contemplate the personalities and the emotional makeups of the chief antagonists to this struggle—the civil rights leaders on the one hand and Chief Parker on the other—without being struck by the similarities. Each is intelligent and strong-willed. Each regards himself as a champion of a beleaguered minority. Each has almost Oriental regard for 'loss of face.' Each is determined to prevail, no matter what the cost to the community generally. Each is currently embarked upon a course of conflict which is designed not to *avoid* violence but to place the blame for violence upon the opposing party. Neither is willing to take any steps to reduce the possibilities for violence. Each has as his motto: 'Not one step backward.'

"Chief Parker does not deserve the reputation for bigotry which clings to him. Chief Parker does not dislike Negroes because they are Negroes, but because they dislike the police department. This, in Parker's book, is the only unforgivable sin.

"I discussed this problem with Loren Miller [a newspaper publisher and attorney, later appointed a superior court judge] at some length. It was his opinion that violence in Los Angeles is inevitable, and that nothing can or will be done about it until after the fact. Then he expects the appointment of a commission who will damn the civil rights leaders and the Chief alike.

"By this memorandum I am trying to convey my opinion that this is a problem to which you and the Governor could give a high degree of interest. I think it is truly a situation where a stitch in time would save nine. I only wish I could tell you where to start sewing—but you know Parker better than I do."

Los Angeles slumbered through the summer of 1964. The memorandum was pigeonholed. When Gov. Brown was asked about it, he declared that he didn't believe it existed.

While right-wing organizations accused the Human Relations Commission of being, at the very least, Communist infiltrated, John Buggs labored on. The battle was being fought on the political front, Negroes were being told that

equality lay through use of the ballot, and a massive registration drive raised Negro registration from 65.4 per cent
to 76.9 per cent in Watts. Proposition 14, which, in effect,
would reinstate the legality of discrimination by realtors
(and which was later ruled unconstitutional by the State Supreme Court) was the focal point. A chapter of the White
Citizens Councils was organized in Southern California. A
writer for Citizens Council publications was named public
relations director for the Committee for Home Protection,
one of the principal groups lobbying for passage of the
proposition.

A major Southern California newspaper carried a full-page
advertisement by the "Committee of One Million Caucasians to March on Congress." It declared that "every white
Christian patriotic group will be allowed to join the march,"
and that "white Caucasians will carry out the traditional
punishment for traitors. It is their right and duty as true
Americans to do this. But they will try one more time before bloodshed to accomplish this with ballots of the elec-
torate."

A poll conducted by Louis Harris showed that 60 per cent
of the Caucasian population believed that Negroes "smell
different," and that over half of them did not want to have
a Negro living next door. When, in November, the Caucasians got the opportunity to translate that opinion into
votes, close to three fourths of them decided that they
wanted to keep America white.

For Negroes, especially lower-class Negroes, it was not
so much the literal effect of the passage of the proposition
as the symbolic—once more two-faced Mr. Charley had
shown his true character. Once more—for, in addition to
the Rumford Act (passed in 1963 and extending the prohibitions against discrimination in private dwellings), a model
fair-housing agreement had been reached between the United
Civil Rights Committee and the L.A. Apartment Owners
Association in July of 1963—they had taken one step forward only to be pushed back immediately. The Muslims,
and the newly emerging Black Nationalists, who had said
all along that there was no place for the Negro in a white
America, gained new stature and new supporters.

In Watts and the surrounding area, according to a study
conducted by Edward Ramsford of the UCLA Sociology
Department, not one Negro felt himself to have equality

with whites. Sixty-six per cent thought that they were "not treated well," and the remaining 34 per cent that they were treated "very badly." Fifty per cent thought civil rights legislation had had no effect on them whatsoever, and 73 per cent considered Negro leadership ineffective. Twenty per cent were of the opinion they were no better off than they had been in the South, and 56 per cent thought that they were only slightly better off. To 74 per cent, Caucasians seemed so unreasonable that they didn't have any desire to integrate with them, and 64 per cent indicated that there were times when they really hated white people.

John Buggs knew this, but he also knew that the vast majority of Americans don't. That the vast majority don't know it because they feel it is none of their concern, and because the government, which at times startles itself awake like a somnolent man about to fall off a chair, is, as in the case of the somewhat exaggeratedly famous Moynihan Report,[1] afraid to tell them. This report, which *revealed* that one third of Negro children live in broken homes, and that close to 25 per cent—in some urban areas more than 40 per cent—are born illegitimately, was, for a time, suppressed by the government after its publication in 1965 for fear that the shock would be too much for the American political system. The fact that any number of books on the Negro family, such as *Growing Up in the Black Belt* by Charles Johnson, published in 1941, had offered that same information, was apparently unknown to the officials of the Department of Labor.

John Buggs knew, as the myth makers don't, that, contrary to the popularly held opinion that as soon as the black man has an education he can command all the prerogatives of the white, the gap between the races actually increases as education increases. Whereas, at age 40, the Negro with eight years of education has a mean income of $3,548 per year, 80.4 per cent of the Caucasian's $4,409; that of the Negro with a high-school diploma is only $4,731, 70.1 per cent of the Caucasian's $6,609; and that of the Negro college graduate is $7,061, 60.3 per cent of the Caucasian's $11,530. John Buggs knew that a blind Negro girl with a

[1] This is not intended to depreciate the importance of Mr. Moynihan's work, but to point out that much similar information had been previously compiled and then quickly forgotten—a fate that may, in fact, be overtaking the Moynihan Report.

master's degree in sociology spent weeks trying to find an apartment in suburban Orange County, the home of Disneyland and Knotts Berry Farm—while the operator of the latter orated that the Negro problem in America stems from the passage of the child labor laws.[2]

John Buggs knew that, while the Negro had made great economic strides in the decade between 1940 and 1950, raising his income from 39 per cent to 61 per cent of that of the whites, nothing much had happened since. That the absolute income gap between Negroes and whites is actually increasing, and that median income in south Los Angeles *dropped* 8 per cent between 1959 and 1965. That, between 1960 and 1964, in a time of unequaled prosperity, the Negro unemployment rate in the poverty area rose from 12.6 to 19.7 per cent, and that in Watts the male unemployment rate stands at 30 per cent. That unions deliberately restrict entry into apprenticeship training programs so as to keep a tight labor market, and that, among the largest of these, Negroes make up 1.69 per cent of the total in the electrical trades; 2.92 per cent in carpentry; 4.28 per cent in auto repair; 3.24 per cent in bricklaying; 1.87 per cent in painting and glazing; 3.05 per cent in printing; 6.48 per cent in roofing; 1.16 per cent in sheetmetal working; and 0.00 per cent in ironworking, boilermaking, and telephone installation. That in Sacramento, Negroes represent less than .5 per cent of the total in the programs; in Bakersfield 0.0 per cent; in San Bernardino .4 per cent; and in Orange County .3 per cent.

John Buggs knew that, despite all the hoopla about the Manpower Development Training Program, its effect was practically nil, because unions oppose government training programs that would compete with the apprenticeship programs, so that the only four classes being held in south Los Angeles were in typing, service station work, selling (a field in which Negroes have had virtually no chance of getting a job), and for nurses' aides. That, even for such a rudimentary job as service-station attendant a seventh-grade reading level is required, and that 60 per cent of the youths applying have a reading level of the sixth grade or below.

To check his own impression that the portents were ominous, Buggs telephoned Dr. Claude Hudson, dentist, lawyer, and president of a savings and loan association. Dr. Hudson,

---

[2] As reported by Paul Coates in the Los Angeles *Times*.

who is 80 years old, is considered the leader emeritus of the Negro community.

Dr. Hudson had already told Arthur Peters of the FBI, when asked what the riot possibilities were, that all ingredients were present. That "with every action there is an equal reaction. And with every act of brutality the Negro resents and builds within himself a desire to return in time. When you think of the lynchings, the hundreds of bombings in the South, the church in Birmingham, the four little children killed, and no arrest! Can you blame us if there is a time when we lapse into savagery because we have been treated so savagely?"

Confirmed in his opinion, Buggs decided to try to save the situation by impressing the Negro community with the importance of avoiding further violence. Probation and parole officers were instructed to call every person for whom they were responsible and warn them to stay off the streets. Welfare workers were asked to call everyone on state aid, and hint that the checks might be withheld unless the area remained calm. Ministers were contacted in the hope they could influence their parishioners. The Group Guidance Section went out to meet with the kids, hoping to persuade them they had more to lose than to gain if they repeated the previous night's activity. Key people in CORE and Non-VAC, and counselors at Youth Teen Posts and NAPP (Neighborhood Adult Participation Program) were similarly called on for help. Finally, to counteract the rumors that "It's on!" Buggs decided to try to form 56 teams of neighborhood people to go around and spread the word that "It's off!" To do this, he began organizing a meeting to be held at the clubhouse in Athens Park, situated about a dozen blocks from the Avalon-Imperial intersection, for early that afternoon.

That accomplished, at 10 a.m. he called Supervisor Kenneth Hahn and Insp. James Fisk of the police department to inform them of the steps he was taking.

*   *   *

Across the way, in the Glass House, the new, ultramodern police building, Deputy Chief Roger Murdock commented: "It was just a night to throw rocks at police."

Chief Parker, at a news conference, blamed the violence on the doctrine of civil disobedience, promulgated by civil rights leaders.

"You cannot tell the people to disobey the law and not expect them to have a disrespect for the law. You cannot keep telling them that they are being abused and mistreated without expecting them to react."

Agitators had moved into the area some time ago, the Chief said, but the majority of the residents, who are good citizens, had rejected their attempts to disrupt the community.

"The magnitude of this affair is not as great as some prepare to make it. You should watch the misreporting done on tv from New York. The riots were nothing like those in New York, that went on day after day. Los Angeles is quiet as far as racial problems are concerned."

Insp. Karl Lee, who has over-all command responsibility for the 77th division, left on vacation for northern California.

11   "It's His Law and Order—Not Mine!"

When Timothy O'Seyre met his older brother Warner near the corner of Avalon and Imperial in mid-morning, there were already between 300 and 400 persons congregating in the vicinity.

"How are you and all the white Negroes in Crenshaw?" Timothy needled Warner. "Has the White Knight hit any of you yet?"

Timothy was referring to the southeast community's latest jibe at the middle-class Negro; seeing the White Knight in the Ajax television commercial turning everything white with a touch of his lance, he purportedly yelled, "Hit me! Hit me!"

Warner O'Seyre had joined the army during the Korean War, and, using the G.I. Bill, had put himself through college. Receiving his teacher's credentials in 1958, he had, for the past five years, been teaching at Jordan High School in the heart of Watts. With his wife, Marian, working, he could afford all the luxuries of the middle-class white world. He had even achieved residence in an integrated neighborhood on the fringe of the ghetto. Yet each step forward was like a struggle through quicksand.

When Marian had first applied for work at a utility company in 1961, the interviewer had explained to her that she was "overqualified." She was overqualified because, since she held a college degree, he was certain that the job would not appeal to her; that she would be able to do better elsewhere. When she had declared that she would like to have the job anyway, the interviewer had said that he was sorry, but it was against company policy to hire people who would be unhappy in their jobs.

Although Marian had not wanted to, Warner had forced her to register a complaint with the California FEPC. A commission consultant had contacted the company and been informed by a vice president that there must be some mistake. The utility had been an equal opportunities employer for a long time, for . . . well, at least since the mid-1950's.

Would, the consultant had inquired, there be any objection to the making of a survey regarding the racial classification of employees? Of course not, the vice president had replied. It would clear up the misunderstanding very quickly.

The survey had shown that there was not one Negro employed in a white-collar job.

The vice president had been thunderstruck. He was genuinely astonished his company had not been hiring Negroes. He called in the personnel manager, who was equally surprised. Although company policy *had* changed, no one had informed him of it, no one told *him* that he was supposed to hire without regard to race.

Marian O'Seyre had been hired. She had been advanced with almost embarrassing speed, reaching a supervisory position within three years. Despite this, there were still only a handful of Negroes in the employ of the firm. Because of past discrimination and rejection, Negroes, feeling that it was no use, did not bother to apply. Of those few that did apply, practically none had the necessary qualifications.

When Warner and Marian had tried to buy a house in a new subdivision, they had, like every other Negro and many Mexican-Americans, found it impossible to do so. A development, if they went to it, would suddenly have been sold out; or there would have been an unexpected freezing of mortgage funds by the savings and loan association the developer dealt with.[1]

Giving up on buying a house in a subdivision, Warner and Marian had started going to brokers. No white broker would show them a house in a white neighborhood—taking their names, he would promise to call them if anything suitable came up. Nothing ever did. Negro brokers had practically no listings in white areas unless a block had already been "busted": that is, unless one Negro family had already been introduced into the neighborhood. Negro brokers are excluded from the Southwest Realty Association; they are barred from multiple listings (exchange of information by realtors regarding the availability of housing). In Los Angeles, over-all, 80 of the 2,080 members of the real estate board are Negro, which is some improvement since 1960, when there wasn't one, and Leslie Shaw, now the city's postmaster, was refused admittance.[2]

The only reason O'Seyre had been able to buy his home— at that time three blocks beyond the boundaries of the forward-creeping Negro area—was that he had been friendly with the Caucasian teacher who was selling it, and had offered him $2,000 more than the market price. He then had had to scrape up a 35 per cent down payment, and, on top of that, pay a loan fee of 3.5 per cent—whereupon the residents had shown the fervor with which they welcomed him by dumping garbage on his lawn.[3]

[1] Many savings and loan associations have a reputation of practicing segregation as rigidly as the brokers. One multiple developer makes a practice of separate-but-equal housing—he keeps one subdivision open exclusively for Negroes. No matter which subdivision a Negro goes to, he always winds up at the one reserved for him— the salesman assuring him that this is the one which is more convenient, nearer schools and shopping centers, and a better deal all around.

[2] In northern California the picture is, if anything, worse. Of 350,000 houses built since World War II, only about 100 have been sold to Negroes. A check of 62 brokers by Milton Gordon, chairman of the California Real Estate Commission, showed that not one would agree to sell a home in an all-white neighborhood to a Negro.

[3] Los Angeles has had no demonstrations of mass indignation by white residents upset at Negro encroachment, because police authorities indicated they would not tolerate them. Nevertheless, there have been hundreds of incidents of petty and not-so-petty harassment of Negroes moving into previously white areas, ranging from broken windows and swastikas smeared on doors to the beating up of Negro children by white kids, the setting off of firecrackers, and the firing of shots in the middle of the night. These go almost totally unreported in the community's mass circulation newspapers, so that the average white person never becomes aware of them.

As soon as the O'Seyres had moved in, the campaign by brokers, both white and Negro, to induce panic selling had begun. They solicited the white residents, warning them that the area would soon be aswarm with Negroes, and that they had better get out while they could still get a good price for their houses. Actually, the influx of Negroes had tended initially to drive prices up, since the Negroes, limited in their choice, were willing to pay a premium for decent housing. Inevitably, Caucasians had stopped buying in the neighborhood, and three out of ten houses in the block were now occupied by Negroes.

The Crenshaw Neighbors Association, to which the O'Seyres belonged, was fighting a desperate battle to keep the area from going completely Negro; but the battle was being lost. "Integration is that period between the time the first Negro moves in and the last white moves out," was the bitter joke among the 650 members, black and white. In the decade following 1955, when the first Negro had purchased a home, the neighborhood had become 35 per cent Negro-occupied— the point at which whites almost invariably begin fleeing *en masse*.

The schools presage the exodus. Dorsey High School, at one time rated one of the best in the city, sleighrode from 35 per cent Negro in 1961 to 85 per cent in 1965. Caucasians pulled their children out because fights between Negro and white groups became everyday affairs; because some of the better Caucasian teachers requested transfers when they were unable to cope with the different culture of the Negro kids; because parents were afraid of interracial dating; because the Negro children, with their inferior grade school instruction, tended to pull down the classroom standards; and because, inevitably, despite the objections and efforts of both white and Negro parents, marijuana peddlers and other camp followers began to hang out around the school.

As Catholics, the O'Seyres were bitter about the head-in-the-sand policies of Cardinal James Francis McIntyre, who laid down the official diocesan line: Los Angeles has no racial problems. Although approximately 25 per cent of the county's population is Catholic, the diocese, unlike in other cities where the church has taken the lead in racial rapprochement, has no commission on race relations.

In an attempt to fill the gap, about 400 lay members formed the Catholic Human Relations Council. In 1964 when

Proposition 14, sponsored by the California Real Estate Association with the aim of repealing the state's fair housing law, had been placed on the ballot, members of the council had undertaken to campaign against it. For ten Sundays they had stood outside Catholic churches—whose priests, by the cardinal's fiat, were forbidden to discuss the proposition from the pulpit—passing out pamphlets carrying Pope John's picture and quoting his words. To their chagrin, many of the churchgoers had greeted them with hisses of "Reds!" and "nigger lovers!"

Proposition 14 had passed in a landslide. When the State Supreme Court declared it unconstitutional, the realtors had begun to devise new means of nullifying the fair housing law. The opening shot in the 20-year struggle had been fired in 1946, when Charles Shattuck, the association's spokesman, had declared, "We can't let the bars down against anyone."

What Shattuck had meant was that war veteran or no war veteran, bemedaled or one-legged, no Negro or Oriental—or, in some cases, Jew—would be permitted to buy a house in a Caucasian neighborhood. The next year a Negro, living in a white area, had been arrested and convicted on a charge of violating a restrictive covenant, which, in the state, had the force of law. When such covenants had been declared illegal by the U.S. Supreme Court in 1948, the Los Angeles realty board had proposed amending the U.S. Constitution.

In fact, the realtors have continued to be 99 per cent successful in excluding Negroes from white areas. Los Angeles today is more segregated residentially than any major city in the South, and only Chicago and Cleveland top it in the separation of the races in the North.

Between 1950 and 1960, of the 400,000 Negroes in the city, only 1,437 were able to find housing outside the central district or the segregated areas of San Pedro, Venice, and Pacoima. In the vast white reaches of the San Fernando Valley (excluding the Pacoima ghetto) where the population increased from 311,016 to 738,831 during that decade, the Negro population actually *decreased*—from 1,164 to 953!

Now Warner and Timothy were trying to convince the ghetto's residents that, despite the fact that they would be as welcome as locusts in white neighborhoods, they should not retaliate against the white presence in the ghetto. As they walked up the street they encountered a pair of long-robed Muslim women passing out handbills: "Stop Police Brutality.

Stand With Us, Brothers." [4] Kids, who had started throwing rocks again as early as 5:30 in the morning—when a fire engine had been hit—were sporadically lobbing them at cars. Timothy asked them to stop, and they looked at him curiously, as if he had some hidden interest in making the request.

"Why don't you go home?" Timothy suggested.

"Man, why should I go home? Them motherfuckers been pushing me around all my life. Now it's my turn!"

Across the street, in the empty lot next to Vivian and Fred's Market, an old Negro, the plantation Negro of every Southern-glorifying motion picture, stood quietly by his pushcart selling peanuts. A little way from him on the sidewalk, a 12-year-old boy was licking an ice cream cone. A red Volkswagen stopped for the traffic light. Running to the side of the car, the boy shoved the cone directly into the white driver's face.

It was a gesture simultaneously comic and ominous.

The O'Seyres stopped to talk to the people, and it was as if sleeping on their gripes had merely intensified them. . . .

It took 96¢ and three hours to make a round trip to the area welfare office. You might be told to get there at 8 o'clock in the morning, but would be lucky if anybody saw you by one in the afternoon. On some lines the buses stopped running at 7 o'clock in the evening, and on others they ran hardly at all—along Imperial Highway they came once every three hours. To travel downtown it was necessary to go on two entirely separate systems that do not honor each other's transfers and have little coordination of schedules. You could be happy if you made it in less than an hour and a half. One old woman remembered it had taken her 20 minutes to cover the same distance in the 1920's, when Los Angeles had had one of the best rail transportation networks in the country. But then had come the freeways, and in 1959 the last of the rail lines had been abandoned.

To get to General Hospital by bus took two hours, and one woman had taken her baby there because it had a fever of 104 degrees, and had had to wait three hours before the doctor would see it, and when he had seen it he had said that there wasn't much wrong with it, and that he would

---

[4] One leaflet, depicting a Ku Klux Klansman stepping on a Negro, said, "The Song is Ended," and then continued, "But the Melody Lingers On," the *Melody* being a policeman stepping on a Negro in the same manner as the Klansman.

give it some aspirin. On the bus trip home the baby had gone into convulsions and died.

There were only two child-care centers in the entire area. A girl who wanted to work because she considered public assistance a form of bondage was unable to do so because she had no place to leave her children. To take a child to have an inoculation or vaccination she had to travel miles to a clinic; if she wanted to have his teeth looked at, she would have to go miles to another.

If she were going to have a baby, she would first have to go to the clinic to register. She would then have to wait 30 days before returning for an eligibility interview. After the eligibility interview she would have to wait another two weeks before seeing a physician, who would spend about five minutes with her. When time came for her to give birth, she would be delivered by a doctor who had never seen her before.

If she was not eligible for state aid, and had to go to one of the eight small hospitals in the area, chances are three to one that it would be nonaccredited, with a dirty kitchen infested with cockroaches, mice droppings on the floor, no nurse or doctor available at night, garbage in open containers, infectious dressings lying around, and drugs and poisons stored together with food.

"*The man's* got everything. I ain't got nothin'! Make Whitey run—that's the only way I get my kicks. They come down tonight, I gonna kill myself one of the fuckers!"

One man told of going to a used-car lot to buy a car, and the people had sold it to him for $800 on $50 down payment. He had signed some papers, and they had made him wait while they checked out his credit. An hour and a half later they had said that he had lied to them, and would have to come up with another $400 if he wanted to take the car. So he'd had to leave it there, and had forgotten all about it. Four months later he'd received a notice that he owed another $200 on the car, although he'd never driven it a foot. When he asked what it was they were trying to do to him, they explained that, on paper, he'd bought the car, and that while it was sitting on the lot it had depreciated, so that they had been able to sell it for only $600 instead of $800, which meant he owed the $200 difference. When he refused to pay, his wages had been garnisheed.

A woman said that this salesman had come around to her

place wanting to sell her husband a course in electronics for $150, and her husband had explained to him that he couldn't read so good. That didn't make any difference, the salesman had declared, the texts were all self-explanatory. When the manuals had arrived, her husband hadn't been able to read a word of them. He had sent them back, but every month the bills had kept coming. When he refused to pay, his wages had been garnisheed.

"I ain't worked in two years. I had my ass kicked all my life. Motherfucking Whitey ain't never done a thing for the blood 'cept kick our ass! I'm tired of it!"

The man couldn't get a job because he had an arrest record. He had an arrest record because he had been in a white neighborhood when a white woman had been held up and robbed, and the police had rounded up every Negro in the vicinity, taken them down to the station, and held them 48 hours for investigation. It did not matter that the man had been cleared, in the Central Criminal Index there was now a file on him. The file said that he had been arrested on suspicion of robbery, but gave no disposition of the arrest. When the prospective employer got that information, he could only take the applicant's word as to what had really occurred. Seldom would the employer be willing to take the risk of hiring him: the double risk of a *Negro* who had been *arrested*. Of those men who were looking for jobs, 44 per cent had arrest records. Of those 44 per cent, perhaps a fourth had never been convicted.

Timothy O'Seyre had had his own brush with the law. It had been shortly after he had gone to work at Douglas. His wife had been in her sixth month of pregnancy, and they had bought a rug and a couch from a furniture company for $299, making a $99 down payment, agreeing to pay the remainder in four monthly payments of $50. Three weeks later a coupon book had come from the H & P Finance and Loan Co., advising Timothy he was to make six monthly payments of $50 each. Since he had never heard of the finance company and was certain he owed them no money, he had ignored the notice. He had, subsequently, also ignored the warning letter. That had been a mistake; but he hadn't been able to see how he could owe money to a company he had never heard of.

The next thing that happened was that a collector had come to his house one day when he was at work and told his wife that, unless the payment was made within 24 hours, the company would come and repossess the furniture, all of the furniture (Which, technically, the O'Seyres had put up as collateral when they had bought the rug and the couch.)

"You niggers think you can live loose and easy and not have to pay up," the collector had said. "Well, let me tell you, I am going to get you if I have to follow you through hell!"

Timothy's wife, who was not the strongest of women, had not been able to understand. She had gone into hysterics and begun hemorrhaging. The first Timothy had heard of it was when a neighbor called to tell him that she was at General Hospital.

When he went there, he learned that she had lost the baby. After spending all night with her, he had gone to the finance company office the next morning. He had gone there to tell them about their mistake, and what their mistake was responsible for. But the manager had retorted that it was no mistake. That the furniture store had turned over the bill to them for collection, and that the extra $100 consisted of service charges and interest.

"Just a minute!" Timothy had said.

"I don't have any more time to waste on you!" the manager had retorted.

He had started to walk off. Timothy had followed him. "Sir! I was talking to you," he had said, and put his hand on his shoulder.

"I don't have to talk to the likes of you!" the manager had swiveled around.

That was when Timothy's fist had caught him flush in the face, breaking his nose, and sending his blood spurting over the screaming secretaries.

Warner and his father had gotten together and hired an attorney. That had cost $1,500, but it had been the right move, rather than to plead guilty and receive a suspended sentence, as the public defender had advised. It had been the right move, because the attorney had threatened to sue the finance company if the manager pressed charges, and the finance company had been sufficiently impressed with the possibility of losing such a suit to agree to drop the matter, if Timothy would. Therefore, he had never gone on trial, yet he still has an arrest record, and it had only been because of his father's long, steady work record at the company, and the influence that he was able to have the union bring to bear that Timothy had not lost his job.

Warner had learned to reconcile himself to the fact that, by and large, the white community did not want him. He had accepted the fact that one does not *integrate* per se: one has to integrate this rest room, that school, such-and-such a restaurant, or even a public golf club—it had taken years and years of fighting before the county board of supervisors had opened all golf clubs to all people, and Marian had been able to join the public links. He himself would have to make an issue of it if he should want to teach in an all-white school. When it had been pointed out to the Board of Education that there were practically no Negro teachers in one school district encompassing the west side, the Board had corrected the matter immediately. It had redrawn the lines so as to include in the district a largely Negro school with numerous Negro teachers. That had added significantly to the number of Negro teachers in the district—but not one to those in the white schools.

O'Seyre knew that many of the other so-called victories are, in reality, Pyrrhic: the Negro exhausts himself to gain foot by begrudged foot of ground, sits down to rest for a minute, looks up—and finds that the whites have *re*segregated him as efficiently as he ever was segregated in the first place.

O'Seyre thought nothing would shock him any more. That he had seen all, and could accept all. And then, a few days ago, he had discovered that his capacity to be shocked had not been exhausted after all.

He had taken his 5-year-old son, Billy, to the zoo in Griffith Park. They had been walking around, enjoying themselves, when Billy suddenly had said, "Look, daddy, There's a nigger man."

O'Seyre's immediate reaction had been anger; then, realizing he could not hold his son responsible, he had asked, "Where did you learn that expression?"

Billy could not tell him. He did not know.

"Well, you mustn't use it," O'Seyre had continued. "That man is a *Negro*. Just like you!"

O'Seyre had never seen such an expression of shock and terror on his son's face as at that moment.

"I'm not either" he screamed. "I'm not Negro! I'm not!

I'm not!" He had burst into tears, wrenched free from his father's grasp, and run down the path.

It had been, obviously, for Billy the most terrible of revelations. He lived in a white world where everything he saw was white. In the comic strips, in the nursery books, on the television shows he watched, there was not a dark face. He lived in a white world and so he himself had to be white—there was no way for him to have identity as a Negro. The *nigger,* he had heard somewhere, some place, is someone who is inferior, it is someone that you don't want to be!

Well, now he knew; there would be no escaping it for him any longer. He could grow up and *pretend* he was white; or he could grow up and turn it all around, and make *black* stand for everything superior, and white for inferior. But he would have to be Job, Solomon, and Confucius combined if —in a society that, while patting itself on the back with platitudes, keeps reemphasizing that black is black and white is white, and black is the color that if you can help it you ought not to be—he could accept the fact of his own blackness and the other people's whiteness; accept it and believe in the equal worth of both.

"What I got to do with this country?" A 30-year-old spat onto the sidewalk. "Motherfucking Whitey talks about law and order—it's his law and order! Not mine!"

12   Infiltration Is Not Integration

Farther down on Avalon, Jim Burks of the Group Guidance Unit of the Probation Department wasn't making much headway with the kids.

Burks is a medium-tall, muscular 200-pounder in his early thirties, who had competed in track and football at San Jose State. He had planned to coach after graduation, but one day his own coach at the school had taken him aside and advised him to change his plans—the chances of a Negro getting a coaching job were virtually nil. There are no Negro coaches, just as there are no Negro quarterbacks in college or pro football—because the system says Caucasians won't respect or be led by Negroes. Mal Whitfield, who won medals in the Olympics for the United States in both 1948 and 1952, was forced to go to Africa to find a coaching job.

So, after four years in the infantry, Burks had joined the probation department.

The Group Guidance Unit is a unique concept, designed to transform juvenile gangs, of which Los Angeles has an estimated 150 with 20,000 members, from negative to positive behavior. It had been created following the zoot-suit and Pachuco riots in 1943, and had succeeded in clearing violent gangs from various areas of the city. The task of the probation officers, some 15 of whom are assigned to the unit, is gradually to gain the confidence of a gang, reduce and ultimately stem its violent activity, and then convert it into a social-type club. If successful, a natural attrition is likely to set in. As the older, hard-core members graduate, either into a productive adult life or to prison, the younger, who at an early age have come under the guidance of the probation officer, are influenced by his counsel and begin to pattern their behavior along socially acceptable lines. The job requires long working hours, infinite patience, and a willingness to expose oneself to danger, since, in the beginning, a gang's attitude is one of suspicion and hostility. More than one officer has discovered that members of a gang had agreed to jug him, and then backed out.

In 1963, the LAPD launched a concerted attack on the Group Guidance Unit.

That was after the police department, in the mid-1950's, had discontinued its own work with youth groups. At one time the department sponsored the Deputy Auxiliary Police, known as DAPS (somewhat similar to the Police Athletic League in New York), introducing youngsters to the functions of the police, taking them riding in police cars, sponsoring outings and athletic activities, holding good citizenship classes, and operating a summer camp in Angeles National Forest. Some 30 officers were involved with the DAPS, and Chief Parker decided he needed them to fight crime, rather than to engage in social work. He announced the DAPS would be discontinued.

The announcement resulted in such a hue and cry from

the parents of the youngsters, that the city council pressured Parker to rescind the order.

The next year, when the Chief submitted his budget, he did not include in it a request of money for the DAPS. No one in city hall noticed the omission. The budget was approved, and once more Parker dropped the DAPS. When the howls began, he pointed out that it wasn't his fault. There had been no appropriation for the program.

(Said Deputy Chief Richard Simon at the McCone hearings: "Maybe we have been confused in eliminating the DAP program.")

Impugning the effectiveness of the group guidance program, Chief Parker told the Board of Supervisors that, actually, what it did was give status to gang activity. As proof, he cited the fact that the incidence of violence was greater among gangs that had probation officers working with them than among those that did not.

The controversy between the police and the Group Guidance Unit stemmed from the fact that the police department wanted probation officers to provide information—such as rosters of gang members, and who had committed or was about to commit a crime—and when they refused, because such activity would immediately destroy the confidence of the gang in the probation officer, the police accused them of not being on the side of law and order. Aggravating the situation was the fact that probation officers would sometimes go to bat for a kid in court, try to get him bailed out of jail, or attempt to adjudicate disputes between the kids and police at the local level, where police felt that there was nothing to adjudicate, since they knew that they were right.

Following Parker's attack, the Board of Supervisors ordered the program suspended. The interruption lasted about three weeks. The probation department fought back, explaining that violence tended to be higher among gangs with which the officers were working, since, with the limited personnel available, officers were placed in those gangs where the immediate need was greatest. What, ultimately, carried the day for the probation department was that it was, under a Ford Foundation grant, in the process of conducting a study on the effectiveness of the program, and it was agreed that this study should be completed. However, new restrictions were placed on the officers: they were to work only with the younger kids, only with groups of 25 and less, and to be very careful of what sort of activities—such as dances, which could lead to violence—they organized. Before the program could really get going again more than three months had passed, and many of the kids, who had no idea what had happened to their counselors, had reverted to previous behavior patterns.

Burks had been working with the Del Vikings and the Gladiators about a year when the program was interrupted, and he had gained their confidence to the point where they would call him at one o'clock in the morning, and say, "Mr. Burks, we going to march!" He would rush down, spend the night with them, and talk them out of marching. He had siphoned off some of the members and formed them into the Ambassadors, a club sponsored by the Miracle Mile Optimists Club. Commented one gang member about Burks and the others, "If they leave, we'll just start laying around the park again, waiting for something to do."

Up and down Avalon Blvd., kids were holding impromptu news conferences with newsreel cameramen and reporters. One cameraman directed a couple of 10-year-olds to stick their heads through a plate glass window that had been broken. Another asked a 20-year-old with a handkerchief wrapped around his head to take off his shirt, and he complied. The handkerchief was there to hold in place his hair, which he had just had processed. To the whites in suburbia, unfamiliar and unconcerned about the cultural and status problems Negroes have with their hair, the youth would appear, bare-chested, piratical and sinister.

It was about that time that Burks ran across Ralph Reese and the Rev. Casper Glenn.

Reese, stocky, 21, was a counselor for the Youth Opportunities Board. While in many ways naïve and unsophisticated, he is articulate and had evolved a philosophy of sorts —characteristics that give him a measure of influence with his peers.

Burks knew him from the time he had worked with the Swampmen, a group in Compton. Trouble had erupted in the early 1960's in that city, just to the southeast of the Avalon-Willowbrook area, when the high school had become heavily integrated and a Negro girl had been elected queen over the white candidate. A white gang, the Spookhunters, had threatened to turn the school into a battleground. However, this threat had had in the long run a salutary effect, since it awakened civic leaders and started them working toward a realistic meeting of the problems of Negro-white relations in the community.

Reese was born in Watts. He came from a united family—his father a bus driver, his mother the assistant manager of the Stop Drive-In on Imperial Highway, his brother in the air force—and he symbolizes the new militant political awareness of the lower middle-class Negroes.

"Without togetherness we don't have anything," he declares. "Unity is an iron hand. In unity we have survival. The conflict with white people comes from the fact that whites are raised to nonacceptance of things they don't understand. They've always preached separation psychologically, and the Negro doesn't know what's happening to him. They kept Negroes from thinking for themselves. They made them feel suspicious of each other. But unless the Caucasians realize that black people who never saw them before are seeing them well, they're in trouble. What's happening today is not integration, but infiltration. Integration means *interfeeling!*"

Reese, like a good many other residents, keeps a German shepherd—police seldom bother a man walking a large dog. His views of the police are way out, but they are worth listening to because they are indicative of the opinion of massive numbers of the residents.

"The police are not the great protectors they are in the white community. Whitey uses his cops to keep us here. We're like hogs in a pen. The police are part of the white syndicate, and we have to build our own syndicate for protection. Every time the guys see a cop, they freeze. They think they're going to jail. It's the police suppression that's at the root of Negro crime. They take the blood to jail so he can't get a job, so he's got to hustle to make a living. The police don't want crime to decrease because fewer policemen would be needed—and that would be less power for the Chief."

Burks, together with the Rev. Glenn, minister of the Bel-Vue Presbyterian Church, one of the largest and most affluent in the area, asked Reese to intercede with the kids. Reese said that the kids were in a mood to fight, but that he would see what he could do. He believed he could do nothing unless the police and the Whips made some concessions. He suggested that Avalon Blvd. be blocked off from Imperial Highway to 120th St., a distance of eight blocks, so that they could hold a dance, which would end at 11 p.m. No nonresidents, either white or Negro, would be permitted to come in. The police would stay at least one block outside the area.

Burks promised he would relay the condition to Buggs. He invited Reese to the Athens Park meeting at 1:30 p.m.

13   The Los Angeles Police—An Appraisal

If Ralph Reese's view of the police department is an extreme and telescoped one, there are few that are impartial. It may, therefore, be helpful to take one that, if not without its point of view, at least has the merit of not having been written for public consumption. Prepared by the University of Southern California Youth Studies Center for the use of correction workers in their dealing with police officers, its "purpose was to capture police perceptions of reality."

Much of the document concerns itself with the relation between the police and juveniles:

"The police argue that since the juvenile is considered not responsible for his acts, he therefore should not have the privilege of the First and Fifth Amendments to the Constitution. Juvenile officers commonly shake down automobiles, girls' purses, and boys' pockets. They exhibit some discomfort in doing this but facetiously remark that what they are doing is perhaps unethical but necessary.

"Police brutality in the form of physical violence does not appear to be an important consideration. Verbal abuse of the suspect is a more common occurrence. Police themselves do not recognize that their interrogating techniques are abusive. Sustained and prolonged questioning of juveniles, using relays of police, is not uncommon. The intensity of the interrogative effort of the police is perhaps heightened by the fact that if a juvenile 'cops out' by confessing to whatever he is charged with, the officer does not have to appear in juvenile court.

"The police have established a sharp dichotomy between

what they characterize as the misunderstood juvenile and the junior criminal. Police agree that there are youngsters whose home environment, mentality, and general deprivation is such that they almost unwittingly come into contact with the law. Juvenile officers are sympathetic toward this type of child and often work with him and his parents over long periods of time in an attempt to straighten him out. They consider this type of juvenile 'reachable' and feel that it is worthwhile to attempt to help him in any way he can be helped. The junior criminal is an entirely different type of person, from the police perspective. He is the 'mad dog' of which J. Edgar Hoover speaks. He is a hardened sophisticate and has usually had any number of brushes with the law without benefiting therefrom. The police see little hope for this type of individual. They point out that exposing the junior criminal to the treatment process of camps, probation, youth authority, parole, etc. does nothing but increase his disrespect for the whole legal process of society. Police feel that since this type of individual is hopeless as far as changing his behavior is concerned, the only thing that can be done is to protect society by insuring his incarceration. Police are somewhat resigned to the fact that they cannot keep the junior criminal locked up for very long. Since the treatment approach is based on returning the individual to society as quickly as possible, the police see their job as that of consistently putting the individual back into the system and hoping for the best until he reaches age 18. At that time, they say, he can be 'stuck in the bucket' and kept there.

"Approximately 90 per cent of the juveniles taken into custody are released without having complaints filed. In 1960 over 19,000 juveniles were taken into custody and just over 900 were filed on. . . . One of the main reasons juvenile officers give for counseling and releasing the juvenile is that they do not want to introduce him to the formal system of juvenile justice until they have to. They point out that the system is a 'soft' and easy approach to the youngster and that once he finds this out he no longer has the threat of juvenile court to deter him from possible delinquent acts. Thus the police, in picking up the 'reachable,' unsophisticated juvenile paint grim pictures of what he can expect if he continues his antisocial behavior. They attempt to impress him with the grim reality of a future of jail and punishment. . . . If the youngster's behavior continues he eventually does reach the court and there he finds, if he has not already been told by some other juvenile, that the system is not at all as severe and harsh as the police had indicated. Police then find themselves confronted with a youngster who has gone through the court process and has, in a manner of speaking, beaten them back to his neighborhood. Police are uncomfortable because they feel that they have not been backed up by society in their effort to impress him.

"The police appear to assume automatically that the petitions against youngsters are sustained. [I.e., that they are convicted.] In talking about the arrest record of a juvenile many point to the fact that a youngster has been arrested 12 or 15 times and they take this as indicative of his delinquency. On the other hand, they do not really know how many times the petitions have been sustained.

"Once the juvenile has been arrested and booked, that record is maintained indefinitely. This means that a routine police check of the individual as an adult will reveal that he was arrested at some time as a juvenile but the record does not reveal what the disposition was.

"While there are a number of exceptions, in general the line-operating enforcement agent communicates with the juvenile in what could be termed the delinquency idiom. The language has an underworld flavor and employs the use of such words as 'fink,' 'cop out,' 'taking a fall,' 'in the bucket,' and so forth. Special words, many of them obscene, are reserved for the junior criminal. In the interrogation process, if the juvenile is of that class called the junior criminal, the language is often spiced with obscenity. Not all officers employ this kind of language but those that do insist that it is the only way they can communicate with some of the juveniles. Police also use the same language among themselves."

There are certain people, the police believe, "that probably will never be fit to live in society, and that the best thing that can be done for them at this point is to keep them locked up. They do not feel that keeping the juvenile locked up is going to be of any help but then they do not feel that anything will help." On the other hand, the "position of corrections people in California is that the state cannot continue to build expensive facilities for detaining juveniles, or, for that matter, adults." It costs a minimum of $4,000 a year—more than it would to send him to the most expensive college in the land—to keep a person incarcerated, and facilities are already so overcrowded that some juveniles have to sleep on mattresses on the floor.

"Police feel that there are too many ways for the juvenile offender to beat the system as it is now constituted . . . he gradually develops a healthy disrespect for the entire system of justice and law enforcement. . . . The police feel that in our modern, complex society, parental discipline has largely disappeared and that, somewhere, some agent has to take on that role."

The very nature of the police as a restraining agency upon the behavior of citizens—as well as a protector of lives and property—tends to create conflicts between them and even law-abiding persons.

"The police very often see themselves as an isolated group in the general community. This feeling of a lack of understanding by, and general isolation from the rest of the community generates a considerable amount of suspicion and hostility on the part of the police.

"Many police feel that the effort of the NAACP is directed, not so much at seeing that justice is done, as far as the Negro and the police are concerned, but at harassing police operations. The NAACP does seem to be somewhat preoccupied with trying to prove police brutality based on prejudice."

It must be remembered that this was written in the early 1960's, and what the feelings of the police are about CORE and the more militant civil rights organizations now may be imagined. With both parties to the dispute—the police and the Negroes—considering themselves the victims of persecution, the mix is so volatile that even the slightest stirring is likely to set off an explosion.

"The enforcement agent realizes that in stopping an individual . . . he is almost bound to incur resentment and some hostility. After a number of such experiences, he comes to expect hostility. . . . Police are fully aware that carelessness can mean serious personal injury or even death. . . . Many officers feel that the one sure way to avoid trouble with a suspect is to demonstrate their own ability to handle the situation. This may take the form of . . . 'grabbing on to you,' or, in general, roughing up [the suspect] in terms of grabbing him by the arm, pushing him here and there, pushing him into cars, and so forth.

"There are enforcement agents who go through their entire career having seldom to display force, draw their guns, or otherwise reinforce their authority. There are other policemen who, almost every time they attempt an arrest, find themselves faced with resistance. . . . Most police textbooks and many training bulletins point out to the neophyte officer that if he is to retain control of a situation, he must at all times be aggressive and authoritative in dealing with others. He is admonished to develop a forceful, loud voice which will convince the apprehended individual that he means business. . . . We can ask the question of whether or not the aggressive, forceful, authoritative manner of a policeman does not, to some degree, evoke hostility and perhaps aggression on the part of the person whom he is attempting to apprehend."

In this context it is interesting to note that the annual number of attacks on police officers increased from 104 to 592—or from 2.5 to 11.9 per 100 officers—between 1952 and 1964. However, the number of assaults with a deadly weapon, which can be interpreted as *deliberate* assaults on police officers, increased only from 13 to 44, and, in fact, since 1958, when there were 33 such incidents, has held fairly steady. On the other hand the number of *batteries* on officers, almost all of which occur as the result of an altercation during an arrest, jumped from 44 to 338, and has continued to increase steadily. Since this period was almost totally concurrent with the administration of Chief Parker, there may be some question as to whether his philosophy that the police should not engage in sociology was one that paid dividends.

"Many policemen pursue the goal of preserving life and property with a zeal that borders on a missionary attitude. The world about the policeman is one of good or bad, right or wrong, and there seems to be no room for anything in between."

The police department, like any other organization, has a pecking order. "Departmentalization and specialization creates distances between individuals and sets up a situation for potential conflict. . . . At the low end is the Traffic Department, and at the high end the Metro [metropolitan] Division. Police officers sometimes characterize officers in traffic as 'firemen with their brains kicked out.' At the other end police feel that only very special highly qualified officers go into

Metro and to be selected is a good indication of continued upward mobility."

As in any bureaucracy, officers sometimes find themselves hampered by the rigidity of doing everything "according to the book." "Juvenile officers, at least at the University Division, feel that they are too closely supervised." In one case, "officers had been making a practice of eating their lunches in various theaters. These theaters had been plagued by a high incidence of vandalism; ripping up seats and general disturbances by juveniles. The officers did not consider that they were stepping out of line. They reasoned that they were actually going beyond what was required of them and providing an extra service more or less on their own time. A lieutenant, characterized as being 'on the make' . . . checked up and found the officers in a theater eating their lunch. He reported this incident to his superior and the officers were reprimanded. These officers now scrupulously avoid going into theaters or doing anything else that might possibly leave them open to criticism."

The police are suspicious, and often resentful, of anyone, including their own members, who attempts to work with juvenile gangs. "At the time of the zoot-suit and Pachuco gangs, members of LAPD juvenile section formed a gang worker unit in an effort to control the situation. One result was that this group of police officers eventually came into conflict with their colleagues in other units who felt they were going outside their proper police role."

As has already been indicated, this conflict is even more pronounced when it comes to the Group Guidance Unit of the probation department.[1] "Since group guidance workers are equated with the general social work groups, the police attitude is more than a little negative. As with other so-called do-gooder groups, they consider that group guidance workers are essentially in sympathy with the juvenile gang and hostile to the police. . . . They often refer to group guidance meetings with delinquent gangs as 'little Appalachian meetings.' This is indicative of their general feeling about group guidance activity. They insist that group guidance is not diminishing gang activity but is providing formal recognition for such gangs, which tends to unify its members. . . .

[1] Following the riot, the unit was, experimentally, transferred from the jurisdiction of the probation department to that of the County Human Relations Commission.

For example, the Gladiators, once they were organized, launched a fund drive in order to buy themselves jackets that would identify them as Gladiator members. These jackets cost about $35 apiece. The front of the jacket, on the left-hand side, has a large patch which shows a gladiator with drawn broad sword standing over his fallen foe with his foot on his chest. Under the patch is the word, 'Gladiator.' The police feel that this certainly is not an appropriate symbol for a group which is presumably being helped to redirect its activities to less violent types of action. Police feel thwarted, challenged, and threatened by an officially sponsored activity. . . . They insist that the group guidance workers are not neutralizing the gang psychopath, they are personalizing him by officially establishing him as the leader of his gang."

Most gangs, actually, have two leaders, the leadership tending to be divided along political-military lines. One is the *talker,* who controls the gang when it is just hanging around; the other is the *fighter,* who leads it into battle.

Police believe that these juveniles have no standards. In actuality, it appears more correct to say that, since they are "denied the opportunity to conform to middle-class values and thus are forced to create their own system," their behavior conforms to what is acceptable to their peers, and it so happens "that these standards are inimical to the rest of the society."

The Negro and white cultures already being widely divergent, and the police and the Negro juvenile delinquent tending to be at the extremes of their respective cultures, at opposite ends of the world in one sense, they are in constant conflict at the other.

14   My Mother, the BPA

Anita Greyson came to work in an angry mood. She could have bit her tongue last night, after what had happened with the officer; but she had thought that he had seen her, that he had been genuinely decent about the whole thing, and . . . what the hell! She was determined to help Barney fight the ticket.

In the southeast area office of the BPA the social workers are packed together in one huge bull pen, desk nudging desk, row upon row, typewriters clattering, telephones jangling, human voices intertwining like a mass of spaghetti—it is a hell of noise and togetherness. Secretaries are not available; and, unless he wants to use one of the dictating machines in the half dozen cramped, grimy cubicles that are sometimes booked for days in advance, the social worker must do all of his own typing and paperwork. The paperwork has grown beyond either human capacity or comprehension. Since funds come from many different sources, and each source jealously guards its prerogative to have its own forms with its own concept of what information they should contain, there are forms for the bureau, forms for the county, forms for the state, forms for the federal government, forms in quadruplicate, forms in quintuplicate, and forms just to keep track of the forms. Each worker is supposed to handle 60 cases. But, in actuality, because of the constant turnover—35 per cent of the personnel quit every year—the case load is often almost double that. Cases get shifted from worker to worker, and sometimes are lost in the transit. It is a rarity when a worker is able to stay with one family long enough to have anything more than a superficial relationship with the recipients of aid. The regulations themselves constitute a stack several feet in depth, and it would take any one person years to become intimate with them. When the director of the bureau attempted to explain to the McCone Commission the method used to calculate the amount of assistance, the former director of the CIA was so baffled that he recessed the hearing.

Anita had gone to work for BPA six years before after a brief stint as a newspaperwoman, and she had just about had it. She had, in fact, been intending to quit for three years. But she was so fascinated by the inanity and illogic of what was happening to the minorities in America that she stayed on, half hypnotized, waiting for the moment when the whole mess was going to collapse upon itself like a bubbling-over pot of porridge that has suddenly had the fire turned off beneath it.

In 1959, her first year, the budget for aid to dependent children had been $40.2 million. Less than 15 years before, in 1945, it had been one twentieth of that: $2.4 million. By 1951 it had grown to $28.2 million, and, since her arrival, it had jumped to $55.7 million in 1962 and $96.2 million in 1965. The projection for 1966 was $110 million. Since 1962 the number of cases had risen by 17,000, and the number of recipients by 89,000—an increase of 77 per cent! Among these are at least 7,500 children on the fringe of total neglect by their parents. Thirty-six per cent of the mothers have *never* been married, and there is at least one illegitimate child in *seventy* per cent of the families.

Despite this spiraling increase of chaos, half the applicants for aid are rejected. It is a rule of thumb that *emergency aid* is never granted the first two times it is asked for. If it is a real emergency, the applicant will come back a third time or will have solved his problem by some other means—such as stealing or robbing.

Every time she heard the oft-repeated myth that women on relief are having babies because it's profitable—"screwing us into poverty" a date of hers had once termed it—Anita went into convulsions of laughter. At $200 a month a woman with four children, having to pay anywhere from $50 to $75 for rent, was hardly living the life of Riley.

The BPA has figured allowances just about as close as they can be figured—if two cents is left over at the end of the month, it isn't the fault of the Bureau. A child is permitted $1 a month for transportation, $1.35 for personal needs, and 50¢ for recreation. A family of 10 is allocated $4 per month for education and incidentals. The monthly food allowance for a woman is $27. A growing boy gets $4 more.[1]

Any woman who already has nine children will get the huge lump sum of $5 monthly for each additional child.

In actuality, because only a certain amount of money is appropriated by the state, and this is not enough to cover all of the cases, 60 per cent of recipients do not even receive the minimum amount needed for bare necessities, as calculated by BPA. For example, the state has set an arbitrary maximum of $51 per month for rent, even though 75 per cent of recipients pay more than this. At one time the

[1] For comparison, a middle-class Los Angeles family of two, living well but not extravagantly, spends approximately $150 a month for food.

rent allowance had been less, and BPA had worked hard to
get it raised by $4 or $5, only to discover that, as soon as
it was, landlords had increased the rents by exactly the same
amount—the recipients had not benefited one whit.

One case handled by Anita had been that of a woman with
nine children living in a public housing project. She had been
receiving $371 per month, the maximum possible amount,
even though her needs, according to the schedule, were almost $100 greater. When this woman had gone to work at
$333 per month as an aide in the Anti-Poverty War Neigh-
borhood Adult Participation Project, her salary—except for
a $25 allowance for on-the-job expenses, and an additional
small work-incentive allowance—had been deducted from the
check. The public housing authority had promptly raised the
rent from $56 to $114, absorbing all of the additional money,
and, in effect, punishing her for going to work.

It was, as Anita kept saying, an incredible system, one that
would not spend a cent for prevention, when the cost of the
cure kept increasing tenfold every year. Among the 85 cases
she handled there were 30 individuals—both adult and juvenile—who had been in corrective institutions, and each one
of these during his incarceration cost the state $4,000 per
year. To maintain one individual in the job corps for one
year cost more than $9,000. Yet to get an extra $25 that
might keep a boy from going over the brink was, literally,
impossible.

Anita had had one case, a 30-year-old girl with four children, for whom she had deliberately stuck her own neck out.
Her name was Teressa, and Anita, on her initial visit to her,
had been sitting there with the forms on her lap, calculating
the amount of eligibility, when Teressa, curiously glancing
at the complicated schedule, had rattled off the exact figure.

"My God" Anita had ejaculated—it was the greatest shock
of her entire social work career. "How'd you do that?"

Teressa had explained that she had always been good at
figures; that mathematics had been her favorite subject before she had dropped out of high school to get married.

"Why don't you go back to school?" Anita had asked her.

Teressa had been completely self-effacing—no one had ever
suggested such a thing before, no one thought her capable
of it. Anita had had to push her like a shy child. In a few
months of night school Teressa had gotten her high-school
diploma, and it had been such an exhilarating experience for

her that she had decided she would like to go on to junior college.

That's where the rub had come in—she would need an extra allowance for such things as transportation and books, and, especially, for someone to take care of the children. Welfare regulations provide such allowances for working mothers—but not for studying mothers.

Anita had gone ahead and granted her the money. Teressa finished two years of junior college, and went on to Pepperdine, majoring in mathematics. She had completed her third year when the case was taken away from Anita and a new social worker was assigned.

The new worker was aghast at what had been going on. Teressa told her that she wanted to be a teacher.

"Don't you think your goals are entirely unrealistic?" the worker had inquired of her. "Don't you think you should be going to work?"

Four years before such a question would have cowed Teressa completely. But now she stuck to her guns. When the worker deleted all the extra allowances from the budget, Teressa made application to the Dollars-for-Scholars program, a community project that provides small amounts, usually not more than $25, to needy students. In Teressa's case she needed considerably more, but several persons were so impressed with her that they had gone to the bank and personally underwritten a loan. Teressa had graduated, received a scholarship to Stanford University, and, ultimately obtained her M.A. and teacher's credentials, becoming a junior high school mathematics teacher.

It was almost 11 o'clock when Anita's supervisor relayed the request that she call all her cases and warn the mothers to keep their children off the street.

Anita knew that she would never be able to reach all 85. That it was, in a sense, futile, since one of the main problems is that most of the mothers have no control over the children. That, in fact, the children can exercise control over the mothers by threatening to drop out of school, so that the allotment for them will be cut off by BPA. Pawing over the case histories, each one anywhere from three to six inches thick, Anita tried to decide where she could make calls that would do the most good.

She pulled out the file on ASPARITA PEDRALLY.

Asparita Pedrally had been born in New Orleans, La., in 1927. Her first contact with the Bureau had come in 1948, when her eldest son, Bogart, was one year old, and her husband, Thorex, had been sentenced to six months in the county jail for receiving unemployment insurance while working. She had been granted $1.68 for an emergency food order, and six tokens for a trip to the clinic.

The next year, Thorex had been sent to the federal penitentiary in Arizona for interstate transportation of a stolen car. He had come home in July, 1950, a big man, quiet and friendly, thanking the Bureau for the assistance they had given his wife. He had returned to his old job as a presser in a cleaning plant.

Case closed.

Three years later the file was reopened. Asparita was alone with a new baby. Her husband, who deserted her every time she became pregnant, had taken the three oldest children, Bogart, 5, Honey, 2, and Pedro, 1, back to Texas. It was suggested to Asparita that she return to New Orleans, but she said she was too weak to travel.

(It is usually suggested to women, when they first apply, that they go back to the state they came from. But since this often sounds to them as if they're being asked to go back to hell, they seldom do.)

After a few weeks Asparita had gone to Lancaster, in the Mojave Desert, where she had been offered a job. In 1954 she was back in Los Angeles with the newest addition to the family, Kyle, whose father was Governor Prender, an unemployed plumber's helper.

Thorex Pedrally brought the children back from Texas. He and Asparita became very drunk. He stabbed her, injuring one of her kidneys. She went to the hospital, and he went to jail. For two days the children were left by themselves, until someone finally called the police, who took them to juvenile hall.

When Asparita returned from the hospital three weeks later, all of the furniture except the refrigerator had been repossessed. The family ate off packing crates, and the Salvation Army donated some mattresses and blankets on which they slept on the floor. The BPA put them on a budget of $125 per month.

Asparita asked if she could have some money to make

payments on the refrigerator, on which she owed $300 to the Bank of America. The social worker said she thought an increase in the budget was unwarranted, and that Asparita should find some other means of saving the refrigerator. The bank repossessed it, and a few weeks later Bogart and Pedro (Pancho) were in the hospital suffering from salmonella.

Asparita was pregnant again, but said she felt badly about it.

Governor Prender came by one night, and knocked Honey all the way across the room, giving the 4-year-old girl a severe concussion, because she kept pestering him, asking him if he were her daddy. Bogart brought a stray dog home, which bit Kyle, and turned out to be rabid. Kyle had to undergo the Pasteur treatment.

Just before Easter, Asparita called BPA and asked if she could have an emergency food order, because she had bought the children some new Easter clothes. She was turned down. The next day she was arrested for being drunk and creating a disturbance. She had 16¢ on her, which, she said, were her life savings.

She spent two weeks in the county jail, "The best vacation I ever had." The children were cared for, in a somewhat haphazard fashion, by a neighbor. When Asparita returned home, the landlord had evicted her, and both the few pieces of furniture she had been able to gather and the children were standing out in the rain.

Asparita's next home was a shed, with rags stuffed in the cracks to keep the wind out. The four older children slept together in one single bed, two at one end and two at the other, Kyle slept with Asparita, and she kept the new baby in a chipped wash basin. She cooked on a hot plate. There was no running water or any sanitary facilities.

In the fall, Bogart started to school, and Asparita moved into a $65 a month apartment. Her injured kidney was bothering her, and she had to go to the hospital several times. In November, the social worker asked her if she were pregnant, and she said, "No."

In January, Tulip was born.

Tulip was the daughter of Charles Doon, whose contributions had enabled Asparita to move into the apartment. He made $45 a week working at an auto reconditioning and maintenance service, and promised to contribute $15 a month for the baby's support. Asparita was very remorseful. She hoped she would not have any more children, and wanted to go to work when the baby became bigger.

The social worker had a special investigator sent out to the house one night, and he found Asparita in bed with Thomas Billings. Asparita was surprised, because she said she had never had any trouble with the county, but that she did know that "The BPA is just like a bodyguard or a mother."

She explained that she had been going with both Doon and Billings simultaneously, and had been sleeping with them on alternate nights, which, she thought, was fair, because it wasn't playing any favorites.

Doon said that he would not make any further payments, because Asparita had "turned me up." Billings said he supposed he might move in with Asparita.

Billings was employed at a Veterans Administration Supply Depot. His take-home pay was $277 per month. He owed the Pacific Finance Co. for tires; the ARC Investment Co. for car repairs; National Loan Co. to pay off the car; the First Western Thrift & Loan Co. for furniture; and Acme Clothing for the suit he was wearing. He had a wife and two children from whom he was not divorced, and he was contributing to the support of an illegitimate child in Oklahoma. The BPA figured that he should be able to pay $111 a month toward the support of Asparita. When he suggested that this was to high, the amount was reduced to $107.

Billings lived with Asparita almost two years. Booker and Roberta Billings were her eighth and ninth children.

Anita Greyson had had the Asparita Pedrally case three years. The first time she had seen her, Asparita had been eight months pregnant, and when Anita asked her why she hadn't told the social worker, Asparita said she had thought that she knew—it was the usual story, the usual evasiveness about pregnancy, and then the inevitable birth.

This time, Asparita promised, would be the last. She was, in fact, thinking about getting a divorce—she had heard one could get a divorce cheaply and quickly in Mexico. Anita, who had not had time to read through the case, asked her if the baby were her husband's, and she said No, it was Mr. Billings's baby. But, as it turned out, Mr. Billings claimed that it wasn't. He thought that it was a Mr. Eagle Terman's.

After the birth of the new baby, in late 1962, Anita compiled a roster of the family.

Bogart (15), Honey (12) and Pedro (11) *Pedrally.*
Forrest *Pedrally* (10). (Husband denied paternity,
and, in all probability, not his.)
Kyle *Prender* (8).
Innerva *Prender* (7). (Prender denied paternity.)
Tulip *Doon* (5).
Booker (3) and Roberta (2) *Billings.*
Siska (3 months) *Billings* (?) or *Terman.*

The BPA was supporting all seven of the older children.
The District Attorney's office had failure-to-provide warrants
out for Pedrally, Prender, and Doon, but they were nowhere
to be found. (Pedrally and Doon were discovered shortly
thereafter: one in jail in Nebraska, the other in jail in
Massachusetts.)

When Anita went back to see Asparita, she found Eagle
Terman in the house, watching the children. She told Asparita that she really should not have any more children, and
Asparita said for her not to worry, that she had gotten religion and found God, and that she had decided she could
get along better without a boyfriend. What about Mr. Terman, Anita inquired? Asparita replied that he was like a
brother to her, and that he only stayed at the house once in
a while, when he slept on the couch.

It appeared that Asparita really had gotten religion, for the
radio was turned on to the "Airmail from God" broadcast
from Temple City. "Do not fail to write immediately for the
free materials offered on this broadcast," the announcer said,
"and send a gift of three dollars or more. Goodby for now,
and may God bless you abundantly." Asparita, as well as
Honey, who had also found God, had joined the Mount
Tabernacle Heavenly Holiness Missionary Church, where
they went to prayer meetings several times a week. The meetings started at 8 p.m., and often went on into the early morning hours. On the livingroom wall hung a metal cast of "The
Last Supper," and another said "Prayer Changes Things." A
colored telephone that chimed instead of rang was prominently displayed. (Everybody in the area has a colored telephone. It is a major status symbol.) On the table stood a pair
of busts of President and Jacqueline Kennedy.[2]

---

[2] A likeness of Pres. Kennedy, a greater hero to the lower-class
Negro than Lincoln or Roosevelt ever were, may be found in virtually
every home.

Asparita was a smooth-skinned, round-faced, smiling and pleasantly plumpish woman, who, Anita assessed, had no willpower whatever. She had a mincing, little-girlish manner, and was a terrible housekeeper. Except for an incongruously fresh-looking vase of artificial flowers, the house, one of the older ones in Watts, reeked with age and dirt. Cockroaches wandered about the scuffed furniture like exploring mountain climbers. Three-year-old Booker was chewing on a beetle he had caught and, when Anita commented, Asparita said Yes, she knew, but that he liked them and they didn't seem to hurt him.

Asparita mentioned that Pancho (Pedro) hated school, that he disliked authority, and that he felt people there were always trying to push him around. Bogart, on the other hand, was a good student, a really brilliant boy.

"Bogart's problem," she said, "is that he don't quite know exactly what race he is. All I can tell him—I don't know myself—Mexican, French, Negro, one of his grandfathers was Portuguese, I think, and another half German. I told Bogart I survived it, and so can he.

"Kids used to call me 'Mex'!" she continued. "I wasn't allowed to play with other kids. My father's mother raised me. They thought she's too good to play with us! They wouldn't even allow me to walk to the store with other children. But as you get older, you don't think much of it. Really, I had no problem.

"Just picture this! Here I am in the front yard all fenced in, with a stiff lace dress on Sunday. Kids all dirty in the street, yelling, 'Mex can't get out'!"

Bogart, Anita noticed, was very interested whenever she and his mother talked, and kept trying to overhear. He seemed to be more alert than the other children, and almost painfully serious.

"I keeps having these nervous spells, faints and everything!" Asparita complained. "They come on all of a sudden like and I can't see. The children, they have to carry me to bed. Bogart, he's real good about it, and he comes and sits with me. He tries to help me all he can. He worries about the money, and about all the things like that. He's real good. Only thing, he get sickly just like me, so we both taking iron tonic. It taste awful, just like rust. But it build you up real good!"

Anita asked Bogart what he planned to be.

"I'm going to the navy. To Annapolis," he said. And then he thought about it. "No. I think I'd probably like Oxford better."

"Bogart's got a problem with the other children," Asparita explained. "They awful rough around here. The gangs won't let him alone. He's got so he just about don't like to go out of the house. Pancho is the one that worries me. He's got these bad eyes, and he won't wear his glasses. He keeps breaking them." Pancho had gotten 13 F's in school the past year.

The house had only two and a half bedrooms, and Honey did not like to sleep with the younger children because they were so noisy, so she shared one bedroom with the four older boys. This didn't bother her, but it did bother Bogart, who was shy.

It was summer when Anita went back again, and the children were teasing 9-year-old Kyle because he had lost his shoes. They had been his only pair, and he wanted to go to the park with the other children, but, whenever he started off, the pavement would burn his feet. When Anita saw him, he was in a tantrum of frustration.

Pancho had held up the bus, and was planning to join the army, so he could really learn to shoot.

Bogart had taken "cafeteria" his last semester in school. He was working in exchange for his lunch, said Asparita, but "he was so good, they give him a grade in it." However, he had failed physical education because he refused to strip.

Asparita complained that she was having trouble controlling 13-year-old Honey, who had gotten herself a boyfriend, and would sneak out of the window at night. She was afraid that she would get pregnant.

Anita asked Honey about it, and she replied, in her slow and thick-tongued way, "Oh, don't worry. I know all about not having babies, and that stuff!"

When Anita saw her again, Asparita said that she had talked to God, and that God had told her He didn't intend for her to be unhappy. So she had decided to go ahead and get a divorce from Thorex Pedrally.

Bogart was having a great many physical problems—diarrhea and general weariness. He and Pancho were fighting constantly. He had told Pancho's probation officer that Pancho was sniffing glue, and that he was undoubtedly crazy. He had also suggested to Asparita that she put a mouse trap in the cooky jar, because the younger children were always stealing cookies. Asparita had thought that was such a good idea that she had gone ahead and done it. The trap had broken Tulip's finger, only Asparita hadn't discovered that until several weeks after it had happened, so it looked like the finger was going to be permanently crooked.

Asparita's spells were coming more frequently, and, whenever she had them, all the children would fall on their knees and pray—except Bogart, who would call the doctor, and Pancho, who would whoop and holler and dance around like an Indian, and then fall, or pretend to fall, in a trance of his own.

Honey was pregnant, but was hoping to marry her 21-year-old boyfriend, a $55-a-week painter's helper.

A few months later, Bogart had to be rushed to the hospital because he was having terrible abdominal pains. He was kept for several days, all kinds of tests were performed, but he had no surgery, and was, in fact, rather pleased. "Everything that ever happened, happens to me!" he said.

Pancho had been shooting craps with some boys in a vacant lot when a policeman had come upon them, and told them that they shouldn't do that, because they were breaking the law.

"What would your mammy think if she saw you?" the policeman had asked.

"I ain't got no *mammy,* you motherfucking white bastard!" Pancho had snapped at him. So one more inadvertent remark had laid the groundwork for hatred and conflict.

Early in 1965, Bogart had refused to go to school any more, and had started spending all his days in a tiny, dark closet. He refused to eat, and said it was necessary for him to stay in the closet to study for the examination to Annapolis, because there were Communists after him who wanted to prevent him from becoming an admiral. His mother said she didn't really believe him, but it was true that other boys wouldn't leave him alone, so maybe there was something to it. He seemed quite happy so long as he could stay in his closet, but would become very depressed when he emerged. "Life seems barely worth living, if it has to be lived like this," he said.

Anita checked his school records. At the age of 7, he had scored 126 on his IQ test; when he had been tested again, at age 11, the score had dropped to 99; the last time, at age 14, it had been 86.

Anita suggested to Asparita that Bogart should have psychiatric care, but Asparita had resisted the suggestion. Finally when, in May, he had refused to come out of the closet altogether, even to go to the bathroom, Asparita had had to give in. Bogart was taken as an outpatient. Eagle Terman took him and his mother to the clinic every day on his way to work, and they had to get up at 4 a.m. in order to ride with him. They had to wait on the sidewalk until 6 o'clock, when the clinic opened, and would be picked up again by Terman on his way home at 3:30 in the afternoon.

As Anita called Asparita's number, she wondered if she would be home. Asparita answered the phone, and gushed that she was so happy that Anita called. Wasn't it terrible what had happened—she had been on her knees, praying all night long.

Anita asked about the children, and emphasized how important it was for Asparita to keep a close watch on them. Asparita said she needn't concern herself, she would do just that. Pancho was being very self-reliant. Bogart was responding well to the treatment, and had decided that he was going to go to medical school.

The next file Anita pulled was that of SARA WILLIAMS.

Sara Williams was 35 years old She had been born in Camp Ruby, Texas. She was married to Allys Williams, whereabouts unknown. She had had six children, ranging in age from 2 to 19.

> Tommy *Williams*, 19.
> Baby Doe *Simmons*, 16.
> Cotter *Williams*, 15.
> Quentin (10) and Doris Elizabeth (8) *Browning*.
> John Kennedy *Cowper*, 2.

Tommy had always been Sara Williams's favorite. But she had had only misfortune with him.

When he was 13 years old, he had been at the playground one evening when the director, who was supposed to supervise the children, had left early. Maintenance was shoddy; the sand pit had had only a light covering of sand over the concrete base.

A good deal of roughhousing had started. Tommy had

climbed to the top of the slide. One of the other boys had pushed him off. He had fallen into the sand pit. Since there was no sand, he had split his head open on the concrete.

He had been in General Hospital for a month, the first 17 days of it in a coma. When he returned home, the hospital had failed to send a release to the school, and the school had refused to readmit him without one. It had taken another month to clear that up, and he missed practically the entire semester.

After that, he started to lose interest in school. He began running with the gangs. He said it was the only way to have protection. If you didn't have a gang, you couldn't even go out at night—some other gang would come over and bust your head open. He became involved in a fight, and ripped a boy's face open with a bicycle chain. The police picked him up, and he was placed on probation.

During the next two years, they picked him up several times more—for curfew violations, for drinking, once for being a passenger in a car that had been stolen. Even though he was barely 16 years old, his gang affiliation made him a marked man for investigation.

One night a salesman was robbed and beaten unconscious by a group of boys. The police came and arrested Tommy at 3 o'clock in the morning. He was taken to juvenile hall. He was kept there three weeks, while the salesman recovered. When the salesman was asked to identify Tommy, he said he had never seen him before.

"Mom," said Tommy. "I spent three weeks for something I didn't do. When I go back next time it'll be for something!"

His whole personality changed. He had never been quarrelsome, but now he seemed to be continually looking for a fight. He hated. He hated everybody, but most of all he hated white men. In juvenile hall he had come under the influence of the Black Nationalists, who told him that the whites were interested in only one thing, the extermination of the Negro. Tommy said that if he ever saw a white man again in the projects he would shoot him.

Sara frantically tried to get psychiatric help for him. At General Hospital they told her they had a long waiting list, so she went from place to place, hospital to hospital, university to university, clinic to clinic—more than 20 in all— and everywhere they advised her they could not take Tommy, so long as she was receiving state aid for his support. Finally, she went back to General Hospital. They told her it did not seem to be an emergency, and that they would let her know about an appointment in four to six months.

It was less than a month later when a terrible quarrel erupted between Tommy and another boy. They were snarling at each other and fighting on the grass right in the middle of the housing project. Sara had called the police. She had asked them to please come quickly before her boy killed someone. She had had to wait 15 minutes, 20 minutes. She had had to wait while Tommy picked up a pair of garden shears. . . .

She had had to wait almost a half hour before the police car had pulled up, and the officers, one on each side, had emerged from the car with deliberate, calm motion.

"Please help me with my boy!" she had cried to them.

"How old is your boy, lady?" one had asked.

That was when she had seen Tommy plunge the shears into the other boy, plunge them deep into his back and wrest them out again, the boy sinking to the ground without a word, Tommy standing there in stupefaction, holding the shears loosely in his hand, then dropping them. Sara had seen, too, out of the corner of her eye, the police officer taking out his gun, leveling it at Tommy, and, thinking that he would shoot, she had knocked it from his hand. Tommy had offered no resistance as they had grabbed him, wrestled him to the ground, and handcuffed him.

That was Tommy. He was at the California Youth Authority Camp at Paso Robles, and one day he would come back. Cotter worshiped Tommy, and Cotter said that Tommy "wouldn't come back no different than he'd went. They couldn't break him no place."

Cotter was probably right.

Cotter had had a paper route, on which he made $16 a month. The money, BPA regulations said, had to be deducted from the check, so Sara hadn't allowed him to keep any of it. It wasn't long before Cotter dropped the route. "I ain't gonna knock myself out for the fucking white people!" he said.

Baby Doe was another problem altogether. Sara had never been able to get along with her. Not, at least, since the time King Cowper had appeared on the scene.

King was 10 years younger than Sara. And she saw, or thought she saw, that Baby Doe, who was a precocious 12½, kept making eyes at him. Sara had told her to stop it; that it didn't become her. Baby Doe had sassed her. "You're just jealous!"

Anita had come onto the case a few months after that. Sara had complained to her bitterly about Baby Doe; about how she wouldn't mind her about anything, and was always lying to her. Anita had asked Baby Doe if that were true. Baby Doe had shrugged. "My mother don't care nothing for me."

"Why do you say that?"

"It's true. She always tells me I'm no good. I had $3, and I asked her for another dollar so I could buy me a pair of shoes. She wouldn't give it to me. She said I'm not worth a dollar."

"Perhaps she was teasing you," Anita suggested.

"No, she wasn't. She's said the same thing a lot of times."

"She's not even 13, and she's having sexual relations with all the boys in the neighborhood!" Sara had declared bitterly.

"I'm not, neither!" Baby Doe had retorted. "Only some."

Anita had suggested that perhaps Baby Doe should have psychiatric care, to which suggestion Sara had replied that she had been trying and trying to get help for Tommy, and no one was interested. As Anita continued to talk to the two of them—though she could easily have shrugged her shoulders, contending correctly as other social workers do that this was not what she was being paid for—it developed that Baby Doe was defying her mother because she resented her, that there had been an incident that had triggered the behavior. . . . "I'm not doing nothing she's not!" . . . That that incident had occurred one afternoon when Sara had left Baby Doe alone with King Cowper in the apartment.

"She's a slut!" Sara said. "She seduced him!"

"Come now!" Anita had ejaculated. "A 12-year-old girl?"

"That don't make no difference. All she needed was the chance."

"Why did you leave them alone together?"

"Why not?" Sara had responded ingenuously.

Baby Doe's version was that it had been King Cowper who had been the aggressor, that she had told her mother this, and that her mother had called her a liar. In fact, the incident had not altered Sara's relationship with Cowper at all. It had been almost a year later that she had become pregnant by him.

Baby Doe had always been more intelligent than the other children—in grammar school she had been an honor student, and on her first IQ test in the third grade she had scored 117. On entering junior high school, however, she had lost interest, and was forced to go through the first semester of the eighth grade three times.

"I can't stand them babies!" she complained about her classmates. At the age of 13 she had the sophistication of a 16-year-old.

Sometimes she would stay away from home and school for several days at a time. She was picked up, and the probation officer recommended she be placed in a foster home. The judge, however, decided to return her to her mother, on Baby Doe's promise that she would behave herself.

Baby Doe wanted to change schools, because the girls at Markham kept teasing her. She cried, and said that she wanted to go to a school where nobody would know her, so that she could get a fresh start. She was afraid she would fail physical education, because her gym clothes had been stolen and her mother refused to give her money for more.

"You know, I could do much better if my mother liked me," she said.

After much persuasion, she was induced to return to school. She dropped out again when her mother refused to give her money to get her clothes out of the cleaners, and in the subsequent argument whipped her with a telephone cord.

Sara was suspicious that Baby Doe was running around with King Cowper, because Cowper had lost interest in her, Sara, after she became pregnant.

"My mother always throws it up in my face—going to send me back to my father! I don't know my father. Only one I've ever known is Uncle Browning. He's the only one that ever treat me decently. I get real hard up for money or clothes and I goes to him. He's a real nice man. Only reason my mother broke off with him, she thought he was too old for her. So she start messing with younger men, and do him wrong."

Sara said that she thought Baby Doe should get married "before something happens."

"I don't want to get married," Baby Doe said. She wanted to finish school, and not make the same mistake as all those other people.

During the first six months of 1964, Baby Doe was taken to

juvenile hall three times for ditching school. She said she
didn't mind so much any more, because the probation officer
was now "her man."

She was referred to a psychiatrist, but went only twice,
because, she said, "He told me my mother was crazy, and
for me not to come back!"

By the fall of 1964, when she was 15, she was coming
home only on odd nights. She had a 21-year-old boyfriend
who bought her clothes. Sara said that wasn't any of her
concern, she'd given up trying to do anything with her. Baby
Doe was suspended from Markham Junior High School because of absences and transferred to Drew. Sara said that
she thought she was going, but, it turned out, she had been
absent the whole first month.

Baby Doe was arrested and taken to juvenile hall for purportedly robbing a cab driver, but, as it developed, her girlfriend had taken her wallet and used her identification.

At mid-year, when she reached 16, Baby Doe was passed
on to Fremont High School because of her age. When she
reported to the attendance office, she was told to go to the
auditorium, but the doors were locked, and she was told that
all the classes were closed.

The next day she was called at home and told a mistake
had been made, that all the classes weren't closed. However,
she did not report, because, she said, Sara wouldn't give her
car fare. Sara said that wasn't so, that Baby Doe had refused
to get up, and then fooled around until it was too late to
go to school.

"I won't pay her if she won't get up in time," Sara said.

More and more, Baby Doe said, she realized that it wasn't
any use going to school, because she couldn't do anything
with a diploma anyway.

On her last IQ test she had scored 82.

For Anita, it was the pattern that was not only discouraging,
but terrifying. In case after case the repetition: Bogart Pedrally, whose IQ had declined during his early school years
from 126 to 86; Baby Doe, whose IQ had dropped from 117
to 82. It did not really seem to matter whether children
lacked innate mental ability or not. By the time they reached
their late teens, chances were that they would all have been
beaten down to the same level. Baby Doe, who had at one
time scored 117, was now functioning at virtually the same
mental level as her stepbrother Cotter, whose score had never

been higher than 76. It was this that made such programs as Head Start, with all their intrinsic validity, so futile. What is the point of bringing the underprivileged preschool child up to the level of the comparable middle-class child, then abandoning him to the same environment that you just picked him out of?

Sara, as Anita saw her, was not a bad woman. She had tried very hard with Tommy, and every facet of the society in which she lived had conspired against her. Transplanted from a rural, backward economy into the sophistication and complexity of the city, she had been utterly unable to cope. She lacked the knowledge to deal with the problems that had beset her with her three older children, and already her fourth, Quentin Browning, 10, was being sucked into the same maelstrom.

Quentin did not seem able to keep his eyes open. He would fall asleep anywhere: sitting, eating at the table; in the middle of the floor of the living room; in the bathroom. When Anita suggested that perhaps he should be taken to a doctor, Sara replied, "I'm not alarmed about it because the child was born sick. He was sick for 15 months. I believe there's something wrong with him." She laughed. "He's one of those strange babies. Born in eight months. One of the biggest jitterbugs in town!"

Anita believed that Cotter did not like Quentin, and picked on him. That Quentin was a completely isolated child in the family, as even his natural sister, Doris Elizabeth Browning, paid no attention to him, but treated the baby, John Kennedy Cowper, as her own. Nor would it do any good to call Sara's attention to this—Sara undoubtedly knew it, but had no idea as to what she might do about it. Sara was typical of the women on relief: unable to discipline her children because they have no respect for her; unable to help them with their problems because she doesn't know how to deal with her own and because her children, by the age of 14, are already more sophisticated than she; unable to exert any moral force because her own position is morally untenable.

Tommy had always been upset about Sara's childbearing. "Mom, you ought to be ashamed of yourself, having so many babies," he had told her.

"It don't look good, having a baby here and a baby there," she had agreed with him. Yet, beset with guilt on the one hand, resentful of her dependence on welfare on the other, when Anita had suggested she should practice birth control, she had flared at her:

"The state just sent you to spy on me! I knows my rights and I can have as many children as I do please. Them is my private rights, and if I wants 'em I can have 'em, and the state will have to support 'em!"

That was, as Anita knew, the awful truth. The state would bitch about it; but it would, in the end, have to provide the support, because the alternatives were either to return to a 19th-century type society, or else to face the facts. The fact that the women keep having children indiscriminately because that was how their mothers had had their children, and their mothers before that; because that was how the Southern gentlemen had encouraged them to have children. The fact that they continue to have children because they don't know how to stop; because, with the difficulty of keeping a man in the house, they are afraid to refuse a man; because they are afraid—

"When I gets to be 50 year old, can't get no job because I ain't been fitted for nothing, too old to train and too young for old-age assistance, what gonna happen to me when I got no supportable childrens? 'Long as I have childrens, BPA they takes care of me!"

The fact that the state has, for all practical purposes, washed its hands of assuming any sort of responsibility for these people, so that, in subsidizing their existence, it is simultaneously subsidizing their misery and their exploitation, refusing to acknowledge that they are as exposed to a plague of plunderers as the unvaccinated person to smallpox; that putting money into their hands, without providing any protection for that money or education in the ways and arts of an every-man-for-himself economy, is like giving a 7-year-old child $1,000 to buy an automobile, and being surprised, when he comes back with an Edsel and 10 pounds of candy.

The fact that with certain persons trumpeting that motherhood is next to godliness—so equaling in perception the assertion that, since the multiplication of cells is beneficial, cancer, being a multiplication of cells, must be beneficial also —politicians can have a field day haranguing about illegitimacy (immoral) but would shudder at the thought of inhibiting anyone's motherhood (moral).

The fact that the state would rather spend (and *would* spend) $1,000 tomorrow to counteract the ravages of crime

and disease than to spend $500 today for the family coun-
seling, psychiatric care, and intensive education, both child
and adult, that would prevent them; because crime and disease, like a flood, are visibly evil, but the prevention of them
is nebulous—why spend all that money building a dam when,
even though we've had an annual inundation, it may not rain
for the next hundred years?

Anita called Sara Williams and relayed to her the admonition she had been asked to. Then she slumped down in her
chair—she had 83 to go. Eighty-three that, with squalid variations, were just like the Pedrally and Williams cases. All
around the room 100 or more of her fellow workers were,
like her, struggling with the telephone.

15   The Meeting at Athens Park

It was shortly after 1:30 p.m. when John Buggs arrived at
Athens Park. The temperature was 89 degrees, and inside the
clubhouse it was sweltering. All the chairs were filled, and
dozens of individuals were standing against the walls. More
than 100 kids had shown up. Television cameras were focused
on the microphone.

Buggs had expected neither the kids nor the television. He
had been prepared to deal with a few of the youth leaders,
such as Ralph Reese, and with responsible adult individuals,
whom he wanted to send out in teams to talk peace—for that
purpose he carried a map dividing the community into 56
separate areas. He had called Insp. James Fisk of the Community Relations Unit of the Police Department and informed him of the plans, asking that the police stay out of
the immediate area that evening and send in plainclothes Negro officers, who, with probation officers and others, would
circulate through the people, passing the word to "cool it."
Attacking the problem from both sides, Buggs had high hopes
that he would be able to ward off an explosion. He had been

able to do so in the past, notably in July of 1963, when a group of Muslims had threatened to riot if they were served with an eviction notice by sheriff's deputies. Sheriff Peter J. Pitchess had called on Buggs for help; he had contacted John Shabazz, the Muslim leader in Los Angeles, and Shabazz, averring that the Muslim sect believed in law and order, had told his people to pay up or go quietly.

Obviously, with the meeting turned into a public forum, Buggs could not organize teams to circulate unobtrusively through the community—they would be known and discredited before they ever started out. He decided, therefore, to deal with the kids, because he had seen them, when won over, disperse a crowd of hundreds in an hour; and, because "they knew where the bodies were."

Both official and quasi-official organizations in the community had representatives present: Opal Jones of NAPP; Curt Moody of the Community Relations Conference; Norman Houston of the NAACP; the Rev. H. H. Brookins of the United Civil Rights Committee; the Rev. Archie Hardwicke of the Westminster Presbyterian Center in Watts; the Rev. Joe Hardwicke of the Praisers of Zion Baptist Church; Cong. Augustus Hawkins; Superintendent Kenneth Hahn; Councilman John Gibson; Richard Jones, of Mayor Yorty's staff; representatives from the sheriff, the district attorney's office, and the probation department; and Sgts. Vivian Strange and Harvey Scott of the Community Relations Unit of the LAPD.

The community relations unit, although it had had its official inception in 1950, had been a stepchild, and virtually dormant, for many years. It had received a shot in the arm only recently, in June of 1965, when Insp. Fisk had been appointed to head it. Very shortly thereafter he had gone on vacation for a month, and therefore had been on the job only a few weeks.

(Sgt. Strange, a vivacious, young-looking woman, is a 19-year veteran of the force, and the holder of a degree in sociology. She had once, in plainclothes, entered a room in which a group of police officers had gathered. One of them, upon seeing her, had inquired in a loud voice, "What is that nigger doing here?")

The gripes of the Negro community, both relevant and not, now started bouncing freely through the room.

"Who's getting all that poverty money?" An irate woman

jumped up. "Big deal politicians sittin' up there in city hall making $10,000, $15,000 a year, and the poor peoples supposed to be gettin' a $1.25 an hour, and they won't even let us have that! Who's puttin' them moneys in their pockets, that's what we wants to know!"

"Amen!"

"You tell 'em, sister!"

"Big fat Mr. Charley, that's who's gettin' it!"

The antipoverty program in Los Angeles had been caught in a classic political snarl. Although the city had been the first funded under the legislation, and $5 million had been allocated by the end of 1964, a dispute had arisen in the spring of 1965 between Mayor Sam Yorty and community agencies regarding the makeup of the governing board. Community representatives had, in February, proposed a 22-man board, a proposal that had been countered by Mayor Yorty in April with that of a 9-man board. This difference had not been resolved until late June, by which time it had become virtually impossible to obtain any federal funds for a summer program. An emergency call to Washington had, finally, netted enough money to inaugurate a crash program for teen posts on the first of August; and a Congressional committee investigating the situation had come to Los Angeles and held public hearings only the previous Saturday.

"Why don't Yorty never come down here? The way he treat us, Watts might as well be in Birmingham!"

"He worse than Birmingham! In Birmingham, the mayor at least come down and see how the soul folk live."

It was true. The mayor had not visited the southeast area since his election. He had been elected the first time largely as a result of the Negro vote, but he was now blaming "Communist agitation" for every Negro demand.

"When we gonna get jobs? How we gonna live if we got no jobs?"

"How we gonna get jobs when the police keep harassing us, so we gets a record and *the man* won't give us no job?"

"Like I was downtown yesterday all day at the state employment office, and I come back last night, and the police grabs me and push me up against the wall, and ask me what I doing and all sorts of silly questions, and then they write up this little piece of paper on me and let me go! Next time I try to get a job, the man gonna say I have a record. So what's the use?"

(The youth had no record. Police had merely filled out a *field intelligence report,* which never passes beyond the local station and is destroyed after a period of time. However, since he *believed* he had been given a record, that belief tended to have more importance than the fact.)

"The police, they don't care nothing about helping the people. Last week some kids come and strip my car clean, and I calls the police and they says they sorry but they can't do nothin' about it, they got no car to send out, if I wants to fill out a crime report, I got to go to the station. So I go down to the station, and I'm crossin' the street, and the man stop me and give me a ticket for jaywalking. Brother, I says to him, if you can hide there in that little alley just to catch people crossin' the street, you can come down to my house and see my car like it been gone over by cannibals. So he tell me just sign the ticket, that ain't no affair of his. But I say it ain't right!"

"That's right. The big operators, they let 'em go, because they pays 'em off. It's the little people they pick on. My son, 13 years old, he was taking a shortcut across the school yard on his way to church one Sunday, and somebody had busted the window during the night, so the police come and say he's a vandal, and they handcuffs him to a pole in the playground and leaves him there 20 minutes. I goes down to 77th to tell 'em that ain't right, and the sergeant, he start talkin' real loud like he want to call everybody's attention to it so that everyone start lookin' at my boy, and he say, 'Lady, you sure this incident happen to your boy?' and I say, 'Sure I sure!' and he say, 'You know it a real bad thing to say a policemans commit malpractice, it a real serious thing!' So I starts getting the shakes, I thinks they going to be molesting my boy everywhere he go, so I goes on home and thinks it over, and then goes to the Glass House downtown, and a sergeant there he take my statement and say he look into it. And that the last I ever hears!"

For many years Los Angeles had had a peculiar ordinance, which made it a crime to file a false complaint against a police officer. In one such case a Negro waitress, getting off work and returning home at two o'clock in the morning, was stopped by a white motorist who attempted to rape her. Able to run to a nearby house, she had called the police, who, refusing to believe her, had arrested her instead. When she subsequently registered a complaint against the officers, it was disallowed, and she was arrested again, this time for filing a false complaint.

Courts had ruled the ordinance unconstitutional in the early 1960's, but its effect lingers on, especially in the minority communities, where citizens feel that it is not only useless to make a complaint, since, in their view, all police officers are brothers-under-the-skin, but dangerous to themselves as well, since officers henceforth will be out to "get them." Aggravating the situation is the fact that the police department— unlike the sheriff's, which sends the complainant a full report regarding the disposition of the case—investigates the complaint and chastises the officer if it appears warranted, but never informs the complaining citizen whether his complaint was sustained or not—the effect being that the citizen, no matter what the disposition, is left to believe nothing was done.

It is this monolithic face that the police department feels it must present to the world, so as not to lose the confidence of the average citizen, that infuriates the Negro, who time and again, personally and through friends, comes into contact with discourtesy and what he feels are unjust and arbitrary actions.

On the one hand, Chief Parker said, in a relatively secluded atmosphere,[1] "I never said there is no brutality. I can't belie my own figures." Figures that show that, over the span of the last 15 years, an average of about 25 officers per year have been separated from the department because of serious offenses. This 25 is an infinitesimal 5 per cent of the 5,000-man force, and, in this context, may be taken as a reassuring indication of the over-all excellence of the Los Angeles police.

On the other hand, considering that Parker himself stated that "it's what a man does at three o'clock in the morning [when there's no one else around] that makes or breaks the force," that each officer separated had a number of years of service at the time of separation, that there may be 100 rotten eggs on the force at any one time, and that each of these works 40 hours a week during which time he may have as many as 100 individual contacts with citizens, it becomes clear that the damage wreaked by even a few officers over a period of time can reach incalculable proportions. In the "Bloody Christmas" beatings of December, 1951, 93 officers were

[1] The McCone Commission hearings.

given lie-detector tests and eight ultimately were placed on trial for battering seven prisoners, mostly Mexican-Americans, who had become involved with two policemen in an altercation at a tavern. As one of the officers had put it: "What happened to the boys was life insurance for the rest of us. When I get through with these guys they'll never jump a policeman again!"

That, under Chief Parker, such offenders were viewed with greater disapprobation than the most confirmed criminal, and were sent packing as soon as they could be weeded out, does not change the fact that they existed.

It is, thus, perhaps doubly unfortunate that, in his most public pronouncements, Chief Parker felt compelled, in his own words, to be "the self-appointed defender of the police departments of America"; to declare, accurately: "We employ only the finest young men. That's why we've become irritated and disgusted. They're not a group of moronic individuals who happen to stagger out in the street, they're the best that society has to offer!" That he felt compelled to lay all criticism of the police at the doorstep of a subversive conspiracy, because the "Difficulty is . . . no organization of police in America. . . . They are under constant attack by heavily organized and nationalized forces without anyone to defend them, and this is part of the revolution facing America. . . .

"Officers [have been] beleaguered and badgered to death about brutality, [which has] been used as a revolutionary tool all over the world. . . .

"This is Custer's last stand, last of the breed that fights for his department—if I'm eliminated it will be the greatest victory that antipolice elements have attained in modern history!"

When a group of ministers had asked him simply to make the statement: "We will not countenance police brutality!" the Chief had demurred, contending that, like the promise to stop beating one's wife, it would be an admission that police brutality had occurred.

(Said Insp. Fisk, "If you use the term 'police brutality' any policeman will sit back and relax because he knows he is not brutal—but it diverts attention from the problem. If you use 'police indignities,' then you will be communicating. . . . I don't think that law enforcement has listened enough to the Negro community.")

That was, precisely, what one speaker after another at the meeting, both young and old, were complaining about. And it was a complaint directed not only at the police but at the entire community, that whenever they tried to air their grievances, Negroes were talking into a vacuum. That whatever they tried to say was always misrepresented in the white press and on radio and tv.

"Look at me!" said a man. "I'm 40 years old, and I fought for my country, and I got a German bullet in me, and I come home, and they say to me, 'White people to the right, niggers to the left!' I'm the bottom man on the totem pole, the last chicken in the pecking order. A few years back, I'm trying to get a job, me, an American who fought for his country, and next to me is a fellow who, it turns out, was a Nazi, and who do they give the job to? The Nazi, because he's blond and blue-eyed. So now they bring in all these Cubans, because they say Castro's discriminating against them, and whose jobs the Cubans gonna get? The American Negroes', who're being sent to fight in Vietnam so they can come home and take the back seat on the bus! Well, man, the Vietnamese never done nothing to the American Negro! But if they want to send me to fight in Mississippi, I'll join up right now!"

There were calls of "Amen!" and "You tell 'em!"

"You treat people like dogs, you got to expect they're gonna bite sometimes!"

"I've got seven sons!" A woman, very emotional, stood up. "And I'd just as soon see them die on the streets of Watts as in Vietnam. But that's not the way to do it! We want our rights, but we don't want to have to fight the police for them!"

"That's right!" a youth said. "We don't want no riots. We don't want no fights. We want to dance tonight!"

"All we wants is that we get our story told, and get it told right! What we do last night, maybe it wasn't right. But ain't nobody come down here and listened to us before!"

One of the ministers had invited Rena Frye to the meeting. She, Marquette, and Ronald had been taken to the Firestone sheriff's station the previous night after being transported from the scene of the arrest.

On the ride to the station there had been, according to allegations, a further altercation. Mrs. Frye had inquired, "Why am I going to jail?"

To which an officer had replied, "Because your mouth is too big!"

The precise sequence of subsequent events is vague, but during their course Mrs. Frye was slapped, an officer was kneed, and Ronald was punched on the nose.

At the booking cage, Marquette had commented, "It was a good bust, but they should have done it different!" and then lapsed into a frenzy of incoherence—shouting, flailing about, and screaming obscenities. He had demanded to be granted his right to make a telephone call, but, when the telephone was placed in the cage, had been unable to make himself understood over it, and flung it against the wall. A few minutes later his tantrum had ended as precipitously as it had begun—he had fallen asleep.

In the morning all three had been taken to municipal court. Mrs. Frye had pleaded not guilty to a charge of interfering with an officer, while Marquette and Ronald had pleaded guilty—Marquette to drunk driving and battery, and Ronald to the latter charge only. All were released on bail.

Mrs. Frye now stepped up to the microphone. "I am the woman who was arrested last night," she identified herself. "But I'm not here to talk about that. I'm here to ask you, please, to help me and to help others in this community to calm the situation down so that we will not have a riot tonight!"

Several voices seconded her plea.

A youth, about 16, grabbed the microphone. "It's like this, the way the policemens treat you round here, I'm going to tell you something. It ain't going to be lovely tonight whether you like it or not!"

Shouts of disapproval, whistles and jeers erupted from the gathering.

"I was down on Avalon last night, and we the Negro people have got completely fed up!" he continued. "They not going to fight down here no more. You know where they going? They're after the Whiteys! They going to congregate. They don't care! They going out to Inglewood, Playa del Rey, and everywhere else the white man supposed to stay. They going to do the white man in tonight. And I'm going to tell you—!"

The catcalls from the audience drowned him out. Ralph Reese grabbed him and dragged him away from the microphone. A half dozen other youths began to jump on him and pummel him, and it was only through the intercession of several of the adults that, frightened and crying, he was saved from a severe beating.

Reese returned to the microphone, declaring that the boy did not represent the consensus of opinion, and that the majority of people wanted only a fair hearing. The Rev. Joe Hardwicke, echoing the sentiments and asking that there be calm and order, ended the meeting with a prayer.

Following a suggestion made by Jim Burks of the probation department, John Buggs met with Ralph Reese and two other youths in a closed meeting in a small back room. Buggs wanted them to contact various groups and gangs of kids, who were known to be preparing to riot, and to pass the word that there wasn't going to be any march. It was a delicate situation, because, if the youths felt that they were being asked to fink on their friends, they would rebel.

The key request made by Reese was that someone go to the community at large and explain that there was a reason for the previous night; that these are kids who had a legitimate reason for what they had done; and that, even if they went about it in the wrong way, they were not just hoodlums.

Buggs said that he would attempt to get someone on television to do this.

"Fine, Mr. Buggs," Reese said. "If you can get the police not starting something, we'll do our best to get the blood to cool it."

It was agreed that they would meet again at 7 p.m. at Bel-Vue Presbyterian Church, south of Imperial.

As the tv cameramen were packing their gear, a group, led by Sgt. Vivian Strange of the police department, pleaded with them not to show the boy who had said the people were going to move out and riot in the white communities. It was pointed out that his was an isolated opinion, and that there might be an unfortunate reaction if his statement were broadcast.

The television newsmen were non-committal. "Everybody has it. We can't say we won't use it, and then have some other station put it on the air."

It was almost 4 o'clock when Buggs left Athens Park. There had been one or two isolated rock-throwing incidents shortly after noon, and here and there groups of a half dozen persons were standing about; but the area in general was quiet.

Insp. James Fisk of the police Community Relations Unit had gone to see Chief Parker shortly after receiving Buggs's request in the late morning that police remain on the periphery that evening.

"Certainly we do not want to be provocateurs by being in the area," Parker had said.

However, there had been disagreement among others present regarding the use of Negro officers in plainclothes. There were only 200 Negroes on the force and they were scattered throughout the various divisions, only seven being assigned to 77th. No record of race is kept on personnel cards, and it was felt it would be a difficult task to round up the necessary number of Negro officers in such a limited period of time.

Insp. Fisk was not invited to the top-level strategy meeting, and spent lunch at a meeting of the Men of Tomorow Club, a Negro service club organization. He taped an announcement for KGFJ, the Negro radio station, appealing for order, then went down to the Westminster Neighborhod Association in the heart of Watts, where a meeting and press conference had been scheduled for mid-afternoon. This meeting never came off, so Fisk returned to his office downtown, unaware that, at numerous listening posts established by Westminster throughout the community, rumors were starting to come in that Watts was going to be burned the next day.

When Sergeants Strange and Scott returned to the police building, they relayed to Deputy Chiefs Roger Murdock and Thomas Reddin the essentials of what had occurred at the Athens Park meeting. Reddin felt "that the dominant tone of the remarks had been one of objectivity, one hoping to bring a reign of reason as opposed to a reign of riot."

Buggs called the CBS television station, KNXT, which offered the Rev. Joseph Hardwicke time at 5:45 p.m. to explain the meaning of the previous night's riot.

Buggs then telephoned Fisk to inquire what action had been taken by the police department on the suggestions he had made that morning. Fisk told him that the department had decided not to pull back its men from the area, but that they were not going to saturate it either. They had decided that they were going to patrol as if it were any other day.

"I've made a commitment." Buggs was upset. "I promised the kids that if they wouldn't start anything, the police would stay out. If they see that my promises don't mean anything, this is going to put me in a very bad light."

Fisk said that he was sorry; that he had not been party to the decisions that had been made.

"Then can't you put a Negro officer in every car?"

"No," responded Fisk. That wouldn't be possible either.

"You've blown it!" snapped Buggs.

16 "If That's the Way They Want to Read It, That's the Way We'll Write the Book!"

At 4:55, Parker called Lt. Gen. Roderick Hill, adjutant general of the California National Guard, in Sacramento, and advised him that the situation was fluid, and that there might be a need for the Guard. Hill explained to the Chief that the Guard was scheduled to go on its regular two-week summer drill the next evening, and that, unless a request were made before then, there might be difficulty in getting them to stations in Los Angeles. He told Parker he would have the assistant commander of the 40th Armored Division in Southern California, Brig. Gen. Robert Elder, get in touch with him. He then immediately ordered Col. Robert Quick, his assistant, to fly to Los Angeles to act as liaison.

At 5:15 p.m. Gen. Elder called Chief Parker, and shortly after 5:30 p.m. Mayor Yorty came to Parker's office to be briefed.

By 6 o'clock, 200 to 300 persons were beginning to gather in the area centered on Avalon and Imperial. By 6 o'clock the Rev. Hardwicke had appeared on television, but, due to the early hour, relatively few viewers had seen him. At 6 o'clock, most of the city's seven televison stations launched their evening news programs.

A meeting had been held, viewers were informed, at the instigation of the County Human Relations Commission, in the Negro community that afternoon, and television news cameramen had been present.

"We the Negro people have got completely fed up!" a boy was orating. "They not going to fight down here no more. You know where they going? They're after the Whiteys! They going to congregate. They don't care! They going out to Inglewood, Playa del Rey, and everywhere else the white man supposed to stay. They going to do the white man in tonight!"

That was the complete television report of the Athens Park meeting, not only to the citizens of Los Angeles, but to those of the nation, CBS carrying the film on the network.

If the Caucasians of Los Angeles were shocked by what they heard and saw, the Negroes were dismayed. They were dismayed, and simultaneously fulfilled in their expectations. They had not expected that the news media controlled by the Whips would present a fair and impartial report of the Negro viewpoint. They never had. That was one of the great and long-standing gripes.

Ralph Reese saw the telecast in company with some of the youths he had been trying to convince to cool it.

"Man," said a boy, "how come you come here stooging us like that? The white man ain't interested in nothin'. Look to me like he want us to riot!"

"Sure, baby!" said another. "If that's the way they want to read it, that's the way we'll write the book!"

Chief Parker, viewing the news, was incensed. He was seriously ill, suffering from an aneurysm of the aorta. He was scheduled to go to the Mayo Clinic, and there was an assumption among many persons who knew of his condition that he would soon retire. He had, as a matter of fact, already offered to submit his resignation to the mayor. He had been given one testimonial, and others were pending. Because the men in the department wanted to protect him and make his job as easy as possible, he was, in fact, becoming more and more detached from the day-to-day operation of the force.

No one had told him of the Athens Park meeting; no one told him that the police department and other agencies had been fully informed and had, as a matter of fact, had representatives present. Like other viewers, he assumed the television representation was a factual report.

"What right do these persons have to sit down with people

who are supposed to have just committed a long series of crimes?" he asked. "This, to me, as a law-enforcement officer presents some real questions as to ethics and authority. We are charged with the security of the city, and they come into a situation and start making deals with rioters without consulting the police, and then leave the mess to us. As long as law enforcement has a problem of maintaining order, we should have something to say about the things that are done in relation to the mob."

Parker, although he had had absolutely no expectation that a riot was brewing, especially because of the previous summer's "absolute refusal of the Negro community to demonstrate," had, nevertheless, at a confidential meeting with city leaders following the passage of the civil rights act a year previously, warned of the potential explosiveness of the situation.

"The sun will rise and shine on the same squalid conditions that it did the day before," he had said, "nothing will be different and still these people will have been led to believe that great improvement would follow." He was concerned about the frustrations, because as part of all the civil rights activity, and all the civil rights conflicts, police brutality was paraded all over the city, the Los Angeles *Times* once carrying a full page NAACP advertisement with nothing but a police dog with bared fangs.

"Some people can relate these things in terms of their own experience, but those people can't, and they are going to get very restless as result of all this propaganda."

Other people outside the area, he believed, "have not had any experience with the negative aspects of propaganda streaming in on people that have been treated badly and done wrong. I don't believe you can shower people with this propaganda without expecting them to strike out some way at people they believe have held them back. . . . The type of democracy they [the NAACP] are trying to sell is represented by *The People's World*.

"Political pandering," he contended, "and the failure of legislation to change the status of people here," could lead to frustration and violence. "The community is allowing the police to cope with all factors, and it is more than we can handle."

Parker was upset because, despite the fact that there was

no question of racial prejudice on his part and the fact that, he felt, he had tried to be accommodating, civil rights leaders were setting him up as a straw man.

It was he, who, as chief, had integrated patrol cars; who had spread Negro officers throughout all the divisions, without regard to race; who had opened up all assignments to Negro officers; who had assigned a Negro lieutenant, Roscoe Washington, as watch commander in charge of white policemen; who had declared that he would not countenance any "second-class officers" on the force.

It was he who had, at the urging of civil rights leaders, stopped identifying race in crime statistics—more than 60 per cent of all crimes of violence being committed by Negroes—because they contended it was hurting the Negro drive for equal rights.

And it was he who, he felt, had been betrayed by them, because: "This inordinate amount of crime is something that has grown out of the dislocation he [the Negro] has suffered in our society, and therefore we should not be putting this [the statistics] out, because actually he may not be nearly as responsible for his amount of crime activity as perhaps other sections. The thing that discourages me is that after we have done this there isn't the slightest flicker of recognition that we have done anything in a cooperative way, and . . . continue to be beaten over the head that we are oppressively policing the area.

"I don't know anything about what has happened to the Negro in Mississippi. [But] Negro hoodlums have taken advantage of the police . . . because they have been held up as people who are deprived individuals, that they have been maligned and abused by the community, that the Liberty Bell never rang for them. . . . Who are they going to lash out against?

"If we just abandon our basic responsibility to try to get into a handshaking situation here to make people like us, I don't know who is going to take care of this tremendous amount of crime."

Parker was now convinced that the riots, if they were to be renewed, would obtain their driving force from "the widespread support of civil disobedience as a tool for social and economic progress. Civil disobedience is a revolutionary tool that . . . has been used to bring about the overthrow of existing governments. . . . It creates a contempt of and dis-respect for all laws and lawful authority."

*   *   *

After talking to Insp. Fisk, John Buggs had called Under-sheriff James Downey and asked him to intercede with the police department, but Downey had replied that he did not have any jurisdiction. It was a few minutes before 6 o'clock when Buggs, together with Leon Smith and another staff member, left to return to the area, stopping at a barbecue stand at the corner of 96th and Central to get a bite to eat. While they were there, several police cars passed going in the direction of Avalon and Imperial, and when Buggs reached that corner at about 6:50 there were approximately 300 persons lining the street. Two blocks farther sough Buggs saw five police cars, the officers having stopped to search two women and a man, whom they had backed up against the building. A tense group of people, among whom were sev-eral kids with bricks in their hands, were standing watching them. The air was heavy and humid.

Ralph Reese, perspiration glistening on his face, arrived at the Bel-Vue Presbyterian Church on 118th St. a few minutes after Buggs.

"Well, Mr. Buggs, I see you didn't make it," he greeted him.

"No. We didn't."

Reese had contacted the Slausons, the Businessmen, the Gladiators, and the Watts and Compton gangs. Two of the five had agreed to stay off the streets. The other three had hedged—they would wait and see what the cops did before committing themselves. The situation was complicated by the fact that some kids who had been arrested the night be-fore had been released on bail and had returned to the area with bloody heads and hoary stories, thirsting for revenge.

"Is it too late?" Buggs asked.

"Maybe not," Reese said. Though by all indications it ap-peared to be.

Urged on by the others present, Buggs agreed to go to the 77th St. police station and try once more to have the police pulled out of the area. The kids were after the police, the reasoning went, and if the police were withdrawn, the target would disappear.

In the half hour since Buggs had driven south on Avalon,

the crowd on the street had swelled from 300 to 2,000. There was a police car driving slowly up the street, and, as Buggs pulled around it, a boy made a waving motion with his arm and yelled, "Hurry up, man!"

No sooner had Buggs cleared the patrol car than he saw, in his rear-view mirror, a score of rocks converging upon its sides.

17   The Magnificent Seven

Police officer Mac Benton's assignment was vice. He had been out on a routine assignment Wednesday night, and knew nothing of the previous night's happenings except that two highway patrol officers had been attacked at the corner of Avalon and 116th St. Since there was an after-hours drinking place just three blocks up, at 113th St., and this often generated disturbances, he had thought it just another caper and paid no attention to it. During the afternoon he had had the radio turned on, but there had been no special bulletins, no warnings of a riot situation—as a matter of fact, no mention of the previous night's incident whatever. Although the final, street edition of the Los Angeles *Times* bannered the story, the home edition, which he, like most other Angelenos, received, carried only a two-inch story on an inside page. Benton, as a matter of fact, like four-fifths of his fellow citizens, had no idea of the seriousness of what had occurred, nor of the thunderstorm that was hovering over the city. When, at 5 o'clock, he received a telephone call ordering him to the 77th St. station in old civilian clothes, he dressed accordingly, and gave it no further thought.

When Benton had come on the force in 1959, assignments allotted to Negroes had been severely restricted. There had been some improvement from the days when almost all non-Caucasians had been herded together in one division and placed in the industrial district, to be kept out of sight as much as possible; but Negroes were still assigned to X cars, which would be sent on an A call only if all A cars with white officers were busy at the time. In a sense, this was only bowing to the pressure of the Caucasian community. On one occasion, responding to a call, Benton had reached the location to be faced by a bewildered white. "But I called for a *policeman!*" he had protested.

That he cannot escape the caste distinction is made clear to the Negro rookie—and, by indirection, therefore, the white rookie as well—the moment he enters the police academy. Because policemen are exhorted that they must be police officers 24 hours a day there is a tendency for them to become isolated from the community at large, and they therefore congregate socially as well as during working hours. During orientation at the academy, cards are passed out to the officers inviting the membership of their wives in the police social organization, and veterans of the armed forces are invited to join the police American Legion post.

Negroes do not receive the invitations.

They do not receive the invitations, and a segregationist element on the department works diligently to keep fraternization to a minimum. Benton went through the academy with a white officer who later became his partner in a radio car. Subsequently they were given different assignments, but remained friends, and often talked to each other at the station. One day, in the parking lot, the friend had taken Benton aside. "Look!" he said. "I hope you'll understand. I'm intending to make a career out of the force. And there are people who keep telling me it doesn't do me any good to be seen buddying up with you. I just can't ignore it any longer."

Benton understood, as every Negro has understood, implicitly, that the oral board would not pass him beyond the rank of lieutenant. ("Don't get big ideas, you're just a black boy in a blue suit," a sergeant had once advised a rookie.) As a result, in August of 1965, there was not even one Negro lieutenant on the force, because such highly qualified men as Thomas Bradley, later elected city councilman, and Earl Broady, subsequently appointed to the number-two spot in the district attorney's office and then to the Superior Court bench, invariably resigned after making lieutenant.

There was in the department, as in almost every other walk of American life, a hesitancy to believe that the Negro could function both intelligently and impartially. On the vice squad, for example, Negroes had been assigned only as *operators,* who, undercover, would make the contacts with prostitutes and dope peddlers in order to garner the evidence, never as *investigators,* who would actually make the arrests and put the case together for prosecution. It was only in the past year that the breakthrough had come, and that Negroes, such as Benton, had been assigned as investigators.

To the surprise of some they have been highly successful, because, as Benton points out, the Negro who often fools the white officer by "shucking it" is much less likely to be successful with another Negro, who knows exactly what he is doing.

Far from being soft on the Negro criminal, the Negro officer is likely to be upset by the dual standard of justice that treats a Negro-upon-Negro assault as something less serious than the same thing in the Caucasian community. In the parlance of the courts these have come to be known as "Newton Street misdemeanors" (Newton Street is one of the police stations in the Negro district) indicating an assault-type crime that would be tried as a felony had it been committed in a middle-class Caucasian neighborhood. Judges rationalize this dual standard by saying that by the time the case comes to trial the victim usually isn't mad any more (true) and that Negro witnesses are almost always reluctant to appear in court (true). The Negro law officer, however, feels that this leniency only acts as a spur to the lawless element. On the other hand, he tends to be more realistic about the reasons for the high incidence of crime in Negro areas, and about the built-in inequities that automatically work against the average Negro citizen.

While the LAPD, officially, has no such thing as a traffic ticket *quota,* there is continual pressure on every man in the traffic department to *produce*—that is, to show that during his eight-hour shift he earned his money, and wasn't taking a nap somewhere. The evidence of this production consists primarily of 1) traffic citations; and 2) field intelligence reports, also known as "shake slips."

The basic concept of the shake slip is excellent. A suspicious person is sighted. He has not, to the officer's knowledge, committed any crime, so there is no cause to arrest him. As a suspicious person, however, he is asked to identify himself, and that identification is recorded. Subsequently, if the police discover a crime has been committed in the vicinity, there is a record of every person spotted nearby, this providing a list of suspects for interrogation.

The catch is that if an officer is pressured to turn in a certain number of shake slips daily, he is likely to start finding excuses for stopping people simply to make himself look good. And, somehow, there seem to be a great many more suspicious-looking Negroes than Caucasians.

(James C. Williams, the executive director of the Los Angeles World Trade Center Authority, a state agency, was stopped 12 times in six years while driving his car. At least eight of these stops were made simply on *suspicion*—the usual explanation being that a car matching the description was seen speeding away from the scene of a crime, or that one like it had been reported stolen, etc. Four times Williams was issued traffic citations, and, of these, three were dismissed by the city attorney's office as arbitrary. Few Caucasians have ever been stopped even *once* for no purpose other than investigation, and even fewer are ever spreadeagled against the side of their cars and searched from head to toe, a common practice in Negro districts. It is this type of action that Negroes refer to when they speak of "police harassment.")

Since Negro areas, because of the high rate of crime, are policed twice as intensively as Caucasian ones, and the population density ranges from two to ten times that of the community over-all, it is a simple matter of probabilities that the law-abiding Negro citizen is much more likely to come into contact with the police than the law-abiding white. Increasing this likelihood even more is the fact that to a great number of Caucasians, police officers and others, "all Negroes look alike"; and the fact that economic factors result in the Negro's higher susceptibility to citations, just as the rundown person has a higher susceptibility to disease. When an officer stops a late-model automobile it is likely to be in good working condition; when he stops a seven or eight-year-old crate that has been pawned off to a recent, unsuspecting arrival from Mississippi by a used-car dealer, it is seldom very difficult, if the officer is of such a mind, to cite the car for a faulty muffler, inoperative turn signals, or some other malfunction.

Imagine then the result when "motorcycle officers [are] told to tighten up and to write more tickets" because they have been "dogging it and if they don't get to work they'll be transferred off the motorcycle squad." [1]

[1] Los Angeles *Times*, March 18, 1955.

Exacerbating the conflict is that the effect on the Negro who receives a citation tends to be much more devastating than on the middle-class white. To the white person who gets a $12 ticket it may be a slight annoyance—he goes, or sends his secretary, to the nearest office of the automobile club to pay it. (There are some 730,000 auto club members in Southern California.) To the Negro domestic, not only is $12 a day's wages, but she must personally appear in court, waiting long hours and losing another half day's salary. The man from Mars, happening to look in on Los Angeles traffic court, would be inclined to think that a majority of cars in the city are driven by Negroes.

The aggressive, canny, often intelligent but semieducated Negro—raised, most likely, in the South where he was systematically pushed outside the pale of the white man's culture and mores so that, not only do they mean nothing to him, but he sees them actually as negative values because they are the values of his oppressor—quickly becomes convinced, because he sees the evidence all around him, that he will never make it by sticking to the white man's rules. That, on the other hand, by catering to the white man's—as well as the Negro's—vices, he will be able to make the kind of money he never could by knocking his head against the doors that prejudice has closed against him.

Bookmaking, numbers, gambling, after-hours drinking, prostitution, and dope peddling—all abound within the confines of Mac Benton's territory. At one corner, that of 60th St. and Avalon Blvd., which became notorious throughout Southern California as a place where one could pick up the "hard stuff," police made more than 1,500 arrests before the peddlers moved on to another location.

It is a wry witticism, not greatly exaggerated, among vice squad members that every telephone booth has its own bookmaker. The people are passionate bettors, and since most of them have neither the money nor the transportation to go to the track, the telephone is their link to the tote board. Numbers, the payoff being based on the total winnings of all the horses in the fourth, fifth and sixth races at a given track so that, unlike the policy racket, a fix is impossible, are widely played, their popularity stemming from the possibility that on a dime bet one can win a fortune.

Prior to the advent of the Harbor Freeway, when Figueroa St. was the main artery between Los Angeles and San Pedro and Palos Verdes, the Negro prostitutes plied their trade along a two-mile stretch, snagging homeward-bound suburbanites who preferred whore to hearth. When the freeway made stops for sex snacks less convenient, the prostitutes moved on to Western Ave. Some smart cookie tipped off the Los Angeles *Times* that a rampant prostitution situation had developed on that street, and the *Times,* in all honest fervor, published a series of articles decrying the situation. The prostitutes, who had been having to work harder to scrape up their tricks, found the togetherness situation improving rapidly.

Central Ave., Watts, Imperial Highway, each has its own nest of prostitutes. Most cater to Caucasians—it's necessary only to drive down the street at night and catch the eye of a slim, dusky girl with bleached hair—but on Imperial, near the freeway, a bevy of attractive white girls play host to affluent Negroes. One coterie of pimps has become popularly known as "The Magnificent Seven."

After-hours drinking and gambling clubs, some operating 24 hours a day, and a number of them integrated, are scattered throughout. Games played include craps, poker, blackjack and Georgia Skin, a cross between dice and poker in which three dice are used—4:5:6 or three of a kind being high, a pair of sixes beating a pair of fives, etc. Many of the clubs cater to fashionable clientele—which have included the relatives of local officials, the mayor of a lilywhite suburban town, and a Southern gentleman well known for his impeccable prejudices. Some masquerade as private clubs and use every means short of snooperscopes and lasers to detect the proximity of police—one keeps a watchdog on the roof, not only to bark the alarm of suspicious-smelling strangers, but also to discourage the disconcerting tendency of the vice squad to bore its way in through the roof.

Until the assignment of Negroes, the southeast area vice squads—whose Caucasian members sometimes tended to be rather naïve—had occasionally generated more smoke than fire, raiding penny-ante rent party poker games and small-time bookmakers, breaking in doors, putting their boots on the beds, and knocking furniture about to make the raids look good. Benton, who had himself, when it was expected as in the raid of a club, battered down doors—and once had actually gone straight through a wall—felt that there was no need to operate so obtrusively, and that there were too many big fish waiting to be caught to waste time on the small fry.

In this atmosphere of lasciviousness and constant temptation, a few Caucasian vice officers have gone to pot. One sergeant became used to drinking a six-pack during every shift. One night he was somewhat befuddled in a bar when his partner shook down a prostitute. "Give me a hard job, or I'll badge you!" he had threatened her.

Unbeknownst to him, the girl worked part-time in the records and identification section of the police department and, after he had taken her outside, filed a complaint. That was the end of the vice squad careers of both the sergeant and the officer.[2]

Central Ave. and 68th St., where the jurisdictions of the sheriff's office and the police department adjoin, was the domain of Big Emma, a local madame. It was the practice of sheriff's deputies to take rookies, clean-cut and Caucasian, who had just graduated from the academy, and introduce them to her.

"We want you to be nice to Emma," they would admonish straight-faced, "because she's one of our best informers."

"How do you do, Emma?" the rookie would say.

"Well there! Hiya! Pleased to meet ya!" Her voice would boom out as she sat there, legs akimbo, scratching herself. "Had your rocks blown lately, boy? Come on and we'll sixty-nine ya!"

The rookie would stagger back as if a skunk had been slammed into his face. The veteran deputies who had brought him would burst into laughter—he would soon get used to it!

As Mac Benton turned off Broadway into 77th, a quiet residential street where the police station stands unobtrusively flanked by single-family residences, green lawns, and palm trees, he wondered what sort of caper they had planned for him tonight. He was surprised to see the station bristling like a fortress—officers stationed at every entrance; shotgun-toting guards peering down from the roof.

---

[2] It is a well-known phenomenon that when officers are left too long on the vice squad—the maximum allowable at any one time being four to five years—they begin to "go over," adopting the behaviorisms and mores of the criminals with whom they are dealing, and shifting their primary allegiance. The same holds true for probation officers working with gangs.

18   There Is Nothing More to Be Said

John Buggs, together with the Rev. H. H. Brookins, was, at that very moment, pleading with Deputy Police Chief Roger Murdock in the division captain's office just to the right of the entrance. The situation was very grave, Buggs said. The kids were spoiling for a fight. A lot of people had guns, and were prepared to use them. He had seen five police cars that, he felt, should not have been in the area.

"They were responding to an officer-needs-help call," Murdock explained. He was, after Chief Parker, the highest ranking officer on the force, having, at the time of Parker's appointment in 1950, been himself considered for the position of chief. A Phi Beta Kappa graduate of USC and a former Rhodes Scholar, he has, as the leader of Southern California's 30,000 Shriners, a considerable following.

"Why was the officer there in the first place?"

"Because," Murdock snapped, "you've been dealing with hoodlums. I know exactly what you're going to suggest. I had a full report of your meeting this afternoon. We know how to put down a riot, and we are going to handle it our own way. We have already decided what we are going to do, and what you have got to say isn't going to change it. You have been no help at all. As a matter of fact, I think you are part of the problem!"

"All right," said Buggs, "maybe they are hoodlums. And I've been dealing with them. But right now they're the responsible people, they're the only ones who have the muscle necessary to control the situation."

"That's your opinion. We are not going to have hoodlums telling us how to operate. The LAPD is going to demonstrate who runs this town."

"Then why don't you try doing it with Negro officers?"

"Because it's not a workable plan. We are in the midst of quelling a riot. We don't have time for social experiments. We don't assign officers according to the color of their skins. Ne-

groes don't respect Negro officers—they call them 'Uncle
Toms.' I've talked with police chiefs all over the country, and
Negro officers have been no more help than any others in
riots—except that they can't be seen as well in the dark!"

"I assure you I'm as interested in the welfare of police officers, Anglos as well as Negroes, as you are."

"I doubt it."

"I have a commitment," Buggs persisted, "if you pull the
white officers out . . ."

"We're not pulling anybody out. There are 3,000 people
rioting down there. I've got 46 patrol cars saturating the area,
and I've got another 46 in reserve. I can call in 50 highway
patrolmen and 150 sheriff's deputies at a moment's notice.
And if that isn't enough, we can always get the National
Guard."

"You don't understand," Buggs said. "I'm not interested in
putting down a riot. I'm trying to prevent one."

"You're wasting your time!" Murdock declared abruptly.

"Then there's nothing more to be said."

"No. There is nothing more to be said."

The hall and entrance to the station were seething with
reporters and television cameras. Isolated shots were beginning to be heard, and there was a rumor that the station
was to be attacked.

"What's happened?" A tv reporter wanted to know.

"Nothing," Buggs replied. "I presented a plan but it was
turned down."

He went out through the people, white and black, milling
about, many frightened and uncertain as if they were in the
borderland of a nation teetering on the edge of war. He went
out and he saw the kids in the middle of the street, running
around playing ball, and eating popsicles. And he thought of
the efforts he had spent trying to involve middle-class Negroes
and Caucasians in positive movements, such as Big Brothers,
for the area; of the efforts necessary just to counter the
charges by right-wing elements that the Human Relations
Commission was a tool of the Communists, efforts little supported by responsible community leaders steeped in their own
noninvolvement. His mind dwelled on the thousands of kids
who had never sat at a table with a tablecloth, who had never
sat down together for a family dinner because the kitchen
table wasn't big enough, to whom the Caucasian is as foreign
as a Negro to a Norwegian. He remembered the continual

rejections, some major, others petty, the Negro steels himself against. And he sat down on the curb, and he took off his coat and his tie; and his shirt had turned translucent with his sweat. And he knew that he was beaten.

II.   The Fires of Discontent

19   Fi-Po, Eleanor, and Animals

At the roll call, the word went out that billy clubs only, no guns, were to be used against the rioters.

"Shit!" Frank Pinter's partner said to him. "This is just like Korea and Vietnam, they want us to fight with our hands tied behind our backs."

"Did you see any of the people when you drove in?" Pinter asked.

"People?" Errol Lawrence spit. "I didn't see any *people!* All I saw was animals!"

Lawrence was a 13-year veteran of the force, and Pinter, in order to avoid argument, usually went along with what he said. Pinter had learned to go along with a lot of things since, shortly after his graduation from the academy four years previously, his veteran partner had said to him near the end of the shift one day, "Let's head for the duck pond and write up a few jigaboos!"

The "duck pond," or "apple orchard," is a corner at which the traffic signals have been engineered so badly that it is always possible to catch a half dozen cars running the red light in the span of a couple of hours.

He had learned, after first being aghast, that one can always *find* a reason for making an arrest on suspicion—that suspicion, like the question of whether a person is under the influence of alcohol, is often a matter of opinion—and that the unsophisticated person is seldom in a position to put up a squawk if he is taken to the station for a few hours and then released. That if he does put up a squawk it can be pointed out to him that he resembles such and such a person who is wanted, or for whom an All Points Bulletin had been issued, and that he is, in reality, lucky not to have been booked—a study by the California Senate Interim Committee on Crime Law and Procedure showed that tens of thousands of persons have been arrested and booked without charges being filed against them; that all of these persons, although never charged, now have arrest records that make it difficult if not impossible for them to obtain any sensitive job.

He had also learned that the police have become so subject to hostility in the Negro community that it is virtually impossible to obtain witnesses in a crime investigation—a body will be lying on the sidewalk and half a dozen persons lounging about, and none of them will have seen anything, heard anything, know anything; or, possibly, even be willing to admit that the body is there at all.

"You know," said Lawrence, "I can forgive the niggers for being immoral; I can forgive them for being stupid; I can forgive them for living like a herd of goats. But what I'll never be able to forgive them for is letting the Reds in the civil rights movement make dupes and tools out of them— this is the start of the revolution to sovietize America!"

Lawrence, like several hundred fellow officers and firemen, was a member of the Fire and Police Research Association, an unofficial social-political type organization which may be accurately described as a "little John Birch Society." Fi-Po, as it is commonly known, urges its members to alertness against "the communist conspiracy operating within the borders of the state," this conspiracy ranging from folk singers to Arthur Schlesinger, Jr., the late President Kennedy's adviser. "We know," Fi-Po warned on April 18, 1963, "the United States will be a socialistic nation that will eventually fall under the domination of Russian rule if we continue our 'New Frontier' progress," but that "according to Khrushchev's openly published schedule of conquest . . . we have at least two more years of 'freedom.' "

Although Fi-Po has no official standing, its philosophy reflects that of enough police officers so that, for a time, it was permitted to pervade every facet of the department. Tickets to John Birch Society functions were peddled by watch commanders. "Communism and the Map," produced by Harding College in Arkansas and considered by the militant Christian Anti-Communism Crusade as inaccurate and extreme, was screened in the auditorium of the police academy. During the 1964 election, police officers, cruising in patrol cars, would drop by Poor Richard's Bookshop in Hollywood and the Dr. Ross Dog Food Co., both hotbeds of right-wing activity, to pick up literature for distribution. Anti-Johnson material was scattered throughout the lunch rooms of police and fire stations, and the right-wing *None Dare Call It Treason* was peddled by an officer in the main jail. Bulletin boards in the administration building and throughout stations in Los Angeles sprouted such material as "Is the civil rights struggle a prelude to class conflict Khrushchev style," "Impeach Earl Warren," and a picture of Eleanor Roosevelt with the caption: "Nigger Lover."

The fact that many of the department's chiefs were appalled when they became aware of the extent of this agitation, and cracked down on it, did not alter the fact that officers of liberal or moderate bent tended to be overwhelmed. Any man of liberal opinion became subject to the suspicions of his fellow officers, and, if he were a militant liberal, he placed his career in jeopardy.

This was made clear in the case of Michael Hannon, a blue-eyed blond of Scandinavian extraction, who undiplomatically argued with other officers, and is an avowed socialist.

Hannon, as a member of CORE, participated at times, off duty and in civilian clothes, in picket lines. Once he carried a sign: "What Khruschev did in Hungary, Johnson is doing in the Dominican Republic," and after he wrote an article, unsigned, in the CORE newsletter, beginning: "The changes wrought by CORE's attack on Chief Parker's bastion of bigotry show clearly that even the LAPD can be forced to modify its behavior by subjecting it to publicity," he became a marked man.

The Internal Affairs Division of the Police Department placed a plant in the guise of a Nicaraguan student within CORE, and, at meetings, he carried a transmitting device which relayed every word to two officers stationed outside in the street with a tape recorder. When Hannon then made the mistake of falling asleep in the station during the early morning watch—a not uncommon foible, for which the punishment is usually a brief suspension—the department moved against him.

When he was brought to trial in late June, 1965, before the police Board of Rights, it was charged that "without considering the pro and con of his convictions, they are held in conflict with the desired objectives and 'mental' attitudes necessary in a policeman for him to fairly exercise his functions. . . .

"He has been an active participant in demonstrations by a 'cause' group whose public appearance always requires extra policing against the contingency of their provoking an incident.

"It is the opinion," that although "over-all value to the department resolves as 'good,'" he is "completely untrustworthy in every respect. His loyalty to the department would seem to be nil and in addition most questionable in regard to the country and the national peace and security," and he therefore "poses a grave security threat."

Hannon was found guilty, and dismissed from the force. Chief Parker decided the sentence was excessive, and reduced it to a six-month suspension.

"Well," said Pinter, "I guess that's what the Chief's been saying, about civil disobedience being a tool of revolutionary forces."

"You're damn right!" Lawrence declared emphatically. "You know what the John Birch Society says." Lawrence pulled out a sheet of paper he had torn off. "'The civil rights movement in the United States, with all of its growing agitation and riots and bitterness, and insidious steps towards the appearance of a civil war, has not been *infiltrated* by the Communists, as you now frequently hear. It has been deliberately and primarily *created* by the Communists!' What do you think of that?"

"I don't know," Pinter replied quite honestly. "But with all this socialism going on, I wouldn't doubt it."

"Okay!" Lawrence said, moving toward their patrol car. "Let's go get 'em. I've got my throwaway knife all ready!"

The "throwaway knife" is a standard inside joke on the force—you carry an extra knife on you to "throw away" next to a suspect if you accidentally, or not-so-accidentally, shoot him, so as to make it appear that he has been shot during an attempted assault. But, like other such jokes, it may be transformed into something not so funny, as when two vice squad officers, Richard L. Price and Daniel M. Samaniego tried it after shooting a 31-year-old Negro musician. Caught at it, Price resigned and Samaniego received a six-month suspension, both being found guilty in Superior Court of "conspiracy to obstruct justice."

"Cut it out!" Pinter said to Lawrence. "We're going to have enough troubles!"

20   The Pot at the End of the Rainbow

Mac Benton was given a handful of dimes, told to go down into the area, stay out of trouble, not compromise his identity by engaging in any police activity, and call in periodically to report what was going on.

At the police administration building downtown the Emergency Control Center (ECC) was activated. Bypassing normal channels, the ECC would control all activity in connection with a riot. Shortly before eight o'clock Code 77—designed to order all extra units from other divisions to the 77th area—was broadcast, and a request was made for the 190 sheriff's deputies at the Harvey Aluminum Plant to stand by. A number of fake ambulance and police calls were coming in, and there was desultory rock throwing, but many motorists were being allowed to go through untouched.

Uncertainty prevailed on both sides. Only five police cars were within the 16-square-block area of the perimeter—as far as crowd control was concerned, they could act only as irritants. Kids like G. T. Godrick, Dandy Briggs, Pancho Pedrally, and Cotter Williams, who had been planning and building up stores of missiles all day, were aching for a fight—and Godrick was not the only one who had brought a home-built Molotov cocktail along. Gabriel Pope who, emotionally, felt every muscle in his body straining to strike at the white man's police, was allowing Lada's reasoning to hold him back. Ralph Reese, seething with as much resentment as anyone, was walking down the street, urging, "Come on, man, don't throw rocks. Wait a while and check things out—we're going to have a party!"

Shortly after 8 o'clock two of the police units in the area inevitably came under attack. Officer Needs Help vibrated the radio. Two dozen patrol cars, sirens screaming their response, shotguns displayed out of the windows, stormed down Avalon. At Imperial Highway some officers dropped off and charged into the crowd, their batons thrusting back and forth

—it was like trying to disperse water with a stick. Among the first to have his legs knocked out from under him by an officer was Ralph Reese.

The police drove in; then they drove out. Their effect was that of an electric current running through a magnet—the particles that had been swirling every which way became rearranged into a coherent, if not orderly, pattern.

Unaware, drivers plunged their cars into the trap of anger. The Revs. Glenn and Hardwicke, assisted by several persons including Timothy O'Seyre, rushed to block off Avalon. At the northern end, Imperial, they pushed sawhorses from a street improvement project out across the boulevard. Leaving Rev. Hardwicke in charge, they ran down the street, turning white drivers aside as they went. At 116th St. a television team had set up cameras and lights, casting a daylight glare over the area.

"Get the hell out of here!" O'Seyre yelled at them. "You'll get killed!"

At 120th St. the Rev. Glenn, O'Seyre, and two or three others cast about for some means to block the street. The only available object was a cement bus bench weighing several hundred pounds. They decided to drag it into the street, and had managed to push it off the sidewalk when they were challenged by a police lieutenant.

They explained to him what they were doing, and asked for his help. He was sympathetic.

"I can't give you authority to block off the street," he declared. But he left them a box of flares.

With great effort they pushed the bench into the middle of the street, lit the flares, and, placing another minister, the Rev. Parnell, in charge, went east on 120th St. toward San Pedro to set up a roadblock there. The Rev. Glenn headed for a supermarket a block away to call police to attempt to get them to block off traffic and announce over television that all persons should stay out of the area.

When Glenn and O'Seyre returned to the corner of 120th and Avalon, the flares were lying ashen in the street, a quartet of police officers were pushing the bench to the side, and the Rev. Parnell was sitting in the back of a police car, under arrest.

"What for?" O'Seyre asked.

"Obstructing traffic," was the reply.

"But the lieutenant himself gave us the flares!" O'Seyre protested.

The officer shrugged.

The car carrying the Rev. Parnell left.

A white Chevrolet with a Caucasian driver approached the intersection.

"Don't let it through!" Rev. Glenn shouted. When the officers made no motion, he himself started to jump out into the path of the driver to wave him away. One of the policemen, grabbing him, pulled him back.

The car proceeded up Avalon and was approaching the vicinity of the television cameras when it disappeared. A minute later a ball of flame shot into the air, engulfing it.

One of the officers looked at the fire, then at O'Seyre.

"You can put the bench back in the street!" he said.

But there were no flares with which to illuminate it.

Said "Wild Bill" Davis, "The communications from the upper level to the sergeants and policemen in the field were ridiculous. At no time in the first two nights of the riot . . . did any of the sergeants at the scene or police officers know what the orders were from the upper level."

Mac Benton was sitting on a wall. All around him girls in halters and men with their shirts off were lolling about, drinking beer, laughing, talking about Las Vegas, the horse races, the Dodgers—the people were the friendliest he had ever seen them, there was a pervasive air of camaraderie. A great many persons had transistor radios on which they were listening to the police calls—the police frequency is so close to the commercial band that, with only a slight adjustment, or sometimes none at all, it can be brought in.

Suddenly there were screams and shouts, flames blossomed amidst the trees, Benton could see everybody running toward a Chevrolet on fire in the middle of Avalon. A police car, traveling along a side street, skidded around the corner into the boulevard. Its back wheels locked against the curb. The engine stalled. Two officers rushed into the mass of people.

Pancho Pedrally saw them coming.

"Hey, you motherfuckers," he taunted them, "come and get me!" He hurled a rock, bouncing it off the arm of one of the officers, and the officer took the dare. He went in after him, around the corner of an apartment house—right into the middle of a mob.

"Get him! He's by himself! Kill the motherfucker!" the cry went up.

The officer's head was ground into the cement, his baton and gun were ripped from him, black fists, black feet pummeled and kicked at him. He would have been killed had it not been for Benton and a couple of the other undercover officers who battered their way through to pull him out.

The Rev. Glenn, O'Seyre, and several others, including Richard Jones, Mayor Yorty's Negro aide, jumped into their cars and drove to the 77th St. police station. Lt. Frank Beeson and Insp. Fisk came to the door to talk to them.

"Please. You've got to block off traffic. People are going to be killed!" the Rev. Glenn said.

"White people have a right to go through there," Beeson replied. "We have enough men to keep order."

"Things are blowing up all over. The only chance—if we could get them to hold a dance on Avalon."

"Go ahead and hold your dance," Fisk said. "The police will not be out in force."

The Rev. Hardwicke asked if he could borrow a bullhorn to make the announcement, and Fisk said that he would get it for him. However, when he went back into the station, so many reports were coming in of white motorists being attacked and of police officers in trouble that he forgot about it.

Along Imperial Highway nail-studded boards, benches, garbage cans, uprooted traffic signs, oil drums—anything of any size that was movable was thrown into the street to create hazards for automobiles.

A 21-year-old Cornell University law student, Roy Calamaro, was driving a taxi for the Yellow Cab Co. during the summer months. Having been asleep during the day he knew nothing of the disturbance, and had picked up a fare at International Airport. As, coming along Imperial, he reached the intersection of Avalon the light turned red—the white woman motorist ahead of him stopped. Rocks started splattering down on both vehicles but she refused to budge—she saw the police cars, she knew the law. As Calamaro frantically tried to maneuver around her, the door of the cab flew open, he was jerked out, a rock crashed into his jaw, breaking it—a minute later the cab was sitting on its top, wheels clawing the air like the feet of a helpless turtle.

The Rev. Glenn and Timothy O'Seyre returned with the others from the 77th St. station. They began walking down

Avalon Blvd. to spread the word that there was going to be a dance.

"The police are pulling back," O'Seyre said.

"Check it out, there's going to be a dance," the Rev. Glenn advised.

A kid with an armful of rocks was aiming them at a street light.

"Look, you don't have to bust those lights! We're having a dance!"

"Is that right?" The boy couldn't have been more surprised if they had told him they'd brought him a cake for his birthday.

"You're a damn liar!" The words were suddenly spat into the Rev. Glenn's face.

He looked up and saw the police, 20 abreast, marching down the boulevard with shotguns and batons in combat position.

"You goddam preachers have been telling us to bear our burdens for a hundred years!" A 20-year-old youth's eyes were flashing. "Now we're gonna let somebody else carry 'em for a while!"

He darted out of the way of the police whose batons moved rhythmically right, left; left, right like scythes mowing down stalks of grain.

Behind the police came an ABC television team consisting of cameraman Ralph Mayer, sound technician Raymond Fahrenkopf, and newsman Piers Anderton. They had parked their station wagon on Avalon south of Imperial, and were following the sweep on foot, filming the action as they went.

When the three television men returned to their station wagon, it was in flames, no police were in sight, and the immediate vicinity seemed to have been abandoned. As they stood, momentarily in shock, illumined by the flames, a barrage of bricks and bottles rained down—behind them, like a phalanx of Indians following the arrows, the youths came rushing. Anderton and Mayer managed to scurry away, but Fahrenkopf, older and less nimble, was caught, the equipment torn from him, his head battered from fist to fist, one youth repeatedly banging an empty trashcan down upon him as if he were trying to flatten a piece of dough. Beaten almost unconscious, he was left lying in the street. Anderton and Mayer, catching sight of an abandoned police car, locked themselves inside. The kids, jumping on it, beat an ear-bursting tattoo against its sides, danced on the roof, and waved their hands in the three-fingered *W* sign that was blossoming everywhere. The *W* of the Watts gang. The mob was molding an identity for itself.

Suddenly the lights flickered, flickered again like a man trying to catch his breath, then went out. Amidst shouts and screams the street was plunged into a tunnel-like blackness.

"Get out! Get out! We're tired of this shit!" Police moved through the Shell Station on Imperial, banging their batons against the fenders of the cars parked there. They pulled open the door to the office. "Get out! Get out!" they ordered the five girls, four Negro and one white, frightenedly standing inside.

"She'll get killed if she goes out there," the attendant argued with the policemen. "I told her she could stay."

"If she wants to stay with you blacks, let her, but I won't take the responsibility!" one of the officers snapped.

The police were moving east along Imperial, driving the people before them. Residents of the area were intermingled with spectators from all over the city who, coming upon the crowd, had parked their cars to watch. A girl in a bathing suit stood next to a man in a tuxedo, a wizened old preacher was going along waving a Bible high in the air.

The police made no distinction. "Get the hell out of here! Run!" they commanded.

A woman fell, and a girl stopped to pick her up, "I said run, nigger!" an officer jabbed her with his baton.

She started to turn on him. Another policeman's gun was pointing at her belly. "You ever been pregnant with a bullet, girl?" he asked.

*   *   *

Frank Pinter was stationed on Imperial Highway beyond the perimeter, several blocks to the east. A lighted liquor store was behind him, and Pinter, hot and thirsty, had twice gone in to get a drink of water—knowing the way the minds of the Negro residents operate, Pinter was sure they would spread the word he was drinking whiskey. Everything was quiet along the street. A gap-toothed Muslim, about 30, wearing an ill-matching assortment of coat, plaid shirt, and woolen tie, a hat a size too small perched on his head, was persistently trying to sell him a copy of *Muhammad Speaks*.

"The Messenger of Allah speaks!" The Muslim circled

around Pinter. "How about it, sir? Read the words of the third of the great prophets, the honorable Elijah Muhammad!"

Pinter remained silent, and the Muslim tried another officer, then approached a customer entering the liquor store.

"The prophetic vision of the prophet reveals all. Only 20¢!"

The Caucasian owner of the store came out to glance around.

"Here you go, sir!" the Muslim pressed the tabloid upon him. "The Messenger of Allah speaks."

"Does he tell me what's going to happen tonight?" The white man was friendly.

"The sins of the father will be visited four-fold upon the sons. That means the 400 years the Negro has been enslaved. It's all in knowing how to interpret. The Bible and the great Koran contain all the history of the world, yesterday and tomorrow. Elijah Muhammad interprets all."

"That's all very well," said the store owner. "But what about those of us who didn't have anything to do with enslaving the Negro? The kids come in and I give them candy and potato chips, and when they don't ask for it I let 'em go ahead and steal it. Whose sins am I going to be four-folded for?"

"The white race has had five great prophets but ignored them. We are 4,000 years from Moses, and Moses was 2,000 years from the creation of the white race. And now the old world must be removed to make way for the new, and today is the day in which the God of Allah is judging between man and man and nation and nation. The American whites are the enemies and haters of their slaves. The white people are very tense. They don't believe in Johnson—things are just like before Kennedy was assassinated." Carried away, he caught and admonished himself; "Now you've got me preaching. I'm not supposed to preach to you. I'm not going to preach."

"I don't hate you," the white man said. "If you were hungry, I'd give you a loaf of bread. If you were thirsty, I'd give you a drink. Come on. Come on in right now, and I'll prove it."

"You're like the devil," the Muslim replied. "You offer food with one hand, and you befuddle my people with drink on the other. Alcohol is evil. The messenger tells us it is the white man's way of keeping us enslaved."

"I'm not asking you to buy my liquor. I don't ask anybody to buy it. I've been here more than 15 years, long before any of your people were around. I'm willing to live with you, to live and let live. Now you're doing exactly the same to me that the Messenger complains about the white people doing to you. You want to be friends with me? Come on. I'll be friends with you." He started to take his hand.

"Man!" The Muslim shied away. "Don't do that!" He had been taught exactly how to behave when ignored or when met with anger, but he was baffled by friendliness. "Don't do that!" he repeated. "You're relaxing me!"

He did a slow jig down the pavement, backing off from this dangerous situation.

"Well, I've got to go now!" he called out.

"Where you going?"

"Back to my people. Back to the promised land!"

That's when Pinter, looking up, saw 15 or 20 persons, scattered on both sides of the street, running east on Imperial as if they were trying to escape an avalanche.

*   *   *

Mac Benton was in a telephone booth on Imperial, trying to call the special number at the 77th St. station that had been given him. It had been busy for 10 minutes, and was, in fact, busy incessantly, since 10 telephones couldn't have handled the calls that were coming in and going out on one. Benton watched the kids, bloody, their shirts torn, running back and forth, declaring, "Man, we gonna get 'em! We really gonna get 'em now!"

As he repeatedly dialed the number, there was a knock on the door—he was startled to see the faces of three white men, who wanted to use the telephone. They were probation officers. No one was bothering them.

Benton decided to return to 77th division to make his report in person. He walked several blocks to get out of the immediate area, then, as he saw a police car coming down the street, stepped out, badge cupped in his hand, and hailed it. The driver halted. Benton approached the window.

"What you want, shitass jigaboo?" the officer demanded.

Benton stopped as if he had been slapped. The two officers looked, and in that instant recognized him. It was as if a terrible truth, long smoldering, had suddenly boiled to the surface.

At 77th St. station, Benton talked to Lt. Beeson and other high-ranking officers who were swarming about. He told them that, in his opinion, there was little point in any police officers being in the area, for they weren't there in large enough force to keep the rioters from acting as they pleased. When Benton had left the station a few hours earlier an air of confidence had prevailed, but now everything seemed to have gone haywire. The brass were confused and astonished. No one seemed to know what, if any, decision to make.

There were 190 sheriff's deputies stationed around the perimeter, but inside, actually dealing with the rioters, were less than 100 Los Angeles police officers, and, because for every two officers there was one patrol car, some were tied down guarding the equipment.

(Said Deputy Chief Murdock: "Our tactics were bad. We should have been out there with a lot of foot soldiers and we're out there with a lot of officers in radio cars. If we'd known then what we know now, we would have had three times as many officers . . . and it wouldn't have gotten out of hand.")

Murdock called the sheriff's office and was told that he could have 500 men in an hour. But 500 men were more than had been used on a detail during his entire 34 years on the force. He decided, instead, to request the assistance of 40 California Highway Patrolmen who were being held in readiness three or four miles away.

*   *   *

Anita Greyson was driving south on Avalon Blvd. She was driving south on Avalon because if there was one person she had sympathy for it was Bill Briggs, Dandy Briggs's father.

Bill Briggs, in his mid-forties, was training to be a janitor in the southeast area office of the BPA. An amendment to the aid-for-dependent-children law, passed in 1964, made it possible for children to be aided when an unemployed father was in the home, providing he agreed to undertake on-the-job retraining. Prior to the change, such aid could be granted only if the father were absent, and it had been theorized that many men deserted their families because, not being able to get jobs, they wanted their children to be eligible for state aid. This theory had been blasted to bits when, after the AFDC-U law, as it is known, had gone into effect, the rate of family breakups continued to soar.

"You can't expect a man that knows he's gettin' the whittlin's off the stick to have any respect for himself," Briggs told Anita. "They paying me $1.25 an hour, but when they get through training me like they say, there ain't gonna be no more $1.25 jobs. You either gets $3, or you gets nothing. Nowadays a man needs some fat in his head to make money —you ain't got no fat in your head, you're lost!"

Briggs came on the job at 4:30 p.m. when all of the social workers pulled out. His family was one of those assigned to Anita, and Anita had talked to him before, but never extensively. This evening, however, it had been 6 o'clock before she'd decided to call it quits on the telephone calls she was making. When she'd looked up, Bill had been only a couple of desks away, pushing his mop, and she recognized that he had been listening. They were alone in the vast, cluttered room, and with the air conditioning turned off it was hot and stuffy.

"What it is," he said, shaking his head, "all they doing is training me for unemployment. I could train for 100 years and I'd never catch up, the way it is now. You think I'm going to be jumping up and down for joy, knowing that? Every time I been retrained in comes some machine and out goes half the jobs, and it's always the black man that goes with them. It's not retraining that I need. It's some re-equalizing."

Briggs had brought his family from Midnight, a small community near Yazoo City, Miss., to California because, he said, "A man's got to have some breathing room. It ain't living right when you always got to be looking over your shoulder, looking out for *the man*." In Midnight, when times were good, Briggs had been able to work as a roustabout in the nearby oil fields, he had worked in the saw mill, he had driven a truck. When times were bad he had gone back to the fields to chop cotton. "You knows you weren't never going to starve."

When he had come to California he had been surprised to find that many jobs that were open to Negroes in Mississippi were closed to them in Los Angeles.

"Like, I had this friend delivering parcels back there. He come out here, and nobody hire him. Nobody hire him because he don't belong to no union, and you come out here and you try to get in, and you might as well be knocking on the pearly gates. I work in construction back in Mississippi, I don't need no lessons. I go to the union and they say you

got to be an apprentice, you got to have a high school diploma and you got to take this test that look like you need a
collegiate degree for, and then when you does all that, you go
to the bottom of the list. 'We call you when we get an opening,' they say. 'When will that be?' I asks. 'Oh, maybe five or
six years if you lucky!' they tells me."

Every day for five weeks Briggs had gone to the hod car-
riers' hiring hall; he had gone as early as 4 a.m., and the
story had always been the same—somebody else had always
been called for the jobs. Finally an acquaintance had taken
him aside. "Billy," he said, "you ain't got much sense. This
here's the public hiring hall, they don't hire people in the
public hiring hall, they hires 'em in the private hiring hall."

The acquaintance had given him the home telephone number of the business agent. Briggs had called him and the agent
had explained to him that life consisted of gives and takes,
and that if he expected to take something he had to give a
little also. Briggs had understood him, and for a while every
morning when he went down to the hiring hall his name had
been on the list. But then, three or four years back, the jobs
had come fewer and were harder and harder to find, the construction industry had gone into a slump, and of those buildings that were going up more and more were high-rise types
using more machinery and fewer men.

"I'd be making near $200 a week, and then'd come a month
I'd make nothin', how's a man going up and down like a
yo-yo to know what to do? How's a man used to workin'
honest and making good money to feel pushin' a mop for a
dollar and two bits an hour?"

Briggs and his wife, Manella, had five children in addition
to Dandy. The youngest was 4, and the oldest, Yolanda, was
23 and already receiving public assistance for herself and her
three children. Yolanda had been shot in the right eye in
Mississippi by a white boy with a beebee gun.

"So they tells us they don't want no trouble, and they going to go ahead and give her another eye. Only it don't look
so good, but what can you do?"

Anita had met and talked to Yolanda Briggs. She was a
pretty girl of, for the Mississippi migrant, average intelligence, with deep blue eyes, one slightly deeper than the other.
The deeper blue one did not move but continuously stared
straight ahead, so that sometimes her eyes seemed to be

crossed, at other times divergent, and one often had the uncomfortable feeling that she was, simultaneously, watching different things in entirely separate parts of the room.

"She never get married and she have these three babies," Bill Briggs said, "and I know it ain't right. But she got this bad feeling 'bout that eye, and she always afraid no boy gonna like her, so she think she got to be real commodious."

Anita asked him about Dandy.

"He don't come home last night. I know he down there in that trouble. Everything going okay with him till last summer when he get his school diploma and go out on that job to the white people, and he come back with this great big hate, saying it ain't no use, that he was a nigger in Mississippi, and he be a nigger in California, and he gonna be a nigger all his life! So finally I gets him over that, and he go down to Trade Tech and sign up to be a mechanic. Everybody say to me it be a free school, but he come home and tell me he got to have all this money to buy tools, and I calls up down there and sure enough, he got to get his own tools that cost $700! So I give him all I got, which is $50, and say you start on that. And he go out and buy himself a set, and he driving home one night at 10 o'clock and the police stop him and make him open up the trunk. And there he got the tools, and the police ask him where he get 'em and he say he buy 'em, and they want to know where he got the slip, and he say he don't have one. So they takes him down to the station and books him for questioning, and they keeps him more than a day, and they lets him go and say he check out okay. They say he check out okay, but now he 19 years old, and he got a record!"

That was when Anita told Bill Briggs she would go down and try to find Dandy.

"You know," Bill said, "we all got some good and some bad in us. And I never know a white man, and that include the policemens, that I could talk to that I couldn't get along with. But the way they got us now, we so filled with this frustration we just aching to bust out. We been to Mississippi, and we been to Chicago. We been to New Orleans, and we been to New York. And everywhere they say, 'Go to California!' California's the great big pot o' gold at the end of the rainbow. Well, now we're here in California, and there ain't no place else to go, and the only pot I seen's the kind they peddle at 60th and Avalon!"

Driving down Avalon, Anita felt quite safe. She had the top down on the little MGB, and she had picked up Manella Briggs who, carrying her 4-year-old, was sitting in the seat next to her. Everyone would be able to see that the car was integrated.

Manella was talking too much. She had little of her husband's sense of proportion, and one minute she would be almost hysterical, worrying about Dandy, while the next she was gleeful: "Oh boy! You white folk are going to get it! You been takin' all the poverty money from the poor folk, and now you really going to get it!"

Approaching Imperial Highway, Anita saw more and more people walking south along both sides of the street, and by 109th St. it was a steady stream. Three blocks farther on she came upon an automobile burning in an empty lot, and, having heard nothing of the riot having spread north of the highway, she became concerned, and wondered out loud if she shouldn't park the car.

"What are you, chickenshit?" asked Manella. "Drive on."

Hardly had she uttered the words when a police car materialized in front of the MG, and rocks began arcing down on both vehicles.

"Hey, it's blood! It's blood!" Manella yelled hysterically, waving her arms over her head. "Not me! Not me!" She was entirely unconcerned about Anita. "Let me out of here!" she screamed, opening the door of the still-moving car, as a rock landed squarely on Anita's forehead.

Another rock crashing through the windshield pounded into Anita's eye; a 10-pound chunk of asphalt smashed into her cheek; she was soaking in her own blood, and, blinded by it, almost ran the police car off the road. The police car was one of the few that had both a Negro and a white officer. They summoned an ambulance which refused to come into the area without an escort.

By the time it finally arrived, more than a half hour had passed. Anita was taken to the hospital where she spit out two of her teeth, the cut above her eye was stitched without anesthetic, and her wallet was stolen. When she returned home two days later, a card, postmarked Glendale, Cal., was waiting for her.

"Niggers and Kikes must go!" it read. "Only the American Nazi party has the final solution."

21   "A Deadly Fear of the Police"

The howling of sirens, the sight of red lights flashing down boulevards, drew an ever-increasing number of people toward Avalon and Imperial where, like bits of paper fluttering into a fan, the police tried to spin them out again, but succeeded only in scattering them over an ever wider area. By 10 o'clock no vehicle driven by a Caucasian could come within blocks of the intersection without coming under attack. Cars were burning like starshells to the west, the south, and the east. As the fire trucks rumbled down, missiles of every description were hurled at them. A full can of beer ricocheted off one fireman's ankle, a massive chunk of asphalt bent the steering wheel of a truck backward out of the driver's hands. Where the ABC-TV station wagon was burning south of Imperial the firemen had just set up their hoses when, coming under attack from all sides, they had to abandon their equipment and run toward the safety of the police command post two blocks to the north.

A rig coming from the station on 103rd St. in the heart of Watts reported seeing people in the streets for almost the entire two miles. Since the truck had been subjected to harassing action from the very start of the run, it was decided to abandon the Watts station. Orders were given for the fire apparatus to move only in task forces of two or more units, and only with police protection.

Timothy O'Seyre was moving east along Imperial Highway. Behind him came the mob, and behind the mob the police. Inexorably moving from intersection to intersection, the riot expanded, the older teenagers and young adults in the van, 14- and 15-year-olds behind in reserve. O'Seyre tried to warn the drivers, he tried to wave them off, but most would only stare at him as if he were a madman. In the bend of Imperial an oil slick had crept across the road, cars were spinning in it, one turned completely around and came to a halt. Immediately it was pounced upon and the occupants pulled out. A Molotov cocktail consigned it to flames.

A pattern was developing: a car would be stoned, halted, the occupants briefly beaten, then rescued by friendly Negroes or else, as if by accord of the rioters, allowed to flee. A young girl jumped out of a Volkswagen as her escort tried to fend off the attackers; nobody bothered her as she ran helter-skelter down the middle of the street between the shores of black faces.

"Go get 'em, man! Blow 'em up! Blow 'em all up!" girls were screaming, urging on the men as car after car, emptied of its occupants, was engulfed by fire.

There was a mindless mania to much of the action. Police were making arrests as if they were intent on picking off individual fleas hopping about on the coat of a dog by thousands. A Negro motorist, Harry L. Atkins, got splattered with rocks, stopped his car, and five minutes later was throwing rocks at other cars. He stood imperturbably as police officers bore down on him. When they grabbed him, he was astonished. "What's the matter with you, man?" he protested.

"You just threw a rock at a car!"

"Sure I threw a rock at that car, man! Other people threw rocks at my car, why bug me? I didn't throw it at your car!"

Newlyn Brunton and Carol Lawson were driving a "first call" car, similar to a hearse, for the Abbott & Hast Mortuary. They had just picked up the body of a man at the hospital in Lynwood when Brunton, driving, was startled to come upon a bonfire in the middle of the street. Momentarily slowing down, he saw figures darting at him from all sides. A bottle spun across the hood, the point of a knife penetrated, ripping through the canvas top. Brunton swerved, accelerated, went right through the middle of the fire. Ducking beneath the level of the dash and steering by watching the line of trees, he careened the vehicle down the street. The body, arms waving, bounced off the stretcher and engaged in its own version of the twist.

Mac Benton had returned to Avalon. He watched as a 1964 Malibu, stopping for the traffic signal, was instantaneously stung by a swarm of rocks. The driver dropped down to the floorboards, the kids closed in and pelted him as he lay there. A half minute later he opened the door and, trying ineffectively to ward off the rocks and bottles, began staggering down the center of the street. A pickup truck swerved alongside him;

the driver opened the door, pulled him into the cab, and the truck spun off.

A motorcycle came roaring down the boulevard, a white youth, his girl sitting behind him, nonchalantly taking in the sights.

"Here comes Whitey again!" the cry went up.

"No! Not them! Let 'em go!" a woman cried.

The motorcyclists chugged through the gauntlet untouched.

There was a crash of glass—Benton looked up to see a youth stepping through the plate glass window of a market, chug-a-lugging a fifth. Within 15 minutes the area was aswarm with people, their arms loaded with groceries, some pushing overflowing shopping carts. As Benton tried to make his way to a telephone, the Bing & Yet Market, which had been looted the night before, began turning red with fire. There were kids in the neighborhood who had a feud to settle with the owner because he kept a baseball bat behind the counter for self-protection—there were a lot of feuds awaiting settlement.

A red-shirted youth, ducking out from between a row of houses eight blocks to the east on Imperial Highway, snapped off a quick shot at an officer, then disappeared. Within the hour a dozen sharp, staccato pops resembling small caliber fire, interspersed here and there by the deep bass-drum sound of shotguns, were heard—there was such turmoil that officers, aiming at phantoms, discovered they were shooting at each other. A California Highway Patrolman, Robert Mitchell, was winged in the leg by a ricochet. A 30-year-old Negro medical technician, Julia Jones, took a shotgun blast in the stomach as she stood at the corner of Avalon and Imperial.

A few minutes past 11 o'clock a colonel of the National Guard called from Sacramento to ask if assistance were needed. He was told that the police were in control.

At the southern edge of the perimeter, along 120th St., where things had been relatively quiet, two police officers were surrounded by a mob of 200 rioters. A sheriff's car was overturned and burning.

Chief Murdock had managed to build up his forces to 500 men—295 sheriff's deputies, 157 police officers, and 47 highway patrolmen—with another 130 in reserve.

"We've been playing games with these kids long enough!" he said. While the sheriff's deputies guarded the perimeter, he decided to have the police and highway patrol sweep the area clean.

The streets were a mass of seething humanity as Benton tried to make his way around the market fire. The action had changed from one involving a few dozen youths performing for a great many spectators, to one of mass participation. In his wanderings Benton crossed a field in which the shadows of huge water storage tanks were beaten down to the ground by the light of the moon, dark figures were scurrying everywhere laden with groceries, sundries, and liquor. . . .

"Hey! Where'd you get that?"

"Store's open!"

"No shit!"

"I got mine. You better get yours!"

The flames from the fire gave shape to the dark horizon. A boy had a girl backed up against the leg of one of the towers —they were locked together in an oblivion of giggles. Benton returned to Avalon Blvd. He returned to hear whistles, the jangling of key chains, the solid tramp of massed boots, to see a line of lights bobbing up and down like a wave washing down the street—it was a frightening combination, and, reflexively, he vaulted a wall to get out of the way. People were screaming and yelling, there were cries of "motherfuckers!" "sons of bitches!" "blue-eyed devils!" and "black bastards!" Benton could hear the sounds of doors being kicked in as officers went after fleeing suspects; again there was a lack of discrimination as policemen prodded and corraled some people who had been sitting peacefully in their doorways, while allowing others, spilling rocks as they fled, to run for cover. The police dropped off half a dozen men at each corner as they went. The firemen moved in behind them to attack the blazing store.

Benton approached the police lines around the fire.

"Hey, blood! Heat's up there!" a youth called out from behind a row of bushes.

Putting his hands above his head, Benton came into the light of the fire. He walked slowly, so as not to startle anyone. Before he had time to say anything, he heard the click of a shell slipping into the chamber of a shotgun.

"One more step, nigger, and you're a dead man!"

He started to explain, but not more than a couple of words managed to cross his lips.

"I'm just waiting to blow some of you bastards' heads off! Move!"

"Okay! Okay!" he said. "I'm going."

He turned around, but had taken only a couple of steps when a boot caught him in the hip and sent him sprawling.

*   *   *

As the police swept down Avalon Blvd., the people scampered out of the way between the houses, then circled back behind the officers. While the firemen aimed streams of water at the market fire, in the next block glass was crashing to the pavement. There was a scurrying of looters, then a flash of fire—a pharmacy and doctor's office began belching rainbow-colored flames.

Motorists, still driving into the area unaware of what was going on, were coming upon unlighted barricades, skidding and crashing into them. One driver detoured by the police got lost on the back streets and emerged face-to-face with a score of armed youths. Along Imperial Highway three more cars were burning. A Negro man was carrying an elderly, sobbing white woman down the street to safety. The mob had lost its cohesiveness—groups of 10 to 12 persons were scattering all over like ants driven out of their hill. Along Imperial, G. T. Godrick was part of a mob that had infested a liquor store. Everyone grabbed whatever he could carry, bottles were tumbling off shelves and being pitched from hand to hand. One enterprising fellow had found himself a cart and was trundling two cases of whiskey down the street.

Inside the store a gleeful Pancho Pedrally kept knocking the tops off beer bottles and, amidst screams and curses, spraying the contents around, until someone slapped him on the head and temporarily knocked him silly.

Raul Milera was a 22-year-old Cuban who had fled to the U.S. in 1959 after the Castro takeover. After several years of working in menial jobs while he learned English, he was now employed as a salesman by Sears-Roebuck. He had been in a nearby city visiting friends and, hearing on the radio that a riot, possibly instigated by Communists, was in progress, he decided to investigate for himself. At the corner of Avalon and Century Blvds., a full mile to the north of Imperial, a brick detonated against his windshield. Several blocks farther on a bevy of kids were bombarding a police car. Pulling to a halt, Milera got out of the car to report to the officers that he had been attacked. As he did, the police charged the kids, and, momentarily, as they ran and he went forward, in the welter of confusion he was caught amongst them. When he disentangled himself from them, the police were upon him.

"Sir—," he started to say.

"You're under arrest!" was the reply.

He was charged with assault with a deadly weapon for throwing rocks.

*   *   *

The Stop Drive-In at Imperial and Central—which had always employed Negroes, and at which Ralph Reese's mother was an assistant manager—was surrounded by a howling mob of kids. Negro comedian Dick Gregory, borrowing a bullhorn at the 77th station, went to talk to them. He had no sooner emerged from behind a police barricade than several shots rang out, and a .22-caliber bullet thudded into his leg.

"Okay. You shot me," he told a straw-hatted, T-shirted youth. "Now go home!"

Officer Larry Fultz had the end of his thumb bitten off in a struggle with a rioter.

Piles of rubbish and a number of small buildings were on fire within an area more than a mile square. Mervyn Dymally, the area's assemblyman in the state legislature, could see several stores being looted as he drove about. On Imperial, two blocks to the east of where Gregory was shot, three cars and a building were on fire. Dymally tried to talk to the kids who were standing about, suggesting that they had done enough and should go home.

"Let's cool it!" he said.

"Man! Where you from?" one challenged him. "You from the west side? From Baldwin Hills?"

"No, man," Dymally answered. "I live here."

"You must live in some big house."

"No, man. I'm the people."

"If you're the people—" the kid handed him a bottle, "throw it!"

"No, man. I'm for peace!"

"Hell!" the kid said. "You're with *the man!*"

Dymally telephoned the 77th police station to ask for help. A handsome West Indian, who looks like a tanned Brian Donlevy, he had become involved in politics in 1960 when he organized the Westside Young Democrats. During this time, while working the swingshift at an electric plant in the area, he had on numerous occasions been stopped by the police in the early morning hours. Despite the fact that he was now a state legislator he still had, as he said, "a deadly fear of the police."

When the officers arrived in response to his call, they charged against every Negro in sight, including several persons who had been sitting peacefully on their steps, watching. Intervening, Dymally approached an officer to explain, and to suggest that such indiscriminate action could only trigger more trouble.

"Take one more step," the officer leveled his gun at the assemblyman, "and you've had it!"

22   "And the Thing Was Boiling!"

Col. Robert L. Quick of the National Guard, the assistant adjutant general assigned by Gen. Hill as liaison with the LAPD, had arrived at the ECC a few minutes before midnight. An hour later he was told that it appeared unlikely the National Guard would be needed.

By 1:15 a.m. rioters had traveled as far as three miles to the northeast, and looting was beginning along 103rd St., the business district of Watts. At his home in Hawthorne, five miles to the west, Glenn Anderson, the lieutenant governor of the state, could see the fires superimposed upon the dull glow of the city's lights. Since Gov. Edmund "Pat" Brown was on vacation in Greece, Anderson was the acting governor, and would be responsible for calling the National Guard if the request were made.

At 1:45 a.m. Lt. Gov. Anderson was informed by John Billett, the governor's press secretary, who had checked with the ECC, that the riot was nearing control.

At 1:50 a.m., Mac Benton, and several of the other plain-clothes officers who had been in the area, voiced the opinion at a critique at the 77th station that the situation was out of hand, and that the National Guard would be needed.

At 1:57 a.m. the sheriff refused to let fire trucks enter the area, because protection could not be provided.

At 2 a.m. the perimeter was considered to have been officially dissolved, because people had spread out everywhere. In the heart of Watts a liquor store owner, barricaded in his store, was blazing away with his gun at numerous people battering at the door.

*   *   *

Cotter Williams was tired. He was lugging a six-pack of beer, two fifths of whiskey, and various sundries from a delicatessen home to his mother to surprise her—they could have another party. He had no sooner opened the door of the apartment in the Jordan Downs Housing Project when a number of shots rang out. Dropping the articles on the kitchen table, he ran out.

People were congregating, rushing out from all the apartments. Shouts and questions filled the air.

"What happened, man?"

"Who doing the shooting?"

"I seen 'em!" said a youth. "It was a yellow Buick with a couple of Whiteys!"

"Yeah, man!" another joined in. "I hear them Klan people is coming down to get us!"

"We needs protection!"

"Sure, baby! That's what we needs!"

It was quickly decided that the protection could be obtained from the pawnshops lining 103rd St. Cotter Williams forgot he was tired. Together with a score of others, he rushed off.

People using boards and crowbars were prying the protective gratings off the windows of several shops along 103rd St. As they worked, one lone police car with two officers made its appearance. People in a clothing store scattered as the car stopped. The officers, calling for the looters to halt, were ignored. One of the officers, in the penumbra of a street light, thought he saw a metal object glinting in the hand of a man who, running, stopped and looked back. The officer fired, the shot spinning Leon LaCour to the ground. As the policemen rushed toward him, some of the people who had been running turned back, while others poured out of alleys and side streets.

"Motherfuckers!" they cried at the policemen. "Murderers!"

They pushed at them and hemmed them in. Threatening words were backed up with threatening gestures, several persons helped LaCour to his feet—there was nothing the officers could do as he was carried off into the darkness.[1]

Among the units answering the Officer Needs Help call on 103rd St. was Sgt. Richard Rankin's. Rankin had already been involved in one altercation in which his service revolver had tumbled out of its holster to the street, and he had almost lost it. As his car passed in front of Larry's Pawnshop, he could see people scurrying and sliding out beneath the pried-up grating. Grabbing the shotgun out of its bracket on the floor, he jumped out of the car, and, on his hands and knees, went beneath the grating into the store. Rising to his feet and moving forward, he tripped and almost went sprawling. Radios, fishing rods, guns, clothing, wheels and tires of automobiles—articles of every description were strewn about. As his eyes grew accustomed to the darkness he saw a figure lurking by a display case—the man gave him no trouble and he hustled him outside.

Going back into the store, Rankin went up the stairs to an atticlike second floor where the darkness was complete. His shotgun was thrust forward, his heart pounding. It was the kind of situation a policeman hates: alone, not knowing how many suspects he is facing, completely at a disadvantage should he be jumped.

The attic was empty.

It was 2:30 a.m. Seventy-four injuries, at least a half dozen from gunshots, had been reported, and 33 arrests had been made. The LAPD released the sheriff's deputies and highway patrolmen, and, with units consisting of two men per car and two cars per unit, began a roving patrol of the area.

*   *   *

Lada Young had been sticking close to Gabriel Pope all night. She knew that he was on the brink of hurling himself pell-mell into the riot, and that only she was holding him back. Avalon Blvd. had the appearance of a battle scene— smoldering cars were emitting wisps of pungent smoke, store

[1] A former narcotics violator, LaCour was traced down by the police and arrested. Evidence presented at his trial proved insufficient to convict him.

windows were smashed, merchandise had been scattered like entrails out into the street, isolated fires threw up their glows as one looked north and east, glass glittered and crunched sharply against the pavement everywhere one stepped. There were small knots of people here and there but they seemed to be cowed by the atmosphere of desolation. Walking along, Lada's attention was caught by a whimpering sound. Turning, she saw in the doorway of a store a small girl, not more than 6 or 7 years old. Her bare feet were studded with bits of glass, and a jagged gash across her arm had turned portions of her pink dress purple.

Lada called to Gabriel. Together they picked up the girl, and Gabriel took her in his arms. A police car came slowly cruising up the street.

"Please help us!" Lada cried, indicating the girl. "She's hurt bad!"

"That's the way you people wanted it!" The officer was impassive.

"But she's only a little girl! We've got to get her to a doctor!"

"That's your problem. We're not allowed to carry her in a police car."

As the patrol car pulled off, Lada began to cry. "Goddammit!" she sobbed. "Goddammit!" She sat down on the curb. "Goddam, why do they have to be that way?"

"You see how it is!" said Gabriel. "Don't nobody respect us, because all that we ever get is what somebody give to us. They give us our freedom, and they give us our civil rights, so they figure they give us what they please, and what they don't, they won't. We gonna have to take it, baby! We gonna have to get up on our hind legs, and take it! We gonna have to do just like Mr. Charley do with his Boston Tea Party. We gonna have to have our own uprising!"

*   *   *

From the ECC, Col. Quick telephoned Gen. Hill that, according to police reports, there would be no need for the National Guard. At 3 a.m. he left the ECC to go to his hotel.

*   *   *

Pancho Pedrally was lying by the railroad tracks. He was lying there because, he had decided, he wanted to wreck a train, and, having communicated this desire to several other kids, they had gone and built a bonfire on a flatcar that was standing on a siding. The idea, although they weren't sure how they were going to carry it out, had been that when the train came by they would push the burning flatcar into it. . . .

"That'll be groovy!"

While they waited they had been eating and drinking, and Pancho who, all of his life, had felt he had never had quite enough to eat, had been gorging himself. He had been standing on the flatcar, drinking from a bottle in one hand, with his teeth tearing chunks off a piece of meat held in the other. He had been drinking and doing an Indian dance, firing a couple of shots into the air from a revolver he had picked up, and, the last thing he remembered, everything had whirled about. Then he had fallen.

When he awakened it was an hour later—though, to tell the truth, he had no idea what time it was—and he was alone. The first thing he felt for was the gun, which was still in his belt. Staggering up, he wandered around for a while, then started for home. As he reached the corner of Central and Imperial, where Dick Gregory had been a few hours before, he came upon the action. The police had left, and the youths, who had been surrounding the Stop Drive-In for three hours, were attacking. A long, wooden table was thrown through the window, a bench was being used to batter at the door, there was milling, yelling confusion. Pancho squinted his weak eyes to try to bring the scene into focus, but the effect of the alcohol had not completely worn off, and all the figures seemed to be surrounded by a teddybearlike fuzz. Pulling out the gun, he started pumping bullets in the general direction of the building.

"Hey, man! Look like Whitey ain't gonna come out!"

"Fuck! Let's blow it up!"

A Molotov cocktail was lighted and punched through the hole in the window. The flames spurted up.

The night manager, locked inside, had been frantically calling the police for an hour. They told him that all their units were busy, and to protect himself as best as he could. At 4 o'clock they finally got through to him with a flying squad of 16 men, who pulled him out of the half-consumed building.

Perhaps 200 guns had been taken from pawnshops, but this was an infinitesimal number compared to the gun population of the area, where almost every person keeps a weapon for

199

self-protection. Some of the guns had come into the hands of kids like Pedrally, and they were using them to take pot shots at police cars and fire trucks. Although cars were still burning, and a lumber yard was on fire on Imperial, the fire department refused to enter the area because of sniper activity. At 4:30 a.m. Deputy Chief Murdock left the command post—

"And the thing was boiling. I had the radio on all the way to West Los Angeles, and it was boiling!"

At 5:10 a.m., the police department, taking into account that there were relatively few persons on the streets, released the extra units and returned to normal patrol duty in the area. A tally indicated that 18 cars had been overturned and burned, and 76 buildings looted or destroyed by fire.

At 6:30 a.m. bus companies rerouted their lines, because the area was unsafe for travel.

At 6:45 a.m. Lt. Gov. Anderson asked John Billett to check on conditions again, because he was scheduled to leave on a 7:25 a.m. flight for Berkeley to attend a meeting of the Board of Regents of the University of California.

Billett called the police department and was connected with Sgt. Jack Eberhardt, in charge of the ECC. Eberhardt told him that there was still some activity—looting, snipers, and fires—but that the department was beefing up its reserves. "The riot area is contained," he said. "We do not anticipate need for the National Guard."

Informed of this, the lieutenant governor left for Berkeley.

23   The Chief Was Perplexed and Disturbed

By the time Col. Quick returned to the ECC an hour later at 8:30 a.m., the stores that had been broken into along Avalon Blvd. the night before were beginning to be visited by curious residents, rummaging to see what they could pick up. People were streaming toward the business district of Watts as if it were the site of a county fair. By 9 o'clock 103rd St. was so mobbed it had become impassable. During the early morning hours hundreds of kids, abetted by some adults who had been on Avalon the previous night, had returned home carrying food and liquor, and the word had spread from door to door with the rapidity of a jungle telegraph that Watts was going to be hit next; that Watts was going to be hit next because Whitey—as Gabriel Pope and others like him framed their thoughts—must be driven out; because this was the day of reckoning with *the man,* the day of retribution when the soul folk would pay him back for all the years of anguish.

At 9 o'clock, Col. Quick called Gen. Hill to report that activity seemed to be building up again, but that police officers at the ECC were expressing no alarm.

At 9 o'clock John Buggs was calling the community relations service in Washington, asserting that it was evident the Los Angeles police could not handle the situation, that the National Guard, and, possibly, even the army, would be needed—that only massive force would be able to restore order now.

At 9 o'clock 15 leading ministers and several other persons, including Douglas Ferrell, the area's second Negro assemblyman, were meeting at the Praisers of Zion Baptist Church to determine on a course of action. A man rushed in to say that the people were getting ready to tear up Watts. All present agreed that the situation had passed beyond the point of control, and that the National Guard would be needed. A call was placed to the lieutenant governor's office to make the request that the Guard be brought in. The ministers were informed that the lieutenant governor was out of town and unavailable.

A few minutes after 9 o'clock, Col. Quick was called to Chief Parker's office, where a staff critique was in progress.

Parker had been informed the previous night that only 200 people were involved in the riot, and he was still upset over "this young man who posed as a representative of the rioters [taking] over the microphone, and he was not interfered with at all."

The Chief, as he said, "was perplexed. I didn't know what to do, we had never had anything like it in our lives, I had never read about a riot that ran this way, where the people rested the first night and then the next night . . . and I was very disturbed." [1]

His men, Chief Parker thought, "were as perplexed by this spectacle as anyone else." They hesitated to move. They delayed in responding to the assaults. "When we finally did decide to clear the area . . . all we did was merely move them [the people] out to other areas and . . . this thing began to spread in almost epidemic proportions."

The Chief now ordered a complete redeployment of the department, with detectives placed in radio cars and everyone put on 12-hour-a-day shifts. As many rioters as could physically be taken into custody should be arrested, he said, because all that the men had been doing the previous two nights was chasing people around.

He had been reluctant to call the National Guard. He had been reluctant because "I thought it was a decision that could really backfire. What it could have meant to me as an individual, if this was an unnecessary move. A thing the chiefs of police of America have refrained from doing, on the fear it would reflect upon their abilities to handle the situation. I could be made to look very inadequate if I had asked for the Guard to stamp out the activities of 200 people."

As he finished his recapitulation of the situation, Parker said, "It looks like we are going to have to call the troops. We will need 1,000 men."

To Col. Quick this seemed like an observation, not a request, and he discussed with Insp. Walter Kinsling, his contact man on the police, how he could get Parker or Mayor

---

[1] The assertion regarding the novelty of the pattern is not quite true. The Washington and Chicago riots of 1919, and the Harlem riot of July, 1964, started and sputtered and started again several times, gaining in intensity each night. The FBI report on the riots during the summer of 1964 declares:

"Each of the seven major city riots, with one exception, was an escalation from a minor incident. . . . In each instance there was first violent interference with the policemen on the scene, followed by the gathering of a crowd. . . . Store windows were broken . . . rocks were thrown, ash cans hurled from roof tops, bottles, bricks, Molotov cocktails and fire bombs were thrown; the latter usually on the second or third day of the riots. . . . Looting followed. As news of the riots was spread by the newspapers, radio and television the riots spread to other sections. . . . Respected Negro and other civic leaders . . . made every effort to halt the riots. . . . In almost all cases only massive and vigorous police action or the arrival of state police or the national guard finally brought about a termination of the riots and the restoration of law and order."

Sam Yorty in touch with someone at the governor's office. It was 10:10 when he telephoned Gen. Hill in Sacramento to inform him that the request to have the Guard called out was going to be made, and that, in his opinion, the troops were definitely needed.

Mayor Yorty, who had been informed of the rapidly deteriorating state of affairs and the need for the National Guard a short time earlier was, at that moment, taking flight for San Francisco. The mayor who, although he had yet to announce it, was already running for the Democratic nomination for governor, was taking flight because "I have to decide whether I am going to disappoint that crowd in San Francisco and maybe make my city look rather ridiculous if the rioting doesn't start again, and the mayor has disappointed that crowd." [2]

24   Watts Black and White—

Wendell Collins, the first vice-chairman of CORE, was at Will Rogers Park on 103rd St. in Watts. CORE, like NAACP and other civil rights organizations, had been steadily losing identity with, and relevance to, the Negro striving. It had concentrated on mock issues and soft targets and all too often appeared to be more concerned with making a *case* than with cracking a tough nut, so that its Los Angeles chapter had declined in a few years from more than 3,000 to less than 300 members. People in Watts were apathetic toward CORE because it was full of white liberals trying to get the middle-class Negro into country clubs. This image Collins was trying to erase. He was trying to show the people that CORE did care, but it was a bad day for anybody appealing to the head rather than the heart.

---

[2] At the Commonwealth Club in San Francisco, where he was scheduled to make a luncheon speech.

Will Rogers Park is a broad expanse of green with a large swimming pool and few trees in the heart of an area that was once called "Mudtown" where cows, pigs and ducks lay in the middle of dusty wagon paths and hootowls and bats roamed at night; an area that, with its narrow "main" street (103rd St.) lined with small, cheap shops and false-front deteriorating buildings, its languid air of palms and tree-shaded clapboard houses, and its considerable number of Negro settlers—first transported west for cheap labor by the Southern Pacific Railroad—had more than a passing resemblance to a small Southern town. It was also more than a passing resemblance that it had been annexed to the city of Los Angeles in 1926 at the instigation of the Klu Klux Klan in order to dilute the Negro vote which was, at that time, threatening to gain control of Watts.

There is, in the minds of many persons, the picture of California as the great, golden land of equality, but this is a historical myth, at least as far as the southern section is concerned. During the Civil War, Los Angeles was a hotbed of secessionist sentiment that, for a time, threatened civil war, Western style, within the state. As late as the turn of the century, Chinese charged with serious offenses were likely to find that court was held under a tree. A few years later the principal enemy had become the union man, blown out of town with dispatch by Pinkerton detectives. Between the two great wars Orientals had been accorded second-class citizenship, which was one class higher than residents of Mexican ancestry, which was one class higher than Upton Sinclair's Socialists. In 1943 bands of sailors roamed the streets looking for Mexican zoot-suiters to beat up in what have gone down in history as the Pachuco Riots. After the last war the menace became the Negro, and any city devoid of the black plague happily advertised the fact.

"Lynwood, the friendly Caucasian city!" was the official designation of the community just to the southeast of Watts. In the 1960's, Alameda Ave., a complex of industry and railroad tracks beyond whose boundaries no Negro is allowed to set foot permanently, became known, in Negro argot, as "The Berlin Wall." When the Pacific Electric Railroad service, which ran through the heart of Watts and had been the artery that connected it to downtown Los Angeles, was leached to death by the freeways in the late 1950's, the people found themselves as isolated from the city as if they lived 100 miles away. They also found themselves in greater numbers than anywhere else—27.3 per acre as against 7.4 in the city over-all—since five public housing projects had been carefully bunched together, out of sight, out of mind of all Caucasians except a few police, firemen, teachers, merchants and the like.

When Collins arrived at Will Rogers Park, it was seething. A long line of newsmen, officials, and miscellaneous persons stretched back from the one telephone booth. A young woman came over from the Westminster Neighborhood Association to say that 300 kids were massed there, milling restlessly, that she was trying to keep them from rioting, and what should she do with them? A youth in Bermuda shorts and sandals declared he was tired of the white people having all the good jobs, and taking all the money to Beverly Hills. An attractive girl in a blue dress said, "I hope they blow it up. I hate this goddam place."

Collins explained that he was with CORE. A woman reared up angrily: "We don't need no black Caucasians!"

"They keeps telling me this is the promised land," a man said, "but I can't eat promises."

"Brother, if this is America, send me back to Africa," another spoke up. "Africa be my nation."

"Well, man, the black man is fighting and dying all over the world, and I'm willing to fight and die right here in Watts," a mustachioed, fierce-looking youth carrying a gun, said. "We got a cause."

"Baby, get ready! We going to burn the street!" another exclaimed.

Collins decided to try to get all the people to come to the park to hold a mass meeting and air their grievances. He went to the police substation a block away to obtain a bullhorn. An officer, who was on the phone to the 77th division, said that he had no bullhorns available.

"Well, you get us the horn in a half hour or it will be too late—they're going to burn the town down!" Collins told him.

When Collins returned to the street, it looked like a combination of market and moving day—people were bedecked with armloads of clothes, armloads of groceries, armloads of sundries of every description. A youth was rolling a wheel and tire down the street with one hand, carrying a portable television with the other. A woman stood in front of a blasted show window with a dozen hats in her arms, carefully trying on one after the other, discarding those that did not fit. A small boy, sweating, dragged a full case of milk across the pavement, stopping every few feet. A girl was trundling a shopping cart filled to overflowing with groceries, her 2-year-old, licking an ice cream cone, sitting on top of the mound like a monarch. A man in his twenties, attired in pointed Italian boots, lavender shirt, tapered pants and curved sunglasses, his long hair flowing down the back of his neck like Daniel Boone's, was directing the transportation of a refrigerator.

The two largest stores along the street were Martin's Department Store and the Food Giant Market. Martin's had opened for business as usual that morning, and people were jammed elbow to elbow in the aisles, one paying for a purchase, the next taking what he pleased, an air of uncertainty prevailing. A woman, watching people help themselves, took a scarf, looked at it, then, muttering uncomfortably that she had never stolen in her life and wasn't going to start now, put it back. Management was desperately trying to move the people out of the store, and at 10 o'clock did actually succeed in locking the doors.

Harvey Claybrook stood across the street, looking at the aluminum front of the two-story building with the prominent signs: "No Finance Co. to Deal With," and "Easy Terms—Glasses on Credit." A salesman at the store for more than 18 years, it was his day off. When he had first gone to work there, it had been a small furniture store attuned to the community, with 75 per cent repeat business, and good public relations engendered by the sponsorship of a boy scout troop. Gradually, management had taken over other small stores—hardware, feed, grocery, a rummage shop, the old post office—on both sides, the contributions to the scouts had lessened, the public relations had deteriorated. As prices had risen, merchandise had become cheaper. A refrigerator that might cost $99 elsewhere, would go for $169, a stereo set selling for $600 in a store located where there was competition would be priced at $1,000. Claybrook had bought his own television set at another store for $25 less than he could have gotten it with a 15 per cent employee discount at Martin's. Service charges varied from 12 to 17 per cent, and "after they got through adding the carrying charges and other things to the bill, then the bill became exorbitant." On a $400 item, after making a $75 down payment, the customer would still owe $400. Customers who could not read were in no position to argue over additions and subtractions, and the only thing most ever asked was, "How much are the monthly payments?"

Across the street at the Food Giant, the management and customers were lost in admiration of each other. "They're scum!" said the manager of the meat department. "They sell us all the rotten meat they can't get rid of anywhere else!" shoppers complained. "They got flies so big they like to carry off a side of beef!" "There's a lady that got toe-name poisoning!"

Next door to the market, and affiliated with it, was a wholesale meat concern run by Carl Margolis. At one time, when the area had been divided fairly equally between Mexicans and Negroes, Margolis had formed the Lancer Club, an organization that got boys off the street and trained them in boxing and other sports. But as Negro migrants moving in from the South had become dominant, as they discovered that it was safe to express the hatred of the white man that during decades of oppression in the South they had had to stifle within them, the homogeneity of Watts had dissolved, and with it had gone the Lancer Club. Margolis still employed many of the boys, tough-muscled and loyal, who had once been in the club, and with them he undertook the defense of the Food Giant market. It was impossible to keep people out of the market entirely, but Margolis and his men made it a revolving door proposition—they would burst in, snatch items here and there, then be hustled out again.

Watts was a body without a soul. Its chamber of commerce had dissolved, its ice skating rink melted, its two theaters closed and degenerated into empty shells that were the hangouts of dope addicts. Its towers still stood, but only because of the intervention of outsiders who seldom visited the area.

The Watts Towers, acclaimed as one of the world's great examples of folk art, raise their intricate, interlaced spires like a mating of Gothic cathedral and Buddhist pagoda a hundred feet into the air. Slim and lancelike they project from a garden of ceramic murals made out of 70,000 seashells, thousands of pieces of pottery and bits of colored glass like Snow White and the Seven Dwarfs strolling amidst a never-never land of flowers. They are the creation of Simon Rodia, an uneducated Italian immigrant who lived in a small house on the property and was 40 years old when he began working on them in 1919. A tile-setter and telephone repairman by profession, he worked by intuition like a spider spinning upward from the ground; like a spider's his handiwork was not symmetrical but of incredible strength. In 1957 when bureaucrats of the city's building department had ordered the towers torn down because of their supposedly unsound structure, an engineering test had shown them to be stronger than a skyscraper.

But by 1957, it had been three years since Simon Rodia had abandoned his monument and disappeared, feeling, apparently, that he was becoming a stranger in the place where he had spent most of his life. Discovered in Martinez, a small northern California town several years later, he would say only, "If your mother dies and you have loved her very much, maybe you don't speak of her."

Simon Rodia himself had died, at the age of 86, in July, 1965.

Only a few young people—the elite among the students at Jordan High School—still cared about Watts. The year before, spearheaded by Richard Townsend, Bill Armstead, and Linda Bryant, they had organized the Student Committee for the Improvement of Watts. In 1964 they had managed to unite the community behind a Civic Improvement Week that had featured a clean-up, family rally, and parade. Michael Lasky with the two or three poor-mouth followers that were the sum total of his Communist Party, Chinese version, had tried to take over the parade by appealing to the "Students of Jordan High School: wake up to the fact that you are not really free. The history of America is a brutal and murderous history of violence, injustice, and mass murder."

Unable to take over the parade, Lasky had tried to disrupt it. "The police department and the city council are putting on a puppet parade to insult the Negro people. The police and the city council through their Toms and white stooges are presenting themselves as friends of the poor by telling us how to put our garbage out. The garbage that needs to be put out of Watts is the authority and the violence of the white ruling class through its brutal police. . . . The cops in Watts are used by the white ruling class to suppress us. . . . The cops are the stooges of U.S. imperialism."

But the last thing the residents had needed was Michael Lasky, and he had been run out of Watts by a group of angry Negroes.

Richard Townsend stood on the grass, watching people running through the housing project carrying every conceivable kind of object, some offering to share their loot—"Hey, man! Try this on for size!"—and thought that, ironically, tomorrow, Saturday, had been scheduled for the start of Watts's second annual civic improvement week. During the past year, the student committee had spent their Easter vacation painting eight houses near the Towers, they had been able to negotiate the tearing down of two dilapidated buildings, and they were trying to save the Watts railroad station as an historical monument. Although they had failed in their efforts to have the dilapidated Villa Maria Hotel, standing next to the modern library, taken over by the city as a library annex —the library, on the outside a shining example of good architecture lacked only a few thousand volumes and a seating capacity beyond 17 persons to make it adequate—they had been able to induce the hotel owner to make some improvements.

It was too bad, Richard thought, that all these efforts were now going down the drain. Last night, the kids coming by had invited him: "Hey, man! We're going down to Imperial to throw rocks. Come along and have some fun!"

A stocky, rock-hard, 16-year-old, Richard has the poise, maturity, and verbal skills of an adult. An only child, born in Selma, Ala., where his grandfather still operates his own farm, Richard lives alone with his mother. ("At Jordan," he says, "father is a dirty word.") During his first five years in school he had been a poor student, uninterested, showing little promise. Then, when he was in the sixth grade, he and his mother had changed their place of residence and he had entered a school that was, for a brief period, truly integrated. He had come into contact with middle-class values—it wasn't square to be seen carrying a book or to spend one's time studying in class—and he had blossomed into a B student and a leader. During the previous summer he and his friend Armstead had written a report on the area that had been included in a government study, "Hard Core Unemployment and Poverty in Los Angeles," which, like the Moynihan Report, had been considered too hot to publish. He had written that too much money is spent on churches and liquor, and that "so-called preachers use churches as stepping-stones to wealth." The kids don't trust the preachers at all—they see them driving big cars and wearing silk suits, while the people going to church buy their clothes second-hand. (There are more than 150 churches in the Watts area, bearing such names as "Sun-

flower Missionary Baptist Church," "Bright Star B. C.,"
"Smith Chapel Holiness B. C.," "Greater Love B. C.," etc.
The ministers themselves usually hold the deed to the land
and buildings as personal possessions, and a great number of
them, supposedly capable of advising their parishioners, are
themselves steeped in abysmal ignorance and incredible naïveté. "There is certain regulations that is drawn up by our
congress giving rules, isn't there?")

"The people of Watts don't understand other cultures because of their limited horizons," Richard had written. "Lack
of pride leads to lack of action." The attitude of the residents
is: " 'I just got here' and 'It was like this when I got here
and it ain't gonna change.' "

The only time that there had been a spirit of unity in the
area, as Richard remembers it, was in the summer of 1963
when the Birmingham uprising had drawn everyone together
and given them a sense of purpose in supporting the Negroes
in the South. At a mass rally, the name of Alabama Ave.,
running through the heart of Watts, had been changed to
Medgar Evers St.

The summer of 1965 had, on the other hand, been the
worst ever: one of chaos, disunity, and suspicion. Usually a
summer athletic league is formed, but in 1965 even this had
not come into being because all the kids who usually participate wanted to make the $1.25 an hour they were going to
be paid working on jobs under the antipoverty program. As
no jobs had materialized, they had lounged around getting
high on cheap wine and marijuana, discussing among themselves which white motherfuckers and Uncle Toms were making a killing on the antipoverty program.

From experience the kids thought they knew that somebody must be getting fat off the poor people. Rejected by the
white world, they had, in turn, rejected all the white world's
values. They ventured into Caucasian neighborhoods only
with self-consciousness and trepidation, full of fear and ready
to burst into anger. At the age of 13, Richard, with other
kids, had gone one Halloween across Alameda Ave. into an
all-white neighborhood. Most of the people had been friendly,
but one woman had opened the door and exclaimed, "What's
this? The black tornado from Watts?" Laughter. "If I give
all you black kids a piece of candy I won't have any for the
white ones!" As she had slammed the door, one boy had
picked up a brick and heaved it.

It was these kids that Warner O'Seyre saw smashing windows, looting and destroying, as he walked along 103rd St., talking to the few who would still listen, trying to get them to cool it.

"We through listening. You better talk to Whitey!" they told him.

"What makes you think you're one of us just because you're black?" they challenged him. "You got no business here."

He tended to believe that was true, even though Jordan High, the school at which he taught, was just down the street a few blocks. There it stood, a symbol of the failure of the system, and here were the products of that failure rampaging up and down the street, breaking the way for their parents. Here were all the dropouts, half of whom quit for no other reason than lack of interest; among the girls an additional 40 per cent because they were pregnant—and 90 per cent of whom, both boys and girls, the schools could have saved had there been enough money and enough personnel. Here they were because they had no skills and couldn't get jobs and because 61 per cent were rejected by the armed forces—more than half that total because they lacked an education.

Unequal at birth because of the color of their skins, they became more and more unequal year by year as they grew older. By the time they reached the eighth grade, children in white, middle-class West Los Angeles were able to do three to four times better on standard tests than they. In reading vocabulary (scored in percentiles), 79 to 13; in arithmetic fundamentals, 67 to 10; in English, 74 to 12; in spelling, 72 to 21. In the eleventh grade—by which time the most hopeless 20 per cent have dropped out of school in Watts—the average IQ of students in Watts is 85.74; in West Los Angeles, 110.79.[1]

By the time the children reached O'Seyre at Jordan they were suffering from so many years of intellectual deprivation and neglect that it would have taken a major operation to reinvigorate their minds. Half of the elementary schools were on double sessions (compared to one-sixth of the elementary schools in white areas), and many of the teachers, despairing, had lost all motivation except to shove their pupils onward into the next grade's teacher's lap. Kids who have a hard

[1] The figures are from a study conducted by Dr. Kenneth A. Martyn, professor of special education at California State College, Los Angeles.

time adjusting are suspended for every conceivable reason, including being "too nervous." A Caucasian teacher who tries to immerse himself in the community's problems is looked upon suspiciously by the school administration. A teacher who attempts new methods to make contact with the kids and bring them out of their isolation is told that he must not deviate from approved standards—standards established by middle-class white professors for middle-class white school children. Subjects are geared so as to enable the maximum number of pupils to achieve a passing grade—"gardening" is a requirement for boys in junior high school. In the elementary schools the children can't take their books home unless the parents request it and sign for them—and most of the parents either don't understand, or couldn't care less. The only time a teacher can get a rise out of them is when some kid has been suspended for ditching, or pulling a knife. Then an anguished mother will appear, demanding, "What are you doing to my baby?" And while O'Seyre had been trying to explain to one that her 15-year-old son was no baby, she had pulled a brick out of her purse and cracked him over the head with it.

Often at school O'Seyre was overcome by the enormity of the situation facing him in exactly the same way as his pupils were overcome—he would have had to multiply himself by six to do an adequate job of teaching, counseling, and motivating—motivating, most of all, because most of the kids saw no point in going to school. They saw no point in going to school because the textbooks they were given were written by whites, for whites, and of whites, and they were deprived of all sense of identity with the society and the country in which they lived. It was as if the black print of the Negro had been wiped away from the white slate of American history.

Under the limitations of budget and manpower, O'Seyre had learned to be callous, had learned to save the ones he could, and forget about the rest. He had learned to forget that the electrical shop wasn't operating because the equipment hadn't arrived, that for every one place open in the auto shop, five wanted to get in; that a boy who was eager to learn could not study because he had no place in which to do it—eight kids in a three-bedroom apartment, the television set blaring and a radio playing rock and roll. He had had to forget about the boy who had sat hour after hour staring at the same page, and, when asked why he didn't study, had replied helplessly, "I don't know how to study. Nobody never showed me how."

He had had to forget what the shock of the honor student would be when thrown into competition with whites; he would discover that he was only average, that both the standards and the demands of the white world were far greater than those of the Negro. He had had to forget his own hypocrisy when he drummed into students that education makes everybody equal—Isaac McClelland, the first Negro principal of Jordan,[2] might be the equal of his white predecessors, but he was the first principal the Kiwanis had "forgotten" to ask to join.

It was getting on toward noon, and the narrow street roiling with people was humid with their sweat. Whenever O'Seyre tried to explain the children of Watts to a white person, he felt as if he were trying to explain an otter to a bighorn sheep—the middle-class white who, in one fashion or another, loves and disciplines his children, has no frame of reference in which to view the actions of kids who have no roots, no sense of security, who lack the ability to feel for others because no one has ever felt for them. In O'Seyre's head spun the words of dozens of kids—

"—guy my age wants to learn how to use tools, in Hollywood where parents own factories and businesses it's swell just to teach typing, but here, let's face it, our mothers and fathers don't own industry . . . don't get out of high school math with addition, subtraction or long division, should be forced to take chemistry even if you fail, at least you're familiar . . . did some research of my own, there is an average of 600 commercials on tv every night, how many of them are geared toward education, would help us if have more commercials toward education . . . lots of times can't understand what the teacher's talking about, and he doesn't have time to help us. . . . Hoodlums in this neighborhood, 75 per cent of my friends, they are the guys who've dropped out of school, told teacher to go to hell, they're the hoodlums, but they're the guys I see every day. . . . I was one of those guys who had the cool walk and talked the cool talk and was supposed to be cool all the way around, but then I came in

---

[2] Since promoted to the position of an area superintendent in the school district.

contact with some teachers who cared and some students who
had achieved something and they instilled a kind of pride and
responsibility that I was worth something. . . . Hardheads just
about ignored, teachers are scared of us, teacher should get
off his high horse and talk to us, I mean, if you come to
school with a D average, who talks to you? Another hardhead with a D average, so the first thing you want to do is
crawl into your shell and get away from all those people who
don't talk to you, you're left out; if you know you're wanted
you'll change just knowing you're wanted . . . teacher should
be given more right to fit programs to shape of students . . .
don't fake, don't be false, don't treat someone like a child,
they'll hate you for it and you'll stink rotten . . . our parents
are lazy just like we are . . . we have no communication
with schools of other communities other than going out to
try and kill them in a football game . . . we know nothing
about ourselves, about where we live, about the school, like
who is David Starr Jordan? . . . cheerleaders dressed and everything, sweating and wondering how to get to game, don't
know how to get to game because don't have transportation
and can't afford it . . . like what's the point, what for should
I sweat studying when I can get a job boxing at the store and
make all that money, they just give me the same job two
years from now if I get my diploma, my father, he graduate,
and he couldn't get no job since I can remember . . . today
sex is very prominent in a person's life, more so than ever
before, I feel it should be faced, because there's nothing embarrassing about sex . . . wait too long in our education to
teach us about dating and sex, and like etiquette, I think the
boys need more sex education than girls, actually they do,
boys are the ones that create the problems . . . okay they
give us guidance, give us aptitude and interest tests, this helps
you fine, but what about your sex problems in growing up
that will hinder you from reaching those goals? . . . You're
nobody till someone talks about you!"

Well, now they were going to be sure that they were talked
about. At the corner of Beach St. was a lone police car, two
officers idly watching two men carrying a large red sectional
with a television set sitting in the middle of it. They were two
policemen against thousands and they had been overwhelmed;
it struck O'Seyre as curious with what apparent equanimity
they had adjusted themselves to the new situation, it was as
if it were almost a relief to be able to retreat from the tensions

of constant conflict. A woman came out of a store wearing a brand-new outfit, carrying an electric iron in one hand and a blender in the other. Seeing the policemen standing there she stopped. She looked at them, and, like a little girl, asked, "Can I take them?"

One officer shrugged. "Wait till we're gone!" he said.

Carefully she stepped back in through the jagged remnants of the plate glass window and sat down.

The kids were not vindictive . . . at least O'Seyre thought they were not. They were resentful, and they would show their resentment by sassing, by deliberate discourtesies, by doing exactly the opposite of what was asked of them. Rejected by their parents, they would come to school without breakfast, without being washed—and they would not come at all if they did not have decent clothes to wear because clothes were the status symbol in the school; it did not matter if you failed, but it did matter if you lacked class in the way you looked. They would come without ever having seen a newspaper or a magazine in their homes, unable to talk in complete sentences because no adult had ever talked to them. Attacked from all sides all their lives, they had become so supersensitive that even the slightest criticism was likely to have hidden meaning read into it and set them off; they would flare into anger because, like the blustering of a blowfish, anger was a symbol of strength and their means of defense. Surrounded by insincerity they trusted no one, and O'Seyre was able to count on his fingers how many of them he had been able to convince that there were some white persons who were honest, that there were some who were not hypocrites.

25   "The Chief Cries Wolf Too Often"

Trouble was also being encountered by Chief Parker in going through the formalities of requesting the National Guard.

Two years previously, on August 21, 1963, a meeting had been held between Col. Quick, Deputy Chief Murdock, and other top officers of the National Guard and the LAPD, regarding steps to be taken in case a riot situation developed. On August 5, 1964, a second such meeting had taken place, and it was Gen. Hill's opinion that "Chief Parker is well aware that the governor's office has the sole authority to mobilize troops."

Gen. Hill, however, was mistaken. Chief Parker was not aware of it. Between 10:10 and 10:30, he was under the delusion that Col. Quick's having talked to Gen. Hill was all that was necessary for the calling of the Guard. When, therefore, Col. Quick asked him whether he wanted to make the formal request of Winslow Christian, the governor's executive secretary in Sacramento, he was more than a little perturbed.

"Why should I have to talk to a man by the name of Christian when I have the assistant adjutant general of the state of California here?" he wondered. Christian was put on the line. Parker told him the National Guard would be needed.

"Fine," said Christian. "I will accept that request."

The Chief's mind, however, was far from easy "I am talking with this total stranger who I had never had any contact with . . . and I have to rely on his statement to me that he could process the request, and I still don't know that I was talking to a man in authority who could do it. As far as I know, it could have been the mate on the *Bounty!*"

And he formed the opinion "that something must be going on."

It was 11 o'clock when Christian reached Lt. Gov. Anderson in Berkeley and informed him of the request for the Guard, and also, as he understood it, that Negro leaders wanted to discuss the situation. He said, further, that he did not have the information on which the request for the Guard was made. Anderson replied that, in that case, he wanted to obtain more information. The lieutenant governor then began a series of starts, stops, and backtrackings that, by comparison, made Hamlet history's greatest man of decision.

Los Angeles–San Francisco is the most heavily traveled air route in the world, with planes leaving on a shuttle service every hour or less, so that Anderson, had he taken a commercial flight, could have been back in Southern California by 1 p.m. Instead, he decided to fly back on the governor's plane, which, at that moment, happened to be buzzing around the wilds of the far northern portion of the state on an errand for the Department of Parks and Recreation. Gen. Hill, who was getting ready to board a National Guard plane to fly from Sacramento to Los Angeles, was informed that Anderson wanted to meet him at the Oakland airport, and cancelled his plans. When Anderson reached the airport he discovered that the governor's plane was, momentarily, nonexistent, and he changed his plans again and decided to meet Hill at the airport in Sacramento. It did not, apparently, occur to him to call Atty. Gen. Thomas Lynch, or Finance Director Hale Champion, or Richard Kline, or John Billett—all members of the governor's staff who were in Los Angeles and could have given him firsthand information.

Instead, discussing the matter with Christian, Anderson decided to call a meeting for 4 o'clock in Los Angeles with Negro leaders and the principal law-enforcement officials, Chief Parker, Sheriff Peter Pitchess, and Highway Patrol Commissioner Bradford Crittenden. It just so happened that Crittenden was in Oregon, and Pitchess in Canada.

Parker, informed at noon of the requested 4 o'clock meeting, exploded. He was involved in one of the most violent situations he had ever seen, he told Kline, the riot was out of control, there was no purpose in holding a meeting in the middle of a riot, and he wasn't going to negotiate law enforcement. Told that the lieutenant governor would like to have a situation report on the riot, Parker retorted that he couldn't spare a man from any of his important duties for such a task, and that if the lieutenant governor wanted a report of the situation, he could come to the ECC and see for himself.

Unaware of this, Anderson droned toward Sacramento, in the opposite direction from Los Angeles, arriving at 12:45 p.m. "We wanted to make sure . . . there wasn't any question about what I was doing and how I was doing it," he said. "There is also the legal side of what, as acting governor, I do relating to the legalities; relating to the responsibilities. . . ."

In Los Angeles, the order mobilizing the Guard was already being drawn up by the attorney general, and was almost ready for the lieutenant governor's signature. Members of the governor's staff on the scene, as well as Negro leaders, were desperately trying to reach Anderson to tell him to get the Guard out.

It was close to 1 o'clock when the lieutenant governor sat
down at the air field in Sacramento with Gen. Hill and three
members of the governor's staff, Sherrill Luke, Lucien Haas,
and Bill Becker, to decide, more or less in theory, what to do.

"Let's not move too precipitously!" Luke suggested. He
doubted that the need was as urgent as Parker had made it
sound. Someone also chipped in and remarked that, "I think
the chief cries wolf too often!"

Gen. Hill said that, according to his information, the need
was urgent, and that Parker had told him the previous night
he would not ask for troops unless it were absolutely necessary. It was nearing 1:30 p.m. and he suggested that he be
authorized to move the troops into position at the armories
now, so that they could be ready to go if the order were
given.

Luke was against it. Any such move would be construed as
giving support to Parker, he indicated, and it was not clear
that such support was warranted. The position of the state of
California should not be compromised until the meeting with
Parker and the Negro leaders had taken place, so as not to
lose grounds for negotiation with the Chief.

A member of Gen. Hill's staff suggested that, since the
troops were supposed to report for regular drill to the armories at 8 o'clock anyway, this time be moved up to 5 p.m.
without any specific mention of a callup being made. Taking
into account the time necessary for contacting the men, 5
o'clock would be the earliest they could start assembling in
any case.

Anderson, agreeing this was a good suggestion, adopted it.

The lieutenant governor was now ready to leave, but the
plane was not. The Los Angeles sheriff's office had requested
bullet-proof vests, and 150 of these, weighing some 20 pounds
apiece, were being loaded onto the plane. It was 1:45 when
the old flying boxcar finally taxied out to the runway. For
the next two hours Anderson and Hill were airborne, unavailable by radio, completely out of touch with what was occurring.

What was occurring was that Los Angeles was turning into
a hell of fire.

26   —And Red Like Fire!

Looting had started along Avalon Blvd. again shortly before 11 o'clock, and by noon mobs were roaming up and down the few blocks directly north of Imperial in numbers at least as large as the night before—with one difference. Everyone was participating, women and older people were not just standing and watching. At noon the V and F Market was invested by a horde of people. Fred, together with his wife and small children, standing guard inside, tried to appeal to them. When the appeal failed he blasted over their heads with his shotgun—they backed off but remained, surrounding the market. The police came. They told Fred that they could not guarantee his safety. They suggested that he and his family leave.

They left. The market was looted. A few hours later it was a burned-out shell.

A car was set on fire at 115th and Avalon, the area again becoming impassable because of rock throwers. Firemen were able to move only with a police escort, and police escorts were few and far between. Police officers in twos and threes were bombarded from the tops of buildings and threatened in alleys. At 1 o'clock a dry cleaning establishment at 107th and Avalon was set on fire. Kids lay in wait for the fire engines as sirens heralded their arrival. The trucks had no sooner halted than they came under attack from every direction. In the shop, bottles of solvent were popping, sending out sharp spurts of fire through the smoke and general conflagration. The firemen had to retreat.

They returned a half hour later.

Buildings in two blocks were burning.

Rumors of every description were pouring into police headquarters: Rioters were arming themselves with machine guns. The Hell's Angels—a white motorcycle gang—was on its way into the area. So was the Rev. Connie Lynch, a Southern segregationist agitator. Four hundred Negroes had left the

Congo Club in Ventura, 60 miles to the north, for Watts. Caucasian citizens were going to drop Molotov cocktails on Watts from the air.

It was 1:20 and 92 degrees in Watts when flames started licking from the first building. Gabriel Pope was of a mind to put the torch to every building owned or inhabited by a Caucasian. He wanted to burn them out, to burn the white man out of his soul. He touched the match to the wick of a bottle filled with gasoline, he threw it into the interior of a debris-littered store. As it burst, spreading its pool of fire along the floor, he felt a great exhilaration, he felt as if, for the first time, he were free.

"Let's all get together and burn!" the Magnificent Montague said on his disk jockey program on KGFJ.

The Magnificent Montague, a smashing success in Chicago and New York, had been in Los Angeles only a few months, and had, ironically, been able to obtain an apartment in an expensive West Los Angeles condominium that had refused a Negro physician only the year before. "Let's all get together and burn!" had no intrinsic meaning, it was a catch phrase he had used everywhere. But, suddenly, as the youths picked him up on their stolen transistor radios, it seemed the perfect battle cry.

"Burn, baby, burn!" they chanted, as store after store, building after building along 103rd St. became alight like old-fashioned gas globes to which the flame was being touched by an orderly lamplighter.

At the corner of Compton Ave. what looked like an array of naked bodies lay sprawled across the street—they were store mannequins that Wendell Collins of CORE had used to block off traffic. Collins was still trying to get people to come to a meeting at Will Rogers Park. Having, at last, obtained some public-address equipment from the United Auto Workers and mounted it on his car, he was driving up and down the street, making the announcement. A youth on crutches propelled his way along, carrying a radio. Women dressed in shorts and bathing suits, curlers in their hair, pushed shopping carts or simply carried what they could in their arms. Collins had never seen the people in such a light, gay mood, never seen them so drawn together in a kind of mystique; and he concluded that he was now in the midst of a war, a war against the authority of the Whips who had forced the Negro into an inferior position in American society. The fires boiling up obelisks of thick black smoke into the yolk of the sun were an expression of the tremendous hatred that had built up in the Negro, that had turned him, potentially, into one of the most violent people on earth because he had been pushed as far back ino a corner as he could go. And Collins thought that if the nation did everything possible now to remedy the situation it still might be too late.

And he gave up and drove back to the park.

Dr. Harold Jones walked down the street. Dr. Jones had been born in Galveston, Texas, some 35 years before, and had been several years into his segregated grammar school before he had learned that "Lift Every Voice and Sing," the Negro national anthem, was not the national anthem of the United States. He had gone on to Fisk University and a desegregated University of Houston Medical School to become a psychiatrist.

A woman carrying an armful of shoes, not one of them matching another, burst from a store into the path of Dr. Jones. "What do you want to steal a bunch of shoes like that for?" he asked.

She looked at him as if he were mad, continuing down the street clutching her prize.

"Man!" said a gangling man emerging from a pawnshop carrying a pair of binoculars, a sports coat, and a fishing rod which he clutched in the same hand as a fifth of whiskey, "I give them people so much of my business they owes me a bundle of money they could never pay back. This ain't stealing! This is redeeming!"

"That's right," a woman, carrying a portable tv, agreed. "It just hit me I been paying $25 a month for three years on a bunch o' furniture that cost me no more than $300 to start with, so the least they can do for me is give me a tv."

A Negro, grunting beneath the heavy load of an armchair pressing down upon his head, walked into a baldheaded Caucasian who, standing on the sidewalk, was being completely ignored. "Oh! Excuse me," the Negro said. "I hope I didn't hurt you." Cars, their rear springs sagging beneath the loot loaded into their trunks, were still stopping at the signal in perfect obedience to the traffic laws.

Trying to reconcile and make some sense out of these incongruities without rationalizing, Dr. Jones viewed them as an almost inevitable reaction—one that was bound to come sooner or later—to a 300-year campaign by whites to convince the Negro that he is slothful, immoral, and worthless; an inferior being who, as late as the 1925 edition of the *Encyclopaedia Britannica,* was considered to be related closer to the lower anthropoids than to man.

It was a campaign that had been singularly successful. With no means of comparison other than those postulated by the Anglo-Saxon, the Negro had accepted the white man's evaluation of himself. He had been slothful, fun-loving, immoral and passive. All ties with his African culture and heritage destroyed, the close-knit pattern of tribal family life transformed into the chaos of slavery in which the plantation owner bred his slaves for profit in the same manner that he bred his cattle, the Negro had neither identity nor sense of his own history, he passed through life without purpose, without loyalties, without any sense of honor or self-worth, without even the development of normal, familial affections—these were a luxury he could not indulge in when the white god who owned him could momentarily sever them for whim or profit.

Had he gained his freedom through his own efforts and the staging of his own revolt against the slave master, the Negro would have tended to regain his manhood. But when freedom was superimposed upon him in the same fashion slavery had been, and freedom was spelled s.e.g.r.e.g.a.t.i.o.n., with all the do's and don'ts of life still issuing from the white oracle, nothing, psychologically or culturally, had been changed; he had become in the classic pattern a subservient caste—and the fact that he existed as a caste within a supposedly casteless and classless society had only exacerbated the conflicts and frustrations generating the turmoil within him.

Then, once again, an extraneous force had exerted pressure: the word, if not the act *integration* had become fashionable; the Negro had been told that, being equal, he should have all the proprieties, mores, and Puritan values of middle-class America—not to speak of the sophistication necessary to implement them—which was like telling a whale that, because he is a mammal, there is no reason he should not be able to ride a bicycle.

But by this time the Negro had already rejected these values, he had found his identity in the awakening of the African continent—instead of darkest Africa it was now a free Africa with which association was salutary instead of degrading. The Negro, instead of having to deny the color of his skin and to prove to the whites that he, alone, was different from the remainder of his race in order to obtain social acceptance and build up his ego, began to visualize power in his blackness. He is casting off the inferiority imposed upon him by rationalizing that, although he is a minority in America, he is part of the world's majority of colored people. He is in the throes of a rekindled racial consciousness that is almost arrogance. And in this arrogance and pride he has rejected all that is white as evil—just as in Caucasian usage the word black as used in *black* day, *black* mood, *black* cloud, etc., has a negative meaning. Even the word *motherfucker* takes on different connotation. For the white it is the image of incest; for the Negro it is the picture of a white man lying with a black woman who is his, the Negro's, mother.

A sense of impotence transformed into action becomes hate. And a person who harbors an attitude of bigotry and hate must labor to maintain it; he must overcome his own sense of guilt by becoming ever more aggressive, ever more prejudiced. Since this hate is simultaneously both involuted and outgoing it finds satisfaction not only in the destruction of the enemy but also in the destruction of oneself. It is typified by the kids who, baiting and throwing rocks at the police, when caught plead defiantly, "Beat me, you white motherfuckers! Kill me! Kill me!"

The irony is that, in Dr. Jones's opinion, these attitudes are being continually reinforced by the fact that the power structure now demands that the Negro integrate himself into American life, while providing him with none of the tools to integrate successfully. Undereducated, underfinanced, undersophisticated, he finds himself largely unable to tolerate the competition of integration. He has difficulty achieving the success that is paramount to self-confidence and a sense of self-worth.

Instead he is beaten down by a plethora of government giveaways that, since they demand little or nothing in return, reinforce the matriarchal structure of the Negro family. Emphasizing the dominance of the female, they continue to emasculate and devalue the male, obviating the necessity for his developing a sense of responsibility.

The Negro man, deprived of the male's normal, dominant position, finds it necessary to prove his manhood over and over by the conquest of one woman after another. The young girl, growing up resentful toward a class of men who cannot fulfill the normal expectations of financial security, family stability, and success, expects the worst from a guy, castigating him with, "You're no damn good!" Which, unable to deny, he will answer, "I know it!"

Unable to deny his subservient position, the new generation male blames it on the fecklessness of the older (the Uncle Toms) and is in violent revolt against the maternal mantle of the white liberal. Lacking the material things that provide a sense of self-worth, he is rationalizing that his blackness is an intrinsic and automatic indication of that self-worth. He is making a cult of race consciousness just as the Caucasian has done in the past. In order to give expression to this, he must not only deny the validity of white values, he must aggressively move against them.

The three blocks of 103rd St. in front of Dr. Jones were being transformed into an inferno. Long tongues of flame licking out from the gaping mouths of stores on both sides of the street were making a chimney of the street itself, raising the temperature of the pavement to 120 degrees, creating an intense updraft that sucked the two flanks of fire together into one towering column of black smoke. The sun was obscured so that a Götterdämmerung-like twilight enveloped the street, a burning telephone pole spit sparks like a giant Fourth of July firework, a dozen burglar alarms jangled together in a nightmare concerto. Fire trucks, under the bombardment of rocks and an occasional bullet, were forced to retreat.

Los Angeles, Dr. Jones thought, was teetering on the brink of a major racial war.

Police Capt. Thomas King at the Watts substation had 12 men with which to attempt to inhibit that war. The field commander of the 77th division, he had rushed back from his vacation at 2 o'clock that morning, and, with his handful of men, had made sporadic sallies from the station for the past several hours. Having served in the area many years before, he deplored what had happened to it, but felt helpless to cope with it.

"People who should be going to church are going to jail!" he said. "A lack of moral character has become evident throughout the United States. Book stores are full of pornography that is stomach turning. Movies try to outdo each other in sexual suggestiveness. There is a lack of respect for living by the rules. Crime in Watts is simply an aggravated manifestation of what is happening elsewhere."

A gentleman who believes in adhering to the rules, Captain King is, nevertheless, realistic: "Police officers are only human. Many times they are severely provoked, and we do have some weak ones. To be honest, I don't know how I would take it if I went out on the street today. I tell my men that no matter what name they're called and what animosity they meet, it's not the face, it's the badge."

Had Capt. King wanted, he could, with his shotguns, have mowed down the throngs of looters by the dozens. As he was not inclined to do so, since, among other considerations, a majority of them were women and children, he could only stand by and observe. In doing so, he was doing what every other police officer was doing that afternoon—standing and watching. Watching and trying to stay out of the way of rocks. Watching and copying down the license numbers of looters' cars. Standing, feeling the hostility radiate from the populace like heat from the fires.

Pancho Pedrally, flaked out on a patch of grass, had two guns stuck into his pants' belt—he had found the additional one as he roamed unmolested in the early morning hours through a previously broken-into pawnshop. Radio and television were broadcasting that thousands of guns had fallen into the hands of the rioters, and Caucasians were starting a run on gun and sporting goods stores all over the county in order to arm themselves. In actuality, the number of guns taken had been in the hundreds, not the thousands. Many store owners were turning over their stocks to the police for protective custody, and some guns that had been stolen had already been recovered. One batch of a hundred or more was found, following a tip, in the wastebaskets of a church. Many of the guns had, in fact, been pawned by residents in the first place, and with thousands of guns already in the hands of the people—police confiscate an average of 25 to 40 concealed weapons every month—it is doubtful that those stolen added significantly to the total number.

But they did give Pancho Pedrally and the others like him a feeling of power. Drowsily he watched the big, silver jets as they banked over Watts beginning their approach to the airport. Drowsily he saw himself as the hero of a war against the white man, as the leader of the black people leading his army against the white police. Startlingly he was awakened by the beat of a giant grasshopper flailing the air two or three hundred feet above him—jumping up he aimed both pistols at the helicopter, and, crying defiance, fired shot after shot as it passed overhead.

*   *   *

Fire alarms had become so numerous that the fire department could no longer keep up with them, and was relying on its television sets to spot new ones. The tv sets were tuned to Channel 5, KTLA, which was flying a helicopter and relaying live pictures from it. The fire department had put two helicopters of its own into the air, but with somewhat less success, since trouble with their radio communications was being encountered.

The Central Library had a run on books dealing with explosives, and withdrew them from circulation.

*   *   *

Traveling along the San Diego Freeway, which curves in an arc around the southeast area, was a convoy of trucks containing the 3rd brigade of the 40th armored division of the California National Guard. The 3rd brigade, located in San Diego, had stopped for lunch in Long Beach, and then resumed its journey toward Camp Roberts, 200 miles to the north, where it was scheduled to begin training the next day.

As the convoy rumbled by and on toward Ventura, one of the men remarked that there certainly seemed to be a lot of fires burning in Los Angeles.

*   *   *

Atty. Gen. Lynch and State Finance Director Champion, despairing of reaching Lt. Gov. Anderson, telephoned Gov. Brown in Athens. Gov. Brown, deciding immediately to return, suggested the imposition of a curfew in addition to the calling out of the Guard.

27   The Businessmen Go to Work

Lada Young's sister, Deborah, had been dating a 17-year-old youth of Filipino-Mexican parentage, Felipe Borrago. Flip, as he was known, had telephoned her in the morning.

"Hey!" he said, "I was just watching tv and I saw 'em busting all up and down Avalon and 103rd. Run over and get me a tv and a radio."

"I can't do that!" she had replied. "I can't steal things."

"Hell!" he said. "If you don't get it, somebody else will."

Flip, tall, sinewy, the eldest of seven children, had high yellow skin pigmentation and, despite his parentage, features with Negroid characteristics that, he pretended, he was not sensitive about. Within five minutes of meeting a person for the first time he would say, "I'm not Negro, you know."

He was not Negro and his parents, who were Catholic, and both of whom worked hard—his father at two jobs, his mother at one—did not want him to associate with Negroes. None of the other children had Negroid features and they thought it was degrading—his mother was constantly nagging him about his going out with Deborah Young and having Negro friends; his father would hardly let a week go by that he did not cuff him. The overt conflict between father and son was the baseball that Flip constantly had in his possession and constantly was practicing with—he was a pitcher, and in his junior year in high school had made the California Interscholastic Federation all-star team.

The family lived in the Santa Barbara district, near the USC–Los Angeles County Museum–Memorial Coliseum complex, an area with an Oriental-Mexican-Negro-Caucasian mix that, in another decade, if things proceed in the classic pattern, will be mainly Negro. The Borrago family was, by the standards of the area, well off. They owned the house they lived in, and, had there been three children instead of seven, they could have lived quite well. As it was, they were making a go of it until a hustler for a building contractor convinced them that the land was too valuable to have just a house on it. They should have the house torn down, the hustler had declared and build a four-unit apartment building—one large unit for themselves, the other three to rent out.

So the house had come down and the family of nine had moved into a two-bedroom apartment—for two months only; that had been the promise. In two months the new building would be up, and they would be landlords with an independent income. But then the contractor had had problems obtaining financing, the rains had come and impeded progress, there had been a shortage of building materials, there had, in other words, been everything to draw the two-month period out to ten. As the family's money had grown shorter so had tempers in the cramped quarters, Flip's father had badgered him constantly about wasting time on baseball when he could be helping the family by getting a part-time job. Flip had retaliated by spending less and less time at home and more and more in the companionship of the Businessmen, the gang which dominated the district.

Attending an integrated Catholic high school, he identified with Negroes, yet felt himself to be a cut above them. At the age of 13 he had already begun to develop a hatred for white persons. "You see some Negro man kicked on tv, cops standing there, doing nothing . . . pictures in *Life*, an old man all beaten up . . . hear about people in Westchester hating niggers. . . ."

Whenever the school he went to engaged in athletic contests against other Catholic schools in all-white areas, they went prepared not just to play but to fight; they would wait outside after the game to waylay the biggest of the opposition players they could find, Flip would try to "Land on the side of some white dude's head. And this white man raking his lawn gets upset when he sees this gang fight between whites and Negroes. So I hit him and I knocked him on his ass, so then this second white man gets in it and I let him have it with the hoe. And a white woman in a car expressed her opinion, and I break her window glass. But the Surfers, especially, nobody I hate worse or'd rather fight than the Surfers!" [1]

One day Flip and a friend had seen a car, with the keys in the ignition, sitting in the parking lot of a market. They

---

[1] *Surfers* is a generic name for middle-class kids.

had taken it and gone on a four-hour joyride, then had returned it to the same parking space from which they had stolen it. They had been arrested within two blocks and charged with grand theft auto—but they had discussed it beforehand and didn't really care: a few months in a camp wouldn't be too bad.

Instead they had been released on probation to their parents. Flip was suspended from school because, he believes, "I refused to beg forgiveness from the priests."

The Borragos had moved into their new apartment building, but conditions had improved little. They were overextended financially, and the three rental units proved anything but an economic bonanza. They were not always all occupied, and, when they were, the occupants would often evidence reluctance to pay the rent. The Borragos learned, as had other landlords in poverty or fringe-poverty areas before them, that a large portion of the potential income could be written off because of deadbeat tenants.

Living in that area, unless you were deaf and blind and never went out into the streets, it was almost impossible not to know where you could make a connection. Flip knew. With the pressure for money, he went out one night and told the man, "Why don't you let me sell some grass for you?"

Flip had looked like he checked out okay, so the man had reached down inside his neck brace and pulled out several joints. Flip had sold them for him, and gotten him some new customers too. But that was small time. He needed $125 to buy a kilo, so he had started robbing a small Japanese market a few blocks away. The owner was afraid of the gang kids, and Flip had had an easy time—he would walk in, grab the money from the cash register, and walk out. He had had to do it four times to get his stake.

He had bought his kilo and broken it up into cans ($7.00), and half-cans and matchboxes ($3.50), and started developing his own runners. That way he could make between $125 and $175 profit on a kilo. Breaking it up into joints, which sell for 50¢ apiece, he could have grossed as much as $500, but that takes a lot of time and trouble. One month not too long after he got his business fully set up he had netted $750.

Some of the best places for business were around the schools, and one evening he and his partner had been walking near Dorsey High School when he saw this car, with the lights off, creeping along. He figured it was the plainclothes

fuzz so he and his partner had split. Ducking around a corner, he had thrown the junk across a wall into the lot of a
post office. The detectives had stopped him a half block farther on, but he had figured he was clean and didn't have anything to worry about.

"What's the problem, officer?" he had asked.

They had stood him up against the wall and searched him,
and asked him how old he was, and he told them 18. They
were about to let him go when a second car, which had
picked up his partner came by. His partner was high and
hadn't thrown his package away. Coming up to Flip, one of
the officers had said, "This is an odd-shaped cigarette, isn't
it?"

"Yes, sir."

"You know what it is?"

"I seen one of those in our science class. It's a reefer, isn't
it?"

They had put the handcuffs on him, and the detectives had
asked him if they were too tight, and he had said they were;
so they loosened them. At Georgia Street Flip and his partner had been put in the room where they have the two sets
of eyes staring from the wall—one normal and the other
loaded, for comparison. Flip's eyes had checked out okay.
But while they were looking at his partner's they had shaken
his shirt, and out had fallen another joint—he said his girlfriend must have put it there while he was necking with her.
So then they had separated them and put them in different
rooms. Flip, figuring he had the case beat, had been real
relaxed.

One of the detectives had come in and showed him the
cigarette package with grass in it that they'd taken off his
partner, and Flip had said he didn't know anything about it.

"Either you're awful dumb, or you're innocent," the detective had told him.

"Yes, sir. I think I should go home now."

Another man, carrying a plant, had come through the door.
"You know what that is?" the detective had asked.

"It's—!" Flip had almost told him, then caught himself.
"It's a begonia, isn't it? I think my mother has one in her
yard."

"This ain't no suspicion," the detective had growled. "You'd
better cop out."

So Flip had started putting all of the case on the other

dude, while the other dude was doing the same to him. He had kept denying he knew anything about the weed the dude was carrying, and, since the cops hadn't found any on him, after 48 hours they had had to let him go.

After telephoning Deborah Young, Flip went down to South Park where the Businessmen hang out. He was chafing to get in on the action, and he figured maybe he could get somebody to wheel down to Watts with him. Since he'd been picked up, his connection didn't trust him, figuring that maybe he was stooling for the cops, so business wasn't good.

At South Park it was hot, and there were the usual couple of hundred jobless teenagers and young men hanging around the tables, playing checkers and Georgia Skin. He saw maybe 20 of the gang there, but it was so warm that only one was wearing the uniform—red vest with black suspenders—and he must have been crazy. Of the rest, many were stripped to the waist, and most of the others had on only white T-shirts on top. Beneath the broken canopy provided by the scattered trees, South Park was as languid and sultry as a Southern town square. The swimming pool was virtually empty, and the poor old bastard at the corner who said "Thank you very much, suh" to every son-of-a-bitching Charley who bought a bag of peanuts from him, was mopping his brow.

"Man!" said Flip. "When we gonna start jiving?"

One of his acquaintances shrugged his shoulders. "I hear they got the National Guards coming in."

A youth came up to Flip and offered to sell him a dozen pink ladies for 50¢. That was when a ripple of excitement started, and some of the people began moving toward the parking lot. Looking over, Flip saw a car standing there with the trunk open. It was a couple of guys that had just pulled in from Watts with a load of liquor they wanted to sell.

He followed everybody over, and there were exclamations of envy when, crowding around, they saw a half dozen cases of the best stuff sitting there. The driver said he was willing to let it go for two bucks a fifth, which seemed like it was too high. While they were arguing about it, they saw the black-and-white car turning into the parking lot. The driver slammed down the lid of the trunk, and began walking away.

There were two officers in the police car. They got out, and one of them was a Negro.

"Where you going?" he called after the driver.

"I'm gonna climb a tree and go ape!" he shot back. "What's it to you?"

"Come back here. I want you to open the trunk of this car."

The driver ignored him and continued walking.

The Negro officer started after him, and the onlookers exaggeratedly parted their ranks, one of them bowing and making a sweeping, ushering motion with his arm.

"Hey, blood!" he said to the others standing around. "The fuzz is gonna come visit the park."

"Yeah, man," another chipped in. "I hears they wants to come and play ball with us."

"Maybe he tired. Maybe he want to come and lie down on the grass."

"Like he want to be initiated. He want to join the gang."

The Negro officer looked at the narrow, 20-foot long passage that the crowd had made for him, and decided he didn't want to go into the park. The passage looked exactly like the gauntlet that new members have to fight their way through on initiation to the Businessmen. Although they weren't visible, there were undoubtedly some knives in the crowd, and any number of the youths had pop bottles in their hands. Virtually all were veterans of one or more encounters with the police. One of the favorite tactics is to get the cops all heated up, then run them a merry chase through the alleys and back yards of houses—if one of them doesn't break a leg or get a rock bounced off his head, at least he'll be practically run to death. The police, when they caught a dude, would retaliate with a billy club to the belly, then drive him five or six miles and make him walk back.

Likely as not, he wouldn't walk very far. He'd spot a car with the keys in it or one that he could cross-wire, and he'd arrive back in style, waving and grinning.

The white officer radioed for help. Few women ever go into the park, and it was strictly a masculine crowd that formed a semicircle around the car.

"Hey, man," a youth called to the white officer. "I saw your mother the other day!"

The crowd laughed, knowing what was coming. "She come down here wanting to know what a real man could do, and I give her the best fuck she ever had."

"That's right, man," another called out, grinning. "She even give me a blow job for six bits!"

The officers ignored the taunts.

"Hey, you motherfuckers! You're chicken!" A young man fired a coke bottle against the side of the car.

The Negro officer leaped on him like a cat. Grabbing him by his T-shirt he spun him around and slammed him backward across the hood of the car. "You goddam punk! I ought to let you have it!" he ejaculated.

Another police car, responding to the Help call, turned into the parking lot.

"Hey, man! That's brutality!" an onlooker protested.

He was arrested also, and, together with the bottle-thrower, driven off. To the south the northward drifting smoke from the fires along Avalon Blvd. was now visible. "Man! We gonna take this lying down?" someone asked.

"Shit no. They want a riot. We give them a riot."

"Like man! The blood down in Watts need our help!"

"Three for one! Three for one!" They began their chant of revenge.

Bottles and rocks, handily available at the maintenance area inside the park, plummeted against the second police car. The mob rushed out onto Avalon Blvd., forming the eastern boundary of the park.

Cars were pelted, regardless of whether driven by Negroes or Caucasians. A white man's automobile stalled in the intersection, and was rocked like a cradle. Although the driver had locked himself inside, the windows were soon broken, he was pulled out, they began beating him with a ferocity that, in general, exceeded anything seen on Imperial Highway.

"Stop it! You'll kill him!" Wendell Collins and several other members of CORE who, having left Watts, happened to come upon the scene, intervened.

"Why not, man?" One of the kids was surprised. "We was gonna hang him!"

The CORE people carried the Caucasian over to their car. The youths couldn't understand. "Why you doing this? Whitey wouldn't do nothing, he wouldn't give you a drink of water if you was in the same fix!"

Right on the corner across from the park is the Southeast Health Clinic. Negro women, who had been there for treatment, poured out. As the automobile was set on fire they were swept along in the current of excitement. "Burn, baby, burn!" they cheered.

White doctors and nurses scurried for their cars. As they

drove off the back way, some of the people who had been patients moments before sped them along with rocks.

Down Avalon Blvd. and three blocks to the east to the Central Ave. business district the mob, gathering new recruits and new momentum with every block, swept. Rocks were thrown, store windows broken. The police hastily set up a command post at the northern edge of the park. Within a few minutes 100 youths were storming it, forcing the officers to abandon the corner and retreat six blocks to the south. The seven officers—the total force available—were buffeted about like flotsam on the ocean as they tried to check the fever of violence.

"We gonna have the biggest and best riot ever!" exulted Flip Borrago. "We gonna show all those dudes in Chicago and New York we're bigger than they are!"

He met a friend of his who had a .45, and the friend said he knew where they could get another one. That was right up Flip's alley. Once his fingers had curled around the heavy, blue steel, Flip said, "Come on, man!"

The two of them headed for a liquor store, and, by the time they got there, there were another half dozen dudes with them. They went in, and Flip pointed to the shelves and told the proprietor, "I'll take this, and this, and that!"

The proprietor put all the bottles on the counter, and said, "Let's see your draft card."

"Is this good enough?" Flip asked, pulling out the .45.

The man raised his arms. Eight pairs of hands flew over the shelves, grabbing every bottle they could carry.

"All right, man, you get down on your knees!" Flip ordered the white-faced proprietor. "Now you don't get up till you count to ten."

"All right. All right," the man agreed. "Anything you say."

Everybody poured out of the store; everybody but Flip. As he was about to leave, he grabbed his friend's arm and motioned him down on the front side of the counter. Together they squatted there as the proprietor counted "One, two, three, four, five, six, seven, eight, nine, ten!" Emitting a huge sigh of relief, he rose to his feet.

"Surprise! Surprise!" Flip jumped up, the muzzle of the .45 not a foot from the proprietor's nose.

The proprietor took one look, and collapsed in a dead faint.

"And then," as Flip recounted later, "we went on and vandalized some place else."

It was an hour and a half after the initial incident before the commander of the Newton Street division, in which South Park is located, was able to get through on the jammed, inadequate communications system to the ECC to report that the riot had spread to his district. It was 7:30 p.m., an elapsed time of four hours, before a full complement of officers could be moved in.

28   "An Unfriendly Foreign Country!"

Chief Parker's office resembled the locker room of a team that has just won the world series. A television crew with live camera was parked there permanently. Up to 20 reporters, filling the air with smoke and babble, were in constant attendance, moving out only to file stories and meet deadlines. Every report, every rumor that came in was immediately relayed raw and without qualification. . . .

Chief Parker will be killed over the weekend . . . 250 pounds of dynamite is to go off at Manchester and Broadway . . . rioters plan to attack through the sewers . . . the bank at Manchester and Broadway is to be knocked off tonight . . . suspects hiding in bushes near Mayor Yorty's home . . . hundreds of Black Muslims are arriving at International Airport from Chicago. . . .

In reality the "Muslims" were postal employees coming into town for a convention—but then, who can tell one Negro from another? Another couple of hundred white suburbanites rushed out to buy guns.

There was neither time nor personnel to check on the rumors. The law enforcement intelligence setup was atrocious. The police department, the sheriff's department, the California attorney general's office, the Los Angeles district attorney's office, and the FBI all had men in the field, but there was no pooling of information. The district attorney's office had, in fact, set up its own intelligence system because the police department refused it access to its files, contending they were confidential. With the sheriff, Chief Parker was not on the best of terms, and with the FBI he was on no terms whatsoever.

Parker's dispute with Sheriff Pitchess was an outgrowth of an attempt by the Special Law Enforcement Committee of the United Civil Rights Committee to iron out differences between minority groups and the sheriff's and police departments. While Parker had taken umbrage at the entire proceedings, calling the committee a "kangaroo court," Pitchess had been fully cooperative. He had invited attorney Thomas G. Neusom, who headed the committee, to make a study of the operations of the department in depth, and he felt that the suggestions subsequently made were helpful. Having integrated the jail after his election in 1960 (although there were dire warnings that massacres would occur, there had, in fact, been no incidents whatever), he had taken pains to look personally into all charges against deputies, and by taking immediate and public action had effectively cut off the water of those persons who made charges with no basis in fact. In order to insure good conduct, he operated an investigative section of 19 "head hunters," who circulate anonymously, monitoring the behavior of deputies. Furthermore, he had, at the time of the riot, five Negro lieutenants on the force. The police department had none.[1]

When Parker had heard of the accommodation reached by Pitchess with the UCRC, he thought "that was not quite a fraternal thing to do. I told him that . . . it was very unneighborly of him to get out and make a deal and get off the stage when the two of us were on it together originally and leave me there by myself."

Parker had also been left by himself by FBI Chief J. Edgar Hoover following a dispute over the establishment of a national clearing house for crime information, which Parker had favored and Hoover had not, a dispute that had been exacerbated during the Frank Sinatra, Jr., kidnaping case when Parker had become incensed because the FBI operated within the city limits of Los Angeles without telling him what

[1] The reason why the LAPD had no Negro above the rank of sergeant, has been explained previously. Since the riot, one Negro has made lieutenant.

they were doing. As a result, although most top men in the sheriff's department have been to the FBI Academy, no Los Angeles police officer has attended the Academy since 1950. Applicants from the LAPD are politely told that there is a waiting list of seven to ten years, which, ironically, is the same method used to discourage Negroes where they are not wanted. The fact that Los Angeles officers are, for all practical purposes, banned from the Academy, may have had some bearing on law enforcement performance during the riots, since "the FBI National Academy has developed riot control procedures through the use of outside experts [because] riot situations are so rare in the United States [that] the highly specialized training required for their suppression has not generally been a regular part of police training or organization." [2]

As the FBI Academy's policy is to permit attendance of police officers from all U. S. cities as well as friendly foreign countries, in Parker's own words, "I guess we are an unfriendly foreign country."

The inefficacy and impotence of the Los Angeles police commission—a five-member body that, according to the city charter, is supposed to supervise the operations of the police department but, since it meets only once a week for three or four hours, in actuality is at best a rubber-stamp body—can be demonstrated by the following exchange between Com. John Ferraro and John McCone at the McCone Commission hearings:

McCone: "Do you think in your responsibility to supervise and control and regulate and manage the police department that [the relations with the FBI] is a satisfactory condition?"

Ferraro: "I don't know. I have never given that any thought."

McCone: "J. Edgar Hoover was out here for two months. Didn't anyone talk to him from the police commission to straighten this out?"

Ferraro: "No, but four or five years ago I saw him at the Del Mar Race Track and I went and introduced myself to him . . . he didn't have too much time, he was busy with the racing form."

*   *   *

[2] FBI *Report on the Riots,* dated Sept. 18, 1964.

Maj. Gen. Charles A. Ott, arriving at Parker's office at 2:45 p.m., was appalled by the chaos he found, a chaos that made any discussion of what to do with the troops once they were available virtually impossible. Parker believed, however, that although "The press just took over my office . . . I didn't have any more office. . . . That's the only way you can stay alive in this business. Otherwise, the detractors will destroy you.

"I'm not a cloak-and-dagger man and I don't work in an area of secrecy. I work on the theory that someone somewhere is listening to everything I say, whether they are entitled to or not.

"The general is here but he can't act yet," Parker told the reporters and the television viewers to whom he appeared at frequent intervals. He was fuming over the inaction of Lt. Gov. Anderson, who, he believed, "wasn't at all interested in my opinion . . . [he] didn't want to talk to me. There is a pattern of deliberate delay here." He had the very definite impression that Anderson didn't want to talk to him until *after* he had made a decision.

"Just between us girls," Col. Quick told Col. Palumbo, another national guard officer, on the telephone, "he's a little upset . . . when the Governor gets here, if he doesn't come through right away, he will ask for whatever it takes to get government troops."

Anderson arrived in Los Angeles at 3:35, which was virtually the same time that Mayor Yorty trundled back; and a few minutes after the incident at South Park had, like an exploding bomb, spread the riot to an entirely new portion of the city. It was Gen. Ott's opinion that, had the National Guard been alerted before 8 a.m.—in other words, before most of the men had left for their regular jobs—between 500 and 1,000 men could have been in the field before noon. That, in all likelihood would have saved Watts and been enough to stem the tide right there. Had they been ordered out at 11 a.m., some could have been in the field by 3 p.m. —that might have inhibited the northward expansion. However, by this time, so many people were involved that just a few troops would, probably, not have been very effective.

Five minutes after landing, Anderson was on the telephone to Finance Director Hale Champion, who told him that he had talked to Gov. Brown, and Brown recommended that the

Guard be called out immediately. Anderson then held a press conference at the National Guard air field in the suburban San Fernando Valley where he had landed, announcing he was ordering the immediate mobilization of the Guard. This information was passed on to Chief Parker by a member of the governor's staff.

Parker, however, misunderstood, or else thought that it was only another delaying tactic, for a few minutes later he was on television explaining that he had prepared a telegram, over Mayor Yorty's signature, to the President of the U.S. requesting that federal troops be brought into Los Angeles, since state officials were refusing to call out the National Guard. Sen. Thomas Rees, the city's lone representative in the state senate,[3] having made his way into the office through the back door—the guards at the front door had refused to let him in since he lacked press credentials—became upset at this statement and tried to usurp Parker's place in front of the camera to explain that Anderson was calling out the Guard, and to suggest to Parker that he go out and fight the rioters instead of holding press conferences. It was an intervention to which the Chief demurred, exclaiming, "I didn't know state senators had anything to do with calling out the Guard!" Thereupon he suggested to Rees that, since it was not the senator's office and since he had not been invited in, he should leave without further ado.

Trying to placate Parker, Gen. Ott told him that, in addition to the 1,300 troops previously allocated for riot duty, he was on his own initiative ordering two more battalions to remain behind for duty in Los Angeles. (The rest were still scheduled to leave that evening for Camp Roberts, 200 miles away.) Col. Quick was in consultation with Col. Irving (Bud) Taylor of the National Guard, a Los Angeles police officer by profession, on deployment of the troops after they would begin assembling at the armories at 5 p.m.[4] It was somewhat disconcerting to Col. Quick that no one on the department seemed to have any ideas as to where, how, or when, the troops were to be used.

---

[3] And now a U.S. Congressman.
[4] It may or may not be of significance that Col. Taylor has never been able to make sergeant on the police force because of the difficulty of the examination.

29   The Fire This Time

Had troops been available, they could have sent a few down to Avalon Blvd. right then. The street was a shambles. Half-melted metal signs tilted downward like wilted flowers, the top of a palm tree presented a brilliant bloom of flames, from sidewalk to sidewalk the street was a spaghettilike maze of fire hoses. Residents, many of them not unfriendly, were running along the shops, grabbing items here and there as if from an open smorgasbord. As one woman said, "It's not like it was stealing when the stuff's gonna burn anyways."

People continued rummaging in stores whose walls and ceilings were already afire. The street was littered with sundry items discarded or dropped in haste—women picked over them and children played with them. The looters ignored the firemen, going about their business as if they did not exist. A driver, loading his car, started off. . . .

"Hey, back up! Get off that hose!" a fireman yelled.

"Yes, sir!" The man made an imaginary hat-tipping motion with his fingers. "I'm sure sorry about that."

The few police officers on hand, sweating in the heat of sun and fire, were being run ragged. Acknowledging their impotence, they confined themselves to driving back rock-throwers and spectators and, when they were able, taking down the license numbers of cars of people who were looting.

Jimmie Hoffman in his 22 years had been arrested more than 30 times—22 of those within a three-year period for being drunk. He had dropped out of Jordan High School at the age of 16 because, he felt, he was going to be expelled anyway. In 1959 he had stolen a car and in 1960 he had been involved in a gang fight in which one boy was killed. He had already spent more than three years in custody. When someone hurled a six-inch chunk of concrete and a red fire-brick at a police car, hitting one officer in the eye, he, together with several others, ran. The officers identified him as the culprit.

He said, "It wasn't my fault. I was standing down the street . . . and the officer was chasing a group of people toward where I was standing. They couldn't catch the ones they was chasing and all at once they runs over and grabs me. Takes me and books me for throwing rocks at cars, assault on two policemen. That's the way it was.

"I mean to work and hold my job and do better than I been doing. I plan to stop drinking like I used to, and stay out of jail. I'm sick of it."

Twenty-four-year-old Robert Jackson, married to a 16-year-old girl, had quit school in Arizona, where he lived with foster parents, in the eighth grade because, at that time, 15 years old, he was "halfway grown." He had been arrested twice for burglary—the first time it was a pop machine, the second a telephone booth—once for armed robbery of a service station, and once for transporting a stolen car across state lines. He owed money on a 1957 Buick, a color television set, and a sewing machine, and the manager of the restaurant where he was employed as a janitor and cook considered him a good, steady worker. He had just taken his wife to the hospital because she was having stomach pains and he thought she might be pregnant, and they were returning home when they stopped at a barbecue stand on Avalon to have something to eat. Suddenly a lot of people started throwing rocks and bottles at the police, and, caught up in the excitement, he threw one too.

Norman Martin, 20, had been, in the past four years twice convicted of petty theft and once for carrying a concealed weapon. At probation camp he had been a troublemaker, several times assaulting other boys. Since his release he had been picked up for burglary, attempted robbery, assault with a deadly weapon, kidnaping and rape—all investigative arrests, without any charges filed. He had an 18-year-old girlfriend who had borne him two children. He emerged from the window of a liquor store looking like a walking alcoholic display case just as two officers drove up. The first bottle he threw smashed against the door frame of the patrol car, splattering one officer with slivers of glass and whiskey; the second hit the other officer on the neck. As he took off, the policemen went after him—through alleys, over fences, across backyards, bottles popping from his arms and out of his pockets. Finally, after six blocks, he was collared.

Bogart Pedrally, Pancho Pedrally's brother, had visited the clinic that morning for his regular psychiatric treatment. After returning home with his mother he had wandered out—he had no clear notion of where he was going or what he was going to do, but the fires and the smell of smoke excited him. For the first time since the death of President Kennedy he felt capable of meeting persons on the street and not cowering before them. For the first time since his booklet of poems and essays, *A Tribute to J.F.K.*, had been published by a print shop, and ridiculed by his teacher at school, he felt as if he might be able to function again. He wandered over to Avalon Blvd., and, seeing the firemen at work, quickly began identifying with them. Wanting to help he began dragging hoses and running small errands. As he carried a ladder toward a burning store, the Caucasian owner met him on the sidewalk.

"What is this?" he wanted to know. "First you niggers set fire to my place and then you come back with a ladder. What do you want to do? Collect the insurance?" The Caucasian gave him a shove that sent him stumbling off the sidewalk.

Like Jimmie Hoffman, Robert Jackson, and Norman Martin, Bogart Pedrally was arrested for throwing rocks at police and firemen. That was how things were on Avalon Blvd. the afternoon of Friday the 13th.

*   *   *

A few blocks away on Central Ave. and 76th St., the block-long White Front Discount Department Store had closed its doors at 3 p.m. Morris Yedwalski remained behind in charge of a six-man security force, both Negro and Caucasian. At 3:30 p.m. the first windows were broken, and the next hour and a half produced a running battle to keep people from breaking into the store. Shortly after 5 o'clock Yedwalski spotted Mardis Dorton across the street.

Dorton was a 24-year-old Louisianan whose parents had separated when he was six and who had, on and off, lived with various members of the family. He had never had a full-time job and, over the course of seven years since dropping out of school, had been arrested more than 20 times for offenses ranging from armed robbery and attempted rape to drunk in public and driving without a license. Three months before he had been nabbed by Yedwalski for trying to pilfer a barber's kit, and had received a sentence of 30 days in jail.

Carrying a bottle with a lighted wick taped to it, Dorton ran toward Yedwalski and shouted a warning for him to get out of the way. Yedwalski stood his ground. Dorton threw the bottle at him. As Yedwalski ducked, it somersaulted over his head and into the store through a broken window. Splattering against canvas, it set it afire.

"I am awful sorry that all of this happened in the first place, and I hope that this never happen again to our wonderful city," said Dorton.

*   *   *

But it was happening. Not far away in an alley an officer and a suspect engaged in a brief pistol-versus-shotgun duel whose outcome was inconclusive—the suspect, leaving traces of his blood behind, disappeared.

At 77th division, Lt. Mead, the watch commander, was preparing to hold roll call for the night shift. Confusion was rampant. Plainclothes officers being called to patrol duty lacked helmets and were scrounging them from regular officers going off duty. Wearing civilian clothes with black-and-white helmets, pistol belts, and detective badges on their shirts, they looked like a curious breed, neither fish nor fowl. There were no shotguns for them—shotguns were in such short supply that the department was sending frantic teletypes to police and sheriff's departments all over California and Arizona in an attempt to requisition them. Sears-Roebuck brought in 100 from its sporting goods store. Officers were borrowing them from their neighbors. Shotguns of every type and description made their appearance; until, ultimately, the department garnered a motley collection of more than 900. Shotgun shells and .38-caliber ammunition had to be rationed. At 77th, Lt. Mead never knew how many men were going to report, or what to do with them once they had reported. Although it was his duty to assign them, he received no information as to what was happening on the streets.

Lacking any specific orders, police officers were still working under the assumption that they were not to use their guns unless coming under direct attack. Sgt. Rankin tried to bluff people running out of stores by leveling his shotgun and threatening to shoot. Women and children would scream, throwing loot up into the air, but this approach did not work with the older kids and the toughs. "Go to hell, you mother-fuckers, they won't let you shoot!" they taunted the police. One kid clobbered an officer across the side of the head with a bat and kicked his shotgun out into the street. Another wasn't fazed in the least when an officer fired a shotgun blast over his head as, emerging from a liquor store, he hurled a bottle at him. "Shit, man, who you think you're kidding, you got nothing but blanks!" he yelled at him, and went right back into the store for another load.

The frustration and humiliation the officers felt at their impotence had brought tension to the point that it quivered like a heavy cable on the verge of snapping; when it did snap there would be an inevitable whiplash.

Lt. Mead felt it his duty to try and bring some order into the situation.

"I can't tell you to go out and kill," he said, "but when someone throws a rock, that's a felony. When they commit a burglary, that's a felony. When they throw a Molotov cock-tail, that's a felony. And don't you forget it!"

A murmur went through the ranks. The officers knew well enough that anyone resisting, or trying to escape from, a fel-ony arrest could be shot.

"Well," said Errol Lawrence to Frank Pinter. "I guess they're finally taking the clamps off. I'm gonna have myself a little surprise for one of those black bastards!"

*   *   *

By 5 p.m. approximately 550 men had assembled in the National Guard armories, and shortly thereafter the number grew to more than 1,300. At police headquarters Gens. Hill and Ott expressed the Guard's readiness to move in.

"Well," said one of the chiefs, "we are not so much in-terested in doing this quick as in doing it right."

It was a euphemism for, on the one hand, doubt as to what role the troops should play, and, on the other, confusion about where they should be deployed. The riot was centered in four separate and distinct localities: Watts, aflame; a mile-long stretch of Avalon Blvd. between Century and Imperial, burning, and almost completely denuded of police; an area extending more than a half mile in each direction from South

Park, where there was still only a smattering of police; and the 10-block stretch of Broadway, not previously involved, where the riot was about to enter a new phase of accelerated violence.

To Manchester and Broadway crowds were being drawn by the reports disseminated on television. Every time people heard a store was being looted, there they went; every time they could identify a burning building on television, they headed for it. ("I told them they were complicating our jobs," said Chief Parker, "but who am I to interfere with the great freedom of the press?")

As Mac Benton went out he saw that all of the gangs were out in force, riding around flashing the V sign of the Slausons, the thumbs-down fist of the Gladiators, the open fingered O of the Businessmen, the W of the old Watts gangs. As they passed each other in cars they would identify themselves, they would be cheered—old enemies forgetting their grudges to go and get Whitey. The Outlaws, the Rebel Rousers, the Parks and Boot Hill—all had representation. At 77th, when Benton had told his superiors that the gangs were marching, they had shrugged—there wasn't much that they could do about it one way or the other. Broadway just north of Manchester was, as Benton knew, a violent section even in ordinary times, there were two pool halls in the vicinity that spawned constant trouble. Mentioning that the way he had operated the previous night, he hadn't been able to report information in time to do any good, Benton suggested to his superiors that he be provided with radio transmitting equipment that would enable him to call in from trouble spots. He was told that none was available.

Benton had hardly left the station, located on 77th St. just off Broadway, when he came upon hundreds of people lying in wait for police cars as they emerged from the parking lot. An 8-year-old kid snatched a bottle from the hand of an older boy, demanding, "Let me throw it!"

Next to him a 60-year-old crone awkwardly overhanded a rock at the police. One car halted, the officers jumped out, and, using the doors for cover, began firing over the heads of the crowd. Everybody ran.

A few blocks farther south a semicircle of police cars guarded firemen trying to put out a fire. At two locations on Broadway, three blocks to either side of the police station, heavy construction pipes had been laid across the roadway

so that cars would have to come to a virtual halt before proceeding over them. As they slowed down, they would be battered from all sides. In the same fashion as it had on Wednesday and Thursday nights on Imperial, normal traffic, unaware
that the riot had spread to the area, continued to flow in.
The rioters, however, were so busy lashing out at the police,
so occupied looting and setting fires, that the ordinary white
motorist had gotten low on the priority list.

Officers in convoys of cars moved down one side of the
street, hugging the curb, their shotguns pointing at the people on the other side—they were not attacked. Shortly before
6 o'clock it was decided to sweep a 10-block area from 78th
to 88th Sts.—one group of officers advancing from north to
south, the other from south to north.

A good many shots were beginning to crackle about, some,
undoubtedly, aimed at the police, others fired by the police
into the air, almost all having the impersonal characteristic
of Fourth of July backyard fireworks. Unlike fireworks, however, each shot left a residue—a bullet that went up had to
come down, and where it came down it was likely to be interpreted as having been fired by a sniper.

As the skirmish line was being formed south of 88th St. a
screaming horde of kids and men descended upon it, un-
leashing the now standard assortment of missiles. The attack
was notable only for its ferocity, a ferocity that drove the
line back and almost caused it to break.

Shooting out of a side street a patrol car, the driver's eyes
barely sticking up over the dash, careened through the crowd,
up onto the sidewalk, then back into the street and through
the line of officers, who scattered. "We are being shot at!"
the driver yelled; and he had certainly been thrown at, since
his partner had a chunk of concrete lying in his lap.

A half block up the street, Leon Posey, Jr., a wiry 20-year-
old with a trim mustache and goatee, was sitting in a barbershop waiting for a friend who was being tended to. Hearing
the crash of glass, the sirens of police cars, a smattering of
shots, seeing people start to run by the window, he stepped
outside to look at what was going on.

"They're going crazy!" a police officer yelled as the mob
appeared on the verge of closing in for hand-to-hand combat.
There were cries of: "Mayor Yorty told them not to shoot!"
"The motherfuckers have got blanks in their guns!"

A ricochet splattered onto the pavement 10 feet in front

of the skirmish line, a chunk of cement bounced off the leg of one officer, a rock hit the jaw of another. There was a shout: "We're losing control!"

One officer fired; two; three. All along the line firing pins drove into cartridges. Some of the men, in the breaking of the tension, pulled the trigger again and again as they aimed their shots over the heads of the mob.

Leon Posey, Jr., a .38-caliber bullet ricocheting off a building wall and lodging in the back of his head, slumped to the sidewalk.

He was the first to die.

Just beyond the barbershop, 88th St. crosses Broadway and, within a half block, dead-ends in the freeway. It is a quiet street of frame houses, palm trees, and numerous cars, parked both along the street and in the driveways of houses. In the first house on the north side, next to a gas station, lived young Donnell and Della McCray and their three children. Together with two friends they were standing on the front porch. Nearby, Edward Jones, an amateur photographer, who had had to park his car because of the riot, was wandering around snapping pictures.

There was continuous firing as police advanced up the street. Most of it was coming from officers on the other skirmish line headed south, but the men did not know this, and, not knowing or expecting it, assumed that the shots must be coming from rioters. As the skirmish line reached the southern edge of 88th St., a bottle exploded at the feet of the officers. Bullets whined about them. One officer looking toward the gas station on the northwest corner saw several persons—the McCrays and their friends, who had also been startled by the proximity of the shots—running inside the house. "There they are!" the police officer yelled. "They're firing at us from that house!"

A score of officers charged toward the house, taking cover behind trees and parked cars, snapping off shots as they advanced, pouring a fusillade of bullets into and through the wooden boards. Jones, the photographer, who had ducked into the house next door, heard a scream as a woman was hit. Putting his hands over his head he emerged, imploring the police to stop shooting. One officer, running up to him, grabbed him and yelled, "Goddam you black son-of-a-bitch, tell those niggers to come out or we'll kill them all!"

Donnell McCray, crying that his wife had been killed—

she hadn't; shot in the abdomen, she survived—came onto the porch waving a white handkerchief. As the adults were lined up against a chain link fence and searched, the police demanded, "Who's got the gun?"

Told that there was no gun, they assured the people that the gun would be found.

But what did not exist could not be found. So, after being taken to the 77th station for questioning, all of the people were released.

The next afternoon, the Los Angeles *Herald-Examiner,* with a half page of photographs, headlined the incident: "White Flag Ends Riot Gun Battle." [1]

*   *   *

A half hour later, two blocks to the north, 21-year-old George Oliver Carter was mingling with a crowd of people looting a furniture store. The son of an unwed, 16-year-old girl, he had been raised by relatives, and had been in and out of trouble ever since the age of 14, when he had begun stealing large sums of money. A psychiatric examination had shown him to be in dire need of treatment, but none was provided. In 1964 he had spent six months in jail as a result of ignoring traffic tickets he had received, and was picked up in front of a theater with a .45 concealed beneath the seat of his car. "I was going to use the gun tonight to get me some bread," he said. He had been married to a 15-year-old girl whom he had gotten pregnant, but, since they could not get along, he had separated from her. He was on his way to work at a restaurant where he made $77 a week as a busboy when he stopped off to see the action.

When the police came in cars and on foot as they swept the street, the crowd scattered, throwing rocks over their shoulders as they went. Carter's aim was good—he broke the rear window of one car, and hit an officer jumping out of the next on the leg. As the policeman came after him he ran between two houses, the pursuit ranging over a fence and through bushes, ending there as the officer brought him down with a shot through the leg.

*   *   *   *

[1] In the Sunday editions the newspaper front-paged another picture, with the caption: "Police Charge House From Which Fusillade of Shots Was Fired on Them." News magazines, subsequently, repeated the error.

The sky was darkening, the fires raising plumes of smoke tinted crimson by the setting sun. Mac Benton went down to the freeway crossing at Manchester Ave. Along Figueroa St. to the west of the freeway there was little disturbance; in Norm's Restaurant whites and Negroes, intermingled, sat together eating dinner. A block to the east firemen worked, guarded by police with drawn guns. Practically next door a large Pep Boys auto supply store was being looted. Benton stopped to talk to a white store owner who was remaining to guard his property. A duo of other Caucasians walked down the street, discussing the situation, nodding "good evening" and remarking on how terrible it all was. A Negro youth came ambling by, walked a few feet beyond where Benton and the Caucasian were standing, then whirled and returned. "What you say, you white motherfucker?" he challenged the man, who had said nothing.

"Why don't you make it?" Benton suggested.

The kid hesitated; then left.

A National Guard jeep looked forlorn and lost as it halted beneath the freeway overpass, the two officers in it surveying the field.

To Oak Park Hospital across the street police brought a constant stream of injured—Caucasians struck by Negroes replaced more and more as time progressed by Negroes wounded in clashes with the police. Doctors and nurses were in such short supply that even administrative personnel were tending to wounds. The anesthetist refused to enter the area, so no anesthetics could be administered, and Leon Posey, who was brought in alive, died because doctors could not perform the operation that might have saved him. Bloody clothing littered the floor, there was no opportunity to sterilize instruments properly, bandages wound about like garland streamers the morning after a wild party, there was no time to cross-match blood, whole blood ran out, plasma ran out, people were being brought in at a rate of one every two and a half minutes. . . .

A Negro man streaming blood carried his eight-months pregnant wife, who had been shot in the head. She was saved but the baby was lost. . . .

A deaf-mute girl who had been on the way to pick up her child had never realized she was in the midst of a fire fight until the bullet drove the fabric of her red sweater deep into her abdomen. . . .

A woman with an arm gashed to the bone sat moaning as a doctor and a nurse worked desperately to tie off the bleeders and save her. When the job was finished she turned on the nurse and snarled, "Now go to hell, you ugly white bitch!"

An angry mob gathering outside, angry at the police, angry at themselves, irrationally vented their anger on the hospital. They threw bricks through the windows, rocked and nearly overturned the ambulances as they drove up. Smoke from encroaching fires snaked through the building, leaving the residue of its pungent odor on everything it touched.

Mac Benton left and drove down to Watts. The police had just finished sweeping the streets, and hardly a person was to be seen—one of the few was Mrs. Ann Miller, director of the teen post at the Hacienda Village Housing Project. Mrs. Miller had scored the only triumph in Watts that day—at the height of the rioting she had organized a volleyball game that had kept her kids off the street.

Fire trucks driven off earlier were returning; coming back to a wasteland of buildings sending thick acrid smoke into the air, their blackened ribs standing out sharply like the carcasses of animals whole-broiled. The legs and buttocks of a mannequin angled obscenely and humanlike out of a trash can into which it had been stuffed. In several places mounds of rubble made the street almost impassable. An orange, propelled by some unseen force, rolled leisurely along. From beneath a heap of bricks in a burned-out store a radio eerily blared rock and roll. Live wires hissed sparks like the flickering tongues of angry snakes. The clear blue flames of burning gas jets illuminated towers of water ejaculated 50 feet into the air from decapitated hydrants.

"Hell!" said a fireman. "There's nothing left but a charcoal alley!"

The name stuck; 103rd St. became known as Charcoal Alley—number one.

Benton drove on. The backwater of the riot was along Imperial Highway. At 120th and Central a complex of stores was being looted. A youth in a cut-down Buick stopped and called to him, "Hey! You want a drink?"

The youth opened the trunk, which was crammed full of liquor, and Benton took a hot beer. The back seat of the car was a jumble of dozens of pairs of shoes. "Three bucks a pair!" the kid offered.

Men came and tried them on and took them for a dollar—it was a buyers' market.

Once more on the move, Benton headed for the triangle formed by Wilmington and Willowbrook with Imperial—it was another one of those trouble spots, a hangout for prostitutes, pimps, and dope peddlers. Liquor stores were being looted on both sides of Imperial, the one on the south side was on fire. Several sheriff's cars, some straddling the center line, were parked on Imperial. Sheriff's officers were running people out of the store.

One shouting, "Run, niggers!" slapped them on the buttocks with his baton as they scurried from the broken show window. On the opposite corner three or four deputies had lined up more than 20 people. Deciding that there were too many to be arrested they ordered them to "Make it! Get the hell out of here!"

One deputy, in frustration, cried, "I'm tired of you niggers messing with me!" He began whipping a girl around the thighs, punching his billy into her groin. . . .

"Goddammit, you white motherfuckers! Leave our women alone!" the people, upset, shouted at him.

It was nearing 9 o'clock, and one of the deputies on the scene was 26-year-old Ronald Ernest Ludlow. He had grown up in the southeast Los Angeles area and had been in his junior year at Pepperdine College, majoring in psychology and social sciences, when, in 1961, after getting married and working at a variety of jobs such as shoe salesman, recreation director, and credit investigator, he had decided to join the sheriff's department. The father of three children, he was of considerably more liberal bent than most of his fellows. He had already been on duty several hours, earlier in the evening having chased looters out of the large Safeway Market and shopping complex two blocks to the west.

Less than a half mile to the east, in the Imperial Court Housing Project, lived 21-year-old Noranyce Allen. Extremely pretty, separated from her husband, she was supported, along with her three children, by the BPA. A friend, 24-year-old Harold Potts, had arrived Thursday evening and spent the night with her. Since he did not have a car, Friday afternoon he called Joseph Levine and asked him to come and pick him up. Levine, together with Philip Brooks, arrived at the Allen apartment at approximately 6 o'clock Friday evening. All four had known each other for many years, and Noranyce was, in fact, Brooks's "play sister"—they had grown up together as children.

Noranyce mentioned that she had no food in the house for the children, and asked if they could drive out and get some while Levine had the car there. The four of them, plus the three children, piled into the car. At the Safeway Market they saw the sheriff's deputies, the doors of the store appearing locked. As they continued driving they could find no market that had not been looted and remained open. Noranyce was becoming nervous about having the children on the street, so they returned to her apartment.

Giving Levine $2, Noranyce asked him and the others to try again. Brooks, 22 years old, the father of four children, a veteran of two years in the navy, took the wheel. Neither he, nor any of the others, had ever been in serious trouble. As the car nodded over the rise of the railroad tracks on Imperial a half block east of the corner of Wilmington, Brooks could see, to the left, a liquor store on fire, in the center and on the south side of the street a bevy of sheriff's cars, deputies and Negroes running this way and that. The light turned red, and Brooks braked the car to a halt. Inside the car a record player was going full blast, outside there were shouts and screams—it was a cauldron of confusion.

Brooks's attention was momentarily diverted by the fire. When he looked up, sheriff's deputies were approaching the car from three sides, the one nearest to him seeming to have his shotgun pointed directly at him. The deputy was yelling something. It was impossible to understand his meaning. Levine and Potts had already thrown up their hands, and Brooks followed suit. There were two deputies on Brooks's side of the car: one approaching the window, the other bearing down in line with the left front fender.

The deputy near the window came to within a foot of the car. The barrel of his shotgun swung sideways, then suddenly kicked up with the blast of a shot. Ronald Ernest Ludlow, who had approached to within a yard of the front fender, was lifted off his feet and turned almost somersault by the force of the pellets. Deputy William B. Lauer, whose gun it was that had fired, dropped it and rushed over to Ludlow, crying, "Ron—are you hurt!"

"Yes. I'm hurt bad," Ludlow answered.

Lauer, almost hysterical, tugged at Ludlow's Sam Browne belt, trying to loosen it, then was pulled away by two other deputies. Brooks, Potts, and Levine were dragged from the car and slammed against its sides. An ambulance was called. The deputies waited, 10 minutes, 15, 20—no ambulance arrived as the dark stain pulsed ever wider across Ludlow's shirt. Finally, placed in the back seat of a sheriff's car, he was driven two miles to the nearest hospital in Lynwood. He was dead on arrival.

Ronald Ernest Ludlow was the second.

Brooks, Potts, and Levine were charged with his murder.

*   *   *

Ten minutes later at the corner of 110th and Main Sts.— just a half dozen blocks from Avalon and Imperial—Officer Frank Alexander, Alvin Miller and several others were passing the Hudson Department Store when they heard breaking glass and saw numerous people moving about inside. As they approached, four or five started coming out through the window, and were placed under arrest.

To Alexander's astonishment, lying amidst the rubble of the street, was a 12-gauge shotgun. He bent down to pick it up.

One of the officers, firing a shot into the air, called out to the remainder of the people inside, "You'd better come out —we don't want to have to drag you out dead!"

As he did, someone threw a tape recorder straight through an unbroken portion of the window, shattering the glass. Several of the Negroes used this moment of distraction to make a break for it. Miller yelled, "Stop or we'll fire!"

One man, his arms full of goods, dropped them and started to spin back toward the officers. Miller fired three shots; Alexander two from the 12-gauge shotgun he had just picked up. The man clutched at his side and tumbled to the pavement.

His name was Calvin Jones, Jr. He was 30 and unmarried. He was the third.

30   The Wave from South Park

To the north, in an ever-widening wave rippling out from South Park, the experience of Watts was being repeated. Eleven major fires were burning. A six-block section of Central Ave. made it appear that 103rd St. had simply been an overture. Broadway, Santa Barbara, Florence, Firestone, Washington, Jefferson, McKinley, Vernon, Wall, San Pedro, 41st, Normandie, Western, Vermont, Adams—street after street became invested with looters and jangling burglar alarms, on street after street fires blossomed, some set amateurishly with piles of paper or trash dumped onto the floor, others burgeoning with the orange-red streamers of fire bombs. As people were looting the Buddha Market a Molotov cocktail plummeted into their midst. A girl's dress caught fire and was beaten out. Screaming, people ran in all directions. Then, while the flames roared up to the ceiling, they came back, risking incineration and suffocation to grab cans and bottles, bread and baby food.

Nothing made sense. With 200 or more rioters for every policeman, the officers would come, grab someone who had picked up a shirt from the sidewalk, and leave to take him to the station. As soon as they were gone, a youth who had been sitting on a shoeshine kit would get up, take a bottle from inside, light it, and blast another store into an inferno. Teenagers picked up a newsstand and heaved it bodily through the show window of a large Thrifty Drug Store. Liquor stores went right and left. One owner saved his by standing in the doorway, a .45 on his hip and a shotgun in his arms; another by placing all of his stock on the sidewalk—people picked it up and did not bother him.

Northward the riot crept. Past USC, past the Sports Arena where thousands of persons were attending a circus, like a footpad through what had once been the city's finest residential district and from whose stables burghers had trotted downtown on their horses. Around the house where Adlai

Stevenson was born, past the cottage where the 108-year-old son of Sitting Bull sat at the window watching. At 28th and Central, only a mile from the heart of the downtown business section, 45-year-old Homer Ellis had doubled-parked his old green Buick in front of a small liquor store. Ellis had only a minor arrest record, but he was among a dozen persons moving in and out of the store, several of them loading liquor into the trunk of the car.

To Officer Gerald Ray, when he arrived at 9:30 p.m., it looked like an assembly line. One of his partners had previously been injured and driven to the hospital, so five officers were doubling up in the one patrol car. When they halted and headed for the liquor store, the people inside came charging out. One officer was hit by a flying case of whiskey, another christened with a bottle of bourbon—there was a sharp rattle of shots as Ray and several of the other officers fired.

Homer Ellis fell. He was the fourth.

*   *   *

At 9:40 p.m., police were estimating that in another four to eight hours the riot would be in the heart of the city. Gen. Hill suggested to Deputy Chief Murdock that, to prevent this, the troops establish a blockade on the northern perimeter. While Chief Parker averred that "less than 1 per cent of the Negro population is involved," a National Guard officer suggested that: "If you know how many people there are in Los Angeles, colored people, I mean, there are about 80 per cent of them involved, with, of course, a few white defectors."

The truth, most likely, lay somewhere between.

31   "This Is the Hate that Hate Produced"

At the Do-Rite Market and Liquor Store at 82nd and San Pedro Sts.—near Manchester and Broadway—Willie Cobb, Willie Tom Little, and Errol Drew were among a host of looters. All had been in some trouble with the law, although Little, who had served for three years in the army and received an honorable discharge, had the kind of offenses that are almost epidemic in the Negro community—a conviction on battery and several driving violations.

One officer flushed Little out of the toilet, and Drew was nabbed after he assertedly threw a bottle. Cobb, 25, had arrived in California only three months before after serving a prison term in Alabama for breaking into a nightclub. As, together with a dozen others, he ran down the street, he was shot through the stomach and critically wounded.

Sgt. Richard Rankin, arriving a few minutes later, supervised the placing of Cobb in an ambulance. After Drew and Little, together with another suspect, had been handcuffed and put into the back seat of the first police car, the convoy started off, the ambulance leading and Sgt. Rankin trailing. He, together with his men, was glad that the mollycoddling had come to an end, that they were finally able to react to the attacks. The thing had built up to a point where it had to pop. The police, he felt, had been placed in an impossible position—no matter what they did, they were going to be criticized for it later. All the normal, orderly routine, the discipline that demanded each officer be able to answer for every one of his actions, had cracked and gone to hell. It was like a tidal wave, and far from trying to stem it all one could do was ride it and try to stay on top. A short time earlier Rankin had stopped a car bulging with liquor; the driver had been arrested, the liquor unloaded onto the sidewalk; an Officer Needs Help call had come in, Rankin had rushed to answer it; when he returned, all the liquor had disappeared.

The officers had traveled only a couple of blocks from the market when, at Main and 82nd Sts., they came upon a large crowd. It was 9:45 p.m., quite dark, and suddenly an officer in the first car spotted the muzzle flash of a gun, a bullet screeched into the front panel of the car. . . .

"Look out—they're shooting!" the officer yelled, drawing his gun and snapping off two rounds at a tall, husky man wearing a straw Plantation hat. As the driver accelerated, the prisoners in the back seat scrambled for cover on the floor.

Sgt. Rankin, who had also spotted the sniper, jumped out of his patrol car as it came to a halt next to a pickup truck. He saw the muzzle of the gun in the hand of the man with the Plantation hat swing in his direction just as the sights of his own .38 Smith and Wesson bracketed him. He pulled the trigger.

Nothing happened. The night before, when the gun had tumbled to the pavement, the hammer had been bent.

A bullet whined into the hood of the pickup truck behind which Rankin crouched. Another cracked through the windshield. Rankin's partner, Gary Beebe, leveled his shotgun and pulled the trigger.

Nothing happened. He had forgotten to take the safety off.

A third shot slammed into the patrol car. People were screaming and running in all directions. Finally Rankin and Beebe got their guns into operation, Rankin pumping off several shots just as the man with the Plantation hat started off, running in a crouched position, silhouetted against the wall of a building. Beebe fired as he saw him disappearing behind a truck parked 20 feet away on 82nd St.

Both went and looked for him, but he was gone; and Rankin was not disposed to enter into an extended search in a dark and hostile neighborhood.

Standing on the corner, watching a store being looted a block away, Eddie Taylor, Robert Louis Crowder and George Adams, Jr., had been renewing old acquaintances. Taylor heard someone in the crowd say, "You'd better put that thing away before it is taken from you!"

A moment later had come a shot, then, as the three of them retreated toward their car parked on 82nd St., a flurry of a dozen more. As they reached the car, Adams collapsed. Crowder, placing him in the car, headed for Oak Park Hospital, seven or eight blocks away. Before he got there, he was stopped at the police roadblock at Manchester and Broadway.

A police officer looked at Adams and felt his pulse. "There's nothing they can do for him," he said.

Adams, 45, had been felled by a shotgun pellet which had struck him in the back and severed his aorta.

He was the fifth.

At 10:30 p.m., 45 minutes after Sgt. Rankin and the other officers had left the Do-Rite Market, the neighborhood had quieted down, and, as 18-year-old Charles Shortridge passed by, he saw the night light on, the windows battered in and the door standing ajar. There was an inviting glow from the beer cooler, and Shortridge thought it wouldn't hurt if he helped himself to a beer.

Concealed behind the counter were three men who had returned to guard the store after it had been looted—John Henry Nichols, Jr., Richard Jackson, and James Lawrence. As Shortridge padded by, Lawrence raised up and fired his 12-gauge shotgun at close range.

Charles Richard Shortridge was the sixth.

Fifteen minutes later 11 blocks to the south 24-year-old Alfred Elliott was struck above the eye by an officer's bullet as he emerged from a market, but suffered only a minor wound.

With that singular ability of pushing their cause at the precise psychological moment to develop the most enemies— a characteristic shared with other crusaders—the Student Non-Violent Action Committee and the Socialist Workers Party sent pickets carrying signs "No More Harlems" to the police building.

At 76th St. and Central Ave. the White Front Store that Morris Yedwalski and his men had been guarding was a block-long grate of fire, the sign advertising "California's Largest Discount Headquarters" twisting to the street. The fire set by Mardis Dorton's bomb had been extinguished, but, after Yedwalski and his men had been advised by the police to leave at 8:30 p.m., because their safety could no longer be guaranteed, the store had been subjected to continuous looting and set on fire again—twice more, in fact.

When Yedwalski left, there had been three young Negroes at a taco stand across the street. Calmly they had finished supper, then one, in white shorts, in a sudden swift motion had picked up a shopping cart and heaved it through a plate glass window. Within minutes dozens of persons had come swarming toward the store. One man carted off a refrigerator, came back and took another, returned a third time and, with all of the refrigerators gone, trundled off a washing machine. A pregnant woman ran across the street with an armload of motor oil cans. Three men loaded a huge stereo set through the top of an open-roofed Volkswagen. Two of them climbed in and the third stepped onto the rear bumper to hold down the stereo protruding through the top. Whenever a police car drove by the people would drop whatever they had and take on the air of innocent bystanders. As soon as the police were gone, they hoisted the goods, and off they went.

By 10:30 p.m. the building was in its death throes, flames thrashing about, emitting belches of blue steam as firemen played streams of water from the ground and a 50-foot ladder. Incredibly, cries of help began to issue from the second story—two looters trapped behind barred windows were desperately trying to claw their way out. The firemen attempted to breach the wall. When that failed they attempted to cut through the roof, but found this an impossibility also. Finally an acetylene torch was located, the steel bars covering the windows were cut, and the two looters, well smoked but alive, were lifted out.

To the north at Jefferson and McKinley, only a few blocks from where, at that very moment, thousands of people were emerging from the circus and making their way without harassment to cars parked on the streets and in lots, firemen were battling a blaze in a small market. A score of youths were standing around. From among them one suddenly darted forward and pressed a small-caliber pistol to the back of Harold Myers's neck declaring, "Man, you are going up to meet the Big Boy!"

Myers turned. The Negro youth fired. As the force of the bullet grazing his neck tumbled Myers forward, he yelled a warning, "Look out! He's got a gun!"

Hoseman Gene Smart, pulling a line from the rear of a truck, ducked just in time, the bullet plowing into his hand.

Five seconds later the youth had disappeared.

Although the fire department had been far better prepared for the riot than the police—bulletins had been issued six weeks before warning of the building up of a dangerous situation and detailing steps to be taken if it materialized—the department, while preparing to mass its equipment, had not been prepared to defend itself. Lacking police protection, it found its operations severely handicapped. Furthermore, the old water mains in the area were so clogged with silt that it was impossible to fight massive fires effectively—the water would just not come through the pipes in large enough quantities.

One hundred trucks and 26 ladder companies were being employed as, at midnight, southeast Los Angeles looked from the air like a city that had been subjected to pinpoint bombing. At almost a dozen different locations ranging in size from one to six blocks fires spotted the darkness, Central Ave. and Broadway coloring the night like a massive steel mill's open-hearth furnaces, tendrils of smoke silvered by the full moon. Despite almost total mobilization of its forces, the Los Angeles Fire Department, rated one of the best in the nation, was, like the police, no longer able to cope with the situation. Priorities had to be established. They were:

1) Valuable property; 2) Buildings in areas not previously fired; 3) Buildings remote from others; 4) Buildings partially destroyed that had caught fire again; 5) Automobiles; 6) Areas made untenable by rioters.

Such a system, however, was a hit-or-miss proposition, since all semblance of order and communications had been destroyed. With the number of alarms received since morning nearing the 1,000 mark, the entire alarm system, unable to handle such a load, had, almost literally, short-circuited itself. Lacking communication links to the police, firemen were relying, like the rioters, on transistor radios tuned to the police frequency to find out where the hot spots were. Sirens wailing, convoys of two or more trucks raced this way and that, crisscrossing the paths of other trucks and police cars, through some miracle avoiding the smashups that might have been expected. As one fire would be controlled firemen would, on the way back to the station, spot another; weaving from fire to fire, rigs would wind up miles from their original starting point. Some firemen worked 12 hours without respite. When they did arrive at some station far from the home base they were likely to find it locked and abandoned, and, having no key, would be unable to get in. At other stations the doors were left open, the buildings unguarded, anyone could have sacked and fired them.

(The next day, when the National Guard began arriving in force, 28 men were sent to guard one fire station. As soon as they arrived the engine company there was transferred to another station that had no guardsmen for protection.)

Although the Civil Defense Office and the Public Health Service had thousands of cots available, none were brought into the fire stations, and firemen, when they did get a break, were forced to sleep, soaking wet, covered with soot, stinking with the redolence of smoke, on hose beds and on concrete floors, heads cradled in their helmets.

While some men worked and worked, others, in the morass of disorganization, were never called out. The fire stations were islands in a sea of antagonism. A fireman went out to buy a paper and the Negro newsboy on the corner snapped at him, "No paper for you, white boy!"

At Vernon and Main a crew returned to the station to see a string of cars lined up at the gas station across the street, kids and young men filling gallon cans with which to set new fires.

One fire engine left the station a man short when he was unable to disengage himself from the john on time. Some distance away the driver was conked on the head and knocked out. The rig came to a halt. The tillerman in the rear was left a sitting duck atop his platform. Pelted again and again, he was seriously injured, the engine returning to the station under the guidance of the one remaining man.

The tension among the firemen, knowing that each time they left the station they were liable to be attacked, was as great as it had been among the police. The number of injuries due to the action of the mobs, as well as the normal hazards of fighting fires, was growing—one man had been hit by a beam, two more had fallen through a roof. Some men, plucking the tops off trashcans, went out with their makeshift shields like Roman charioteers. Others—although it was against the law—began arming themselves with guns. Standing atop their snorkels, some of them 70 feet high, they knew they would be sitting pigeons for any sniper intent on picking them off.

A three-block-long stretch of Broadway from 45th to 48th St. was ablaze on one side, the lights of cars along the Harbor Freeway, paralleling the street, providing an eerie, fireflylike effect as they flitted through the smoke and flames. A large, angry crowd jeered the firemen. "I wish I was white so I could be a fireman!" taunted a youth. One fireman was hit by a lightbulb, another had a monkey wrench cracked against his skull from point-blank range, a third received the benediction of a bottle of perfume.

"This is the hate that hate produced, white man!" said a youth with matter-of-fact venom.

At the corner of 47th St., tenants in an apartment building heard people screaming, "Fire! Fire! Get out of there!" Carrying whatever they could of their belongings, they tumbled out into the street. Among them was slight, 40-year-old Rita Rena Johnson, who had come to the city from New Orleans, La. As sparks shot out from the cleaning shop burning on the first floor of the building, and the wavering light highlighted the gold tooth in the front of her mouth, she wandered about dazedly.

For the past seven years she had been living as the common-law wife of a man named Leroy Robinson. Until the past spring they had been a quiet, unobtrusive couple, but then something had started happening to the mind of Rita Johnson.

Tenants would be startled to hear her run, screaming at the top of her voice, up and down the hallways in the middle of the night, as if she were being chased by some monster. Birdie Lee Pagoda, who lived in the apartment below her, would receive strange visits from her. Rita seemed to her like a small child, unable to perform even the slightest task without hesitation, unable to speak without twisting her hands about themselves.

"I want to say something, but I don't know how to say it!" she would plead desperately, attempting to wring a declaration from her mind.

Leroy Robinson had brought Rita dinner from the Thrifty Drug Store in the next block earlier in the evening, and then had gone out again. Now, as Rita stood gazing into the flames, an old memory apparently began tugging at her. The last her neighbors saw of her she was running down the side street, in the direction of the door to the building.

When Robinson returned, nobody could tell him what had happened to her, and he searched futilely. Not until precisely one week later did she reappear—beneath the rubble of the building, a skeleton whose flesh had been almost entirely consumed. By her side lay a ring that Robinson had never seen her wear.

Rita Rena Johnson was the seventh.

*   *   *

No sooner had the fire in a market been reduced than people would scramble inside once more to grab redhot cans and anything else that had not been burned. The police would come and hustle off a few. A police officer and a fireman, both breathing heavily and sweating profusely, stopped to take a moment's rest.

"Doesn't take much for them to revert to savagery, does it?" commented the officer.

"As a race they're just lazy and indolent!" the fireman replied.

"Put them in Beverly Hills and in five years it'd look just like Watts."

"It's about time we shipped them all back to Africa."

"I'd put in my thousand bucks to get them out of the country."

"I've never seen such a bunch of happy people! They're having a real good time with this riot!"

"What do you expect? With their simple minds they take it as an invitation to riot every time President Johnson and those other people make those statements about how they've been mistreated!"

Five Negro firemen appeared on the scene. They had been off duty and had returned voluntarily, without being called.

"Get out of here! We'll take over. You're only making things more difficult for us," they told the white firemen, who were glad to take their advice.

The five Negro firemen were almost 10 per cent of the total representation of Negroes on the Los Angeles Fire Department. Ten years before there had been 81 on a force of 1,500. Now only 59 were left on a department that had grown to 3,400, and of those 59 only 5 had come on during the past decade. In the last class of 50 there had been one Negro, and he had resigned before graduation.

Atty. Arnett Hartsfield, Jr., had won his battle to integrate the LAFD, but, as he himself is the first to say, the war has just about been lost.

By all criteria Hartsfield is a moderate among Negro leaders, and his experience is an indication why he and others like him are rapidly being pushed to the side in the onslaught of militant black nationalism. His personal battle had begun as a student at UCLA just prior to World War II when, despite a high rating and full qualification, he had been refused time and again admission to the advanced ROTC course, leading to an officer's commission. Only after the situation had become so embarrassing for university and army officials as to make it more painful to reject him for the fourth time without reason than to let him take the course, had he received his appointment, becoming the first Negro to obtain his commission at the southern branch of the state university.

Shipped to the Pacific as an infantry officer, he had never seen combat duty. Gen. Douglas MacArthur had refused to use Negroes in any but quartermaster tasks.

Upon his return, Hartsfield, already a fireman, had rejoined the department. A fireman's job, with a salary range of from $600 to $940 per month, is, in Los Angeles, ideal for the man who wants to moonlight or go to school—the men work one day, then have two days off. Hartsfield used his spare time to attend law school.

The department was totally segregated, all Negroes being assigned to two stations in the south central district. Fire Chief John Alderson was determined to keep it so, even though many Caucasian-manned stations were shorthanded, while the two Negro ones had men hanging from the rafters. Chief Alderson, a former Rhodes scholar and a highly respected man, was not a racist. He was against integration because it was his opinion that his men were not ready to eat, sleep, and live with Negroes for 24 hours at a time, and because he believed, therefore, that it would impair the morale and efficiency of the department. Integration, he thought, should wait for the time when all men had learned to live with each other as brothers—a position that Hartsfield and the NAACP did not accept, because it was like waiting for heaven.

Another key facet to the drive against segregation was the fact, that, as long as Negroes were restricted to two stations, there was, in effect, a quota system, not only for rookies but also for higher grades, since no Negro could make captain until a Negro captain had retired.

The issue began to come to a head with the election of Norris Poulson as mayor in 1952. The NAACP threatened to file suit, and since Poulson and Alderson were not on the best of terms politically, the new mayor backed the NAACP, and, in September, 1953, initiated steps toward the desegregation of the department. The battle between the chief and the mayor dragged on for more than a year, the mayor bolstered during this period by the Supreme Court's school desegregation decision and an opinion by the California attorney general that segregation in the fire department appeared to be a violation of state law; the chief backed by a militant majority of white firemen, ranging in estimates from 50 to 98 per cent,[1] and by various "instant" right-wing organizations, such as the Police and Fire Recall Committee. It was the end of 1954 before the mayor finally triumphed, and early 1955 before the first four Negroes were assigned to previously all-white stations.[2]

That was the end of the battle and the beginning of the war.

Although it was part of the integration agreement that Negro firemen would not try to force their way into nonduty activities of white firemen, that they would not attempt to control the television set, and that they would not go into the kitchen with the other men, at certain stations the Caucasians were not willing to let it go at that.

They would turn off the light in the room in which a Negro was sitting, then station at the switch a man who, every time the Negro turned it on, would flip it off again; so that there was nothing for the Negro to do but to sit in the dark. When the Negro went to bed they would come with dishpans and iron spoons and beat them in his ear. They would pick up his blanket, throw him into the air in it, and play "Catch the nigger baby!"

One Negro, Reynaldo Lopez, had been taking a shower when the captain and all of the white firemen appeared. "Don't stop to dress!" said the captain. "Get a scrub brush and clean every inch of the walls, floor and ceiling. Every time you decide to take a shower, notify me and this will be repeated."

Carl Cotterell, another Negro, found many of the whites willing to accept him. One day the captain approached him. "There are some men in my company who resent that other men will speak to you," he said. "So I want you to stop speaking to everybody so as not to create trouble!"

Cotterell refused, and was transferred as a troublemaker. The captain justified his action by asserting that, by continuing to talk to other men, Cotterell was stimulating argu-

[1] This should by no means be interpreted as meaning that that many of the firemen were prejudiced. Hundreds of them have, at one time or another, worked to help Negroes. What it did mean was that, having tremendous respect for the chief, they supported him and believed, like him, that integration could not work.

[2] Those readers who may be interested in the many ramifications of this dispute are referred to *The Mayor and the Fire Chief* by Frank P. Sherwood and Beatrice Mosley, published by the University of Alabama Press in 1959.

ments between white firemen, and that these were resulting in dissension.

One station, in particular, became known as The Hate House. The men took the pillow of Negro fireman Ernst Roberts into the toilet, defecated on it, and replaced it on his bed. They then waited with great merriment for bedtime to come, and made certain that, when Roberts went upstairs, all of the lights had been turned out. Roberts, knowing something was afoot, but never suspecting what, lay down on the bed, letting his head drop directly into the mess. The white firemen, lurking just outside the door, erupted into howls of laughter.

Instead of punishing these malefactors, Chief Alderson gave every indication that he was in sympathy with them. One captain who supported integration was disciplined for "falsifying records." Another resigned, charging that Alderson was waging a subtle war against those white firemen who wanted integration to work. In December of 1955 the chief ordered all Negro firemen resegregated in order to avoid, he said, "bloodshed by outside interests."

This was too much for the mayor and the fire commission —which, like the police commission, lacks effective power— and charges were filed with the civil service commission against the chief. Alderson, who was nearing retirement age anyway, submitted his resignation, and it was accepted.

By September of 1956 integration of all Negro firemen had been completed. While antagonism, obviously, did not diminish overnight, as the years passed certain of the ground rules were amended. Negroes were given the right to participate in all drills and examinations for higher grades, and were no longer assigned isolated beds and lockers.

Nevertheless, the silent war continued. Examination for jobs on the fire department was in two parts, written and oral, and, as it became evident that practically no Negroes were coming into the department, Hartsfield believed that this was due to prejudice on the part of the oral board, which contained among its members some of the same captains and chiefs who had resisted integration. After another struggle, he and civil rights organizations succeeded in having the oral examination abolished.

This changed nothing. Negroes who applied failed the written exam, and those who could have passed failed to apply —for many there are better opportunities elsewhere, and others, cognizant of the battle that had taken place, did not want to go where they were not wanted.

On another front Hartsfield had more success. Following integration it became the practice, when a Negro passed the examination for captain, to transfer white firemen, higher on the list, into his station so as to prevent him from receiving his promotion and being placed in command of white firemen. An agreement was reached in the early 1960's to discontinue this practice. Now more and more of the Negroes—54 of the 59 on the department having more than 12 years service—have made or are close to making captain. This is creating a peculiar situation in which there soon will be many Negro captains but practically no Negro firemen, and, ultimately, no Negro firemen whatsoever on the department.[3]

One of the 59, Frank J. Harrison, was the only Negro fireman in the half dozen engine companies that began, at 10:30 p.m., to fight the fire at the Shop-Rite Market at 120th St. and Central Ave., the place where, two hours earlier, Mac Benton had met the youth combining the liquor and shoe stores in his car. At first the firemen had police protection, but soon the officers were called away. Cars drove back and forth across the hose lines in an attempt to sever them. Sporadically rocks and bottles curved out of the jeering, cursing crowd. One fireman, Gene Plotkin, employed the lifegun—a tool firing a steel projectile and used to hurl a line to the top of a building—to hold them at bay. As the fire came under control the area became darker, and by 12:30 a.m., as the men were winding up their task, virtually the only illumination came from the headlights of the trucks, and from the moon, hanging ghostlike over the ruins. One hose line remained on the sidewalk in front of the market. As a captain and three men began picking it up, a 15-foot ornamental arch on top of the 18-foot-high front wall collapsed inward, pushing the wall out.

"Get out of there!" the battalion chief cried. The captain and one of the men managed to jump free. The other two, Roger Laxague and Warren Tilson, were pinned beneath the wall.

Within seconds some of the same Negroes who had been standing, crying "Go to hell, white devils!" were clawing at

---

[3] Of 16,000 municipalities in the United States, only 62 employed Negro firemen in 1953.

the rubble with bare hands in an attempt to free the trapped men. Laxague, pinned in the gutter along which a rivulet of water was rushing, was moving and talking, yet slowly but inexorably beginning to drown. Jacks were positioned beneath the wall. Inch by inch it was raised until there was space enough for Harrison and Malen Jacobs, a white fireman, to wriggle beneath the rubble and carefully pull Laxague free.

Tilson, 31, was not so lucky. He was the eighth.

32   The Deluge

As the evening progressed, the riot, previously confined to the east side of the Harbor Freeway, moved across to the west. At 11 p.m. 26-year-old Don Lockhart, who was returning home after having gone to the drug store to buy aspirin for his baby, was passing the Academy Appliance and TV Store at 61st and Vermont Ave., just south of John Muir Junior High School. There was general confusion, some people running in and out of the store, others watching or, like Lockhart, simply passing by. Police officers arriving on the scene saw two men carrying a console television set. Ordered to halt, the two, Julius Riggins and John E. Kirk, both from Althimer, Ark., began running toward a white Chevrolet. The police opened fire.

As the shots resounded and Kirk caught a bullet in the leg, some of the bystanders ran. Running in such a situation is dangerous—one is likely to be shot. On the other hand, not running is not an ideal solution either, since the police assume, in many instances correctly, that anyone in the vicinity of a looted store has no business being there. Lockhart, having dropped to the pavement at the first shot, was beginning cautiously to stir, preparatory to rising, when he heard an officer's voice, "Move, and you'll get your ass blown full of holes!"

He was arrested and charged with burglary, first for taking a lamp, then, when it developed the store did not carry lamps, for taking a television set. His bail was set at $5,000, and he spent the next week in jail. Although the charges were ultimately dismissed, there is no way for him to recoup the lost time or lost money, and he now has, of course, a record.

Shortly thereafter the Home Furniture Store in the next block was set afire, and when Officers Ronald Borst and Larry Bradfield passed by at 12:15 a.m. a fireman high atop a ladder was pouring streams of water into the building. In the next block the officers, both of whom had participated in the gunfight at 88th and Broadway five hours earlier, saw two cars, their trunks open, parked in front of a Pep Boys Auto and Hudson Department store, numerous people passing back and forth through the broken windows. Borst collared one of the looters and, his right hand holding the revolver, was searching him with his left when he heard footsteps crunching on glass. Whirling, he saw, four feet inside the store, a figure moving toward him. As he yelled for him to halt the man jumped through the glass.

Bradfield caught sight of the action just as Borst was knocked sprawling. The man sprinted south on Vermont Ave. Following him, Bradfield fired one shot from his shotgun, but lost him in the trees and bushes surrounding the junior high school. Afraid to stalk him amidst the shrubbery, the officer walked along the hedge. Then, seeing a figure dart from tree to tree, he fired again, but missed again. A moment later the man emerged, running, into the open directly in front of the steps leading to the main entrance.

Bradfield fired once more, and Montague Whitmore, a husky, 37-year-old Texan, went down. His prior criminal record was minor.

He was the ninth.

Inside the school, being used for a National Guard staging area, troops thought, as bullets and pellets whizzed about them, that they were being subjected to a sniper attack.

The two cars, which had caught the officers' attention in the first place, were driven off during the confusion.

*   *   *

On Western Ave., a mile to the west of USC, Milton S. Ackerman had been besieged in his apartment above the

Friedman Furniture Co. since 10:30 p.m. Ackerman had
come to Los Angeles from San Bernardino and obtained
employment as a furniture salesman in the store only two
days before. At 9 p.m. he locked the store and set the burglar alarm. An hour and a half later two cars with four
boys and two girls stopped in front, and, sitting by his window, he heard one girl say, "Baby, I'd sure like that stereo
there!"

No sooner said than done—one of the boys kicked in the
window, out came the stereo set and two large lamps, and
then, as Ackerman said, "the deluge started," carload after
carload of "souvenir hunters" coming by and helping themselves.

Having no telephone in the apartment and afraid to ven-
ture out, Ackerman was able to do nothing but watch, hoping no one would set fire to the store. Not until an hour
later did he see the first prowl car. As he went downstairs
to meet it, it drove off.

Going inside the store, he turned on all the lights and
called the store owner, who called the police, and reported
back that the police said that they had no men available
and were unable to come down, and "I'm not either!"

Ackerman, no longer young, feeling somewhat like a condemned man awaiting his executioners, turned on the one
remaining radio in the store and waited. A Negro man from
across the street came and kept him company, and together
they went back upstairs. Ackerman was nodding when, an
hour or two later, he was jerked awake by shot after shot.
Shouts and curses, the sounds of crashing glass and furniture
made it seem as if a number of outsized cats and mice were
clattering through the reaches of the building. Looking out
of the window, Ackerman could see policemen running back
and forth in the street, firing through the remnants of the
plate glass window. Inside the store five Negroes were
darting back and forth. Five, six, seven, eight . . . twenty,
twenty-one, twenty-two—the number of shots mounted.
Thirty-year-old Allen Arnett Browning, a construction boss
at the new Music Center project downtown, scrambled out
of an office, and, as he did, was shot and wounded by Officer
Dexter G. O'Day. Browning claimed that the only reason he
had ducked into the store was to get out of the way of the
shooting.

Although O'Day and his fellow officers had been on the

job for more than eight hours and had been in the midst of the area being looted, these were the first arrests they made.

*   *   *

In a straight line three miles to the east of the Friedman Furniture Co. is the intersection of Vernon and McKinley Aves. As Officer Ronald D. Rouse and his partners passed the S and L Market, they could see the glass broken out, the doors wide open, several heads, illuminated by a dim light in back, ducking back and forth inside. While the driver of the patrol car made a U-turn, Rouse jumped out. Two men emerged from the market, running toward a white 1959 Thunderbird. As Rouse yelled for them to halt, one, carrying a box of canned soft drinks, dropped it and sprinted into an alley. The other continued toward the Thunderbird, which was full of bottles of wine and beer, and tv dinners.

Rouse and his partner each fired one shot from their 12-gauge shotguns. Tall, 22-year-old Thomas Ezra Owens, an ex-marine and motion picture projector operator, fell, fatally wounded.

Five minutes later Rouse heard a girl ask, "Is that my brother?"

Thomas Ezra Owens was the tenth.

Ten blocks directly to the north, just a block from where slightly less than two hours before the two firemen, Smart and Myers, had been shot, Thomas W. Hooker and Michael Bergman, together with two other officers, heard the loud ring of a burglar alarm. A large group of Negroes were standing in front of a liquor store, the window of which had been shattered. As the police car came to a halt in the middle of the street, Hooker jumped out and shouted at a youth emerging from the doorway of the store with a box full of liquor in his arms. Dropping the box, the youth took off. Hooker was starting after him when, out of the corner of his eye, he noted another man reaching into his pocket—he whirled to cover him. Bergman, as he was still sliding across the seat of the car, fired one shot at the fleeing youth as he turned the corner into the next street.

For the next few minutes all of the officers were occupied searching the large number of people in front of the store. Nothing was found on any of them. They were admonished to go home and stay off the streets. That done, Bergman and

Hooker went around the corner, looking for the youth who had gotten away.

Two cars were parked in front of a barbecue stand. The first was empty, but in the second the two occupants were calmly eating sandwiches.

"All right. What's going on here?" Hooker demanded. When it appeared that not very much of anything was, he gave the pair the same advice he had offered the people at the store—go home!

The two officers then left.

Vincent Alexander, who lived on 36th St., had gone downstairs a few minutes earlier to talk to Claude Chaisson, the owner of a service station and garage. As they were standing, watching the action, a youth had come sprinting around the corner. Simultaneously there had been a shot, and they had seen the youth stumble and roll under the second of the two cars parked at the curb. Alexander thought that the shot had missed, and that the boy was hiding beneath the car. Of that opinion, he went home, where 15 minutes later, at 1:45 a.m., his mother suggested he go see if the boy was still beneath the car.

The car had driven off, but a body was lying in the gutter where it had been parked. Slight, 17-year-old Carlton Elliott, a massive wound in his chest, had been killed instantly.

He was the eleventh.

33   The Kamikaze Attack

Not until shortly before 11 p.m., more than 12 hours after Chief Parker had requested the Guard, and almost six hours after the first troops had reported to the armories, did the National Guard presence begin to manifest itself.

The first unit to move out was the Glendale contingent, which, having the year before received semisecret riot training—semisecret because of the political connotations—was

272 THE FIRES OF DISCONTENT

considered the shock troop. When it left the Glendale armory between 7:30 and 8 p.m. 500 Caucasian citizens assembled there cheered.

It was almost 9 o'clock before these troops reached the Manchester Playground staging area, located just west of the Harbor Freeway, within a block or two of where Mac Benton had watched the mob surrounding Oak Park Hospital. The Glendale troops had a relatively easy passage, but others —having to rely on service station maps, since neither the Guard nor the police were able to supply any of a more detailed nature—became lost on the freeway. One unit from northern California, arriving on Saturday, got itself so tangled in the maze of the city that it did not get into action until 8 o'clock Sunday night. Another was brought to a dead halt by a guard at a toll bridge—he refused passage to the convoy until it paid up, and none of the officers had authorization or money to pay. Signal Corps line-of-sight radios would not function in the city, a problem that was solved later to some degree by placing them atop tall buildings. Officers, concerned about the minimum quantities of ammunition available, were startled to hear the Los Angeles police department inquire if it might borrow 2,000 rounds of .38 and 2,000 rounds of 12-gauge shotgun ammunition.

(This was one of many ironic situations that developed. There was, unbeknownst to the police, within the riot area itself, a warehouse containing $100,000 worth of ammunition. Yet, ultimately, 10,000 shotgun shells had to be flown in from Pittsburgh.)

Except for the Glendale contingent, other troops had to be given emergency riot training as they arrived. Some, trained with the M-14 rifle but now armed with the older M-1, had to be instructed on the functioning of the latter. Yet, according to National Guard officers, the principal delay in getting the troops into action was the lack of planning by the police.

"We've been trained in putting people in the field and to operate, the police weren't and we had to wait on them. When we did get together with them they still didn't know what they were going to do. Although they could operate individually effectively, it was chaos when more than one carload was involved."

A command post had been set up by the police at the 97th St. school, just off the freeway, and it was from this

that the actual field operations were controlled. A high-ranking Guard officer described the situation there Friday night
as "Gangs of people milling around. They didn't have any
operations plan as to what they were going to do next.
They had men just sitting around the hallway and out in
back, and when a call would come in they would throw half
a dozen of them in a couple of cars, poke the shotguns out
of the window and away they'd go!"

(In all fairness to the police, it must be pointed out that,
lacking the manpower to institute any kind of control, there
wasn't much else they could do.)

It was decided that—since, from a logistics standpoint it
would be the simplest operation—the first assignment for the
troops would be to replace police officers as a security force
in Watts. As the convoy moved out on its three-mile journey
many of the guardsmen became, for the first time, aware of
the seriousness of the business they were engaged in—police
standing with shotguns pointed at the heads of Negroes, Negroes, loaded with contraband, walking unperturbed between
the vehicles of the convoy, firemen crouched beneath their
trucks as shots reverberated about them, avenues of warlike
destruction never before seen in an American city.

The arrival in Watts was an even greater shock. Beyond
the police station, where the Guard command post was established, 103rd St. was a wasteland. The illumination provided by the backdrop of street lights that, beyond the rav-
aged area, were still working, by the glowing fields of embers
in the burned-out stores, and by the garish gas jets, gave to
the towers of water from the hydrants a semblance of un-
capped oil wells. The side streets were pitch black and deserted. Ammunition had been issued only to the squad leaders,
and, as guardsmen took their positions between 10:30 and
11 p.m., they were understandably nervous. It was a nervous-
ness that was not eased when, at midnight, from a Cadillac
speeding down 103rd St., four random shots were fired into
the police station. Following this incident, Lt. Col. Thomas
Haykin, the commander of the battalion, set up a perimeter
defense, establishing roadblocks and sending guards up to
the roofs of buildings.

Between 10 and 11 p.m., it occurred to Gen. Hill that in
the northern sector the troops might best be employed in a
block-by-block sweep of the area. A problem developed because the LAPD lacked any kind of powerful public-address

system; and Lt. Col. Irving Taylor was forced to use a hand-held bullhorn, which, because of its limited range, was hardly satisfactory in ordering the people off the streets.

Those found with stolen goods were ordered to walk ahead of the trucks until the arrival of a police patrol. One woman, carrying a large sack, was crossing the street in front of a looted grocery store when she looked over her shoulder at the guardsmen, tripped over a fire hose in the street, and fell, sending canned goods from the sack rolling in all directions. The police arrived, made her pick up the goods, had her return them to the store, and then forcefully told her to go home.

The first sweep concentrated on a mile-square area directly to the west of South Park. This was completed, in a little more than an hour, at about 12:30 a.m. The troops then moved over to Avalon Blvd., the next objective, on the east side of the park. They were being accompanied by a number of reporters and photographers, as well as by several state officials and National Guard officers, including Gen. Hill himself.

A half dozen blocks south on Avalon Blvd. from Santa Barbara Ave., where the troops were forming a skirmish line across the street, 42-year-old Charlie Edward Rhone and his friend, Brooks Berry, were staggering out of the Tom-Tom Café. Rhone, big and husky but pleasant and easy-going, had served honorably in the army and lived the feast-and-famine existence of the construction laborer: when he worked, he averaged $130 a week; when he didn't, he made nothing. He had been raised largely by his grandmother in Alabama, and he had been married once, briefly. Since then he had lived on and off with various girl friends. Between 1951 and 1965 he had been arrested 15 times in four states, mostly on misdemeanor charges, but once for the sale of marijuana, an offense for which he had served four years in prison.

Berry had come by in his 1956 Buick early that afternoon to Rhone's place of work. Together they had decided to drive out to Cabrillo Beach to go fishing. They had done more drinking than fishing, however, and, upon returning to the city, had decided to stop off at the café to get something to eat—while continuing to drink. Rhone had had at least a half pint of liquor and two beers, and quite likely more. Berry, so drunk that he could not see, asked Rhone to drive the car; which was, literally, asking the blind to drive the blind.

Since Rhone could see very little in any case, he did not bother to turn on the headlights. As he swung the car out onto Avalon Blvd. at 60 miles an hour, he was in a direct collision course with the National Guard skirmish line, now only four blocks to the north.

As the troops advanced with fixed bayonets they were accompanied by a number of U.S. marshals and sheriff's deputies, and were followed by several two-and-half-ton trucks and jeeps. They were meeting little opposition. A block away a car with its headlights on was approaching slowly. Suddenly, a Buick, without lights, swerved around it and came screaming down onto the skirmish line.

"My God!" someone exclaimed. Someone else just had time enough to cry, "Look out! Get out of the way!" when the Buick, its brakes taking hold at the last moment and sending puffs of blue smoke up from the wheels, skidded sideways through the line, knocking Sgt. Wayne Stewart of Long Beach 60 feet beneath a truck. As the Buick crashed to a halt against the side of a marshal's car, marshals and sheriff's deputies weaved shot after shot—an estimated 50 to 60 in all—about it, sending everyone scurrying for cover. At least ten of the shots hit the car.

When the firing died down Rhone could be seen slumped behind the wheel. Everyone assumed he was dead. In actuality, although he had suffered a fractured ankle, he had not been hit—he had just passed out cold. Berry, by some miracle also untouched, was yanked out of the car by the marshals. His face was ground against the pavement. One officer pulled his head back, so that he was staring upward into the lights. "You've just committed murder!" he said. "You have a right to remain silent. Do you have anything to say?"

"No comment," Berry mumbled, staring around befuddledly.

Sgt. Stewart had been injured seriously but not critically, suffering a concussion and a fractured leg. To the orderly Caucasian mind, the attempt to run down the skirmish line could not have been anything but deliberate, and Gen. Hill likened it to a kamikaze attack. He immediately ordered that all guardsmen be warned, and that ammunition be issued to everyone. It was a decision that was to have a far-reaching effect during the course of the next several days.

Different commanders viewed the problem differently. One told his men, "Hold your fire! Feel sure you've got the right man, because there are a lot of hotheads, they drink a lot, and some things don't get through to them right away." He had his men fire into the air rather than directly at vehicles, and they managed to stop all within their area.

Lt. Col. Robert Dove instructed his men they could not shoot unless they specifically knew whom they were shooting at and why. "You cannot fire unless you are in personal danger."

However, he believed, "There isn't such a thing as a warning shot. You're either the boss or you're not going to shoot. If you're going to shoot, you're going to kill!"

In Watts, Col. Haykin had been warned by the police that if any cars penetrated the roadblocks, chances were that they would fire upon the troops or throw Molotov cocktails. When the guardsmen heard this, when they were advised—as they were issued ammunition—that one of their fellows had been run down in a kamikaze attack and police had shot and killed the driver, and when they themselves could hear numerous shots, with some bullets twanging close to them, they naturally became more and more apprehensive.

Lacking any kind of equipment, such as street barriers, to set up their roadblocks, the troops found it necessary to improvise. At Wilmington and 103rd Sts. a crudely lettered sign said: TURN LEFT OR GET SHOT. At Compton Ave. and 102nd St., just in back of the Watts police station and opposite a white Catholic Church, a trashcan and an overturned table indicated a roadblock. Behind it were a dozen guardsmen, as well as several police officers. The street lights on Compton Ave. were still functioning, but there were no flares for illumination.

A few minutes before 2 a.m. an old pickup truck came chugging along. It stopped at the barricade, then started up again, and, in the opinion of Lt. John Ewing, a Los Angeles *Times* advertising representative in civilian life, seemed headed straight for him. Several men shouted a warning to the driver. When he did not heed it, all fired, the pickup wobbling drunkenly into another car and pushing it against the wall of an office building.

Fifty-five-year old Ben Bennie Steel, a flesh wound in his leg, staggered out of the cab of the truck, and was ordered up against the wall of the building to be searched. He coughed repeatedly, and—although he did not know it because he had neither the money nor the inclination to go to a doctor—was suffering from advanced tuberculosis, presenting a greater danger to the guardsmen as he stood there than he ever had in the cab of his truck.

Hardly had an army ambulance departed with him, when, at 2:10, a Rambler station wagon halted in front of the barricade. As Cpl. Richard Martinez went to interrogate the driver, he could see the headlights of another car approaching.

Albert "Al" Flores, Sr., 40, his brother Richard, 37, and Richard's two teenaged sons, Ricky, 14, and Ronald, 13, had gone out to get a late snack, and then decided to check on Richard's in-laws in the area. Albert Flores had been drinking, and his breath smelled of alcohol and onions.

Squinting, he could make out, as he drove south on Compton Ave., some kind of barricade consisting of several objects strewn about in the middle of the street. A car had been halted at the barrier; beyond it were the headlights of a truck that seemed to have crashed.

Momentarily, Flores braked his own car. He did not quite understand what it was that was happening ahead. His headlights picked up the figure of a man waving at him. He feared it was a trap that had been set up by rioters, and in his confusion he could not make up his mind whether or not he should stop. Finally, he pushed down on the accelerator.

Cpl. Martinez had just told the driver of the Rambler to turn around when he saw the maroon Mercury, accelerating, swinging around the barrier. There were tense shouts of "Halt!" Moments later the muzzle flashes of a dozen guns split the darkness, most of the police and a half dozen of the guardsmen firing. The Mercury, veering out of control, rammed into a light standard.

Inside, the car was a gory mess. Capt. Michael Patzakis, the battalion surgeon, rushing over from the command post, found Flores dead—he had been hit four times, in the arm, eye, cheek, and chest. On the front seat next to him, Richard, critically injured, was bleeding profusely from wounds in the back and leg. In the back seat the two boys had blood welling from numerous cuts caused by shards of flying glass. As the surgeon worked desperately, more than one of the guardsmen went quietly into the darkness and threw up.

It was a busy half hour for Capt. Patzakis. In addition to the wounded occupants of the car, he had to give aid to two guardsmen. Pvt. Larry Mitchell had caught a dum-dum .22

in his hand, and Cpl. Percival had been nicked in the back by the ricochet of a spent bullet.

Mitchell and Percival were the only two guardsmen hit by sniper bullets during the entire riot, although, somewhat later, a private was thought to have been shot in Will Rogers Park. As it turned out, he had merely stumbled and injured his shoulder. Another trooper, a Los Angeles police officer by profession, had the misfortune of blowing off part of his thumb with his own .45. A sergeant shot himself in the leg.

It was, as one Guard officer said, "surprising that not more police and national guardsmen were hit. The snipers seemed to close their eyes, and to have trouble firing in the dark."

A lieutenant colonel had a different idea: "If 50 rounds are fired one way, 50 rounds have to land, and somebody is going to fire back. We would get sniper fire, and police would point to the top of a building and say it's coming from over there—open up on that building. I believe lots of sniper fire was due to false reports."

That, however, was an afterthought, and at 3 o'clock Saturday morning in Watts it seemed very real. It seemed very real and menacing to men who had arrived in a strange and hostile district in the middle of the night, who knew that there had been a kamikaze attack and that a deputy sheriff had been killed in a gun battle, who heard that "all white hats and blue uniforms" had been marked for extinction by snipers, and who were warned over and over again by police about the violent and unpredictable nature of the people with whom they were dealing.

An hour after the shooting at 102nd and Compton, a white 1959 Oldsmobile failed to stop at another roadblock, this one at Wilmington and 103rd Sts. As a fusillade of bullets poured into it, it crashed through a service station and collided with a frame house beyond. One of the two Negroes was wounded in the shoulder, the other in the neck, and, as they were held at gunpoint, kneeling on the ground, one of them cried in rage, "You'd better kill me, you white motherfuckers, kill me! Or I'm gonna kill you!"

The Oldsmobile contained no contraband, but several cars driven by white youths from LaPuente, a nearby community, did—they were loaded with Molotov cocktails. The most intriguing catch was a Caucasian who had in his car a nearly empty gallon jug of wine—and a bikini-clad girlfriend. Shortly before dawn two Caucasian reporters ran into a volley of fire at a roadblock. Two bullets shattered the windshield of their car—and their nerves—but otherwise they escaped unscathed.

At the command post on 103rd St., "things really started coming to life," as one officer put it, "and we were all looking for nice holes in the sidewalk." One building with a national guardsman on top of it burst into flame, and, as he scrambled for safety, a bullet spun out from behind the wall of fire. Lt. Col. Russell W. Porteous, a battalion commander, was making a telephone call from a booth as he had never envisioned—flat on his stomach.

At 4 a.m. there was a flurry of shots, ricocheting off a two-story brick store building across the street from the police station. Pfc. Douglas Warren Mercer was stationed on the building's roof. At the sound of the shots, he ran forward. As he looked down, he could see directly in front and below him, crouched against the side of the station, several police officers. They had their guns unholstered, and were pointing them toward the roof of the Villa Maria Hotel—that same hotel which the Student Committee for the Improvement of Watts had tried to get the city to purchase for an extension to the library.

Shifting his glance slightly to the left, Pfc. Mercer's eyes focused on a small iron balcony accessible only from the second-story hallway of the hotel. Standing in the doorway of that balcony, at about 30 yards distance, Mercer was startled to see a T-shirt-clad man.

He came to an immediate, and what seemed to him obvious, conclusion—the man must be the sniper the police were looking toward. Placing his rifle to his shoulder, Mercer fired a "warning shot" into the wall of the building next to where the man was standing.

The man moved out of sight into the hallway. A few seconds later he reappeared. Mercer believed he intended to shoot at the officers in the street.

Mercer fired again, the .30-caliber bullet careening completely through the skull of 41-year-old Andrew Houston, Jr., a spindly six-footer from Louisiana. He was, as it turned out, unarmed.

Albert Flores, Sr., had been the twelfth, and Andrew Houston, Jr., was the fourteenth.

34   The Goddam Congo!

The thirteenth was 23-year-old Theophile Albert O'Neal, whose body was discovered by firemen at Jefferson Blvd. and Denker Ave. on the west side at 2:30 a.m. A .38-caliber slug was in his head, and a trail of blood led to Sam's Liquor Store at 1650 W. Jefferson Blvd.

A witness, Harry Clay of 900 E. 28th St., said, "They broke the window in Sam's Liquor Store and five minutes later it was empty. Twenty minutes later the police came and started shooting at people in the store. Three people in the store were shot, and one was killed."

According to police, however, they knew nothing about the shooting, and the death was listed as a criminal homicide by person or persons unknown.

Four blocks directly to the north, at a market at 1552 West Adams Blvd., the riot was creeping to within shouting distance of the Santa Monica Freeway. There Elvin Wharton, 39 years old, lived on a disability pension of $100 a month. Born in St. Louis, he had served in the army and been discharged in 1950. The next year, while working at the army medical depot in Missouri, he had had his back broken in a motorcycle accident and lost most of the use of his legs. Nevertheless, he managed to get around with the aid of a pair of hand crutches, and, being of a self-reliant nature, refused to depend on anyone, living by himself in a rented room. He had, briefly, taken an apprentice course in auto parts repairing, and for two years had tried running a pool hall in San Francisco. During the last four years he had, however, withdrawn more and more, spending most of his time reading and, to a considerable extent, drinking. When he saw a mob breaking into the store, he slowly followed after them, and "accidentally" stepped in.

He was stuffing liquor bottles into his pockets when someone suddenly yelled, "Police," and everyone scattered. Everyone, of course, but Wharton, who could only move foot by foot.

The police officers spotted him standing behind a counter. On the counter lay a meat cleaver. As the officers came toward him, one saw his hand slide across the counter toward the cleaver. The officers said that they called upon him to surrender, and that he replied, "Fuck you!"

Wharton says that all he remembers is a red flash.

The .38-caliber slug entered his chest, and spun out of his back. By some quirk it touched no vital organ, and he survived.

*   *   *

About an hour earlier, a few blocks away at Adams and Western, Baby Doe Simmons [1] had picked up a white trick. The character was driving a Mustang and had a honey voice and a young face with old lines. She figured that if she treated him right he might be good for 25, 30 bucks—maybe more.

Baby Doe wasn't just pretty. She was really good looking. Light skin with chestnut brown hair, an oval face with full but not thick lips—if she'd been Caucasian she would have been competing in the Miss Teenage America contest or been a model for *Seventeen*, but since Negro girls know they can't make it into the Miss America contest or the Miss Universe contest or the Rose Parade in Pasadena, she was out hustling.

The trick's name was Charles Tandy—she peeked at the car registration to get that—and it turned out that before doing anything he wanted to talk. If they'd been in some motel on the south side, the operator wouldn't have stood for it—he had an intercom to every room and a timer he set exactly for 20 minutes. When 10 minutes was left, the speaker in the room would boom out: "Ten minutes!" Then it would announce: "Five minutes!" It was like a countdown. When the five minutes was up it would say, "Now." And if *now* hadn't come yet, you had to pay overtime.

But on the west side they kept up the pretense that they weren't in the business, so they didn't bug you that much.

What Tandy wanted to explain to her was that he was originally from the South, but that he wasn't prejudiced at all. . . .

[1] See pages 45–48 and 138–41.

"Just being here with you like this proves that, doesn't it? Why, when I was a boy we had Nigra families living within a block of us, and I used to play with little black boys and girls all the time. I came from a poor family, and we lived in a little frame house and didn't have much more than the darkies. But now I'm driving a fine car, and my wife drives a fine car, and we have three fine children. I don't mind telling you I'm making more than $20,000 a year as the sales manager for an important company. So you see, my humble beginnings haven't handicapped me at all. Not at all. Why is it that you people, generation after generation, can't get out of the hole you're in? What makes you so slothful and irresponsible?"

"It's because we're no fucking good!" said Baby Doe. "Now, come on, Charley, take your pants down!"

Forty-five minutes later Charles Tandy was fast asleep. Baby Doe was going to wake him, but then she got a better idea. Slipping her dress on over her head, she took the ignition keys of the Mustang out of his pants pocket—man, she liked that car! Carefully she went out into the court. Stepping into a telephone booth, she dialed her mother's number. She hoped her brother Cotter was at home.

Cotter had gotten his share of the loot from 103rd St. in the afternoon. After that they'd partied it up in the projects, and by nightfall, after two days of excitement and practically no sleep, he'd been ready to call it quits. When he heard the telephone chiming, he sleepily padded toward it.

"Hey, cat!" Baby Doe said. "I got us some real classy wheels. How about spinning 'em a little?"

The two of them were spinning up Vermont Ave. when they came to a complex of stores that were all busted up, people running in and out. As they passed one shop, Baby Doe saw on a mannequin in the show window the most beautiful dress she had ever seen in her life—it was low cut, satiny white with sequins.

"Hey, man!" she said. "Hold up!"

She got out of the Mustang, carefully climbed past the jagged remnants of the plate glass window, and tried to take the dress off the mannequin. It kept sticking as she tugged, giving her a real hard time, and while she was still at it, she heard a shout of: "Cops!"

People were running in all directions, there was the *bang-*

bang of shots, so she just grabbed the mannequin under her arm and headed for the car.

"Let's make it, cat!" she cried to Cotter, who had the engine running.

She had just stuffed the mannequin into the back seat, and was sliding into the front, when the policeman, revolver pointing straight at Cotter's head, appeared at the window on the driver's side.

Charles Tandy did not believe in being vindictive, and so told the police that he would not press charges against Baby Doe for taking the car.

*   *   *

Flip Borrago was really scoring. He'd started smoking grass at 5 o'clock in the afternoon, and everywhere he went somebody offered him a drink, there was so much free liquor you couldn't have sold a pint for the price of a Pepsi Cola. With all that grass and booze in him he was really flying. He was so high it would have taken him a day just to land. They were all out there jiving—the Slausons who had no soul, the Farmers who were the worst, and even one of the Roman Twenties with the gold ring in his ear—tonight it didn't make any difference what you were, so long as you were blood. Sure, they'd done one blood in, but that was just for kicks, some old drunk bastard who looked like he was going to walk straight into a fire. There was only one place in the whole block that hadn't been in flames. That was a laundromat. So they'd taken him, shoved him into one of those big dryers, and pressed the button. Round and round he'd gone. When the thing had finally stopped, he'd tumbled out right into the path of the police. He told them he was an astronaut who'd just come from the moon, but that made no difference, they'd taken him in anyway.

Somewhere along the line Flip remembered heading for the big Sears store after he heard on the police radio that they'd opened it up, but when he got there *the man* had arrived ahead of him, and there must have been a million people shuffling around, doing nothing. They never did get anything. He remembered being on a roof some place where people were looting. These three cops came, jabbing and pushing the people against the walls. There he stood on that roof bigger than old Wyatt Earp, and put a shot from the .45 right at the feet of the fuzz. When they turned, he had that cannon leveled right at them, and he said, "Let them go!"

And the police didn't say a word, but climbed back into their car and drove off.

After a while somebody said that the Hell's Angels were coming, so he and a bunch went down to the freeway and waited for them. One of the blood had stolen a shotgun from a police car, and they were really ready for them. But they never did show.

He was over at a furniture store trying to figure out how he could get an eight-foot hi-fi out when somebody came and threw a bottle and *boom*—there went the hi-fi. It was like they'd turned on a big Christmas tree. He was so mad he ran after the car, pumping shot after shot from the .45 at it, blood or no blood. He was still standing there, grieving, when the police came, and said, "Stop!"

He asked, "What's the matter, officer, I'm just standing here, lighting my cigarette from the fire."

"Put your hands up against that wall!"

Flip looked at the officer, and then at the wall; then back at the officer. "You're crazy!" he said. "That wall's on fire. You might just as well shoot me!"

Instead he lay down on the pavement, in the glass and all, and while the officers were rounding up the other people, went to sleep.

*   *   *

Police Officer Frank Pinter's eyes were so red it was almost as if the fires he kept seeing were burning there right in his pupils. He no longer had any sense of time or location, one place looked to him just like another, and he couldn't have said whether it had been at the liquor store that they'd picked up the little white boy who turned out to be a Negro albino, or whether it had been at a market, or whether it was in the market that Errol Lawrence had shot the dog that jumped them, or whether that might not have been in the furniture store with the crazy, revolving light that made the people running back and forth each seem to have six shadows so that you would grab for someone and find you were grabbing air. It was insane. A good portion of the rioters were hopped up, or drunk, or both—in one place a 16-year-old boy who couldn't have weighed more than 125 pounds had launched himself from a chandelier like Tarzan. Zoom-

ing through and out of a plate glass window feet first he
had landed squarely on an officer, they had both gone down
in a heap of jagged glass. Other officers had grabbed the
boy, pulled him away and pummeled him as he snaked
through the glass. He was bleeding from numerous cuts, but
it was the funniest thing that had ever happened to him, all
those cops and all those clubs and all that blood sticky on
his skin—he had laughed and laughed, and finally one of
the officers had said, "Christ, man, the son of a bitch is
crazy! Let him go!" So they had abandoned him on the scene.

Pinter saw officers do things that they would have gotten
busted for in 10 minutes in normal times. Lawrence said,
"I've been waiting all my life for something like this to happen! I'm gonna make mincemeat out of some of those
motherfuckers while I've got the chance!"

Out of all the hundreds of officers, there were perhaps a
couple of dozen like him, and what could Pinter say? It was
now a war, and in war you had to fight with the people on
your side, good and bad—the Negroes had started it, and
they were only getting what they deserved.

The inside of one store was burning with a greenish fire
—Pinter had never seen fire burn with so many colors as he
had the past few hours. Behind the fire a head was ducking
back and forth. . . .

"Shit!" said Lawrence. "I'm not going in there!"

He fired his shotgun through the fire and the head disappeared. Perhaps he had scored a hit and perhaps not, there
wasn't time to worry about such things.

A television set sat on the sidewalk and they figured somebody had left it there and was going to pick it up, so they
staked it out. Within 10 minutes there came a car with a
couple of guys. They drove past it, hesitated, then backed up.
As they loaded the set into the car, Lawrence and Pinter
nabbed them, then got another patrol car, which already had
a couple of prisoners in it, to take them down to the station. After that they staked out the tv set again, in 15 minutes here came another car cruising by, stopping, the guys
getting out and starting to heft the set. . . .

"That's one way to get them off the streets!" said Lawrence.

They went over to the National Guard assembly area at
Riis High School, where the helicopters were landing and
taking off, and the kids in the green fatigues were standing

around. One group was being given training in how to drive back rioters with fixed bayonets.

"What's it like out there?" one of the soldiers asked.

"Like the goddam Congo!" Lawrence answered him. "You've come to the right place, my boy. Just load up your rifle, you're gonna get in some fine practice for Vietnam. We've got a couple of hundred thousand spooks sneaking around, and as far as I'm concerned, a gook and a spook—they're all the same. They're a bunch of filthy, lying bastards working hand in glove with the Commies!"

Commented Capt. Richard W. Baer of the 160th Infantry: "The attitude of the law enforcement agencies toward the Negro population had a distinct adverse effect on the battalion. There were many instances of negative attitudes toward everything Negro, police officers making such statements as 'Shoot the SOB's!' 'Rough them up every time you get the chance!' and similar statements soon gave our men the impression that the Negro was an enemy to be destroyed in every way. For a short time this attitude prevailed within our ranks. Quick action by the battalion commander and other officers soon restored discipline. . . ."

But by this time Lawrence and Pinter were long gone. At a fire they dispersed a crowd standing on a lawn on the opposite side of the street, watching. One of the men started to give them some lip about how they had a right to be there, and they had no cause being so rough with the people. Lawrence lost his head and screamed at him, "You black bastard! I'll show you how rough we can be!"

He gave him a short upstroke to the groin with the butt of the shotgun, then slugged him in the mouth and threw him into the car. As they drove down the street with him, the man was spitting blood out of his mouth, and his jaw was already swelling.

"Look!" Pinter said to him. "We've been given a hard time. My partner lost his head for a minute. We can take you down to the station and book you for resisting arrest, or we can let you go, and you forget about it."

The man decided to forget about it, so they took the cuffs off him and let him go.

*   *   *

It was a war, with all the latent hatred that war releases, with all the moral righteousness that war gives both sides. It was not only the have-nots against the haves, it was the settling of old scores, it was the unassimilated middle-class Negro finding a cause. Betty Pleasant and Brad Pye, two reporters for the Negro Los Angeles *Sentinel* were picked up by a biochemistry graduate from Wayne State University in Detroit:

"Hiding the fact that we were newspaper reporters and trying to put up a bold rioting front," Miss Pleasant wrote, "Brad and I rode in a car which we later realized was stolen, full of goods looted from pillaged stores, driven by a drunkard who, with his companion, drank stolen brandy in the car, and who kept a loaded pistol on the dash board ready for use at any provocation—cops or otherwise.

" 'I'm a fanatic for riots,' he said. 'I just love them. I've participated in two in Detroit but they were far, far better than this one. In Detroit, blood flowed in the streets!' "

There was plenty of blood if you happened to be in the right place, and Gen. Hill's assessment of the situation was so somber that, deciding the 40th armored division by itself would not have enough men to handle the situation, he ordered elements of the 49th division flown to Los Angeles from northern California.

The police were beginning to learn a few lessons. Late the previous night they had placed two buses, Brushfire No. 1 and No. 2, in operation. Each carried 30 men, six of them armed with shotguns. In this manner a full platoon could immediately be dispatched to any hot spot without the confusion resulting from sending the men in individual units. This, plus the practice of placing three or more men in each car and running the cars in tandems of two, was leading to far greater efficiency in rounding up looters. The one fact that had been established beyond contradiction was that, once the normal inhibitory power of the police had been destroyed, groups of two or three officers at widely scattered locations lost all ability to cope with a mob.

The fire department was sanguine enough to send some of its men home. Department heads had established to their own satisfaction that, despite the great conflagrations, the arsonists were a most unprofessional lot. Less than one out of three Molotov cocktails was igniting. In some the fuses separated from the bottles as they flew through the air. Others were made of thick-glassed, virtually unbreakable bottles, in which the wicks sputtered out harmlessly. While losses to commercial property were heavy, these were nothing compared to what the loss would have been had the rioters attacked industrial property, manufacturing plants, and public utilities. Although there were hundreds of such targets within the area, they remained untouched.

At 4:30 a.m. a convoy of bedraggled men—the same convoy that had been moving along the freeway as Watts was just starting to burn—arrived back in the same place it had been 15 hours before.

*   *   *

In Compton, Monrovia, Pacoima, Pasadena, Venice—everywhere that Negroes in Southern California live, the riot fuses smoldered, but quickly sputtered out.

Compton certainly might have been expected to catch fire. Just across Alameda Ave. from the Los Angeles ghetto and now more than half Negro itself, Compton is the city where five years earlier Swampmen and Spookhunters had gone at each other during the integration of the high school. Yet it is also a city that has faced the facts of life, one in which whites and Negroes have established a dialogue. Neighborhood organizations were keeping kids off the streets. Negro citizens were stopping police cars and asking what they could do to help. As a result, outside of one burned car, damage was less than $4,000. On Sept. 16 a Caucasian police officer wrote a letter to the Compton *Herald-American* thanking the community for what it had done—it was the sort of gesture that has been so desperately lacking in police-citizen relations elsewhere.

Pasadena, just as explosive as Los Angeles, smothered its fires by the intelligent cooperation of Negro and white community leaders with the police. The police chief, in turn, met with and listened to the grievances of Negro youths.

At an action committee post in Venice, a district of Los Angeles bordering on Santa Monica and the ocean, a worker kept youths talking into a tape recorder, a local radio station having promised to air their gripes. At 11 o'clock things were relatively quiet. Then a car load of youths came by, telling Shyrlee Williams, another worker, "Shyrlee, they're going to burn down Ming's!"

Ming's is a market, and when she went there, she found 200 kids standing on all four corners, throwing bottles and rocks. Someone fired a shot into the crowd, and the kids decided to barricade the street and knock out the lights. Feeling that she needed help to get the kids off the street, Miss Williams went to make some telephone calls. When she returned, the police had arrived. As she went over to a patrol car to explain what she was attempting to do, she was arrested for failing to disperse. Although the charges against her were subsequently dismissed, she could not, of course, recoup the $55 it had cost her to make bail.

35   The Bloody Dawn

Even though, at 4 a.m., the daily early morning lull set in, it was a respite only of degree.

James Allen had been at home Friday afternoon when Freeman Waterhouse had come by with a stereo and two television sets. Earlier a pickup truck loaded with tv sets had idled down the alley, the driver peddling them as if he were a Good Humor man with a truckful of ice cream. Every kind of merchandise that had been in the stores a day or two before was now available in the side streets, and late Friday and during the day Saturday some locations took on the air of bazaars.

Allen asked Waterhouse where he had obtained the goods, and Waterhouse told him he'd gotten them from a furniture store at 73rd and Vermont. He offered to sell the stereo for $55, and Allen was unable to resist the bargain. Waterhouse then asked if he could leave the tv sets for a while, and Allen told him "Okay, stick them in the closet."

Freeman Waterhouse was 40 years old, and made $548 a month as a brick tender. Born in Oklahoma, he had arrived in Los Angeles in 1941, and he had a passion for gambling. It was partly this that had gotten him into trouble in 1951 when he had lent his car to some fellows who had gone and used it to rob a liquor store, and then had given him part of the proceeds in recognition for his services. It wasn't a good bargain since, as an accomplice, he had received a sentence of five years to life.

At 10 o'clock Friday night Waterhouse drove his 1964 Cadillac to a friend's house to play poker. He remained there till after 3 o'clock Saturday morning, and then started home along Normandie Ave.

Between 3 and 3:30 a.m. Henry J. Barlow, one of the owners of Harlow's Liquor Store, received a call from friends in the 5600 block of S. Normandie that the store was being looted. He called the police department, receiving the standard reply that they were doing whatever they could.

About half an hour or an hour later, Sgt. Kenneth H. Matthys heard on his radio in the patrol car that looters were in the vicinity of 56th and Normandie. Arriving there, he saw the front door of the liquor store broken open, and a Cadillac parked in front.

As Matthys went into the store, he noticed a man, several cartons of cigarettes in his arms, rise up from behind the counter and start running toward the rear.

Matthys yelled for him to halt. When the man paid no heed, the officer aimed his shotgun and fired.

Freeman Waterhouse threw up his hands. "I quit! I quit!" he exclaimed.

Matthys approached him. Waterhouse chided him: "What did you shoot me for? I'm only doing the same thing that everybody else is doing around here now."

The two walked together to the front of the store, where Waterhouse collapsed. He spent the next nine weeks in the hospital, and had two operations, during one of which a kidney was removed.

*   *   *

Like Freeman Waterhouse, Louis Curtis Wharry had been gambling. A 35-year-old maintenance man, he had been at an all-night card party, and was being given a lift home when the driver stopped in front of the Academy Appliance and TV Store at the corner of 61st and Vermont, a location where looting had been going on for more than six hours.[1] The show window was broken, and people were scurrying in and out like busy ants. It was just a few minutes before 5 a.m. as Wharry alighted from the car.

[1] See page 267.

Twenty-three-year-old Calvin Joe Jones was coming from the opposite direction in his Volkswagen. He was up early because a friend, Lawrence Charles Jacques, had spent the night at his house, and had to go to work. As Jones drove down Vermont Ave., a fellow on the street hailed him. "Hey, man!" he said. "Go get yourself a free tv!"

Jones continued on. He was a hard-working young man who had graduated from high school at the age of 17, and supported himself ever since. Even though he was the father of two children, he had no serious financial problems—he was making $475 a month as a cook in an hotel, and his wife earned $275 a month working in an electronics plant. He was active in his church, and everyone thought well of him.

When he came to the store that was being looted, he could not resist pulling the car into the Shell Service Station next door, just to watch what was going on. The showroom was rapidly being stripped, color television sets, radios, and pieces of furniture rushing by him and disappearing in all directions. He would not, ordinarily, have stolen 50¢, but there was an excitement to all of this; the stigma of theft was being removed because everyone was thieving. It seemed to him that, "with all the confusion and the flowing of merchandise, I had a chance to get something for nothing!"

That, perhaps, had also been the thought Montague Whitmore had had prior to his being shot and killed two blocks away less than five hours before.

A man had just stepped through the show window, dragging a grandfather clock behind him, when Jones heard shouts of: "Police! Police!" and, looking up, saw a half dozen officers jumping from two cars. It seemed to him that the officers began firing immediately. In order to get out of the way—without really thinking about what he was doing—he dived behind a couch just inside the store. A half minute later the nose of a shotgun, like that of an unerring bird dog, sniffed around the corner and pointed itself at his head.

Officer John R. Walton's first impression of the scene was that of two men carrying a color television set across the sidewalk. As he dashed toward them, shouting that they were under arrest, one, Louis Wharry, threw up his hands. The other took one look, then headed around the corner of the store. Because the moon had set, it was quite dark, and Walton, right on the heels of his man, could just catch sight of his silhouette as he attempted to flatten himself behind a tree. Dropping to one knee, the officer shouted for the man to come out.

He came out, according to Walton, sprinting away down the street. The shotgun bucked into the officer's shoulder. Three of its pellets struck 28-year-old Miller Chester Burroughs in the back and leg. He stumbled, then fell.

While Walton had concentrated on Burroughs, one of his partners had gone after a T-shirted man who was loading a television set into the trunk of a green 1957 Ford. Called upon to halt, the man decided, instead, to make a break for it. When the officer fired, all 12 pellets of the charge hit 31-year-old Leon Cauley. Both Burroughs and Cauley had been drinking, and neither, except for one misdemeanor conviction acquired by the latter, had a prior record.

When the shooting had broken out, Lawrence Jacques had decided it was time for him to retire from the scene. Getting out of Jones's VW, he began walking across the apron of the Shell Station. He was just passing a red pickup truck parked there when Cauley was blown off his feet in front of him, and he himself was confronted by an officer.

"Don't run, nigger!" the policeman advised.

"I'm not going to run. I haven't done anything," Jacques replied.[2]

He was frisked and made to lie face down on the ground. Shortly thereafter other officers came up, and he heard them say that two of those at the scene had been killed.

Burroughs and Cauley were the fifteenth and sixteenth.

*   *   *

It was 5:15 a.m. when, five blocks to the east, directly across the freeway, 21-year-old Fentroy Morrison George was awakened by the siren of the ambulance coming to pick up the bodies of Burroughs and Cauley. George had lived an exemplary life, but, with an inevitability that is terrifying, he had already stepped onto that escalator that kept wanting to take him DOWN, he already had to run faster and faster just to keep his hold on the same place. His mother and father were separated; so, at the age of 16, he had come from

---

[2] At the trial, Jacques was found not guilty; Jones was sentenced to 30 days in jail; Wharry, who had a considerable prior record, received a longer sentence.

Texas to shine shoes in his father's barbershop in Los Angeles. If he hadn't been a cut above the average he would, right then, have been out of school and running with a gang —that would have been the easy, the expected, the *normal* thing. But even while he shined shoes he enrolled at Fremont High School. He was in his last semester when he fell in love with a pretty, petite girl named Janice, and they decided to get married.

Both dropped out of school. There was nobody to advise them, nobody to warn them that they had just pressed the button to start the escalator moving.

Temporarily, Fentroy George arrested it. He joined the navy and became an aviation machinist's mate. He and Janice lived on the base, and by the time he was discharged in March of 1965 they had three children—the escalator was starting to roll again.

When the riot started, George might well have been in the middle of it—as a policeman. On April 14 he had taken the examination for the academy, but failed. When he tried to get a job as an aircraft mechanic, he was turned down in three places. Day by day it became harder to go out looking for work, and he became more and more discouraged. In June, Janice lost her position as a salesgirl, and Fentroy had to take a job as a sanitarium orderly. The family of five was living in a one-bedroom apartment above the Hudson Department Store on Broadway and 62nd St. They had bought a television set and some used furniture and a 1961 Corvair—which were costing them much more than they were worth. They were being squeezed from both ends, and the escalator was rolling faster and faster.

Friday afternoon Harold Battle, a barbering student and an old friend of Fentroy, came over. After the South Park incident they could see the flames and the funnels of smoke starting up all about the area, and, after supper, Fentroy decided to take his family to his wife's sister's place, where they would be safer. He returned to the apartment at 9 o'clock, and he and Battle watched the rioters roaming up and down, going in and out of the bar advertising "Girls, Girls, Girls!" right across the street. After midnight the department store was broken into, the police came, then left, the looters returned, the police came back—it was a regular merry-go-round. About 2 o'clock Battle went down and asked the people please not to burn the store because there was a family living above it, and about 3 o'clock things began to quiet down.

As George awakened, his senses were stung by the smell of smoke. Looking into the store, he could see it was on fire. Calling to Battle, he had him go around to the back to get the Corvair and park it on Broadway, in front of the stairs leading to the apartment. Both then began carrying down the family's possessions.

Cruising through the area was Houston Hall, an NBC newsfilm cameraman. Attracted by the smoke, he stopped in front of the Hudson Store. As he began to film the action, he saw two Negroes, carrying clothes to a parked car, run in and out of the building.

"The first thing that entered my mind was that the burning building was being looted!" he said. He conveyed this impression to Robert E. Fawcett, the owner of two tow trucks which, at that moment, arrived on the scene.

Fawcett maneuvered his trucks into position, one in front and one behind the Corvair. He suggested to Hall that, for his own safety, he get into one of the trucks since, he thought, the men must have a gun. Hall acceded to the suggestion. As he did, the tow trucks began bouncing the Corvair back and forth, crunching it between their massive bumpers in an attempt to disable it.

It was 5:15 a.m., and the sky was beginning to brighten. Bisecting the thin streak of amber on the horizon a trail of smoke came to the attention of officer Michael Wilson. He suggested to his partners that they go take a look.

As the officers arrived, they saw an NBC station wagon, a pair of tow trucks performing a strange minuet with an unwilling Corvair, and two Negroes, who began running.

Said Houston Hall, "The first I saw of the police was as the Negroes were around the corner of the building nearest Gage St., with several police firing at them. I was unable to hear anything other than the gunshots as the wrecker was banging into the parked Corvair!"

According to the police officers, they shouted, "Halt!" and then began firing. Officer Wilson got off three shots, Doty, two, Mowac four, and Streitberger five. Harold Battle tripped, fell, then scrambled to his feet and took off again.

Fentroy Morrison George fell. The bullet that had burned through his aorta made him the seventeenth.

*   *   *

Hurlbut Hardy could hear the sirens of the fire engines and was unable to sleep. He might, also, have been thinking about what his wife was going to say. A mail handler at the main post office he had, like a good many of the other Negroes there, been in wholehearted support of the uprising Wednesday and Thursday nights.

"It's about time we got off of our bellies and show them ofays we got some backbone. If I was down there, I'd like as not be peppering a few rocks myself."

As Friday had turned the uprising into mass looting and burning, however, there had been a change in attitudes. What had started out as a little roughhousing was turning deadly. . . .

"Like you was crying, 'Enough! Enough!' but nobody don't listen no more!"

After getting off work Friday night, Hardy had gone to visit an old girlfriend. One thing had developed into another, and, before he knew it, here it was, almost 6 o'clock in the morning.

When he stepped into the street the smell of charcoal was like a fragrance in the air. Directly across from him the shell of a market was still smoldering. As he crossed the street, he suddenly spotted a police car. In what has come to be an instinctive reaction in the Negro community, he ducked out of the way.

Hardly had he rounded the corner of the alley back into the street, when the two officers nabbed him. He protested that he had done nothing. One of the officers was positive, however, that he had seen him inside the store room of the market, lighting a fire.

"You think I'm crazy?" he said. "That place done been burned long ago!"

There was no disputing that, and there was a half inch of water on the floor to boot, but he was arrested for arson anyway. Bail was set at $2,500, and when his wife found out where he had spent the night, she refused to bail him out.

"He can rot there in jail for all I care!" she avowed.

So for the next two months Hardy resided in the county jail.

At his trial he was found not guilty.

36   Pat Alexander and the Jews

On store windows everywhere hastily lettered notices were blossoming: NEGRO OWNED, SPERE THE SOLE FOLK, WE ARE BLOOD, BLOOD BROTHER—*We shall overcome*. Many had the X X X indicating Muslim sympathies. Orientals were inscribing COLORED OWNER, and some Caucasians, figuring that they had nothing to lose, scrawled BLOOD on their shops. One white liquor store owner boarded up his place, dumped glass and debris in front, scorched and smudged the outside, and then hoped for the best. The ruse worked. Figuring that the loot was already gone, rioters passed the building by.

Some merchants who had good reputations were spared, sometimes because of the action of the rioters, more often because people in the community protected the stores. One of these was the ABC Market at 52nd and Main, whose owner employed a Negro manager and contributed to scholarship programs. Another was the drug store at 103rd and Beach Sts. right in the midst of the heaviest destruction in Watts, where Amos "Big Train" Lincoln, Cassius Clay's sparring partner, sat cradling a shotgun in his lap. Across the street the Food Giant Market was still standing, not because it was beloved, but because Carl Margolis and his men refused to abandon it.

In his five-and-ten-cent store Nathan Finckel had been without sleep for more than 24 hours, and, at 62, he did not know how much longer he could last. Finckel, a German Jew, had arrived in the U.S. in 1937, and it had taken him eight years to save enough money to open the small store. He did not make a great deal of money, and he had been robbed more than once, but he had gained the respect of the more stable element of the community. Friday at noon, Bill Black, a six-foot-five 250-pound Negro had come, carrying a machete, and sat down in the doorway.

"Mr. Finckel," he had said, "they going to burn this town down. But we gonna see that they don't do nothing to you."

For years the business practices of many of the merchants had terrified Finckel. They would brag about how they could get away with adding 10 or 15¢ to a customer's check, about how they could play their little switching games, substituting a piece of inferior merchandise for one of higher quality marked at the same price, about how they could get away with almost anything because the Negroes were so ignorant.

"Look, look! You see how you do it, Nathan!" an acquaintance had, helpfully, tried to show him. "You add a little here, and you subtract there, and then you add some more, and they don't know what it all comes to. You see, this is what I mean. . . ." He had pulled out a bill of sale for a television set:

$285.00	base price
$ 14.95	90-day warranty
$299.95	selling price
$ 12.00	tax
$311.95	total
$ 31.95	down
$280.00	balance
$ 88.42	carrying charges (24 months)
$368.42	grand total

"That grand total is a really fine gimmick—my own thinking!" he had said. "You subtract the down payment, so that doesn't figure in at all—otherwise it comes to over $400, and that would be no good, no good—they wouldn't buy. And then, the 90-day warranty, that's pure gold. The carrying charges, well, if you want to know the truth, after you take the down payment away, they're between 25 and 30 per cent a year. But you've got to do it, Nathan! It's the only way to come out. These people, there aren't half of them that are going to pay for two years, so you've got to figure—one year! One year, and you make a profit. I have this woman, and she comes to me and she still owes me $100, and she tells me they have cut her check, and she cannot afford to pay $20 a month. So I tell her, 'Okay, you're a good woman, I trust you. Just pay me the interest. Five dollars a month.' So she has paid me now $5 a month for two years, and she still owes me $100. I can't complain!"

It wasn't only the Jews, of course, all the merchants operated in the same way. But the Jews were overrepresented, and Nathan would implore them: "These people have been exploited, they have been beaten, they have had everything done to them that we had in Germany!"

"But *we*," a woman had said to him in astonishment, "were ladies and gentlemen!"

Nathan was terrified because in the writings of Mrs. Pat Alexander, the Negro editor of the Los Angeles *Herald-Dispatch,* he was reading for the second time in his life what he had read in Germany in his youth.

"I have **accomplished indeed a rare feat in America**—I am the Editor of an **independent Newspaper,** not subject to the control of the **American Jewish Conspiracy.** Thus, while you have run almost every other Negro and Gentile owned newspaper out of business or **pressured them into printing only material which you and your gang approve,** you are at a loss to know what to do about me, **whom you cannot control.** You have tried to murder me on two occasions. This is unfortunate, because all you succeed in doing was to expose your viciousness—your hatred of all and I mean all **"black people" Negroes** rendered your ability to work with me as an equal, **impossible.**

"Relative to Zionists, all Jews are not Zionists and all Zionists-Communist-Fascists are not Jews.

"People are beginning to **realize** that the Jews, and not others are Anti-Semitic—that **Jews** are Europeans—European White people who stole Palestine from the Semitic people, the **Arabs,**—by **deception, murder and robbery—teach** them that the **day of reckoning** is coming and that will be the **day.**

"If you were familiar with Negro history in **this country** you would know that the Negro **became** passive when the Negro preacher joined **you and your crowd** and ganged up on the **Negro masses. You are using business fronts** in the Negro **community today—in conjunction with the Negro preachers—their days are too—like yours, numbered.**

"If we could get you and your **entrenched gang** out of your **Federal Government** maybe we would all be **better off** —I am expecting changes in these United States in **1966— the end** is near for you—your days of murdering, **bombing** and poisoning people are coming to an end. . . ."

An aristocratic lady with prematurely white hair, Pat Alexander is the living embodiment of hell's having no fury like a woman scorned. As a student at Columbia University's School of Journalism she had marched alongside Jews in antifascist demonstrations, during the course of one of which she had been severely injured. In 1949 when she and her husband had purchased the Negro *Herald-Dispatch*, it had been a fairly healthy weekly of 20 or so pages.

It was, however, a weak sister compared to the fat and well-financed *Sentinel*, and the support that Mrs. Alexander expected from the area's merchants had never materialized. An attitude of indifference had turned to outright hostility when the paper became Nationalistic in tone, and, for a time, accepted paid advertisements and material from the Muslims. As merchants boycotted the paper, she had retaliated by more and more strident Jew-baiting. Today the paper averages only 8 to 10 pages per edition.

While the paper's claim of "one million readers" is probably exaggerated by a factor of 20 or more, there is no gainsaying that among Nationalist elements Mrs. Alexander has considerable influence. She is not only anti-Jewish, but virulently against the war in Vietnam, anti-Communist, pro-Castro and pro-Chinese (Communist), and if such a combination makes no sense at all to the American Caucasian, it seems eminently logical to Mrs. Alexander and the Negro Nationalists.

"The HERALD-DISPATCH submits the fight against Communism is not in Africa, Asia, nor Latin America, it's right here in America from the poverty stricken area of Watts all the way to the White House.

"The HERALD-DISPATCH believes that China should have been a member of the UN years ago. China represents 700 million people. The Chinese people are as human and possess far more dignity than any other member nation in that august body. . . .

"If the United States were honest in its claim of fighting Communism, why are we sleeping with the Russians? They are the original Communists. We make love to White Communists in America, Europe and Russia, but travel to Latin America and Asia to fight Communism. Are we fighting Communism or 'Colored People'?

"Every so-called Negro who thinks he is a leader had better wake up—he had better try to understand the Communist Conspiracy in this nation—its designs to 'Get the Black Man' and the American Whiteman into the streets into Physical Violence."

Mrs. Alexander believes that: "The war in Vietnam **is not**

a war. It is a **'Human Furnace,'** a politically designed 'Furnace' to get millions of young men out of the United States.

"The 17- and 18-year-old youth which have been literally **burned to death** in South Vietnam swamps were considered the 'unreachables.' They were for the most part unemployed, and with automation, and increasing **unrest**, they would have posed a serious problem, they would have taken to the streets to fight for what they termed **their rights.**

". . . and since the United States has not and I repeat has NOT been attacked, both Negro and whites have every right to say and refuse to go to war. This is a war of aggression against an innocent people. . . . Fight Communism in Russia. . . . Fight Communism in Washington, D.C. . . . but to go to Cuba, Santo Domingo and other black countries to bomb and use lethal gas on those people under the pretext of fighting Communism—this is an untenable position."

Her reasoning is that "more than 60 per cent of those fighting in Vietnam are Negroes," and that the war "will, of course, **kill the majority of the young men.** Thus, this opens the way **for a real Communist take-over in the homeland."**

Her predictions of what will happen if the war is not ended are dire: "The inhabitants of the Flying Saucers are **Asians** —small people—laugh if you will—time will tell. . . . We discussed the Flying Saucers or the visitors from the 'Mother Ship' several years ago. We informed you then, if and when the United States decided to declare **all-out war** against the Asian people—that the Mother Ship would release the secret weapon and defend the Asians on **American soil.** The method in which the defense would be launched is from **outer space.** . . . Thus the Flying Saucers are indeed a very real thing— they are not striking yet—but according to prophecy they will as surely as the **sun rises in the east and sets in the west.**

"If you read and study carefully the Bible—15th chapter of Ezekiel—there will be some indication of what to expect. The Mother Ship was launched early in 1930 and is quite capable of defending the **Asian people.** . . . They will strike unless we are intelligent enough to leave Asia, which we are not."

By this time Arthur Goldberg, for whose advancement Adlai Stevenson was done away with, according to Mrs. Alexander, will be in the White House.

"We did not like the manner in which Stevenson went to England to have his now famous 'heart attack.' . . . Stevenson died in order that Arthur Goldberg, former Supreme Court Justice, could gain nation-wide status as Ambassador of the U.N. Hence Stevenson's 'heart attack' in London. Goldberg, as you know, is scheduled to be our next vice-president, then president. . . .

"In 1968 the lineup is to be Hubert Humphrey, President; Arthur Goldberg, Vice-President—this makes good the prediction of the **Jewish citizens** that they will have a Jewish President in the White House **by 1970.** This is how it will work—LBJ may have a heart attack—so HH becomes President. HH runs in 1968 with Arthur Goldberg as his Vice— then Hubert Humphrey has a heart attack and **Goldberg is President by 1970. All that is necessary for people to accomplish their goals is to have a 'Plan.'** . . . Plans for Goldberg to become President in 1970 were made **last fall** on a ship out in the Pacific Ocean."

The combination of Jews and liberals in "The Anti-Christian Communist Conspiracy is well heeled. They finance the **KKK, American Nazis, Civil Rights Movement, NAACP, CORE,** Trade Unions, and certain elements in the **John Birch Society** and the Republican Party. . . . The conspirators usually convince the GOP heads, Birch group that Negroes are all **Communists-Democrats** and it's a lost cause even to talk to them.

"The White American is a little confused. You see, he **eats, sleeps, marries,** raises families with the Communist Conspirator and thus he is unable to **identify** him so quickly as the Negro.

"The Negro had better wake up before it's too late—he has until 1970—then somebody is going into the CHAMBERS. Oh, by the way—speaking of the **Gas** Chamber—we hear HITLER is in South America laughing like hell at the American People—He said, 'I told you so.' " [1]

There were many who ridiculed Pat Alexander, but Nathan Finckel was not one of them. He knew that, though to the white American her convoluted logic might make little sense, there were many Negroes who believed her, whose own experiences made it easy for them to accept her assertions that the Jews have too much power, and that the United States

[1] The quotes are from various writings of Mrs. Alexander in the *Herald-Dispatch.* Care has been taken to reflect her viewpoint accurately and not to quote out of context. The somewhat eccentric typography is reproduced faithfully.

is engaged in a war against the colored people of the world. As Watts began to burn, one of Nathan's acquaintances came by, his car full of merchandise that he had managed to save from his store. He was lamenting that even as he had gone out of the back door someone had thrown a Molotov cocktail through the front. He was asking rhetorically what was going to happen to him now, and Nathan had not the heart to remind him that for years, when warned of the enmity he was creating, he had shrugged and said, "So. These people come and these people go, and when the time comes I will go too. You are deluding yourself, Finckel, if you think this is Wilshire Blvd. These people are the dregs of the earth, and if they have a chance they will steal you blind, so while I have my chance I will make what I can. And when I go I will have a little put away, but you, when you go, you will have nothing!"

But, with Bill Black there in the doorway, Finckel was not going. Up and down the street roamed the youths who were breaking the way, smashing windows with boards and crowbars or bricks held in hands wrapped with protective towels. Coming up to the store they would look at Bill Black, then pass on. Late in the afternoon one kid, swacked to the gills, approached, carrying a bottle with a wick attached.

"What you say, soul brother?" he said to Black with a curious, questioning look.

"I say that if you throws that thing, I'm gonna have myself one soul brother in heaven!" Black replied.

"No offense, brother," the youth explained. Pulling a pint bottle out of his pocket, he sat it on the sill, and left.

The looting and the rioting continued all night. Several times police drove by, and it was magical the way the people knew that they were coming and melted into the alleys and yards. In the darkness there was no way to protect the store completely: the front window was broken, and a barrel full of trash was set on fire and placed against the rear. Otherwise, however, Bill Black's presence was respected.

Saturday morning Finckel and Black boarded up the broken window. At 9 o'clock, when he saw the National Guard had arrived, Finckel decided to go home for a few hours. As he walked up the steps to his apartment, a neighbor opened her door and met him. "I am so sorry, Mr. Finckel," she said.

"It's all right," he soothed her. "Everything is all right."

"But your store—?"

"My store is all right."

"Come with me!" she said, and led him into her apartment. There, on the television screen, was a burning building. It was Finckel's store.

37   The Eighteenth in Fifteen

A short time earlier, 37-year-old William Vernon King had taken his 12-year-old son, Larry, and Larry's 15-year-old cousin out walking through the neighborhood. It wasn't long before they happened upon a liquor store whose window had been broken. Inside they could see a number of persons rummaging about. King, who already had had several drinks that morning, decided to join them. He was followed by the two youngsters.

King's life, like that of so many of the others, had been a checkered one. Born in Louisiana, he had first been arrested in St. Louis at the age of 14. The next year, 1944, he had been sentenced to the Nebraska state penitentiary for burglary. Two years later he had been convicted of auto theft, and returned to prison. Since then, however, he had in many ways settled down, giving his four children a home superior to many others in the area. After the death of his wife in 1959, he had cared for the children by himself.

As they hunted around the store, Larry found in a drawer by the cash register a black .38 revolver. Taking it, he showed it to his father.

It was shortly before 9:45 a.m. when Officers P. H. Thompson (a Negro), and his partners Nicholas McKay and Charles C. Hutson received a report of looters in a liquor store. As they arrived, Thompson saw a man coming out of the window with a stack of clothes in one hand and several bottles of liquor in the other. Running to him, he placed him under arrest.

Simultaneously, the other two officers, entering through the window, saw three persons moving about the store. One of these, catching sight of the officers, looked up startled. As he did, a revolver became visible in his hand.

"Drop the gun!" McKay shouted.

The man did not react.

"Drop the gun!" McKay called again. This time, as the man straightened up and took a step back, the revolver began to rise menacingly in his hand.

McKay pulled the trigger on his shotgun at the same time that Hutson fired his .38. William Vernon King staggered backward, then dropped to the floor.

"That's my father!" said Larry.

King was the eighteenth in the 15 hours since Leon Posey had been killed by a ricochet.

After the police had taken away his body, the people in the neighborhood burned the store.

38   Fear and Flusteration

The Rev. Seely James had not been to bed for two days. Thursday afternoon he had been at the Athens Park meeting, and Thursday night he had been one of those on Avalon Blvd. trying, simultaneously, to talk to the police and to cool off the rioters. Friday night he had sat, cradling a .22 rifle, in his office opposite the Safeway Store and shopping center on Imperial Highway. Looting had begun at 6 o'clock, and continued on and off until midnight, when sheriff's deputies had come by and rounded up everyone. After that the Rev. James had sat there, keeping people out by yelling, "Don't go in there. You'll get killed!"

About 2 o'clock in the morning he had noticed a figure

moving inside the store, and, going over, found a Caucasian of Mexican appearance pouring gasoline over the floor. Running him out, he had resumed his vigil. It was not so much a labor of love as the fear that, if Safeway were set ablaze, the whole neighborhood would go up in flames.

Seely James had been born in Oklahoma. He had come to California in 1938 to pick cotton in Bakersfield. Moving to Los Angeles, he had gone to work in a used car lot, and then, during the war, in a shipyard. When, in 1948, he had bought a house in Watts it had been a pleasant area. The big change had come in 1952 when the Los Angeles public housing authority had congregated five housing projects together in the one general location, inundating it with children—children with little parental supervision.

The big change in James's personal life had come five years later. Until that time he had operated a small, profitable auto retailing business with four to five employees. Then automated car-wash racks had sprung up all over, and he had been unable to compete. For the past half dozen years he had, for all practical purposes, been unemployed. Most of the little money he did make came from his preaching; like most of the other preachers, he owned his own small church.

Although, behind his glasses, the Rev. James is a meek-appearing person, years of manual labor have given him the shoulders and arms of a heavyweight. He is disapproving of Negro women, and, within his own family, had always run a tight ship. It was a practice not without its troublesome consequences.

As Rev. James tells it, his wife was a "jealous-type woman" and, on the occasion that he took "about the fifth switch-blade knife" from her, he had "hit her a little bitty lick just to calm her down."

The police, "who always believe only the women," had come and taken her side. A disputation had arisen over whether the police were or were not needed. Seely James had emphasized his point by slugging one officer on the jaw. Locking his arms around the other one, he had carried him toward the door, and "he was leaving like a little baby" when his wife "had started inciting again."

The upshot had been that, although his wife refused to press charges, Seely James had been tried for battery on a police officer and fined $52.

Inevitably, perhaps, his marriage had come to an end.

"Women would rather not have a husband if they find you're strict," he says. "No woman wants to listen to a man. They've run the men out of their jobs, and turned the world upside down and given it to the women and children.

"The old ones [among the kids] are almost gone," he believes. "Their minds have been poisoned. They've gotten their education on the streets. They look at tv, and lust after everything they see. They'll knock your brains out if you so much as sneeze—my brother was nearly killed for 57¢. There's not enough of nothing in the home. My children go out and come into contact with these kids, and say, 'Daddy, you're cruel, you're doing me wrong!' just because I make them go out and work. But when he was 18 years old my boy could go out and make $140 a week, and of the 15 boys on the block only three came through clean—the rest of 'em all have records!"

The two dominant characteristics of Watts are "fear and flusteration. At night you fear walking the streets. You hate to meet anybody. I don't know which is worst—the police harassment or the gangs. A boy that don't join a gang, they're gonna get him. If he do join—and he don't have to join; all he got to do is be hanging around—the police will get after him, and sooner or later they'll get him involved."

The Rev. James resents the police because "it's a money business. They're after the people who can afford to pay the fines. They're all the time after the working people, and closing their eyes to the crime that's going on."

He bases this assessment in part on the fact that the Safeway shopping center had been a hangout for winos, prostitutes, and dope addicts, and he had never seen the police do anything about *them*, but there had always been two motorcycle cops hiding behind the building ready to jump on any errant driver.

"You take a cop and he's only human," the Rev. James asserts. "You put him down here and he starts wrestling with some of these hoodlums who've been turning up dung heaps, and pretty soon he smells just as bad as them. But he can't smell himself, so when you tell him he ought to get himself cleaned up, he gets mad. And he takes his mad out on the poor people, and then they get mad, and you get this situation where you couldn't have stopped the riot with a thousand tanks! The kids was glad the police was here. That's what they wanted, was to fight 'em!"

About 9 o'clock Saturday morning Rev. James fell asleep in his chair. When he awoke two hours later, a black, 50-foot-wide column of smoke was rising from the Safeway Market. By the time it had finished burning, the entire shopping center had disappeared.

39   Charcoal Alley Number Two

Right on schedule, between 7 and 8 o'clock in the morning, looting had resumed everywhere, and by 11 o'clock some 50 different stores had been hit, with rioters reported at as many as a score of different locations simultaneously. Gov. Brown arrived back in the U.S., and, in a telephone conversation from New York, insisted that a curfew be placed on the area at the onset of darkness.

Chief Parker was against it. He did not believe such a curfew could be enforced.

As Marvin Goldsmith, the man who drew up both the orders for the call up of the National Guard and for the curfew, recalled, he told the police, "We [the attorney general's office] are going to do it. You can cooperate or not, as you like."

And he went over to the ECC, and drew the boundaries on the map.

Only Watts was quiet. In Watts the National Guard was firmly in control. From the post office—which, except for one brief foray, had been left untouched because "They're the feds!"—issued the mailmen, walking down 103rd St., where hardly one address remained standing. The director of a mortuary was permitted to proceed with three funerals. A wedding party appeared at a roadblock. The father of the bride, it turned out, was a former sergeant of the 40th division. They were allowed to pass through the devastated area to the Catholic church at 102nd and Compton, across the street from which, a few hours earlier, Flores had been killed.

Twenty-eight-year-old Raymond Wrenn had arrived from Texas with his parents and his sister in 1951. A Negro, he had graduated from Pepperdine College, and gone to work as a systems engineer for IBM. Friday night he returned to the area in which he had grown up as a second lieutenant in the National Guard. Early Saturday afternoon he was patrolling with six men near Main and 110th Sts., just a few blocks from where the riot had originally erupted.

Just to the south a furniture store was on fire. The driver of a fire truck hailed him and asked him to provide an escort, since the 200 to 300 persons surrounding the building were refusing to allow the truck to go through. Lt. Wrenn ran interference for the rig, then tried to keep the people back as the firemen laid their lines and set up their hoses. His men, who were white, received a good deal of verbal abuse, but there was no rock throwing. The shells of overturned cars, stripped of their wheels and anything else that might be of value, still lay hulking in the street.

Numbers of people were emerging with canned goods, soda pop, soap, and the like from a small grocery store. Lt. Wrenn took some of his men into the store to clear them out. After the people had been rounded up, one of the white troopers stood looking at a display case of wormy meat and a table of blemished fruit and vegetables. "Lieutenant, you mean people really eat this stuff?" he asked in astonishment.

Wrenn went to check the alley in back of the line of businesses. The door of a clothing store was open, and, he believed, he could see movement inside. A patrol car came cruising through the alley. Wrenn pointed out the open door to the policemen.

"Okay, we'll clean 'em out!" the officers said, and fired a couple of blasts from their shotguns into the store.

Lt. Wrenn returned to Main St. Ten minutes later he noticed smoke puffing from the clothing store, and within a minute fire was licking out of the windows. One of the onlookers came up to him to warn him that he had better get the people back—the owner had one or two five-gallon cans of gasoline stored in the rear of the building. Hardly had Wrenn been able to get them to clear the area in front of the building when a ball of flame roared up to the height of the crossarms of the telephone poles. Within a half hour, four separate fires were burning in a three-block area. Residents were standing on their lawns and directing water onto the roofs of their houses. One woman with a hose in one hand held a rifle in the other. A sign that heralded:

Stop   Look   Listen
REVIVAL
Healing for Body, Soul, Mind

looked as if it had been plunged into the coals of hell.

About two hours after he had arrived, Lt. Wrenn noticed a blue panel truck being driven at high speed down the street. As it passed, he saw the glint of metal in the window of the cab, then heard a *pop-pop-pop* similar to small-arms fire. Believing that he and his men had been shot at, Wrenn, running after the truck, saw it turn into an alley at the end of the block. He caught up with it just as the driver, trying to maneuver, stalled the engine.

Jerking open the door to the cab, Wrenn ordered the two men, both Caucasian, to get out and put up their hands. He was offered no resistance, and police officers, who were standing on the roofs of surrounding buildings, came to his aid. Although several rounds of loose ammunition were found, no weapons were discovered.

Lt. Wrenn later received the California Military Cross for his actions at the fire.

*   *   *

To the north, Central Ave., with its many older buildings, was burning with the intensity that Watts had the afternoon before. There was the same spaghettilike snaking of hose amidst the brilliantly-colored litter left behind by looters, the same bright red fire trucks extending their giraffelike ladders up into the smoke.

In the intense heat—the thermometer was nudging 95 degrees, but amidst the fires it was nearer 110—metal and glass were melting, uniting and re-forming themselves into a myriad abstract shapes. The high-arched streams of white water disappeared hissing into the orange-black fabric of smoke. An armless mannequin in an unsullied white dress, one side of her head smashed in, sat propped against a telephone pole like a pensive victim of rape—the pole was ablaze with short, crackling thorns of fire. Down the street one of the mannequin's erstwhile mates hid behind a pair of sunglasses that had somehow come to be perched on her nose, across her bosom was scrawled, in lipstick, BURN BABY.

It is a little thing, but in America even the store mannequins are all white.

A watermelon split open by the heat came tumbling into the street, Battalion Chief Ken Long and his men grabbed it, and, without letting go of the hose they were training on the fire, divided it among themselves—it was the best thing that had happened to them in two days. Some of the buildings that were going up were of such old and rickety construction and had for years been in violation of so many fire laws that what surprised Chief Long was not that they were burning now, but that they had not burned long ago. The firemen, like the police, had abandoned standard operating procedure, and, adapting themselves to the new situation, were working more efficiently. Instead of attempting to knock down every fire completely, they were concentrating on gaining control and keeping the flames from spreading to other buildings, then abandoning the smoldering shells to go on to more urgent tasks.

Chief Long was not surprised by the riot. When, after a four-year absence, he had returned to the area in 1964, he had been shocked by the change in attitude of the residents. Prior to 1960 he had been able to move about without fear or harassment, going into even the most tawdry bars to make fire inspections at night. Since his return, however, he had met with constant verbal abuse, and relations between the firemen and the populace had deteriorated to the point where there was little communication between them.

Of moderate Republican bent, Chief Long has no use for the Bircher element in the department—some of whom were, according to one of the other chiefs, "tickled to death that Kennedy was shot." He believes that their number has been exaggerated, although there were some who, like their counterparts on the police force at the time of the 1964 election, were running around during duty hours distributing right-wing literature.

Keenly aware of many of the dual standards that exist, Chief Long is, nevertheless, appalled by some of the attitudes and practices in the Negro community; by the differences in mores for which his own upbringing had done nothing to prepare him; by the explosive violence and the casual indifference to suffering exhibited by the people.

One night he had been with the rescue squad when it was summoned to a bar called "The Saints," because a woman had fainted. She was lying on the floor, her head propped on her purse, while people continued, literally, to dance around and over her. As Chief Long had knelt down and checked her for vital signs, one man, stepping between her legs, had looked down and asked, "What's wrong with her?"

"She's dead!"

"No shit!" the man had said, and danced on.

Yet the Negro accused of lacking sympathy will give the white man that quizzical look: *Who you trying to put on? Why should I care about somebody when nobody's ever given a damn about me?*

It was Charcoal Alley Number Two. It was the fire burning away the humiliation that not even the most respected Negro could escape. Two years before, right across from the buildings at which the firemen were training their hoses, Leon Washington, Jr., the publisher of the influential Los Angeles *Sentinel* had been spreadeagled and frisked in front of his own office. To the Negroes looking on there had been no missing the point. If the white police could do that to the most powerful in their ranks, then there was no hope for the ordinary black man in a white America.

40   A Sniper Attack

Rumors, spreading throughout the environs of the state, continued to proliferate.

The freeway interchange is to be bombarded unless all rioters are released . . . a Major of the Minutemen is preparing to move into the area with 2,000 men who have orders to shoot . . . the Beach cities are to be hit late in the afternoon . . . numerous suspects on building roofs . . .

Wilshire Blvd. and downtown are to be hit next . . . 1,500
white men are going to show those niggers they can't take
over the U.S., they're all Commies anyway . . . rioters are
sucking eggshells and filling them with gasoline to make
innocent-looking Molotov cocktails . . . anything red displayed in the window or mailbox of a house will protect it
from rioters . . . the Shrine Auditorium is burning . . . vans
are dropping off Negroes with red armbands . . . a city
water tank is to be blown up by Low Riders who have
walkie-talkies and wear black rags on their heads . . . Hollywood is to go at 7:30 p.m. . . . men seen loading shotguns
at DeLongpre and Wilcox Aves. in Hollywood . . . employees in a car lot at 15th and Figueroa Sts. in downtown
Los Angeles are besieged by heavy sniper fire.

The snipers who had the car lot under siege were 24-
year-old William Henry Shufflebotham, Jr., and 23-year-old
Grover Lee Talley.

Both worked for an automobile dealer in the area, and
Shufflebotham, a kind of self-made mechanical wizard, had,
within a year of his arrival from New Jersey, been promoted
to service manager of one of the largest Chevrolet dealers
in the city. After closing up shop at noon, the two had cashed
their checks at a nearby liquor store. They then had retired
to Talley's panel truck for some serious discussion, meanwhile sucking at the half-pint bottles of whiskey they had
been forced to purchase in order to get their checks cashed.

Apparently, as they talked it over, the situation had begun
to look darker and darker to them, for, after a while, Shufflebotham had driven his Corvette the few blocks to the
Broadway Department Store downtown to buy shells for his
.32-caliber revolver. After he had returned and they had sat
there in the sun some more, the level of whiskey in the bottles slowly sinking, Talley had taken a 7-Up bottle, set it
on the sidewalk, and begun firing at it. Since the 7-Up bottle
had presented too small a target, he had next aimed at a
garage. Shufflebotham, taking a hand, had fired in several
different directions, in one of which lay the used-car lot,
where employees scattered and dived for cover, perhaps
thinking an unsatisfied customer had returned to wreak vengeance. After that, Shufflebotham had fired at the truck itself, as if trying to execute it. Soon thereafter the police had
arrived to lift the siege.

Television and radio faithfully transmitted each of these

reports without evaluation, and the listener, who was in no position to make any judgment, and who never learned that the ominous snipers downtown were a couple of drunks, or that the location of the men seen loading shotguns was that of the Hollywood police station, assumed the worst and made it a banner weekend for gunshop owners, with sales up more than 250 per cent.

41   Barney Goes to Jail

About noon, Barney Wateridge,[1] sitting in his Hollywood apartment, watching the riot on tv, received a call from the radio-tv director of the advertising agengy. "Got a favor to ask of you," the director said. One of the agency's clients, a local radio station, had no man—i.e., Negro—whom they could send into the area for a personal report of the situation. How would Barney like to put on a reporter's cloak for the afternoon, go in and tape some interviews, get some firsthand impressions, etc.?

Barney wouldn't. The tv director made it sound like a picnic, and Barney would just as soon have picnicked in hell. Anita Greyson had depended on her acquaintances in and her knowledge of the area to pull her through, and she had discovered, painfully, that it isn't enough to speak the language—you have to *look* right! To the police and National Guard Barney knew that he wouldn't look right, and he had no confidence in their being impressed with his language.

But that's a difficult thing to explain to a white man who fancies himself as making no distinction between black and white. Barney suggested to him that it might already be past the time when a Negro could be more effective than a white man in the area, but it was no use. The tv director had

[1] See pp. 83–91.

decided that he had discovered the ideal man for the job; he considered it a feather in his cap that he had, for the station's benefit, been able to come up with Barney; and Barney knew that, if he refused, he would take it as a personal affront.

Barney met him at the office. The tv director had an expensive Uhr portable tape recorder waiting for him, and he also handed him a Rolliflex camera.

"What's that for?" Barney asked.

"Well, you know, you might get a chance to snap some pictures. I'd like to have a few for myself, and, you never know, you might come up with something unusual."

Barney didn't argue. "What about identification?" he asked.

The director hadn't thought of that. "If you really think you'll need it," he said, "I'll write a letter for you."

Barney thought he really would, so the director typed a note on agency stationery explaining that Barney was an official representative of the radio station. Thus armed, Barney started for south Los Angeles.

Traveling down the Harbor Freeway he had a rooftop view of the houses and streets. They looked peaceful enough. Except for the columns of smoke rising at scattered points, the area was just as he had always known it—somnolent, parching in the dry sun, a midwestern flatness presided over by brown-bearded palms. Heading for the Manchester Ave. off-ramp he had no plans as to where he was going, or what he was going to do. As he reached the street he had the impulse to turn west and forget all about it. But an excitement was beginning to grip him, he was being torn by conflicting emotions—he knew that many whites would look upon the looting and burning as simply an act of depravity that proved once again the savagery of the Negro. That, no matter what he himself had done or accomplished, they would automatically classify him as one of those savages. That the pillaging would make his own acceptance by American middle-class society more difficult. Yet this knowledge of Caucasian rejection and Negro assertiveness rekindled some of his own aggressive instincts; for the first time the whites were really afraid of the Negroes, and it was a good feeling to have the power to be feared. If the radio station honestly wanted to know what was happening and what the people were thinking, well, he would give it to them. He turned the car toward a beacon of smoke on Main St.

Police were rounding up people in a looted market. They had about a dozen women and children lined up, and were making them open up shopping bags and old shirts that they had tied into knots. A motley assortment of cans and packages were tumbled onto the sidewalk—all together they could not have been worth more than $25. A skinny teenager with curlers in her hair was crying and saying that she had never stolen in her life; she was only looking for some Lady Clairol because all the stores in the neighborhood had been burned and looted. A young mother claimed she was in the market looking for her 7-year-old boy who had wandered off —there was no way to check the veracity of the statement, and she would be bundled off with the rest.

As the police were occupied with their prisoners, an old man, by his appearance at least 70, emerged from an alley and began padding furtively across the street. Beneath one arm he carried a shoe box. Barney held his breath—it looked like the man was going to make it. Then, one of the officers, glancing over his shoulder, happened to catch sight of him.

"Hey, you!" he called to him.

The old man stopped, half poised on one foot, as if trying to convince himself that it wasn't really he whom the officer had yelled at.

"You!" the officer called again.

"Yes, sir," the old man said, shuffling toward him.

"Come here."

The old man's hands began shaking. Slowly he approached the policeman.

"What have you got in that box?" the officer demanded.

As if in response, the box slipped from the old man's grasp. Out tumbled a half dozen packages of snuff.

These were the scavengers, and they were pathetic in their scavenging. On the east side of the Harbor Freeway there was little of value left to be taken in those places that had been broken into, yet Barney saw people everywhere—even in those buildings that had been completely burned—grubbing amidst the rubble. It was mostly the women, the children, the older men; there were comparatively few males between the ages of 18 and 40 about, and those that he did see were congregating about the usual hangouts, the pool halls and the shoeshine (bookie) stands.

At a barbecue stand on Central Ave. Barney stopped. There were eight or nine persons, including several kids, who had gathered, and he figured it was as good a place as any to tape some opinions.

There were the usual complaints about the police. A woman asserted that "police with bayonets on their riot guns" had "busted in the door on the house" and arrested her husband who was sleeping, after rioters had made "a freeway of the yard." Another was intensely troubled by the fact that not a market in her neighborhood was left standing. "When the babies start crying for milk, that's when we'll really have a riot!" she prophesied. A couple of 17-year-olds decried police harassment and brutality in the same breath that they bragged how "this white dude had went out of his head when they blew up his car and started running through the gardens, and all the people went in and killed him." As Barney knew from personal experience, much of what they said was fantasy. Yet they were not deliberately lying; it seemed true to them.

"Freeze!" one of them exclaimed. Barney, looking out to the street, saw the black-and-white car with three officers pulling up. "Man! You better get rid of that thing!" The youth indicated the tape recorder, assuming that Barney could not have come by it legitimately.

The officers looked into all the cars parked around the stand. One, especially, attracted their attention, and they came up to inquire whose it was. A trio of men, sitting at one of the wooden tables, acknowledged, without saying a word, that it was theirs. All three of them, it turned out, were deaf-mutes.

The officers beckoned them over to the car, and, as they stood there, lifted a case of beer from the rear seat. Where, they wanted to know, had it been obtained? The deaf-mutes expressed astonishment. By signals they indicated they had not even known it was in the car, and that someone must have placed it there during the time the automobile was parked. The police said that that was unfortunate. The mutes were handcuffed and arrested.

One officer walked up and asked Barney about the tape recorder. Barney showed him the letter.

"Okay." The officer, who was not unfriendly, returned it to him. "You got a few hours to listen, I could tell you some stories myself!"

Barney left right behind the police car. Going along Florence Ave., he turned onto Central, soon realizing his mistake.

Ahead of him the street was blocked by fire trucks, numerous looters darting back and forth. Looking over his shoulder he could see, a couple of blocks away, a line of national guardsmen advancing. The distance between the troops and the fire trucks was shrinking rapidly. Deciding that prudence dictated he get out of there, Barney had just turned his car around when a patrol car drove directly into his path.

Barney slammed on the brakes and reached for his letter. Scarcely had he done so, when a police officer, revolver in hand, dashed up to the door.

"Get out of there!" he shouted.

"I have—" Barney started to say.

"Out!" the officer yelled.

Simultaneously, another policeman jerked open the door. Before Barney had time to realize what was happening, he had been lifted bodily from the seat, and was thumped down onto the pavement. Hardly was he down, when there was another command: "Get up!"

He was spreadeagled against the side of the car, boots kicking his heels apart until it felt as if his legs must split. Hands patted him down from head to toe.

"Now, buddy boy, who are you?" one of the officers asked.

"I was taping some firsthand re—" Barney started to say.

"I didn't ask you what you were doing! I asked you who you are," the officer demanded.

Barney took his driver's license out of his wallet, and the officer scanned it.

"What's all that stuff in the car?" The officer indicated the tape recorder and the camera.

"I have a letter, explaining," Barney said, trying very hard to remain calm. He began reaching for it on the floor of the car, where it had fallen.

"You just keep your ass right where it is!" The officer pushed him back, reached down, and picked up the letter.

He read it. "You have press credentials?" he inquired.

"No. You see—"

But the police officer was not listening. "Bill of sale," he demanded.

"For what?"

"For those things."

"I'm trying to explain to you. I'm on an assignment. That letter—"

"That letter don't mean nothing to me, buddy boy. Nothing at all. You've got no bill of sale?"

"No. I've got no—"

"You're under arrest. You've got a right to counsel. You've got a right to remain silent. Anything you say can be held against you. Now what about that watch?"

"What watch?"

"Right there on your wrist. You trying to be a smart ass?" The officer grabbed his arm and twisted it, so that the face of the watch pointed upward.

"That's my watch!"

"It's a new watch!" The declaration brooked no controverting. "Bill of sale?"

"You got a bill of sale for your watch, you b—" Barney started to lash back, then caught himself.

"What's that?"

"No, sir," he replied. "I do not have a bill of sale for the watch."

The watch was taken from him for evidence. Another one of the officers, standing by, appeared somewhat discomfited by the proceedings, and, as the first officer went back to the patrol car, Barney appealed to him.

"I'm sorry. I can't help you," the officer replied. "You're in an area where you've got no business being, with stuff that you've got no business having. The judge is going to have to decide, that's all."

While they had been standing there, the line of national guardsmen had passed by. Following behind the guard was a mobile jail—a sheriff's department bus with barred windows. Barney was added to the two dozen or more men already aboard. They were a motley crew, many of them drunk, unable to control their bodily functions—the interior was stifling and stinking. Block by block they crawled along, here and there adding new passengers. As the guardsmen went down the streets they ordered all the residents back from the doorways and windows. "Close all your doors and windows"— the bullhorn commanded. It was an order that, on an afternoon of 90-degree heat, was not lightly obeyed. Its purpose was to cut down on the danger from snipers. The troops were quite conscious of the possibility of someone shooting at them—there was a constant scanning of second-floor windows and of roofs.

Barney's companion became a 27-year-old Caucasian service-station owner named Dale. Blond and blue-eyed, with a Southern accent, he was mad as hell.

At 3 o'clock that afternoon, a 1956 Chevrolet with five youths in it had come by his station in the industrial district of Avalon Blvd. Exhibiting a bunch of Molotov cocktails, they had threatened, "We're gonna get you, man!"

Virgil, the Negro attendant, had told them that he owned the station, and that Dale was only his helper, so they had left. Although the station had been open all through the riot up to this time—actually, in that particular section, a matter of only one day—Dale had decided it was time to close up. Taking his shotgun, he had climbed into the cab of a truck that was parked beneath the overhang. Virgil had joined him, and they had opened up some beer. Across the street two other Caucasians, Harvey Denison and Ed Cunningham, were similarly guarding their property, a truck and car leasing company. Earlier in the afternoon, a police officer, checking on them, had provided them with ammunition for their guns.

Less than a half hour after Dale had closed his station, the National Guard had set up a roadblock at the corner, and a few minutes later a patrol car had come by. Checking on both Dale and the other two Caucasians, they had demanded to know what they were doing with guns.

To Dale it had seemed self-evident. They were protecting their property. The police officers, however, had theorized that they were drunk and were waiting to bushwhack Negroes.

"Hell!" said Dale to Barney. "If I'd wanted to shoot me some, I had five of 'em in my station that wouldn't have been no sweat at all!"

The police, however, had refused to believe him, and Dale, Virgil, Cunningham and Denison had all been picked up.

"It's a rotgut deal!" said Dale. "I don't have no more respect for the fucking law now. They can't protect your property, and they won't let you protect it yourself! I keep six lights burning at night, and the station's been broke into twice in six months. One night they hit all four stations on the corner, and the cops never knew it! Last night they burned two cars and an auto parts store down the street, and the cops were crying like little babies: 'Protect yourself the best way you can!' Now all of a sudden they get the Guard in, and they're big shit! Hell, the way things are, I don't blame you niggers!"

It took the bus three hours to reach the staging area, where a booking and mugging station had been set up. With bureaucratic thoroughness entirely unconscious of other considerations—such as the public image being created—the police were mugging everyone they picked up, including 8- and 9-year-old children. In this they were following standard operating procedure of photographing all delinquents, no matter what the age, and filing their pictures in "mug books."

As Barney and the others were sitting there on the bus, waiting to be processed, several police officers were standing around. One, handling a shotgun that, apparently, was unfamiliar to him, was trying to throw a shell into the chamber. As he maneuvered the pump back and forth, there was, suddenly, an ear-splitting *boom*. The shotgun kicked back into his stomach, the pellets whooshing inches over the heads of the other officers.

*   *   *

The prisoners were processed in groups of about 10. Stacks of recovered loot were sitting about, and the police insisted on photographing many of the arrestees with some of these items, whether they had any specific connection with them or not. When he heard Barney's story, the processing officer frowned, inquired about the letter—which no one seemed to know what had happened to—and then said he could do nothing. Together with the rest Barney was taken to the old Lincoln Heights Jail, which had been closed down several months before, but had had to be reopened to take care of the hundreds of prisoners—ultimately, almost 4,000—who were pouring in.

They were placed in large tanks holding 80 to 100 or more persons each. The bunks were without mattresses. Some of the prisoners, arrested in the heat of the day, were half naked, without even undershirts in their possession. Many had bumps, bruises and burns, and one was wearing a blood-soaked handkerchief around his head. Most claimed they were innocent, and had simply been standing on the street, watching—and in some cases, like Barney's, it was undoubtedly true. A few, on the other hand, bragged about a building they had burned, or a cop they had bloodied. There was a boy wheezing with asthma, and another who had a rheumatic heart. One Negro man said he thought he must be going out of his mind: he and a Caucasian were partners in an electrical shop, and, after the place had been broken into early Friday morning, he had remained on the premises. Saturday the police, chasing people on the street, had seen the broken window and come and arrested him for being a looter. Late in the evening an 82-year-old man was brought in—he had just returned from "preaching the gospel" in Texas and had been picked up by his wife at the bus station. The police, halting the car, had noticed the luggage inside, and arrested him for burglary. A deputy sheriff saw his own nephew arrive in handcuffs. On the top floor some of the juveniles who happened to be brought in after dinner and hadn't eaten since that morning got hungry and started tearing things up. Jailers pulled them out and doused them in cold showers.

It was bedlam. Never before in American history had there been an instance of such mass arrests. Food was a problem, but it was solved by providing each prisoner with two tv meals a day. Toilet and sleeping facilities were inadequate, but, in general, the sheriffs department coped with the inundation remarkably well.

The one system that, for a time, threatened to break down completely was that of keeping track of the people who had been arrested. A considerable number gave false names when they were booked, so that, when relatives, frantic with anxiety, called up, there would be no record of them. Others had, somehow, been booked two or more times, and, with more than one booking number, it was difficult to trace them. A few had been arrested without being booked at all, and, as far as the sheriff's department was concerned, did not exist. In the confusion one seven-months-pregnant woman spent almost two weeks in jail, even though a judge had ordered her released.

Barney himself resided two days in Lincoln Heights before the tv director was able to find him and bail him out. The charges against him were dismissed at the preliminary hearing.

42   The Glitter of Gold's

Sitting on Washington Blvd. near Central Ave. is Gold's, a large department store. It is just south of the Santa Monica Freeway, which had remained as the northern restraining line of the riot. Gold's had first been broken into early on Saturday morning, and the police were running a shuttle service from the store to the jail. Officers would come, pick up a batch of looters, and take off. Ten minutes later the place would be full of people again. In an hour the police would come back, grab another dozen, and the whole cycle would commence anew. Perhaps as many as 200 persons were picked up at the one location.

Dandy Briggs found himself there a little after 5 o'clock Saturday afternoon. When he had returned home late Thursday night—or, more correctly, early Friday morning—and learned that his mother, Manella, had been stoned while riding with Anita Greyson, the realization that in the chaos he might well have come to throw rocks at his own mother had shaken him. His father had been even more upset, lecturing him that just because the white people had committed injustices, that was no excuse for becoming a hoodlum. So Friday he had sat at home, watching the riot on television, wishing every minute that he was there where the action was —not to take part, he told himself, just to see what was going on.

Everybody seemed to be loading up with stuff except him. He was really getting upset about it when this friend of his came by with a truck, and told him that they'd opened up this big department store, and didn't he want to come along? Dandy decided he did.

A Thrifty Drug Store and Shop-Rite Market were burning on Central Ave. as Dandy's friend pulled around to the loading platform at the rear of Gold's. The large, roll-up type door had been pushed back, and people were running out of the store, carrying every conceivable kind of merchandise.

Dandy's friend boasted that this was the third department store "opening" he had been to—he was accumulating quite a stock of appliances, refrigerators, television, stereo sets, and the like.

Dandy was helping him carry out a stereo, when, suddenly, there were shouts that the police were coming; and, as Dandy looked out the window, he could see that they had arrived. There seemed no chance of making it out of the store, so Dandy, dropping the stereo, headed back in. At least a dozen others had the same idea, and they were all running around, looking for some place to hide. Even though outside it was bright daylight, much of the interior was dusky, and some of it quite dark. He had headed into a narrow hallway leading to a storage room when, suddenly, here came a plainclothes officer with helmet and shotgun right in back of him. There was no place for Dandy to go. He threw up his hands.

Sgt. Len Leeds, normally assigned to the narcotics division, poked him with the gun and shouted to his partners, "Get ready! Here comes one!"

Sgt. Leeds had already been at the store several times previously. He was armed with a .12-gauge shotgun and two .38 revolvers. To his right was the door to the store room. Without lights or windows, it was utterly dark, and he could hear the movement of several persons inside.

"Come out. You're all under arrest!" he ordered.

There was no response.

Quickly he ducked inside the doorway and pressed against the wall, shotgun extended in front of him for protection. Suddenly someone jumped from his right, from behind the doorway. As the sergeant shook him loose another person made a dash for the door. Colliding with Leeds, the looter shoved the gun aside. As Leeds was spun around, his finger tightened on the trigger, and the gun, held at waist level, went off, sounding like a cannon in the confines of the room.

As the reverberations of the shot stopped ringing in his ears, Sgt. Leeds could hear other people moving and breathing in the cellar-dark confines. He could see no one.

"All of you—this is a police officer!" he addressed them. "Come out with your hands up, or I'm going to fire!"

"Hold it. I'm coming out!" a voice said.

A moment later a man materialized not a foot from Leeds. They both jumped, as if simultaneously receiving an electric shock. Unsure of the man's intentions, Leeds shoved the barrel of the gun into his chest. Then, moving around behind him, he poked him out into the passageway.

"Here comes another one!" he called.

With his eyes becoming adjusted to the darkness, Leeds spotted the figures of two more persons crouched against the side of the room. He repeated his command for them to come out. They rose, and he started them toward the door.

"Here come two more."

As they departed, another person entered the room, and Leeds heard the voice of one of his partners, Sgt. Glen A. Bachman, "I'm right behind you, Len."

"Do you think there's anyone else in here?" Leeds asked.

Bachman expressed the belief that there was, over on the right. Leeds walked along the wall, where there was a three-foot deep shelf approximately three feet off the floor. As he did so, a figure, leaping up and off the shelf, grabbed at the shotgun. As Leeds tried to free the gun, there was a brief, violent tug-of-war. The butt of the gun hit against the wall, shattering. With a violent wrench, Leeds regained possession of the gun, his momentum causing him to stagger backward. A second later the silhouette of the man appeared as he headed toward the doorway. Leeds fired, seeing simultaneously the flash of another gun to his right.

Curtis Lee Gaines, 24, a five-foot-ten 200-pounder, spun to the floor, his back ripped open by the shotgun blast and a .38-caliber bullet. He had never been arrested before.

He was the nineteenth, the first to die since 10 o'clock that morning.

*   *   *

An hour later, at 87th and Broadway, right in the area where all hell had broken loose 24 hours earlier, Officers Kenneth Henderson and James Benton, riding in an unmarked, dark-blue Plymouth, spotted three men loading clothes into a maroon Cadillac convertible in front of Harry's Men's Store. As the officers made a U-turn and doubled back, the Cadillac started up, turning into an alley at mid-block. Following behind the Cadillac, the officers saw it stop. The three men, jumping out, headed for a fence bordering the alley. The first two vaulted over successfully. The third was hanging there, trying to pull himself up, when Henderson and Benton both fired their shotguns.

Willie Curtis Hawkins, a 31-year-old Texan, toppled back. He was the twentieth.

43   The Roadblocks of Watts

Lack of any comprehensive intelligence or news dissemination network continued to plague the law enforcement agencies to the extent that many of the National Guard troops received most of their reports of what was occurring by listening on transistor radios to XTRA, an all-news station, located in Tijuana, Mexico.

From what they did hear, certain opinions were being formed by troops at the roadblocks. One was that cars that would approach within half a block, screech their tires, then back off, were "testing them." Another was that it was these cars they could expect trouble from that evening, and that they should keep a sharp eye out for all vehicles they had seen in the vicinity earlier. A third was that there were groups of Negroes with red armbands roving about—the red armband story was proliferating fantastically. They were seen "casing markets," spotted in ten cars on the Ventura Freeway, viewed in a yellow school bus on the Golden State Freeway, and discovered in Santa Barbara and elsewhere. In Watts a police officer told guardsmen that the armbands designated Muslims; someone else reported that they identified a sect of "blood brothers"; a Guard officer indicated that according to intelligence reports available to him, it was the Viet Cong who were behind it.[1]

As it ultimately developed, neither the LAPD, nor the L.A. County sheriff's department ever were able to discover one Negro wearing a red armband. Undercover agents, attempt-

---

[1] Perhaps he had heard the statement by Harold Stassen, made at a distance of several hundred miles, that the three-fingered sign—which, of course, indicated *Watts*—identified the rioters as adherents of Mao Tse-tung.

ing to trace the origin of the rumors, came to the conclusion that they were probably the result of one more misconception or misinterpretation grown out of all proportion.[2] The only *known* persons to be wearing red armbands were four high-ranking National Guard officers, who were using them so that they themselves could be more easily distinguished by the troops.

As darkness approached, the situation at the roadblock at Grape and 103rd Sts. was tense. This was the same corner where, in 1964, a riot had almost been ignited as a result of the shot robber,[3] and which, in normal times, is a hangout for dropouts and other disaffected youths. There had been considerable verbal harassment of guardsmen at the roadblock during the day—*"We're gonna get you and burn you tonight!"*—and Sgt. Victor D. Subian reported that he could see about a dozen people wearing red armbands, plus one *leader* with a red rosette in his lapel, at a tavern a couple of blocks away. There was apprehension that they were preparing to charge the guardsmen. There was also anxiety about an orange-red Chevrolet that had been seen in the vicinity several times, and which was thought to be "scouting." Later in the afternoon the troops heard that two cars, a white Cadillac and a maroon Mercury, had passed through and fired shots at another roadblock.

Shortly before 8 o'clock elements of the 49th division, which had been flown down from northern California, began arriving at the roadblock to relieve the Glendale troopers, who had now been in Watts for almost 24 hours. The northern Californians were, of course, entirely unfamiliar with the area, and, although they had heard a good number of hoary stories, they had very little idea of what actually to expect.

Ramon Luis Hermosillo was a 19-year-old of Mexican descent who lived at 95th and Hickory Sts. Hickory is the next north-south street parallel to Grape, and 95th is eight blocks north of 103rd. Hermosillo and a friend, William Robert Gomez, had been driving around the area for an hour or more. For 20 minutes they had sat parked behind a brick wall within a couple of blocks of the guardsmen. Apparently, as they talked to friends, there was some discussion as to

---

[2] This author was told that in later stages of the riot some members of civil rights groups engaged in food distribution were wearing arm bands and berets for purposes of identification.

[3] See page 57.

whether a Mexican would be treated differently than a Negro by the Guard, or whether Mexicans had as much courage as Negroes. Shortly before 8 o'clock Hermosillo started down 103rd St. toward the roadblock.

He was driving an orange-red 1957 Chevrolet Bel Air.

At some 75 yards distance from the roadblock, troopers had placed rubber cones as markers, to warn approaching drivers. Glendale guardsmen were still at the scene, talking with their replacements from the 49th, the attention of most of them being directed toward a white pickup truck which, approaching from the east, had halted at the barricade.

It was at this moment that one of the newly arrived sergeants from the 49th spotted an orange Chevrolet heading toward the roadblock at approximately 40 miles per hour from the opposite direction.

"Look out for that car!" he shouted, leveling his rifle.

To a noncom, Sgt. John W. Jackson, who had been there all day, it seemed as if the car would halt. Momentarily it hesitated, then started speeding up again.

The sergeant from the 49th fired. His action was followed by a fusillade from other 49th division troopers. Ramon Hermosillo slumped over behind the wheel. The car veered out of control and halted in front of a poultry market.

As Capt. Randall L. Woods ran forward toward the car with a medic, he was driven back by fire that exploded from behind the block wall surrounding the Jordan Downs Housing Project. To one noncom it sounded definitely like automatic weapons fire, although an officer believed "it was more like a string of firecrackers." (It is obviously impossible to determine which of the observations is correct, but from the viewpoint of availability of automatic weapons, and what is known of those weapons that were confiscated by police, the latter seems considerably more likely.)

At any rate, there was no question that bullets were bouncing in the vicinity of the roadblock and the wrecked car. Capt. Woods ordered the fire returned, and, for a few minutes, it seemed as if a small war was in progress. When it became feasible to remove Hermosillo from the car, it was found that he was critically injured, and he died on the way to the hospital.

He was the twenty-first, the second to be killed at a roadblock in Watts. Both, curiously, had been Mexican-Americans.

Within the hour, two other cars were fired on at the same roadblock, one man receiving a slight leg injury. All police vehicles were ordered to turn on their red lights when approaching National Guard roadblocks. To those in unmarked cars, it was suggested they proceed with extreme caution.

Following the shooting of Hermosillo, it was decided to set up an additional roadblock at 102nd and Beach Sts., midway between the ones at 103rd and Grape, and Compton and 102nd. This particular intersection, a comparatively narrow one, had the two-story Westminster Presbyterian Center situated on the northwest; across from it lay an empty lot; to the southwest was an empty one-story office and store building, subsequently taken over by the McCone Commission, with a tavern in mid-block and, beyond it, the smoldering mass of the business district; to the southeast stood a large, white-fronted mortuary.

Sgt. John Sutherland with 11 men was assigned to take command of this intersection. As he led his men the four blocks to his new assignment, he could hear considerable firing, and—as hundreds of other men were discovering—it was disconcerting to know that shots were going off, to be able to hear the occasional tinkle of glass and to see the spatter of a ricochet, yet be unable to tell from where, or from whom the firing was coming. At the corner, Sgt. Sutherland and his men set up a trailer and some trash cans, and then made themselves as inconspicuous as possible. They had halted one or two cars when they noticed another proceeding east on 102nd St.

Sgt. Sutherland reports: "I went into the street with two men. We fired two warning shots into the air. The vehicle accelerated, proceeded to run the roadblock; I ordered one shot to be fired at the tire, one shot was fired, the tire went out, the vehicle skidded to a halt about 25 to 30 meters in front of my roadblock where I had two men posted. We proceeded to the vehicle, searched the vehicle, and pulled the occupants out. There was a female Negro and a male Negro occupant. The female Negro was wounded in the leg, which was a minor wound, wasn't bleeding too bad. We applied a handkerchief to her leg and the male Negro held it on there and stopped the bleeding.

"A squad car came, and left in a minute to get an ambulance, and by that time we were back in our positions."

Since the area north of 102nd St. is a residential one, numbers of persons came out of their homes to look on as the woman was taken away in an ambulance. Two blocks to the east on 102nd St. someone else was watching: lean, tall, 25-year-old Charles Patrick Smalley.

Smalley had not been drinking, but he may have been stimulated by bennies, for he had been released only two days previously from the custody of the sheriff, having served 30 days for illegal possession of "red devils." In his short life, he had rocketed to fame, then just as swiftly begun plummeting toward oblivion.

In 1955, at the age of 15, his voice had led him from church singing to his first nightclub date. Under the name of "Charles Fizer," he had become part of The Olympics, a five-man group that hit the big time with "Hully Gully," a record that almost reached the magic million mark. Other well-selling records had followed. Nightclub dates had multiplied and become bigger.

Smalley had been, although he didn't know it, teetering in the middle of the entertainment world's seesaw—he could go one way and be a hero, or he could go the other and three months later nobody would even remember they had known his name. He had been, also, in that stage of transition in which, as an emerging individual aware of his talents, the slings and arrows of prejudice had been not only racial but individual insults. He was the Sammy Davis, Jr., whose white army buddies had him drink piss out of a beer bottle to emphasize to him that, no matter how people might applaud him, he was still a *nigger* to them.

In 1963 the good life had started blowing up for Smalley. Because he was too edgy to get along with people, The Olympics had dropped him. By the time he was released from jail on August 10, 1965, he was reduced to taking a job as a busboy at a restaurant.

Early in the evening two days later, dressed in bright yellow shirt and black pants, he borrowed his uncle's 1955 Buick to pick up a girlfriend. Although he never reached the girl's house, he was headed in the direction of home when he halted two blocks short of the National Guard barricade at 102nd and Beach Sts.

Sgt. Sutherland, bluff, young, well-muscled, was keeping one eye on the Buick. At 9 o'clock he noticed it approaching, and . . .

"One man from the squad flipped a lighted cigarette into

the street. The car stopped, turned out its lights, backed up 50 yards, and sat there for five to ten minutes. It turned on its lights and proceeded slowly toward the intersection. At this time I walked into the road with another man from my squad. I shouted 'halt' several times, the vehicle still proceeding west on 102nd St. I fired two gunshots into the air as warning shots. The vehicle accelerated extremely at a fast rate of speed—he was doing approximately I'd say 35 maybe 40 miles an hour—and headed directly for the barricade. There was one man in front of the trailer and one man behind. At that time I figured he was either going to run down my men or he was going to turn the corner, and he was heading right for the barricade. The man in front of me, I commanded him at that time to fire one shot into the tire, and the car still headed right for the barricade. I commanded then for two men to fire into the vehicle, they fired into the vehicle. As the men jumped out of the way, and one fell in the street, it went completely out of control, turned the corner and headed up Beach St. It ran into the building and caromed off that, then wedged between a telephone pole and the brick wall and stopped there."

Smalley was pulled out of the car. He lay on his stomach on the pavement, legs apart, propping himself up on his elbows, hands clasped together in front of him. Although the young guardsmen did not know it, he might, at one time, have communicated with some of them in their living rooms, a communication that was now lost in the creases of blood that flowed across his cheek and nose from a blotch—as if an ink bottle had been spilled—above his left eye, dripping down steadily onto his forearm and hands. Surrounded by national guardsmen with fixed bayonets—except for one who was kneeling by his side to administer first aid—he had both eyes open, focusing, seemingly, on a far vision.

He was dead shortly thereafter, a .30-caliber bullet having lodged in his brain. He was the twenty-third.

44 The Taste of Ashes

A half hour earlier, Joe Nelson Bridgett, in a gun battle that outdid anything seen on television, had become the twenty-second.

A quartet of deputy sheriffs were checking business establishments along Florence Ave. at 8:30 p.m. when, around the corner from a Thrifty Drug Store, they noted two men loading a Pontiac with bottles of liquor. After placing them under arrest, two of the deputies, Paul Wilson and Jack Innis, started for the shattered windows of the store.

Inside they could see two men, from the midriff up, moving back and forth behind a cardboard display as if they were part of an animated advertisement.

"Police! Come out with your hands up!" Innis ordered.

The two men advanced momentarily. Then a shot rang out.

"I'm hit! I'm hit!" Wilson cried as he toppled to the pavement.

Innis ran toward him. Wilson, he was able to see, had been wounded in the groin. Several more shots spurted from the store. Crouched, Innis sprinted toward the patrol car to radio for help. He had almost reached it when a bullet thudded into his thigh, sending him sprawling into the gutter.

The third deputy, Bryan Keenan, ran to where Innis lay.

"I'm shot!" Innis told him.

"Where'd it come from?"

"Inside the store."

Keenan, joined by the fourth deputy, Donald Kennedy, fired his shotgun into the darkened reaches of the store. The sharp crack of small-arms fire responded. The avenue was brightly illuminated by street lights, placing the deputies at a disadvantage. The wounded Innis, lying in the gutter, attempted to shoot out the lights with his revolver.

There was a sudden shout of "Here they come!" and two Negroes, firing as they charged, plunged through the shattered window. Momentarily the deputies were against the pair at point-blank range, shotguns against pistols. As the direct blast of a shotgun tore one Negro apart, the other dashed around the corner, disappearing into the darkness. In the confusion, he, and the other pair who had first been spotted at the car, escaped. None was ever identified.

Sirens split the darkness like the prows of speedboats slicing through the water. More shots resounded as the deputies, fearing snipers, methodically shot out all the surrounding street lights. Joe Nelson Bridgett, 22 years old, lay still, the debris of the city intermingling with the shreds of his own life. Few would shed a tear for him. Yet in his death Joe Bridgett was telling his story better, perhaps, than he would ever have been able to in life.

He had been born in Shreveport, La., the only child of a marriage that dissolved while he was still a baby. Neither parent had wanted him, and he had come to Los Angeles to live with his maternal grandmother, who doted on him and thought he could do no wrong.

But he had lived in a neighborhood where doing wrong is no more difficult than going to get a milkshake is for the Caucasian kid. Where some things, like playing craps and smoking marijuana are, for all practical purposes, not considered wrong at all. And Joe Bridgett, who might have led a productive life, started sliding into the abyss long before he himself was able to realize he was on the skids.

He was intelligent. He was articulate. His English tended to follow the speech pattern of the Southern Negro—which was, of course, what he heard every day—but, except for the idiosyncrasy of always using a lower case *i* in place of *I,* he was a good speller. He was handsome, and he could have charmed a tiger into a purring pussycat. To an objective observer his dropping out of school in the eleventh grade at the age of 17 made no sense. To Joe Bridgett it seemed quite logical—who needs it? For his teachers it was impossible to cope with—there are just too many Joe Bridgetts.

He had already had his first brush with the law. The year before leaving school he had been arrested for stealing an automobile. He was placed on a year's probation, and returned to his grandmother. In 1961, at the age of 18, he married a 17-year-old girl, Kathylen. They immediately had a child; and then quickly began expecting another. Joe had no skills. He was a glut on the labor market. He worked as a packer in a frozen food plant, but he was too smart and too ambitious to be satisfied with that kind of job. He knew, as every Negro knows, that the money lies in hustling.

Police officers were cruising down Avalon Blvd. a few minutes after midnight on April 16, 1963, when they spotted a car in which Joe and two friends were riding. It was, for the area, a typical pullover—the officers said a robbery had been committed, and the car in which Joe was riding looked suspicious. In the southeast sector it is a simple matter of percentages, a certain number of cars halted are bound to be carrying narcotics, concealed weapons, or other contraband. In this case the officers found two marijuana cigarettes inside the automobile, and, in the gutter, a bag of marijuana seeds that Joe was attempting to get rid of.

Joe was found guilty of possession of narcotics. But he did an excellent job of shucking it with the probation officer.

"His own attitude toward the present offense appears to be serious and responsible and it is believed that the defendant is an excellent subject for probation," said the officer.

"You are only 20 years of age," the judge told Joe, "and I assume that you do not want to spend a goodly portion of your life in the state prison, is that not true?"

"True," Joe replied.

"There are certain types of offenses in this state, Mr. Bridgett, which an individual simply dare not repeat. One such offense is the possession of any type of narcotic . . . on the next occasion . . . you may have a very long time to serve in the state prison. . . . Is that clear to you?"

"Yes, sir, it is."

The judge fined Joe $210 and placed him on five years probation.

Up to this time Joe Bridgett had been a good father and husband. He had brought home the money he earned. But, as the probation officer said, "The defendant has no salable skills and it is expected that employment will probably be a problem with him in the future."

Having lost his job in the packing plant, he began drifting from place to place: four months in a car wash; three months in a hand laundry. He hated it, and he began taking out his anger on his wife. Early in 1964 they separated.

After that, Joe was through working. Several appointments were made for him at the Department of Employment, but he usually did not show up. He lived off his girlfriends and his grandmother, who was a soft touch, and

whatever he could make by hustling. He was supposed to contribute $40 a month to the support of his children, but contributed nothing. Kathylen could barely make ends meet by working in a laundry.

Said Ralph Merola, president of the Probation Officers Union, "The department has long been so understaffed as to make a mockery of proper investigation, guidance and rehabilitation. Officers' individual caseloads are often as high as 230 probationers, four to five times the average recommended by the National Council on Crime and Delinquency. Members have reported having to dismiss juveniles, sometimes after a year, without ever having actually seen the youngsters they are supposed to supervise and rehabilitate."

The Board of Supervisors and county officials pooh-poohed the charge. Nothing to it, they said.

Yet Joe Nelson Bridgett violated one condition after another of his probation. Time after time he failed to report as he was supposed to, and in one 12-month period he didn't report at all. In 24 months he paid precisely $3 of the $210 fine that had been levied against him. The harried probation officer, with 200 other cases to handle, was unable to track him down, much less exercise any influence over him. If the question arises, then, why was the probation not revoked, revocation is usually a last resort. A warrant has to be issued; the man has to be found; a new court appearance has to be scheduled. And the jails are so crowded that the last thing they want is more prisoners.

In early 1965 Joe Nelson Bridgett was arrested for illegal possession of barbiturates, and sentenced to 30 days in jail. He was now clearly in violation of his probation, yet, after completing his sentence, he was released. On June 8, the probation officer wrote, "The defendant is living a worthless existence . . . an extended period in custody may be needed."

Joe didn't want to go to prison. Desperately he tried to explain his way out. "It happened like this on or about the 28th of February i was picked up for possession of pills on 59th St. and Avalon [1] one night. But the most biggest part of it was i did not have any pills on me i happen to be passing by there and i seen an old associate of mine, so i stop and was chatting with him and drinking a cup of coffee in front of the hot dog stand when these two policeman walked up

[1] One and the same location as 60th and Avalon. See page 163.

pulled me away and started patting on me so one of them sayed look in his sweater pocket that's where it's suppose to be remember.

"So he reaches down in my sweater pocket and comes out with one roll of pills, but why should they have picked me out of all them people that was standing around. I seen them when they got out of the car but i didn't have no reason to leave just because they was coming. But like i told the police if i had something like that on me do they think that i would of been a big enough fool to have seen them coming and wouldn't leave. But the only thing that i could figure is that someone planted them on me, because i use to live around there and i use to know plenty of the women's round there and a lots of them liked me. So it started getting around that i was taking everybody girlfriend. But it wasn't true. But one night one of the girls husband walk up and accused me of going with his wife and some of the others did the same thing two. But it was untrue so i had made enemys and hadn't even did nothing.

"So i figured since that had happened someone or one of the husbands planted on me. But what i can't figure out Mr. Thomas that's my other probation officer he told me that he wasn't going to violate me. . . . So now they tell me i am going to have to go to court and most likely get violated but i don't think that's fair. You goes and look on a mans past record so you figure when it happens once more he's guilty. But i am not guilty in 1961 yes i was, but now i didn't do anything and looks as if im going to do time for something that is false. A little bit after i was accused of being taking everybody's wife's three men's jumped me one night when i was coming from work they must have been waiting on me. Because when i step in the hallway to go to my room someone hit me and one of them cut me with a knife i had to have stitches in my leg, so that put me up on crutches for three weeks. If it hadn't been for a friend of mine i would have bleeded to death but he saved me buy putting a turneqet and tying it tight. So i figured it all happened behind them women, because i heard one of them say that he won't mess with nobody else wife no more. So i lost my job by being unable to go to work. Well i guess that's all of my story."

*   *   *

At 15 minutes before 10 p.m., Officers Richard Young and Ronald Wagner were driving down San Pedro St. in the lower reaches of the riot area. As they passed a large hardware store, they observed two men emerging from the broken window and turning down the alley at the side of the store.

While Young went after them, Wagner circled around the block, a long one, the other way. In the maze of small paths, backyard fences, bushes and jetsam—including the rusting remains of an automobile—that comprised the mixed business-residential area, the men passed out of Young's sight and hearing, and he halted. Irregular patches of light and shadow were cast by the fading rays of a street lamp and a naked bulb on the back porch of a house.

Breathing hard, Wagner came around from the other side of the building, just as Young was startled by the rustle of some fronds not more than a dozen feet from him.

"Come out of there!" he called to the person, whose shoes he could see peeping from beneath the vegetation.

There was no response. As Young repeated the call, Wagner warily approached to within a foot or two of the foliage screening the wall of the house.

In the uncertain light he believed he saw something glinting in the man's hand. Afraid it might be a gun, he fired.

Thirty-two-year-old Juan Puentes, a Mexican-American, toppled forward. He had been very drunk, and he was now dead.

He was the twenty-fourth.

*   *   *

Robert Ernest Pegues had decided it was time for him to get in on the burning. A poorly educated, 31-year-old laborer, he made no bones about it. He told all his neighbors and then went down to a vacant store at 4807 S. Broadway, a block from where the night before the burning Allied Furniture Store had consumed Rita Johnson. Kicking in the plate glass window, he stuffed a wad of burning paper through it.

When, at approximately 10:30 p.m., Chief Ken Long [2] and his task force, returning from a fire at 62nd and Broadway, came upon the location, the building was already totally involved. No other units were on the scene. Fluffy clouds of smoke and fire poured from all the openings, capping the

[2] See page 310.

roof with orange-black whipped cream. Hooking their lines to a hydrant, the chief and his men went to work.

A half dozen blocks to the northwest, across the barrier of the Harbor Freeway, the National Guard had set up a roadblock at the corner of Vernon Ave. and Figueroa St. It was 11 p.m. when an old Cadillac, throbbing up to the intersection, failed to halt. Troops opened fire. Both front tires of the car went out, the driver slumped over the wheel—although seriously injured, he survived—and the car skidded to a halt 100 yards away.

As the guardsmen approached the vehicle, they, in turn, began receiving fire.

At the conflagration on Broadway, there was the usual accompaniment of noise from the engines of the pumper, the *whoosh* and crackle engendered by the flames, the occasional collapse of a timber, and the *pop-pop-pop* of exploding aerosol cans and bottles of carbonated drinks and inflammable liquids. It is an accompaniment a fireman is so used to he pays no attention to it. Chief Long was startled to hear one of his men calling to him, "Chief! Chief! They're shooting at us!"

It was 11 p.m., and the crack of small-arms fire was enmeshed indistinguishably with the explosions from the fire, but there was no mistaking the occasional *ping* of metal, or the splattering sound of a bullet flattening itself against the concrete.

No police were present, and Chief Long did not hesitate. "Let's get out of here!" he ordered his men.

They stayed out until the police arrived and began laying down a barrage of covering fire, aiming for the top of a building next to the United Industries Store, on the roof of which someone had glimpsed a figure. By this time both sides of the street had been enveloped by flames, and a two-story frame residence in back of the commercial buildings was burning as well.

In the latter part of the afternoon, James Sanders, Jr., the landlord at 4612 S. Broadway, a two-story building that contained two small shops on the ground floor and apartments on the second, was "having a little party with Delilah, L. J. Hutchison, Ocie, and Jake," about eight people in all, "when the soldiers came down the street and said lock all the doors and close the windows." As in other buildings, the locking and closing was temporary, and the party was soon under way again.

Shortly after 5 o'clock, one of the tenants, Neal Minor, had come in to pay his rent, returning shortly thereafter with three large bottles of orange pop, and possibly some other provisions, that he had bought at Mike's Liquor Store, which up to this time had continued to remain open and unviolated.

Sanders, an electronics assembler, lived in the same apartment as but in a separate room from Ann Randolph, an older woman whom he was taking care of because she was ill. The former operator of a creep joint, she is recalled by police officers on the vice squad not without a certain fondness as "good old Black Annie." On Monday, five days previously, she had sent Sanders out to buy for her a 12-gauge Savage shotgun for $59 at Fred's Jewelry and Loan Co. down the street. The gun, together with a box of birdshot Sanders had obtained, had been placed in a closet in the apartment.

Hardly had the firemen returned to their hoses, when another flurry of shots drove Chief Long behind a wall and his men beneath their fire rigs. More and more buildings were igniting along a three-block stretch—three furniture stores, a junk shop, two drug stores, a bar, a knitting mill, offices and apartments—creating a flaming hell of incarnated shadows and myriad sharp explosions. Ground glass and water imparted an icy texture to the pavement. Reflections of green-glinting street lights and police car red lights twisted about each other amidst the red glow of fires on the mirrorlike surface. A score of police officers were crouched behind their vehicles, behind light standards, behind boxes and other jetsam, trying to draw a bead on the elusive sniper or snipers. A National Guard convoy of seven or eight vehicles, called to protect the firemen, rumbled onto the scene, the men hitting the bottom of the trucks as several rounds whistled over their heads. One round creased the helmet of a trooper; another thudded into the radio receiver of a jeep sitting in the center of the intersection. To several of the police and National Guard officers, it appeared that the sniper must be located on the roof of the apartment building at 4612.

Breaking their way in through the front door of the building, which Sanders had locked, they pounded on his door, demanding to know if he were the landlord. Sanders, who to some degree was feeling the effects of the party, acknowledged that he was. A police officer asked if anyone in the

building had a weapon, and Sanders replied that a gun, belonging to Ann Randolph, was in his apartment.

Going along the corridor, the police kicked open the doors
to the other rooms. An officer inquired whether there was an
attic.

"There is a door. You push it up, but no ladder," Sanders
replied.

A trooper, jumping on top of a box, pushed open the
door, and threw several canisters of teargas into the space
above, letting the door drop back down.

"All of you niggers stay in bed!" an officer ordered. The
police and guardsmen withdrew from the building.

As Officer Jerry Miller drove up in his patrol car, he noted
the muzzle flash from a gun in an upstairs window of the
apartment building. Simultaneously, Sgt. Charles F. Buckland
of the detective division saw the same flash, heard a boom,
and noted the ripple of birdshot on the pavement in front of
him as he dashed along the street. Another flash brought the
remains of a broken window tinkling to the ground just over
his shoulder. Buckland, aiming at the window, was joined by
Miller in returning the fire.

At almost the same instant 2nd Lt. Ernest L. Childs of the
National Guard spotted what he believed to be the figure of
a man behind a Burgermeister Beer sign atop the roof.
Mounted in his jeep was a .30-caliber machine gun. Swivel-
ing it about, he aimed, then fired.

As its sharp chatter resounded, troopers all along the line
took it as their cue to open fire on the apartment building.
Every window collapsed. The entire front of the building
was riddled, police and troops combined directing 200 rounds
in its direction during a span of two or three minutes.

Only a determined effort by the National Guard officers
brought the firing to a halt. As the shots died down, Sgt.
Buckland called out to the building's occupants, "Come out
with your hands in the air, or we are going to open fire!"

There was no reply. He repeated the order.

"Don't shoot! Don't shoot! We're coming!" a voice replied.

Seven persons, in various forms of undress—including Ann
Randolph and her friend Delilah in short nightgowns—
trooped out of the door of the building, their hands in the
air. All were made to lie down in the street, their heads
pointed in the direction of the gutter. A mongrel, who had
followed them out, trotted around, sniffing at them curiously.

Miss Randolph, ill and heavy-set, spotted Sgt. Buckland. "I know this officer," she said.

"Yes, Ann. I've known you for several years, just like I know Delilah," he replied. Turning to Delilah, he asked her if she had a gun.

She replied in the negative. Buckland repeated the question to Ann Randolph.

"Yes. I have a shotgun," she responded.

"Where is it?"

"I would have to show you."

"Okay. Let's go."

"I'm not going back into that building unless you hold my hand!"

"Well, come on." Buckland had known Ann for many years, and liked her. "I'll take your hand, and we will go get the gun."

Hand in hand, Buckland and Ann Randolph went back into the building, Officer Jerry Miller following. In her room, Miss Randolph pointed behind the sofa, and Buckland reached down and pulled out the shotgun, handing it to Miller. Miller removed one shell from the chamber, and two from the magazine of the gun, sticking them into his pocket for evidence. Shortly thereafter, in a further run-in with rioters, he absentmindedly slammed them into his own shotgun. It was the first time that the evidence in a case was, literally, shot to hell.

Hardly had the officer returned to the street when two cars, a green Buick in the lead, barreled around the corner. The sight of guns red-winking from their windows sent officers diving to the pavement alongside the civilians still lying there. As all continued prone for two or three minutes, not knowing what to expect next, Miller asked Neal Minor, one of the occupants of the building, to whose apartment the third window belonged?

"That's my room," Minor replied.

Since that was the window in which Miller had seen the gun flash, and since a search of the building developed that Ann Randolph had possessed the only gun in it, Minor and Miss Randolph were arrested and charged with assault with intent to kill. At their trial, both were judged not guilty.

A few blocks away, several police cars, alerted that shots had been fired from two cars along Broadway, picked up the headlights of a speeding automobile. Behind the wheel of the 1957 Ford, the transmission of which was emitting an unhappy growl, sat 29-year-old Joseph Glenwood Wallace. He had left home a short time before and, somewhere along the line, had had two or three drinks.

Wallace, born in Mississippi, had spent 9 of the past 13 years in prison. He had first been arrested at the age of 16 in the small Gulf Coast town of Moss Point for stealing a bicycle, an offense that had netted him a conviction on burglary and grand larceny charges. He had been incarcerated from 1952 to 1955.

In 1957 he had become involved in an argument with a girlfriend, and had broken into her house to retrieve some clothing. That had cost him a conviction on a charge of burglary, and the next six years of his life.

After his release in 1963 he had come to California on behest of his brother. He had gone to work as a janitor for a pie company. He had acquired a girlfriend, and she was carrying his child.

At the intersection of Slauson and Avalon Blvds., 2nd Lt. Troy Hill was patrolling in a jeep, with four men in a three-quarter-ton truck following behind. He heard the sounds of the pursuit and saw the red lights of several police cars in the distance. Stationing the two vehicles across the road, he ordered his men to take cover behind them, and to load their weapons.

As the car being pursued by the police approached to within half a block, Lt. Hill fired two shots across its hood from his .45. When this did not halt it, he aimed six shots directly at the driver. At the last round, the car skidded in the intersection, ran up onto the sidewalk, and began rounding the corner. Uncertain as to whether the driver had been wounded or was trying to escape, the lieutenant motioned for his men to open fire. As the fusillade poured into the Ford, Joseph Wallace collapsed over the wheel. The car rammed into a power pole in the middle of the block.

Wallace was the twenty-fifth. No weapon or contraband were found in the car.

*   *   *

Hardly had the firemen and others along Broadway regrouped, when a new series of shots showered down from the direction of a two-story building a block away. Petals of fire were already engulfing this building on all sides. As

Buckland and a lieutenant dashed toward it, there was the wink of a revolver in an upstairs window, a slug slamming into a light standard six inches above the lieutenant's head.

Buckland shot back. The heat from the fire was so intense it was impossible to approach within more than a few feet of the building. As firemen came up and began training their hoses, a national guardsman, thinking to protect them, fired a tear-gas shell onto the roof. The gas immediately drifted down, felling a half dozen of the firemen. Five minutes later the building was crackling like a huge bonfire.[3]

With several of the firemen laid *hors de combat* by the tear gas, and the rest withdrawing because of the sniper activity, Lt. Col. Robert Dove—a fire captain in civilian life— suggested to Chief Long that the men leave their lines loaded, and that he and his troops continue to fight the fires until the area was secured.

He next offered the suggestion, immediately adopted, that four troopers be placed on each fire truck as protection for the firemen. Within a few hours the firefighters regained complete freedom of movement, and were no longer subjected to harassment. As one chief said, "Up to four hours ago we were getting licked. Now we're in control."

The conflagration along Broadway was the last major fire threat. Sunday and thereafter, there were only scattered reports of burnings, and most of these were the result of earlier fires reigniting.

*   *   *

In addition to Wallace, two others died in the span of the hour bisected by midnight. The twenty-sixth and twenty-seventh were both 19 years old; they both were shot far beyond the boundaries of what is known as the riot area; they both were caught during the commission of liquor store burglaries.

Frederick Maurice Hendricks was the first. He had been at Avalon and Imperial Thursday night, and there is con-

---

[3] Several police officers believe snipers and looters were trapped in various burning buildings. Were this so, there is considerable probability that some of their remains, as in the case of Rita Johnson, would have been found. It cannot be denied, however, that in the haste to clean up the wreckage afterward, a few bones might have gone unnoticed and been shoveled off with the rest of the debris.

siderable evidence that he participated in the looting and burning of a pharmacy. Later he spent a few hours in jail for being picked up drunk on the street. He lived in the Aliso Village Housing Project located near the intersection of the San Bernardino and Santa Ana Freeways, a deteriorating area of overlapping Negro, Mexican and Japanese homes. He had been ensnared in the typically vicious maelstrom of a broken family living a marginal existence, too engaged in simply staying alive to contribute love or understanding to a growing boy. He had learned first to rebel, then to direct that rebellion at the white society that, because of its studied prejudices, he believed to be at the root of his trouble. Like a manic-depressive he alternated between periods of the most intense hatred and the greatest determination to transcend it by proving his own worth. In probation camp at the age of 14 he was a constant troublemaker, then became a model student and worker upon his release to a foster home. A high-school dropout in his junior year, he was highly motivated in the Youth Opportunity Agency classes in which he enrolled.

At a liquor store within a block or two of his home, the brightly illuminated city hall towering over the dark and shabby streets, Hendricks and two friends—one a 14-year-old boy on a visit to Los Angeles from Louisiana—decided it was time to get high. After rattling the handle of the door, Hendricks plucked a bottle from a trashcan, and thrust it through the window. It was his bad luck that an unmarked patrol car happened to round the corner at that moment, and that, when all three of the boys ran, it was he who caught a bullet in the neck.

The second of the two, Eugene Shimatsu, was a college student of Japanese ancestry. Officers spotted him and another person in a drug store on the approaches of Culver City. When he attempted to escape, Shimatsu was shot and killed.

*   *   *

There were others who, not officially listed as victims of the riot, were victims just the same. There was 14-year-old Bobbie Cannon, accompanying her boyfriend on a looting expedition. She was standing near the loading platform at Gold's

Department Store [4] when he backed his truck sharply, crushing her head between its body and the building.

There were those who, in the swift collapse of law and social organization, were stabbed, shot and beaten in the settling of long-festering feuds that the canopy of the riot made easy. And then there was Bruce Moore.

Bruce and Garland Moore were the sons of Betty Jean Moore, a divorcee. Early Sunday morning she, the two boys, and a friend of hers, Otis Darton, were sitting on the lawn in front of the house, dimly illuminated by the lighted doorway behind them. It was cool and pleasant, and, for the first time in several days, the darkness was not split by the sound of sirens.

All at once a half dozen shots, fired by a jealous former boyfriend of Mrs. Moore, stabbed wildly from the bushes across the street. One struck Garland in the hip, another plowed a fatal path through the body of Bruce.

Garland was three years old. Bruce four.

45   "The Way Things Can Be Twisted"

At midnight, police officials estimated they would need 17,000 troops to restore order. This would have committed virtually every national guardsman in the state, and Gen. Hill was already concerned about the Oakland-San Francisco area, in case a sympathetic uprising should occur there. It was, therefore, decided that the force already in Los Angeles would have to suffice.

That force now numbered more than 13,000 men. They had helped to arrest more than 2,000 persons. As dawn approached, this combination of overwhelming strength and arrests was restoring a semblance of order. One major problem the troops were encountering was the inadequate publication of the curfew over radio and tv, as a result of which many residents were confused.

[4] See page 322.

There were many tense moments at roadblocks. At one, a man approached, a bottle under his arm, a cigarette dangling from his mouth, his lips moving as he grumbled to himself. The troopers, eyeing the bottle apprehensively, became even tauter as the man halted 50 feet away and began a fumbling attempt to strike a match.

Suddenly, one of the guardsmen could stand it no longer. "Hell! If nobody wants to shoot him, I will!" he exclaimed, leveling his rifle.

An officer knocked the gun away, and he and two other men went to get the Negro, who, it turned out, was simply a drunk trying to light a cigarette.

Commented the officer, "That's the way things can be twisted by one's imagination, but it looked like we were about to be scorched out of our little holes there."

Another drunk was 41-year-old Lonnye Lee Cook. She had, as a matter of fact, been drinking whiskey with friends all night, and when she turned down Vermont Ave. at 5 a.m. and approached the roadblock where a captain had told his men that "at another roadblock a couple of the boys have been hit by a car, and you should fire in self-defense if a car tries to run the roadblock," she was so besotted she had no idea where she was, and she was not even certain that she was in a car, much less that she was driving it.

It was a deadly combination.

In the brief engagement between the troops and Lonnye Lee Cook, she took round after round in her body, the bullets fracturing her pelvis, perforating her kidneys and bowel, and almost severing her legs. The wonder was that she did not die on the spot, but awakened in the hospital, to ask, "What happened?"

Told that she had been shot, she inquired, "What shots?"

She died 36 hours later, to become the twenty-eighth, the fourth within a three-block area of Vermont Ave.

*   *   *

Almost at the same time, officers, cruising by the Shop-Rite Market that 12 hours before had been on fire when Curtis Lee Gaines had been shot and killed in Gold's Department Store just across the street, heard the noise of people moving about and things dropping off shelves. As they entered the building, water and sodden foodstuffs sloshed about their feet. Spotting a man—a metal object seemingly glinting in his hand—who was about to duck behind a display case, one of the officers fired three times. All three shots hit their mark.

"Now what you do that for?" 53-year-old Paul Edgar Harbin, who lived a half block down the street, asked sorrowfully. "I was only getting me some meat."

He was the twenty-ninth.

*   *   *

In Watts there had been sporadic firing all through the night, and the National Guard made one search after another for the will-o'-the-wisp snipers. Buildings would be surrounded, people flushed out and searched, but no weapons found. One squad *was* assaulted with a shotgun—it came sailing out of a second-story window, landing at the feet of the startled troopers.

One of the most poignant moments of the entire mad week undoubtedly came at the roadblock at 103rd and Grape. Troopers discovered 104 pints of whiskey in a car and, methodically, broke the bottles one by one as a drunk looked on sorrowfully.

Near Will Rogers Park a Pvt. Gonzales found it necessary to journey to a chemical toilet that had been set up. Hardly had he settled himself comfortably when a round pinged into the street in front. A few seconds later, another crept even closer. When a third appeared as if it were attempting to join him within the small confines of the cubicle, he tumbled out, pants around his knees, and scurried for cover.

There were enough troops on hand to make an impressive show of force. Men were spotted on strategic rooftops everywhere, and each key intersection had its .30-caliber machine gun; .50-caliber machine guns, for which there was not one round of ammunition, had an even greater calming influence.

It was being discovered, in fact, that where there was a significant *show* of force, the utilization of force became unnecessary. It had been feared that the populace would consider such a show of force insulting, but nothing brought respect for law faster than the sight of two tanks—which, actually, were just being transferred from one armory to another—rumbling down the street. One officer voiced the opinion that the fastest way to curb any future riot would be to send a column of tanks down the street and a flight of jets buzzing low overhead.

Commented Col. Dove, "I came up to one man who looked like a Muslim. I said to him, 'You'll be very intelligent if you don't say a single word to me. There's a hundred troops around here. You lean against me, and I'll lean you six feet under the ground.' It was pure corn, but the people ate it up." [1]

One national guardsman, taking no chances on snipers, had ensconced himself in a large, open-topped container for trash, from which, whenever a car approached, he popped up like a jack-in-the-box.

At another roadblock, where rifle fire had resounded the night before, a shapely Negro girl approached the soldiers, and began bantering with them. "Why don't a couple of you boys come take me home?" she suggested.

Laughing, two or three volunteered that they would like to, but that they could not leave their posts.

"Well, man, they got to let you go some time."

They agreed that was true.

"So when they does, you come visit me." She gave them an address near 102nd and Beach. "You all come! I got friends!" she invited them.

The prostitutes were back in business.

As the intensity of the violence diminished, troopers were discovering that they had arrived without any toilet articles, or money, or change of clothing, and that in 90-degree heat this could be a sticky business. Some found time to shower, and even use the swimming pools at the parks and schools at which they were bivouacked. Pepsi Cola contributed 5,000 bottles of soft drinks, and See's brought in candy. Vendors appeared, selling ice cream and sundries at inflated prices. Many of the troops were aching to quench their thirst with a beer, but the officers made teetotalers of them.

Gov. Brown, who had arrived late Saturday evening, toured the area. By noon several hundred sightseers, both Negro and Caucasian, jammed Central Ave.

That afternoon, the Glendale unit, which had been the first into the area, was the first to be rotated back to its armory.

---

[1] There are undoubtedly those who will take umbrage at such an approach, and there are far too many ramifications, for this author to begin probing into them at this point. Nevertheless, there is no gainsaying that, at that particular time under these particular circumstances the best approach was to make clear that there would be no pussyfooting around.

One of the last things its commander, Lt. Col. Thomas Haykin, had done in Watts was to confiscate the tape from a tape recorder being used by a reporter from radio station KPFK. He had done so after being told by one of his men that the station was operated by Communists—a charge that, although disproven many times, has continued to be repeated by the extremists of the right. Enlightened on the true nature of the station, the colonel returned the tape with apologies.

As the troops settled themselves back at the Glendale armory, the colonel was confronted with a new situation. One of his men reported that a quartet of Nazis had appeared, and were haranguing the soldiers.

As he emerged onto the grass in front of the building, Col. Haykin saw a gray pickup truck, two swastika-banded men in the cab and two in the rear, passing out leaflets and fulminating against niggers and kikes. Spotting a German Mauser rifle in the middle of the front seat, the colonel ordered the two men out of the cab. When they did not move, he repeated the order.

The man on the right responded by swinging the door open quickly, hitting the colonel's helmet, and knocking his glasses askew. The colonel thereupon grabbed him and "helped him out." He was all for taking drastic action, but the Glendale police advised him he "had better take it easy with these people—there was some legality involved." The Nazis, as a result, were released, with a warning not to come back.

46   The Top and the Bottom

Chief Parker went on television and reported that the police, after having lost control of the situation, were in command again. "Now we're on top and they're on the bottom." (He referred to the rioters, and was promptly quoted out of context.)

The riots had started, he said, "when one person threw a rock, and like monkeys in a zoo, others started throwing rocks." Besides this being a not entirely accurate appraisal— there were quite enough people willing to throw rocks on their own initiative—he was speedily misquoted.

The Chief of Police of Jackson, Miss., called the Chief of Police of Culver City—for all practical purposes a part of Los Angeles—to warn him of an uprising of Muslims there.

As it happens, Culver City is virtually devoid of Negroes, Muslim or otherwise.

Gen. Harrison of the Alabama National Guard dispatched a telegram to Gen. Hill: "You and your guardsmen are doing a wonderful job. Keep up the good work. I have 17,000 guardsmen to offer you at any time."

It was an offer that was as welcome as if it had been made by the chief of staff of the Russian army.

Marquette Frye appeared before a Sunday gathering at the Muslim Mosque to explain the circumstances of his arrest.

The police log was replete with such entries as:

"Shots at Harvard and San Marino." "Firecrackers." "Code 2, shooting at 42nd and Normandie." "Code 4, no shooting." "Manchester and Hoover fire department station reports sniper, requests assistance . . . area sealed off . . . suspect in school, and school surrounded." "No evidence of shots at station. Not reported by station."

Rumors continued to flow in. A serious food shortage was developing in some portions of the riot area, and several civil rights organizations were preparing to establish food distribution centers. They were using walkie-talkies to co-ordinate their activities, using such jargon as "Millies" and "Pollys" to refer to the National Guard and police. This led some citizens to believe that they were rioters planning further lootings and burnings.

One Willie Owens called to say that, "The Blood [Muslims] will play the grand finale tonight. Manpower will come from Hollywood, Beverly Hills, Encino, and other points. The Watts debacle was formulated last Christmas by a 300-member syndicate and scheduled for Friday, August 13. They changed their mind, causing a new party to be formed within called 'The Blood'—and members and former Muslims are to go along with the original plan which erupted prematurely because of younger, impatient members, before heavy weapons could be brought in."

47   "The Sad Thing About These Shootings"

However, it was not in Los Angeles but in Long Beach that violence erupted as darkness fell.

As on Avalon Blvd. on Wednesday night, it was a misdemeanor arrest that started things off. Cruising through the Negro district, Officer Richard Lee Zylstra and his partners received a report of an intoxicated woman. When they attempted to arrest her, she resisted, and, as they wrestled with her trying to handcuff her and place her in the patrol car, a covey of men suddenly came at them, throwing cinder blocks and bottles. Retreating, the officers had to release the woman.

A crowd of about 100 had gathered on the scene by the time other officers arrived. Carrying shotguns and forming a skirmish line, they began driving the people back. Suddenly three men, darting out of the crowd, made a break for it. As they dashed through the skirmish line, one brushed the shotgun carried by Officer Stewart C. Gordon.

A shot reverberated. Seven feet away 23-year-old police Officer Richard Raymond Lefebre spun to the ground.

"Watch out! They're shooting!" an officer cried.

The skirmish line broke. As Lefebre writhed on the ground, officers milled about in confusion. Standing directly beneath the street lights, they felt exposed to the sniper whom, they were certain, had felled Lefebre. Aiming his gun at the light overhead, one officer fired, blasting it to bits. Others, following his example, quickly immersed the area in the hazy darkness of late dusk. Additional police help was called for. With tempers of both officers and Negroes honed to razor sharpness, there is no telling what might have happened if

the National Guard had not immediately dispatched a unit
to help restore order.

Not until an investigation could be conducted was it determined that Lefebre had been hit by a shot from Gordon's
gun. Gordon, himself, never realized that his gun had fired.

Lefebre was the thirtieth.

*   *   *

An hour and a half later, at 9:30 p.m., 67-year-old Neita
Love and her 77-year-old husband, Claude, were approaching the National Guard roadblock on Avalon Blvd. and 51st
St., the corner of South Park where, Friday afternoon, the
riot had exploded into the north-central area. Claude Love
had gone to the Dodger baseball game, then he and his wife
had been to a friend's home for dinner. They were in violation of the curfew, but: "We thought, probably, not having
anything in the car, we will say, stop and search us."

As the 1958 Chevrolet approached, the guardsmen said
exactly that. "Halt!" cried Sgt. Gerald Garcia twice, then a
third time, simultaneously ordering the driver to turn off the
headlights.

The car slowed. The headlights went out. Then, apparently, Mrs. Love, extremely nervous, let her foot slip off the
brake and onto the accelerator. Suddenly the car plunged
forward. Pfc. Yasua Kita, approaching from the front, barely
had time to leap out of the way.

The reaction was immediate. The firing intense. A police
car, approaching the roadblock from the other direction,
maneuvered to head off the escaping car. As the two vehicles
came together on a collision course, the police fired.

Forty-three shots in all, 35 by the guardsmen and 8 by the
police, were aimed at the car. Two struck Claude Love, injuring him seriously but not fatally. One found its mark on
his wife, severing her spinal cord.

She was the thirty-first.

*   *   *

A certain awareness was beginning to manifest itself in the
minds of some high-ranking National Guard officers.

Commented Col. Dove, referring to cars fired on at the
roadblocks: "We found out that these people are scared to
death. The type of people that give you trouble are not the
type of people most of the time that were hurt. The type

of people that give you trouble give it to you in a different way. They're on the rooftops, they're in apartment windows and things like that, they're not the people down in cars."

Said another colonel, "I believe some of our trouble was caused because our people were not plainly visible. The roadblocks themselves were not plainly visible. We expended thousands of flares, but they were not available in sufficient quantity to keep roadblocks illuminated all night long."

"The 'no fire' policy was not developing," Col. Dove went on. "It took a couple of days to learn under what circumstances people should or should not fire. . . . This is the sad thing about these shootings. You shoot some of the wrong people. Fifteen per cent cause all the trouble, but the 15 per cent hide behind the 85 per cent, and you harass the 85 per cent trying to find the 15 per cent that you can't get."

Despite the reemphasizing of the "necessity for holding the fire of the National Guard people to an absolute minimum," Sunday night produced a constant flow of reports of "shots fired." In Watts, troops bivouacked in the park felt exposed beneath the lights, and shot them out. At a number of intersections guardsmen had been given orders that, whenever they halted a car and needed police help, they should fire their rifles into the air. Sometimes as many as a dozen shots were loosed simply to summon the police. Residents of the city—many of whom, driving along the freeway, had the impression that the shots were going off right in their faces—believed that a guerilla war was in progress.

Not all of the shooting was, of course, due to the National Guard and the police. There were dozens of rioters with weapons who, at one time or another, fired them, both indiscriminately and with specific targets in mind—although by Sunday night, it later became clear, if it was not then, the snipers had been cowed. Yet there were people like the two white youths who drove around Fort McArthur, an army installation, firing guns every which way like an Indian raiding party. And the man who, dressed in army fatigues, wandered into the ECC downtown, requesting 9-mm. ammunition for his .38 Walther, and was almost given it before a suspicious guard officer questioned him and discovered that he was not a member of the National Guard, but merely wanted to go into the riot area *to help!*

Although any accurate assessment of the number of rounds fired in the three-day period commencing Friday evening is impossible, the very fact that one National Guard unit alone expended more than 1,300 means that it is likely that the total passed well over the 10,000 mark. Since the Guard was using armor-piercing ammunition—the only type it had available—which could go through an entire row of houses and still travel more than two miles, the wonder is not that so many persons had rounds land near them, but that not more were hit by them.

*   *   *

In the hour between 12:30 and 1:30 a.m. Monday morning, police received ten reports of shots having been fired.

It was 1:30 a.m. when Pfc. John L. Freitas, stationed at the corner of Broadway and 93rd St., jumped, then flattened himself to the pavement as a bullet skipped across the intersection. The round seemed to have come along 93rd St. from the direction of the freeway. The street was deserted, but Freitas could see one porch light on.

Police Officer Glen Roy Mozingo was northbound on Broadway when he noticed a black convertible driving at high speed. Two blocks past 93rd St. it made a U-turn and halted. The excited driver shouted to the officer, "My wife is going to have a baby! I am trying to find the Broadway Hospital!"

Mozingo was talking to the man, when he heard two shots. Looking down the street, he saw two national guardsmen running from the intersection. Quickly he headed his car in their direction.

Aubrey Gene Griffin, 38, and his wife, Rowena, were asleep in the bedroom of their home at 314 W. 93rd St. when they were awakened by a shot. A native of Oklahoma, Aubrey Griffin had, for 10 years, been employed in a furniture factory. His wife worked in a laundry and dry cleaning establishment. They had two sons in the service, one of whom, Aubrey, Jr., an air force man, was home on leave, and was sitting in the darkened front room watching the late show on television. They were the solid, middle-class American family of which the Negro community is so much in need.

Mrs. Griffin, hearing the shot, became frightened. Her husband, telling her to remain in the bedroom, put on his pants and told her he would go to see what had happened. Passing through the front room, he stepped out onto the porch, where he was illuminated by the light.

At the moment that officer Mozingo drove up, Pfc. Freitas, again looking down the street, saw a figure in a white T-shirt standing beneath the porch light of a house.

"What happened?" Mozingo asked.

"We've been shot at from down the street there!" Freitas exclaimed, a national guard sergeant simultaneously pointing in the direction of the house. It was the only one with a light on. It was the only one with a person visible.

Although the people at the scene did not know it, the situation was curiously similar to two that had occurred earlier.[1] The street was a quiet cul-de-sac of frame houses, ending in the freeway, exactly the same as 88th St. where, Friday evening, police had spotted a group of persons on a porch. It resembled, likewise, the incident at the Villa Maria Hotel Saturday morning, where, after a flurry of shots, a soldier's eyes had focused on the one person visible—a man in a white T-shirt.

Two sheriff's cars, disgorging a half dozen deputies, brought the number of lawmen at the scene to more than a score. As they dashed down the street, they saw the man in the T-shirt turn and go inside the house.

"Police, come out with your hands up!" an officer yelled, men fanning out to surround the residence.

Hardly had the words issued from his mouth when a shot went off. Within seconds revolvers and shotguns in the hands of law officers began converging their fire upon the walls of the house. Officer Gary Walter Boyd, carrying a shotgun borrowed from a civilian friend, made his way around to the back yard. Discovering there that two national guardsmen had preceded him, he told them to go around to the front and warn other officers that he was making his way into the house from the rear.

When Aubrey, Jr., heard the tattoo of shots beating against the walls, he jumped up from the television set and dashed into the hallway. There he collided with his mother, who, upon hearing the front door close and the shots speedily following behind, had run out from the bedroom. As Mrs. Griffin stumbled into the darkened front room, illuminated

[1] See pages 246 and 279.

only by the flickering light from the television tube, she saw her husband down on one knee.

"Mom, call the police!" he said. "I've been shot!"

The police were right at hand. Officer Boyd, tumbling in through the back window, was crawling forward on his hands and knees. As he arrived in the living room, several other officers burst in through the front door. On the floor lay Aubrey Griffin, blood seeping in a circle about him.

He was dead, 11 shotgun pellets having caused a massive wound in his chest. He was the thirty-second.[2]

                              *   *   *

A rumor that the Hell's Angels were gathering in county territory just to the south of the city had been received both by the police department and the residents of the area, who were organized in the Gardena Home Owners Association. During the daytime the streets have the same appearance as that of any other subdivision, but at night, without a single street lamp, they turn pitch black. Since it is one of the few subdivisions into which Negroes have been permitted to buy, it is almost totally segregated.

One of the homeowners was 33-year-old Willie Walker. Born in Birmingham, Ala., he had served in the army from 1951 to 1958, receiving an honorable discharge. In August, 1965, he was working as a welder at the Caine Steel Co., making $110 a week, supplementing this by about $50 a week by doing maintenance work at night and on weekends. Married, with five children, he has a home valued at $14,500, and furnishings at $2,500. He owns a 1959 Dodge.

This was the story, as he told it: "We started guarding our neighborhood on Saturday night, August 14, with rifles, shotguns, and pistols because my neighbors and I were afraid that rioters might come in and destroy our neighborhood. The president of the Gardena Home Owners Association called the sheriff's office and told them to send someone to protect our neighborhood, and he said to protect it the best way we could ourselves.

"On Sunday night, we heard from three men who I imagine live in the neighborhood, and who went from house to house, that the Hell's Angels were in the district. So we

_____
[2] Searching the house, police discovered a .32-caliber revolver, but laboratory tests determined it had not recently been fired.

all got together—the whole neighborhood—to protect our homes and property from anyone who may have wanted to come in and destroy our homes. We stayed outside from about 9:15 to 2 a.m. Monday morning. At 2, we went inside the houses. Shortly after going home, a neighbor came over to tell us that there was a fire at Alondra, between Main and Avalon, in a store or business. We all came out again, woke the rest of the neighborhood, women and children, because sparks were flying and we were afraid our houses might burn.

"We stood on a corner lot, on private property, with our guns because we didn't know what to expect. A national guardsman and a sheriff's deputy came over, and the national guardsman started talking to Chester Perry, a neighbor. I heard a whistle, and more sheriff's officers, two of them, came out of a vacant lot. They asked five of us who were standing in Mr. Perry's yard to go with them to a building in the vacant lot.

"We did so, they disarmed us, shook us down in the field, and then took us to the building in the center of the field. They shook us down again while we stood against the building, and made us stand there approximately 45 minutes.

"A sheriff's officer came down the line asking which one of us set fire to the burning building. He hit each of us with a flashlight in the stomach while we were leaning, spread-eagled, against the building. Later he came back down the line asking who owned the shotgun and hit me again, this time with a blackjack or billy club right in the stomach. None of us offered any resistance, nor did we talk back—or even ask any questions. They had no reason to hit us. While we were against the wall, one officer said, 'Let's take one bullet and finish them all off.'

"One officer said, more than once, 'If any of you fellows want to leave, go ahead. Take off. Run so we can kill you.'

"Then they handcuffed us—hands behind us—and put five of us in the back seat of one sheriff's car. . . . On the way to Firestone station, they pointed out some of the buildings that had been burned. They said: 'These are some of the buildings that you people burned out!'

"As we passed through a National Guard roadblock on Avalon, the passenger officer said, 'We would be lucky if we got shot at.' At Firestone station, they shook us down again, then put identification bands on our hands. My back hurt from where a sheriff's deputy had put his cigarette out against the skin on my lower right back. Jones and Frank Sanders were burned with cigarettes too. There was no reason for them to do this, burn us with cigarettes."

The reader may form his own opinion regarding the validity of this account. It was the first time in his life that Walker had been arrested. He was, initially, booked for burglary and arson, then these counts were dropped, and he was charged with violation of the deadly weapons control act—carrying a concealed weapon—because he had had a sawed-off .22 rifle in his waistband, covered with his shirt. When he did not show up on the job Monday morning, and it was learned he had been arrested, the steel company fired him.

At his trial he was found guilty; but the judge, recognizing it was a technical violation, sentenced him only to the one day in jail he had already served.

Charges against the others arrested at the same time were dropped.

*   *   *

Among the reports Sunday was one by two excitable women that, when their car had been surrounded by a band of young Negroes on a dark street, they had been rescued by a squad of Minutemen. These Minutemen, wearing green berets and uniforms, their pants tucked into their boots, had ordered the Negroes to disperse or face arrest, and offered to escort the ladies home.

A reporter, apparently as excitable as the women, had taken the story at face value, and it was repeated over the radio and appeared in the metropolitan press. It obviously did not occur to the reporter that the description of the Minutemen was precisely that of national guardsmen clad in green fatigues, and that Minutemen were hardly going to threaten Negroes with arrest. (Many of the soldiers were wearing soft caps, which could easily be mistaken for berets.)

It was perhaps this story that preyed on the mind of 56-year-old Joseph Irving Maiman as he drove through the darkened streets at 4:25 Monday morning. A Caucasian, partially bald, he had grown slightly hard of hearing, but he was determined not to let the riot interfere with his job as a milk delivery salesman for a dairy for which he had worked 28 years. In order to get to the dairy to pick up his truck with the milk, he had to pass through a portion of the curfew area.

He had halted his Corvair at a signal only four blocks within the curfew area, and, possibly, did not even know he had passed its boundaries, when a jeep pulled up at an angle to his car. A man jumped out, and approached the driver's side. The man was clad in a green uniform with pants tucked into boots, and what looked like a beret on his head.

Maiman panicked. He pulled out, and began driving up the wrong side of a divided street. Two National Guard jeeps took up the pursuit.

The lead jeep had a .30-caliber machine gun mounted, but it was not loaded. As the jeep barreled down the dimly lit street at 60 miles an hour, with one man firing his M-1 rifle at the Corvair, which was gradually gaining ground, Pfc. Gary Rogers frantically attempted to slip the ammunition belt into the machine gun.

It took him two blocks. After he had gotten the first round into the chamber, he steadied himself in the swaying vehicle, and the gun's chatter cut through the quiet of the residential district.

Joseph Maiman had just turned his head to glance at his pursuers when the .30-caliber slug caught him beneath the nose and continued on into his skull. He was dead even before the Corvair came to rest on one of the neighborhood's well-kept lawns.

He was the thirty-third.

Two hours earlier, Los Angeles County General Hospital had withdrawn all of its ambulances from the curfew area, because, as a result of being continually halted by over-zealous National Guard troops, it had become impossible for them to operate.

48   "Next Time It's Not Gonna Be a Gentle War!"

For Garban Tivoli Godrick and a few of his buddies, it had been one continuous party. In the garage where he lived a variety of stolen merchandise was scattered about—transistor radios, a movie camera, a .22 rifle, shoes, and clothing, and bottle after bottle of liquor. As dawn broke Monday morning, a quartet of youths were lolling around, exhausted, slightly high, but, for the first time in their lives, feeling as if they had accomplished something. They could not say why they felt that way; they could not say what it was that filled the void that, before, had made a shell of their bodies. They only knew that, never having known success of any kind before, this they could call success.

Two of them had been picked up during the riot. One had spent Thursday night in jail for being drunk, and then had been released Friday morning. The other had simply been taken for a ride in the police car.

"Man, that was the meanest little cop I ever did see!" he said. " 'Nigger boy,' he said to me, 'how'd you like to meet your maker right now?' He had these little pinpricky eyes, and I said to myself, shit man! This character ain't foolin'! So I said, 'No sir, I sure wouldn't. I was just on my way home from Bible class when I seen all these people,' and I makes it up to him like I don't really cotton to all this stuff. So he says, 'Well, nigger boy, you go on back and you tell all those black motherfuckers down there we gonna come and blow 'em up!' And then he stops the car, and gives me a kick that I thinks puts me all the way across the freeway!"

"Shit, man! You got no soul. I'd 'a told that white motherfucker to fly up his own ass! The days of Old Black Joe and Aunt Jemima done gone!"

"Yeah. Well you and Old Black Joe'd be playing Georgia Skin together in heaven, and I'm here!"

"What you get busted for?" Godrick asked the fourth of the group, who had spent the night in jail.

"Bunch o' nothin! We was on the corner at one o'clock, waitin' for four dudes to come from a party. Just standing there, getting loaded. We was waitin' for them dudes to come out, so we could fight 'em. The police come round, and say: You can't wait there. I asks 'em, how come! And they say: Boy, you're it! So they takes me in to Georgia Street, and I asks 'em: Aren't you going to call my parents? They says, no, they gonna put me in this cell, and I looks in and it's all dark and dingy, people yelling and stuff! So the other one says: No, let's give him a shower first. I tell him, I ain't gonna take no shower. My hair'll get wet!" He halts momentarily. "But they persuaded me to doing it!"

They all laugh.

"The police, they real mad now. I seen 'em come down on the set last night, shootin' shotguns and bustin' stuff and all! They real mad!"

"Yeah, man. Like they knows we beat 'em good. They put them nationals in here, but that don't mean nothin'! They knows anytime we wants, we can beat 'em!"

"Like we had that cop, we could'a killed him! We gets 'em there on Avalon, and we got this car burning, and they chasin' everybody all around, and I yells to him and hits him right smack on the nose with this little bitty iron ball. So the stupid motherfucker comes after me and I'm laughing like hell, running between the houses there, and he come in and there's 20 of us. We gets him down, and he's hollering like a stuck pig, and we was all set to beat him to death when here comes this dude and says: Don't do it!"

"Shit! That wasn't nothin'! I had one of them mothers chasin' me, so I just kinda stops and scoots down, and give him this little nudge, and he go right through this plate glass window that's all busted up. He looked like he been messin' with an airplane."

"I got myself one! He's standing there, by this fire, and I've got this gun out of this Jap market, so I says to myself, shit, I'm ever gonna use this thing, now's the time! So I really blast him a few times, and he flops down and don't move. Then this damn thing gets a shell stuck in it, and I'm banging it, trying to get it out, and the whole fucking thing comes apart!"

"Man, we really got that one Jap place. It was like somebody says Go, and everybody went. It was like a tornado going through, and he just standing there, watching, and he don't say nothing. So then somebody say, shit, we gonna burn this place, baby, and he start pouring this stuff all around, and the little Jap, he say, No, please, take the things, but don't burn, don't burn. And everybody's laughing, the way he acting. Then somebody throws this bomb, and *boom* it all goes up!"

"Yeah. I seen this one blood. He set up a row of bottles filled with gas in this furniture store. Then he pulls out this gun, and pop-pop-pop he gets 'em one after the other. That place went up like it was stoking time in hell!"

"Fuck! I got nothing against the Japanese. They got it tough, too!"

361

"Yeah, man. And the S.A.'s. The cops treat 'em just as bad!"

"Shit! I got no truck for the S.A.'s. They on Charley's side. I'll have myself a little set-to with them any time they wants!"

"You see them get that confederate dude at the *World* Thursday night? Maybe three, four thousand people all around, and he standing there, big as shit, saying: You can mess with me, but don't mess with my car! So one guy up and gets this sledgehammer, and cracks his head open!"

"This one man, he had a wreck right there by Nickerson! And he all confused and starts running through the gardens, and they killed him!"

"Yeah. And then there was this little broad, driving this little bugsy car. She got her face smashed so bad, she'll never look the same!"

"That's what they get for coming down and messing all the time. I seen these motherfuckers beat these little kids, and hell! They wasn't doing nothing."

"Like, they had this soul sister, and they pulls her arm in back of her, and this one fuzz, he's standing there, handcuffing her, and he's got his foot planted right in her back, like he's gonna break her in two. So I says: 'God damn, man! You think she made of rubber?'"

"Man, let me tell you! It was wild! And if they don't stop fucking with us, we gonna burn some more!"

"That's right, baby! We got some soul, now!"

* * *

Gabriel Pope was going back to work. It wasn't even 7 o'clock yet, but already people were out in the streets everywhere. That's the way it is in the ghetto, people are up at 5 and on the buses at 6, so they can get to work by 8. This morning there weren't even any buses, and on the corners he could see little knots of people, wondering how they were going to make it to their jobs. At one place he saw a National Guard truck stop, the driver motioning to the people to get in, indicating he would take them across town to where the buses were still running.

The Guards were everywhere along the main streets and boulevards. Away from them, off along the side streets of the residential district, you didn't see a one, and you wouldn't ever know that anything had happened in the last four days.

Not a house was burned, not a window was broken, not a piece of rubble lay in the street. Even along the boulevards you could go for long stretches, and the sun's rays slanting low across the rooftops and in between the palm trees would fall only on neatly spaced, one- and two-story buildings with but the usual odds and ends of trash in the gutters. Then up would come a stretch of a block or more, twisted steel, skeleton walls, the street like a rocky field, wisps of smoke curling into the air as from the ashes of yesterday's camp fire.

Gabriel Pope had a sense of grim satisfaction. This was the way he wanted it. He was through with integration. Maybe integration would work one day, but he didn't think he'd live to see it. Integration was the cover the whites used to leach the Negro of his life's blood, the name they gave to taking his money in their stores and restaurants, the excuse by which they could set up their businesses in the ghetto, the way they could keep their police down on his neck to stifle him whenever he cried "Freedom!" He was convinced that all of this police harassment hadn't been haphazard. It had been deliberately planned and carried out to give as many Negroes as possible arrest records, so that they wouldn't be able to compete for jobs with Caucasians.

After he had made up his mind at midnight, Thursday, Gabriel Pope had gone out and burned. He had gotten together with a couple of the blood, and they had taken his car and started on their path of destruction. It was the "Easy Terms, We Carry Our Own Credit" places that he hated most of all. They'd had a disagreement among themselves—one of the guys had said that if they were going to burn it all anyway, they ought to get some stuff first. But Gabriel had said *No,* stealing wasn't his intent. The object was burning.

The object was burning, and when he saw all those people running around with stuff in their hands, Gabriel had the feeling that it was this that had been twisting his guts—he couldn't blame the people for making off with food when all the time they had to count every nickel and dime, he couldn't expect them not to grab what they could while they had a chance to when they'd had such little chance, but it was detracting from what *he* was after. He wanted it to be the Boston Tea Party, and the Civil War, and the Emancipation Proclamation all thrown into one; he wanted to show the whites that the Negroes didn't need the big fat liberals throwing them crumbs, that the Negro was a proud man who could stand on his own feet and do his own fighting; he wanted to erase the shame he felt because all the *leaders* of his people had always needed some great white protector; he wanted to wipe out the humiliation that had stained him when he had seen his grandfather humble himself in Mississippi just to protect that little patch of land—as if that was worth living for!

At first they had had a couple of misfires, but they had learned quickly. Molotov cocktails—made from big, cheap bottles that they dug out of trashcans—were the quickest and surest way. Light the wicks, break a window, fling two or three of the bottles into a store, and within 15 seconds it would be an inferno. There was never a time when police came even close to them; they simply drove along the side streets and the alleys, and the more the police chased the looters and the kids that were raising hell, the easier it had been for them. Even after the National Guard had arrived, passage along the side streets had never been blocked. They had burned down one place from the rear while a whole truckload of troops was standing right in front. With 100 cars and 200 men, Gabriel Pope thought he could have destroyed Los Angeles.

For the moment, if not satisfied, Gabriel Pope was willing to wait and see. They had burned out the white businesses, so that the police could no longer say that that's why they were there, protecting the business establishments. They had shown the white power structure that they were no longer afraid—it was the Whips that were now running scared.

"I'm willing to die," he said. "Maybe I'm not ready, but I'm willing. We'll give this country a chance. We'll give 'em a chance to make up for what they've done in the past, we'll give 'em a chance to say, 'We know we've done you wrong, and we're gonna do our best to change it!' But I'm not gonna have nobody tell me what to do, I'm not gonna have nobody tell me be grateful you've got what you got, because you didn't have nothing before! I'm gonna be the master of my life, and if they try to run over me, I'm gonna demolish them! And next time, baby, let me tell you, it's not gonna be a gentle war like it was, it's not gonna be the soul people doing all the bleeding. We didn't have nothing when we started this. No plans. No organization. But we've learned some things. And if we get pushed again, it's gonna be goodby, baby!"

49   Musical Merchandise and Doberman Pinschers

Long lines were forming at the half dozen food distribution points that had been set up in the area. Some houses had had no electricity, and hence no refrigeration, for days. A good deal of spoiled food, much of it scavenged from stores after they had burned, was being consumed, and a rash of food poisoning cases ensued.

The National Guard was still halting people at roadblocks, and a not insignificant number, both Caucasian and Negro, were arrested. They were arrested for carrying guns for self-protection; but self-protection or no, they were in violation of the law.

(Perhaps they had been stimulated by watching the Joe Pyne conversation-type television show on station KTTV Sunday night. Pyne, an articulate needler of conservative bent, had as one guest Ernie Smith, a Negro Nationalist. In the middle of a shouting match, Pyne pulled out a pistol, slapped it on the table, and indicated he was ready for whatever might come. Whereupon Smith flipped back his coat, revealing a shoulder holster, and declared Pyne wasn't any readier than he.)

The tremendous job of picking up the pieces began. Damage estimates, which first ranged in the neighborhood of $200 million, were gradually scaled down to $35 million. Several insurance companies, which had said they viewed what had happened as an insurrection and would, therefore, use the escape clause in their policies not to make payment, changed their minds. As far as the over-all effect was concerned, it made little difference. Insurance rates for Caucasian-owned businesses were quadrupled or more, raising them to prohibitive levels. In effect, the insurance companies, run by hardheaded and realistic businessmen, indicated that, unless drastic changes are made, a man could expect to be burned out again within five years. A year after the August, 1965, convulsion, not more than a handful of businesses that had been destroyed had reestablished themselves in their former locations, and acres of commercial property, cleared and bulldozed of debris, presented the scarless appearance of skin worked over by a plastic surgeon.

(The city insisted on immediate removal of the rubble by property owners in order to forestall any possible outbreak of disease. Where property owners did not move quickly enough, the city sent in demolition crews—in some cases before insurance adjusters were able to inspect the damage— and billed the owners.)

The police began to collect on the chits they had written— mostly on Friday—when they had had to stand by and watch store after store being looted. Every owner of a car whose license number had been jotted down by an officer became due for a visit from the lawmen. A goodly number of tips were being received from residents regarding a neighbor's possession of a looted television set or piece of furniture. City trash collectors were instructed to report the number of every house to which they were called to pick up an old refrigerator, or the like. Police cars mounting portable address systems cruised around advising people to place all items of looted merchandise on their lawns, promising that if they did so, they would not be prosecuted.

Unfortunately, every one of these methods for recovering merchandise had certain margins for error. Given, to start with, that some license numbers might, in the confusion of the moment, have been jotted down incorrectly, it did not necessarily follow that a person seen getting into a car lived in the household of the car's owner. Further, the lists were simply lists of suspects—they did not indicate *what* a person was suspected of stealing.

Tips received from residents about a neighbor's misbehavior during the riot had to be taken with a grain of salt. There were so many vendettas and grudges to be settled that it was an opportunity that could hardly be missed, and suspicions and second-hand tales abounded.

Nor was the location where an old refrigerator or a new stereo set made its appearance necessarily a reliable indicator. The guilty tended to distribute such items about in random fashion everywhere except in front of their own houses. Whereupon the person spotting them on his lawn would rush to trundle them to the next house in line, and it was marvelous how peripatetic even the largest items became. Unfortunately, with the police going on the assumption that whoever had a washing machine in front of his residence must have been guilty of stealing the laundry, more than one innocent person discovered himself holding the bag in this game of musical merchandise.

As police knocked on the doors of residences on their lists, they were followed by 2½-ton National Guard trucks. At each place they would ask permission to enter and look around, and there is no record of this having been refused. Merchandise that could not be accounted for by the householders, and which appeared new, would be loaded aboard the trucks. At some places only the children were at home, and when the parents returned they would find the house stripped. In many instances it was a matter of just retribution, but in a few it was the kind of mistake for which police, in minority areas, have gained their notoriety.

In addition to the fact that there were now *no* food markets—and other stores—where before there had been largely second-rate ones, people in the area were discovering that they had other problems. One family had had practically all of its clothes in the cleaners, and the cleaning shop had disappeared. A woman, resolutely making payments on the layaway plan for a television set, dashed down to the store when she heard it had been broken into, but there was only an empty space on the shelf where the set had been. A man who had told his wife he had taken her mink stole to be stored for the summer but had, in actuality, pawned it, prepared to leave town when his wife spotted it gamboling down the street on the arm of another woman. A deaf gentleman who, in return for a $5 loan, had checked his hearing aid for the week, discovered he would be deaf longer than he had bargained for. Everywhere people were left holding pawn tickets, laundry stubs, and the like for articles in shops that no longer existed, and whose proprietors, in numbers of cases, simply disappeared. On the other side of the coin, some stores had had all of their credit records destroyed, and a few persons were pleasantly surprised to realize they owed nothing to anybody for the first time since they were children.

*   *   *

A German journalist, who had wandered around the area

for three days and been overcome by the idyllic vision of palms and greenery, trooped into the 77th police station to inquire desperately, "Where are the slums?"

*   *   *

From his own experience, Lt. Robitaille of the National Guard was of the opinion that the forces of law had regained control.

He and his men halted a vehicle at their roadblock, the driver explaining that he was trying to get to the police to report that his store had been sacked. As they were checking him out, nine sheriff's cars with four men each pulled up. All of the deputies got out, inquired as to what was going on, and began questioning the man.

As they were thus grouped, a Los Angeles police car approached and halted. Four officers alighted. Hardly a minute had passed when one of the soldiers exclaimed, "Here comes one more!"

And sure enough, it was another police car with four men. They, too, got out. For a few minutes, there stood a dozen troopers and 44 lawmen questioning one not-so-very-hot suspect.

*   *   *

Yet with the onset of nightfall, no one knew quite what to expect. It was not long before the police received the report that a National Guard armory had been blown up.

This was amended to the information that a bomb had been exploded in front of it.

This was resolved to three kids in an old car having thrown some firecrackers.

*   *   *

In a collision between an automobile and a jeep, two guardsmen were seriously injured.

Despite the fact that ammunition had been withdrawn from men below the squad leader level, there continued to be some tense moments as troopers made their rounds. One patrol caught sight of a fellow who, guarding his store, was sitting with a shotgun in his lap. The colonel advised him that it might be better if, the situation still being somewhat uncertain, he stayed out of the light.

Inside one liquor store a group of people were spotted.

The National Guard officer yelled, "All right! All of you come out with your hands up!"

And the first thing that came out was a huge Doberman Pinscher.

As it became clear that they, and others like them, were protecting their stores, measures were taken to forestall accidents.

A slightly intoxicated driver hailed a National Guard jeep carrying Col. Irving Taylor.

"Hi!" The Negro waved. "I just wanted to tell you I think you're really great! What we need around here is more men like you, colonel!" Driving off, he little realized he had been talking to a Los Angeles police officer.

"Maybe the solution to the problem," said a National Guard officer, "is to change the uniforms of the Los Angeles police department. If we'd had on blue uniforms we'd have been dirty dogs. As it was we were great guys. Everybody seemed glad to see us. The population thought we were going to protect them from the police—and the police thought we were protecting them from the population!"

                    *   *   *

At 11 o'clock Tuesday morning the curfew was lifted. At noon bus service was partially restored. Crews from the gas and power companies went in to begin hacking through the tangle of fallen wires and twisted pipes.

Gov. Brown announced he was appointing a commission, headed by former CIA chief, John McCone, to investigate the causes of the riot.

                    *   *   *

Sniper activity was still being reported, even in broad daylight. A crane operator said he had been shot at. Along the southern reaches of Vermont Ave., a guardsman reported hearing a shot and seeing a muzzle flash from an upper window of Teddy's Rough Rider Post 516 of the American Legion. Troops and police returned the fire, but, momentarily, were unable to force a padlock with which the front door had been locked from the outside. A tear-gas shell was fired into the interior. After a few minutes, the lock on the door was broken.

Guardsmen charged in. The building was empty. A woman living in the rear said she had seen three men jump a fence.

                    *   *   *

The Rev. Martin Luther King announced he was coming to Los Angeles. When he arrived, he held a meeting with Chief Parker that only confirmed the Chief in his belief that civil rights leaders were irresponsible agitators. When he went down to Watts, he was met by a jeering crowd.

"All over America," the Rev. King started to say, "the Negroes must join hands—"

"And burn, baby, burn!" a youth interrupted him.

The same kind of reception met members of Gov. Brown's staff when they went down to the Westminster Presbyterian Center—on the sidewalk in front of which was the stain where Smalley had died—to listen to the grievances of residents. Teenagers made up at least 50 per cent of those present, but it was an alcoholic harridan who first took the microphone: "Four score and seven years ago . . ." she commenced, going on to explain for 10 minutes that she had been born the day the *Normandie* sank, and that this had affected her whole life. One youth said that rats had grown so big and bold that they sat up and begged for food on the counters, and another countered that they didn't beg; they "told" you. A man who got up and asserted it was no use blaming everybody else for their troubles, was shouted down as an "Uncle Tom"! A teenager called Gov. Brown "chicken," and another indicated that they didn't need "all these white motherfuckers down here," that that was the trouble, they'd already had too many. One of the governor's staff members, a Negro woman, said that *she* certainly understood the Watts problems, causing the auditorium to erupt into a clap of laughter.

It was like a shouting match between a deaf-mute and a blind man.

50   The Muslim Mosque

Pickets appeared in front of city hall with signs: END POLICE BRUTALITY, BRUTALITY BREEDS VIOLENCE, and WE'VE NOT BE-

GUN TO FIGHT. One waved a BURN, BABY, BURN placard, but it was torn up by a CORE worker. STOP counter pickets demanded "Stop Tormenting Our Police."

Chief Parker told the press he continued to believe the rioting was unorganized, but that "I will say that other elements moved into it." The Los Angeles *Times* "interpreted" this as: PARKER HINTS MUSLIMS TOOK PART IN RIOTING.

At 10 o'clock Tuesday evening an anonymous informer called to say that Elijah Muhammad had given the order to stop rioting until the National Guard left, and then begin again.

At the Los Angeles Coliseum, located within the northern portion of the riot area, the charity football game originally scheduled for Saturday, went off without incident Tuesday night.

Shortly thereafter, however, an event occurred which, Gen. Hill felt, might retrigger the riot if it were played up in the press. Directly across from the Coliseum, at 11:30 p.m., police were called to the home of Mrs. Kitty Lester to help settle a domestic dispute. During the course of the heated argument, a police officer's shotgun was jostled. It accidentally discharged, the load striking Mrs. Lester and killing her.

The newspapers ignored the incident, and there were no repercussions.

*   *   *

At 12:45 Wednesday morning, at a roadblock at 109th and Avalon, just a half dozen blocks from where the riot had begun six days before, guardsmen were checking one car when another drove up. Three men alighted, and began approaching the troopers. For some reason they began running.

As the soldiers called on them to halt, one of them stopped. A second made it around a corner and disappeared. The third was shot through the chest and critically injured, but survived.

He was the last man to be wounded by a National Guard bullet. His name, curiously, was Charles Stewart. The name of the first guardsman hurt was Wayne Stewart.

*   *   *

Negro plainclothes Officer Mac Benton had just visited the club catering to transvestites, noting with wry amusement that several of the female impersonators were wearing new high-heeled shoes, form-fitting dresses and wigs—a wig store had been among those that had fallen before the onslaught—when, at 12:47 a.m. he picked up a police call that an informer reported seeing many guns carried into the Golden Ring. The Golden Ring is one of the clubs periodically raided by the police in search of gamblers. To Benton the report of someone seen carrying guns into the club made no sense. If anyone wanted to make a delivery of guns, there was a well-concealed back entrance, and he believed someone with a grudge was attempting to set something up.

He became even more suspicious when, a little less than an hour later, at 1:40 a.m., he picked up an all-units call: "Suspects seen carrying guns inside 5606 S. Broadway. Caution, this is the Muslim Temple."

This message was based on a telephone call from a woman, who refused to identify herself. It had been received at the ECC at 1:35 a.m.

"They're being sucked in!" Benton said to himself.

Col. Taylor, also, had been concerned "with the alarming nature of rumors of Muslims moving into the area, as much as with the Muslims themselves." He ordered checkpoints at all freeway crossings to cut off the flow of Muslims, some of whom were already receiving calls that they should immediately come down to the mosque, because police were attacking the building.

Some 25 to 40 police and sheriff's cars, plus national guardsmen, responded to the all-units call.

Within minutes the two-story mosque, located just 10 blocks south of Saturday night's action along Broadway, was surrounded. Next to the mosque is a two-story building, which, in the rear, drops off to one story, so that it is possible to jump from the roof to the ground. The two buildings are close enough to each other so that it would be no problem to cross from one to the other.

Scarcely five minutes after the call had gone out several officers were pounding at the back door, and a police lieutenant was knocking on the front.

The front door was opened.

A few seconds later, while officers from the front were making their way toward the rear to unlock the back door, one of the dozens of officers surrounding the building saw a flash from an upstairs window on the south side. He is corroborated by a National Guard lieutenant. It is believed that this shot took out the red light atop a sheriff's car.

When Mac Benton arrived on the scene 30 seconds later, the fire aimed at the mosque was so intense that police officers and cars were literally enveloped in a blue haze from the powder of the cartridges. One officer, caught in front of the building, was standing there, looking up startledly, as the shots crashed into the wall above his head.

The firing knocked out the electrical system, plunging the interior of the mosque into virtual darkness. A score of Muslims were inside. In the darkness they and the officers went chasing about, colliding, falling, wrestling, through the warren of rooms—kitchen, nursery, auditorium, photographic dark room, printing shop, cloak rooms, restrooms, living quarters, boiler room—while the firing from outside gradually subsided. Through some miracle no one was seriously hurt, and police were herding some 20 suspects together when, a minute or so after 2 o'clock, smoke and flames began pouring out of the building. Firemen quickly brought the blaze under control.

The Muslims who had been captured were unarmed, and police officers were just beginning their search for weapons, when, at 2:25 a.m., six police officers reported that they had been fired on from the roof of the United Veterans Club two blocks to the south. Again, there was mass retaliatory fire.

The Veterans Club happened to be, like the Golden Ring, one of the places that officers consider a trouble spot. Breaking into the building, they discovered it empty, but launched a thorough search for weapons, prying open vending machines, ripping the covers from pool tables, and pounding holes in suspicious-looking walls.

At the mosque, an even more thorough search, lasting well into the daylight hours, was in progress. Floors and ceilings were torn up. The stage was broken open. A stairwell which appeared hollow was ripped apart. Every possible hiding place was investigated for weapons. None were found.

Even the sewers did not escape. At 4 a.m. a National Guard officer, noting a manhole cover open four blocks from the mosque, theorized that the Muslims might be cavorting about beneath the street, and thereupon saturated the lower depths with tear gas.

Forty-five minutes later a block away a police officer, unaware of the National Guard bombardment, reported, "Shots and yellow smoke from storm drains!"—leaving it to others to decipher this phenomenon.

In the early afternoon a new, more damaging fire—which the fire department assesses as having been of incendiary origin—broke out in the mosque. It was the *coup de grâce* in reducing the interior to a shambles.

Charges against all those arrested being dismissed at the preliminary hearing, the Muslims believe the police deliberately staged the incident to gain access to and desecrate the mosque. Police officers who were on the scene are equally certain that they were fired on, and that the weapons were spirited out of the mosque to the easily accessible building next door.

51   The Guard Withdraws

It was 7:30 that evening, Wednesday, when 18-year-old Carlos Cavitt, Jr., picked up two friends, Nelson Chew and Mitchell Williams, both 14, because he wanted to go and look at the riot area. As they drove around, Carlos remarked that he was mad because he hadn't gotten anything during the riot.

When they came to the 4700 block of Broadway, where fire had destroyed almost every building, Carlos halted the car in front of a furniture store whose windows had been smashed. The interior, charred by fire, was sodden with water. Near the show window, however, two marble-topped tables stood virtually undamaged.

"Man! Look at those tables!" Carlos exclaimed. "You guys look out for the National Guard!"

Parking the car around the corner, he went into the store. Mitchell sat down on the fire hydrant in front.

Carlos emerged from the store, awkwardly carrying a table. "Come on," he said irritatedly. "Help me!"

"What for?" Nelson asked. "My father gives me money, and besides, he wouldn't let me keep anything that was stolen."

"Then you can just damn well stay here!" Carlos snapped. "You're not going to ride in my car no more!"

Cowed by the threat, Mitchell helped Carlos carry the table to the automobile. Although they didn't know it, they were passing right by the building where Rita Rena Johnson's body lay moldering beneath the rubble.

Carlos returned for the second table. While he was inside the store, a police car containing Sgt. Ronald Lopez and his partner cruised by. Spotting Nelson and Mitchell loitering on the sidewalk, the officers became suspicious.

Making a U-turn, they returned just in time to see Carlos carrying the second table down the sidewalk.

"Police officers! You're under arrest!" they shouted.

Carlos dropped the table, the marble top breaking off as it hit the sidewalk. All three boys began running. A shot was fired. Chew and Williams halted.

"Stop, Carlos!" Chew cried.

Cavitt paid no attention. He continued in his flight, desperately trying to make it into the shelter of an alley. The shot caught him in the head just as he was rounding the corner.

As the officers were handcuffing Chew and Williams and radioing for an ambulance, a large crowd gathered. A National Guard convoy was passing by at that moment, and Sgt. Lopez hailed it, and asked for protection.

Cavitt died Friday morning. He was the thirty-fourth.

The National Guard convoy Sgt. Lopez had halted was in the process of withdrawing from the city. The withdrawal of the troops had commenced quietly at 10 p.m. Tuesday, and even the newspapers remained unaware of it for almost 24 hours. Except for slightly more than 1,000 troops remaining to guard the Hall of Justice and other civic buildings, by Thursday morning almost all of the soldiers had been withdrawn.

As the National Guard officers were sitting around, attempting to bring the events of the last few days into focus, they were still shaking their heads. One commented that people had told him that stores in the area were selling Harlem goods at Hollywood prices. "Now isn't that ridiculous!" he said. "They couldn't stay in business that way!"

Another was unable to believe that the sniping had not been organized. "One sniper on Normandie Ave. had three different telephones in the apartment. I believe he was in contact with various buildings where people were sniping. He was the head of a sniping organization. He had two high-powered rifles. And he had a peculiar uniform—dark green shirt with white circular emblem on back and a red triangle with a red checkmark in the middle of the triangle!" [1]

Commenting on the police, a colonel said, "Although I don't blame them for brutality, I blame them for frustration and I claim that they have more of an attitude of hazing and they fire their guns independently. They fire with little provocation. . . . Although I don't have anything against the police, I think we do a better job because of this record of being independent and not controlled, and a few things like that!"

The police, conversely, were not enchanted with much of the firing the National Guard had done, or, even, with some of the actions of their own men, since under normal circumstances an investigation is immediately launched if an officer so much as fires his weapon at a skunk. Said Deputy Chief Roger Murdock, "We were a little concerned . . . we might get some corpsmen who might be 17 or 18 years old that might kill somebody."

It was Chief Parker who had asked Gov. Brown to withdraw the Guard because, "frankly, when I looked at the tv film of Little Rock . . . I rather regretted having to see the people punched in the butt with bayonets . . . and I didn't want the Guard in any longer than we needed it."

Mayor Yorty, unaware that his own chief of police had made the request, was incensed. "I don't know what the governor is doing," he said, charging that Brown had failed to clear the withdrawal with city officials. "He's making a mistake to take all of them out now. But then he's too busy with press relations and holding press conferences to tell me what he's planning to do."

And Mayor Yorty, ever the compleat politician, was already too busy running for the governor's job to find out.

On August 22, eleven days after Marquette and Ronald Frye had gone to see some girls, the National Guard pulled out the last of its men. The ECC was deactivated. Early the next morning the police eliminated 12-hour shifts, and returned to normal operations.

---

[1] He was, quite likely, a bookie.

III.   The Legacy

52   The Trials

Beginning on Monday, the 16th of August, and for several
days thereafter, the Hall of Justice was a pandemonium. A
total of 3,952 persons had been, or were in the process of
being arrested in connection with the riot. Of them, 3,438
were adults and 514 juveniles. Of the adults, 3,162 were
Negro.

When it had become apparent that there might be an unprecedented influx of prisoners, Kenneth Chantry, presiding
judge of the Superior Court, had met with William McFaden,
the presiding judge of the Juvenile Court, to work out procedures for the processing of suspects. Twenty Superior Court
judges were assigned to the Municipal Courts for the purposes of arraigning suspects and holding preliminary hearings.
In the two years since Chantry had become the presiding
judge, the Los Angeles courts, through a unique system of
organization and scheduling instituted by him, had reduced
their backlog from two years to six months, best of any
major city in the country. Weathering as stiff a test as they
would ever get, the courts proved that, provided with com-
puter-type scheduling, they could handle even the massive influx of 4,000 cases in a single week.

On television, Chief Parker asserted that more than 76 per
cent of those arrested had prior records. The police department's own figures listed 78.2 per cent of adults and 57.8
per cent of the juveniles with "criminal backgrounds."

This, it turned out, included all contacts with police, including pickups for investigative purposes. The district attorney's breakdown is more informative.

	Adults	*Juveniles*
No prior record	1,232	257
1 or 2 convictions with sentence of 90 days or less[1]	930	212

3 or more convictions with sentence of 90 days or less[1]	234	—
1 or more convictions with sentence of more than 90 days[1]	698	43
State prison terms	344	2[2]

The Los Angeles County Probation Department did an in-depth study of the juveniles arrested. In only 26 per cent of the cases was the family intact. In but 55.8 per cent was the head of the household employed. According to the evaluation of probation officers, 19.2 per cent of the arrestees had unsatisfactory or seriously maladjusted family relationships, and of those 70 per cent had previous records. Of the 9.6 per cent whose family relationship could be termed as "good," only 15 per cent had been arrested previously. In 24 per cent of the cases other members of the family had criminal records.

Families were, in general, large, only about 35 per cent of the juveniles coming from what may be considered small or medium-sized families, while 40 per cent came from very large ones.

Roughly 71 per cent of the families had an income below that of the city-wide median, and, of these, 37 per cent fell clearly into the poverty class designation.

Fifteen per cent of the arrestees had already dropped out of school, an astonishingly high rate considering that most had yet to reach the tenth and eleventh grades in which most of the dropouts occur. Of those in school, 47 per cent were rated as doing poor or very poor work, and most of these could, likewise, be expected to drop out before graduation. Only 12.4 per cent were doing "good" work, which, recognizing the rating system of the schools in the minority areas, means that they were about on a par with the "average" student in middle-class districts.

Of those whose place of birth could be determined, 2,057 of the adults and 131 of the juveniles had been born in the Southern states; 590 adults and 109 juveniles in California;

---

[1] These are County Jail terms, or in the case of juveniles, commitments to Los Angeles County Probation Department camps.
[2] California Youth Authority.

and 460 adults and 40 juveniles in other states. The South, in other words, contributed 65 per cent of those arrested.

Offenses originally charged were as follows:

Offense	Adults	Juveniles
Homicide	36	0
Robbery	93	2
Assault	326	46
Burglary & Theft	2,448	417
Misdemeanors	535	49

Actually, many of these charges were technicalities. In the case of the homicides, 33 of the 36 persons had merely been on the scene at the time that police officers had shot and killed another suspect, and the homicide charges against all of these were dismissed. Only one person was actually tried for murder: Philip Brooks, for the death of Deputy Sheriff Ronald Ludlow.

Most of the robbery and assault cases were, similarly, tried on lesser charges, and a large proportion of the burglary cases wound up as trespassing convictions.

In juvenile court, 25 per cent of the petitions were not sustained. (I.e., charges were dismissed.) Of those whose petitions were sustained, 62 per cent were released on probation, either to their own or foster parents, and 13 per cent were committed to camps.

In charges against adults, approximately 700 of the 2,249 felony cases were dismissed in Superior Court. Of the remaining 1,500, 350 were found not guilty, 800 were adjudged guilty of misdemeanors, and 350 found guilty of felonies.

Of the 1,133 misdemeanor cases, defendants in roughly 75 per cent were convicted. The disparity between this and the felony conviction rate of approximately 55 per cent is interesting from several perspectives.

Much as they may try, courts are unable to work in a prophylactic atmosphere. Judges, like other human beings, tend to absorb the general attitude, usually termed "popular opinion," toward an event. Never was this more clearly indicated than in the trials of the riot cases. The sooner a case came to court, the harsher the penalty was likely to be. As a few months passed and there began to be a better perspective on who the persons arrested were and what their roles had been, sentences meted out began to be noticeably lighter.

So it was that suspects charged with misdemeanors often came out worse than those charged with felonies, because misdemeanors by law must be tried within 30 days. In some misdemeanor cases persons received terms of as much as a year in jail.

Yet, in the felony cases, not only was the rate of conviction lower, but, with two-thirds of those found guilty convicted of misdemeanor rather than felony offenses, a sentence, for the same offense, was likely to be considerably less in December than it had been in September. Fewer than a dozen persons in all received state prison sentences, and virtually all of these—like Mardis Dorton [3]—were returned as parole violators rather than for the offenses committed during the riot. Most county jail terms were short. Two hundred persons, at the most, received sentences of more than 90 days.[4]

One of the judges, Adolph Alexander, however, complained bitterly about background reports and recommendations on convicted persons submitted by probation officers. ". . . How these probation officers can be so generous with these looters during the riots, I don't know. . . . Now here is a character, who came into this county in 1964—all kinds of commissions to inquire into the cause of these riots. . . . The answer is very simple. We have just got a pack of thieves, and this is one of them, and why we are so lenient with these people, I don't know. . . . Maybe there is some sociological reason behind it that I don't understand, so I defer to the better judgment. . . . If it were up to me, I'd slap them all in the State Prison where they belong." [5]

The truth of the matter is that few of the serious offenders were caught. Sometimes they were caught, but only in the commission of a minor crime. Not a single sniping case came to trial. In only one case, that of Ann Randolph and Neal Minor,[6] was there even a preliminary hearing, and, with even

---

[3] See page 241.
[4] On Dec. 7, 1965, a reporter for the Los Angeles *Herald-Examiner* wrote: "More than 80 per cent of persons charged with felonies have been convicted and sentenced to terms in prison ranging from one year to life."
[5] Judge Alexander's words were uttered during a probation hearing and sentencing.
[6] See page 337, et. seq.

some of the officers on the scene believing that it was not they who had done the shooting, the district attorney's office made no serious attempt to convict. The case was submitted on the transcript of the preliminary hearing, and the judge found both Minor and Miss Randolph innocent.

Arson investigators for the fire department found their task difficult. Ultimately, a half dozen persons went on trial for setting fires, but most of the cases were rather pathetic. In one, a man threw a wad of paper into a store already burning. In another, a boy was corraled near a panel truck that was slightly scorched. In a third a suspect was discovered sitting in a car with a can of lighter fluid, and for him to have started a nearby fire would have been completely out of character.

Only Dorton and Robert Ernest Pegues [7] of all those who might be termed major firebugs were caught. However, another case, which developed subsequently, is of worldwide interest because of its precedent-setting nature.

In a special program on the riots during the fall of 1965, CBS television interviewed a youth who bragged of setting a building on fire. His face was not shown, but arson investigators obtained a tape of the program, and, through various statements made by him, began establishing his identity.

Subsequently, a person by the name of Edward Lee King was arrested. His trial was held in late 1966. The prosecution's principal piece of evidence was the television tape. It was the prosecution's contention that the voice prints of the person on the tape and that of King are identical, and that he therefore stands self-convicted of arson.

It marked the first time in history a voice print has been introduced in court, and, on the basis of it, a jury found King guilty. If higher courts concur, voice prints may become as important as finger prints in crime detection.

Defendants represented by private attorneys fared noticeably better than those represented by the public defender's office, which simply did not have the manpower to devote much time to any single case. A check of more than 300 cases handled by attorneys showed that the conviction rate was less than 50 per cent, and that of those convicted only between 25 and 30 per cent actually were sentenced to jail.

[7] See page 336.

Although a handful of attorneys—more Caucasians than Negroes—donated their services free, the going rate, generally,
was $1,500 per case, and not many of the arrestees could
afford, or were willing to undertake, such an indebtedness.
Other attorneys offered their services for $50 a day, which,
judges agreed, was cheap enough, but there were no funds
to pay them.[8]

As might be expected, there were inequities. A man, accompanied by his two nephews, was walking down the street
carrying a shopping bag. Police stopped them, finding in the
bag an odd assortment of a half dozen items, with no record
of payment. All three were arrested for burglary. At the
preliminary hearing, the charges against the man were dismissed. In juvenile court, the petition against the two boys
was sustained.

A Bakersfield man, concerned about his father-in-law who
lived in the riot area, drove down to pick him up. As they
started back, the father-in-law's personal belongings piled on
the rear seat, they were stopped at a barricade. Both were
arrested for burglary.

A woman who heard on a broadcast that people who had
property illegally acquired during the riot would not be prosecuted so long as they returned it, called police to say that
her son had brought home a radio he had found on the
street. The police came, picked up the radio, and arrested
the entire family for burglary and receiving stolen property.

Some defendants heard their cases dismissed at the preliminary hearing, only to be rearrested on the same charges
as they left the courthouse. (Since the case had not yet come
to trial, this is not considered double jeopardy.)

Dale, who had been on the bus with Barney Wateridge,[9]
was released, after spending a few hours in jail, on bail of
$25 on a charge of plain drunk. When he returned to court
for his preliminary hearing, he discovered that he was
charged, additionally, with violations of Sections 404, 407,
409, and 415 of the California Penal Code, which are, re-

---

[8] Under California law, public funds may be used to engage private attorneys for indigent defendants only if the public defender's
office declares itself unable to handle a case. In the matter of the
riot, the public defender decided his staff would be able to take care
of all the cases referred, even though these numbered in the neighborhood of 2,000.

[9] See page 319.

spectively: *Riot, the use of force or violence or threat to use force by two or more persons; unlawful assembly; riot, remaining present after a warning to disperse;* and *disturbing the peace.* His bail had been increased from $25 to $2,500.

Sections 404, 407, 409 and 415, together with 485 (theft) quickly became known at the courthouse as the "famous five," because so many of the defendants were charged with violating them.

In the welter of confusion about the riot, and what did or did not occur, an examination of what happened to three of the leading characters may help in gaining perspective. These three are Rena Frye, Joyce Ann Gaines, and Philip Brooks.

*   *   *

Charged with interfering with an officer, Rena Frye went on trial before Judge George Dell in Los Angeles Municipal Court in mid-October. The American Civil Liberties Union undertook her defense. Representing her were Attys. Stanley Malone and A. L. Wirin. The prosecutor, from the City Attorney's office, was 28-year-old Rayford Fountain, a likable, recent California law school graduate.[10]

A. L. Wirin is the elder statesman of the ACLU, a white-haired, spade-bearded man of gentle manner and soft voice, not necessarily a good trial lawyer. Malone, a light-skinned Negro with handsome features, could pass for a tanned Caucasian, and appears 10 years younger than his 40-odd years. Of middle-class parentage—his father was an accountant, his mother the principal of a Washington, D. C., school—he had attended USC in the early 1940's and became the first Negro student to use the university swimming pool.

In any case involving a racial question, the selection of a jury is a process of baffling complexity. One is dealing not only with the normal human proclivities and frailties, but with ingrained attitudes and biases that the potential juror himself may not be aware of. It may even be said that, given the conditioning processes of American life, there is

---

[10] Felonies are tried by the district attorney's office, misdemeanors by the city attorney's office. The city attorney's office serves as a halfway house for law school graduates between college and private practice, with few staying longer than eight or nine months. As a result, Fountain, although he had been on the staff little more than a year, was senior prosecutor.

virtually no adult without predisposition, one way or the other, where race is concerned.

In such a situation, Wirin did not appear astute in his questioning of the jurors. He stuck to a set of standard, stereotyped questions: Are you from the South, or do you have ties to the South? Were you active in the campaign for passage of Proposition 14 (repealing fair housing)? Are you or were you ever a member of a white supremacist group?

These questions were, for all practical purposes, irrelevant. Far more pertinent would have been inquiries as to whether the person had contact with Negroes, would he be willing to have a Negro live next door, did he believe there has been equal opportunity for Negroes? The lack of validity of Wirin's questions became evident when, after both sides had accepted the jury, one man acknowledged he had already made up his mind on the case, indicating that, in general, he was predisposed against Negroes.

Fountain, conversely, was determined to take no chances on any juror who might have even the slightest unfavorable image of the police. He knocked one girl off the jury because her sister was a teacher at Edwin Markham Junior High School in Watts, and he peremptorily challenged and eliminated every Negro.

"I'm under the gun, too," he explained. "Can you imagine what would happen to the city attorney's office if we had a couple of Negro jurors and this resulted in a hung jury with them voting acquittal? What the white people of this city would say, what questions they would ask about my not knocking them off? I can't operate in a vacuum. My experience has been that every time in a criminal case when there is a Negro on a jury in a case involving another Negro, or when it comes to anything involving the police, they will vote 'Not Guilty.'

"It may be their intent to be eminently fair. But sooner or later the matter of their or some relative's discourteous treatment by the police will come up. I'd like to integrate Negroes into juries and assimilate them into society. But they'll have to measure up, too!"

The final jury consisted of 11 Caucasians—two of them women of Mexican background—and one woman of Japanese-American ancestry. Another woman was of foreign birth, and one was the wife of a Hollywood director. There were an equal number of men and women.

Fountain used Officers Lewis, Minikus, and Veale J. Fondville, in that order, to present the people's case. As they recounted the happenings on the evening of August 11, there was concurrence that, as Lewis said, "Marquette Frye was very friendly toward Minikus," and that, at the beginning, the crowd was not at all hostile. There was, in fact, so little concern that, when Marquette began walking around amidst the crowd and Lewis decided they had better get him back to the car, Lewis had to call to Minikus two or three times before the latter, deeply engrossed in a conversation with Ronald, heard him.

Minikus testified in cross-examination that he could not tell precisely when the change had come over Marquette, but that "he was moving from one side to the other like a boxer," and that he was "obviously mad, a complete reversal. It appeared he'd gone off the deep end." Despite this, Minikus said, there had been no contact between him and Marquette before Officer Wayne Wilson hit Marquette across the left eye and in the pit of his stomach with the riot baton. It was then, as Minikus led Marquette toward the patrol car with his head tucked under his arm in a "choke hold," that Rena and Ronald had kept tugging at him. After he had placed Marquette face down on the front seat in order to handcuff him, Minikus said, he felt someone pulling on his back and on his arm.

The defense's case began with Rena Frye's testimony. A small woman, sad and mild-eyed, she said that Marquette told her, "Momma, they want to take me to jail." "Go with the officers and make it easy on yourself," she had advised. That was when the officers had come up and told Marquette, "Come on, let's go. You're under arrest." "I don't want to go!" he had replied. Moments later, after Larry Bennett had placed the barrel of the shotgun to his head, he had begun screaming, "You'll have to shoot me, you motherfuckers, I'm not going!"

The jury took the several references to "motherfuckers" during the course of the trial with apparent equanimity, though it is impossible to tell to what degree, if any, it affected them.

Rena said that, when she accosted Minikus, she was "telling him don't beat him [Marquette] because they was hitting him with stick and fists."

The second defense witness, Rosalie Sanders, might have

been better left off the stand. She forgot her teeth and could
hardly be understood. Completely thrown by such words as
"contact," she was utterly confused, her most profound statement being: "I put my child's diaper across my face and
wheeled and ran."

Things improved little with the other defense witnesses.
Marquette Frye spoke almost in a whisper, was quite vague
and confused about what had happened, and, with his arms
crossed in front of his chest, obviously felt under the gun.
Cocking his head to one side, he would think over each question before answering. He appeared quiescent, but it was the
quiescence of a coiled spring.

After the defense had placed its six witnesses on the stand,
the overriding impression was that, although the prosecution's case had by no means been overpowering, the defense
witnesses had not helped Rena Frye, and might actually have
hurt her. It was, therefore, surprising that Fountain decided
to call Officer Wayne Wilson as a rebuttal witness.

Wilson, about 40, light hair graying at temples, red-faced
and wearing glasses, was a veteran of eight years on the
Highway Patrol. He testified that he received an "Officer
Needs Help" call at 7:19 p.m., and arrived two minutes later.
There was a large, hostile crowd, with two officers appearing
to be in a fight. He said that he saw Ronald near Minikus,
and that Minikus appeared to be getting up off the ground.
Although he saw no contact between them and did not ask
Minikus if he had been hit, he assumed a fight was taking
place between him and Ronald, and he therefore jabbed
Ronald in the stomach twice with the baton. He then went
up to Marquette, who grabbed at the baton. Wilson said he
was able to wrench it from him, thereupon striking him a
glancing blow on the forehead, followed by a jab to the
stomach.

There was noticeable shock among those in the courtroom
at Wilson's testimony. It was an anguished Ray Fountain
who, as court recessed for the weekend, went out into the
corridor, banged his fist against the wall, and exclaimed,
"Damn it all! I've blown it!"

The impression left by Wilson's testimony was, at best,
similar to what "Wild Bill" Davis had told district attorney's
investigators: "I never seen any undue force used. There
might have been some foolish force used."

On Monday, November 1, when the attorneys met with Judge Dell in his chambers to discuss instructions to be given to the jury, Fountain acknowledged: "If the police had beaten that boy and had used unreasonable force, the mother had every right to interfere, and the police officers would be in serious trouble. . . ."

Said Wirin, "The whole question is whether or not the officers used reasonable force, and if they used excessive force . . . resistance by that person or by a member of the family is not illegal."

Judge Dell summed up his impressions: ". . . There is evidence from which the jury could find that there was use of excessive force on Ronald. . . . I think you can properly agree that all the jury is to be concerned with is whether excessive force was used on Marquette. . . . I hate to put something special in that last instruction which would have perhaps the effect among other things of my almost telling the jury that there was excessive force used on the person of Ronald. . . ."

It was, perhaps, the feeling that he was on the verge of losing the case, that led Fountain to bring up the matter of the riot in his closing argument: "Because of Mrs. Frye's actions, taking the law into her own hands . . . we have 30 or 40 people dead, and we have millions of dollars worth of destruction, and we have a blight on our city's history that is going to take 50 or 100 years to erase!"

This was, of course, not only a gross rationalization, but entirely unfair to a woman who had pleaded at the Athens Park meeting for calm and order. Judge Dell's instructions to the jury were: "If you feel Officer Wilson or other officers acted in a manner that was not discreet or even that Officer Wilson may himself have been guilty of violation of some law, this is not a matter with which you are concerned.

"As far as the matter of the Watts riots, we cannot try a case in a vacuum. [But] you are not to speculate on this. . . . Counsel for the people made a remark which I think was perhaps unwise. . . . I don't agree with it and I don't think it should have been made. . . . I want you to, if you can, banish it from your mind completely."

It appeared, however, from some of the juror's listless attention as the long set of instructions was given, that some probably already had made up their minds. The issue was complicated by the fact that, on the last day of testimony at the trial, the district attorney had released the voluminous, four-volume report of his own investigation of the actions of the highway patrol, and concluded—not having had the benefit of Officer Wilson's testimony—that no undue force had been used. The conclusions of that investigation had been prominently reported by the press and on radio and television, and had been seen or heard by at least some of the jurors.

The jury deliberated a little over three hours before bringing in a verdict of guilty. Judge Dell fined Mrs. Frye $250, and placed her on probation.

The defense appealed, on the grounds that the combination of the release of the district attorney's report plus Fountain's linking of Mrs. Frye's actions to the ensuing riot, had unduly influenced the jurors. The appellate court, agreeing that there was an "unfortunate 'totality of circumstances' climaxed by the prejudicially improper prosecution argument," reversed the conviction in July of 1966.[11]

*   *   *

In the matter of Joyce Ann Gaines, Dist. Atty. Younger believed that "the act [of someone spitting] might have been ignored under the circumstances," and that, in any case, "I don't think they got the woman who did the spitting." Charges against Miss Gaines were dismissed, and she was never brought to trial.

*   *   *

Not until April, 1966, after spending almost seven months in jail, was Philip Brooks brought to trial on a charge of second-degree murder in the death of Deputy Sheriff Ronald Ernest Ludlow.[12] His two companions, Joseph Levine and Harold Potts, similarily charged, had had the indictments against them dismissed by the California Supreme Court in December. They, too, had spent the months between August and December in custody.

The prosecutor was Deputy Dist. Atty. McCormick, a 45-

---

[11] Rather than go through another lengthy trial, Mrs. Frye's attorneys agreed to submit the case to Judge Dell on the basis of the transcript. He found her guilty once more, and reimposed the $250 fine.

[12] See pages 250–52.

-construction laborer, aircraft
ction agent—before joining the

ing at the driver of the black-
e on when he stopped short of
. He said that he did not think
posed any danger to the offi-
e approached, did not say any-
was one foot from the door.
hell out of here!"

e car, he had been holding the
neared the auto, however, he
mbat" position, pointing more
When he came directly up to
said, Brooks's left hand had
mechanism. It was at this
ward on the gun, it

t out that, after
n Ludlow fall,
of the car, where
occupants to reach
point, as it tended to
een concerned about violent or
f the people in the car.

of the trial that a tall, slender
m and took a seat in the front
, Kelly-green suit and was wear-
Ben Franklin type glasses tinted
ke an incarnation of the Jolly
nutes after his appearance some
terested in him than in Thomas's

ttorney afterward. "I wish these

was Harold Potts, Noranyce Al-
player, he testified, had been go-
tion of Wilmington and Imperial,
inting shotguns approaching the
ince, he said, he and the others
done, and since, with several per-
e record player drowning out the

year-old graduate
stocky, serious, be
career in public se
  The defense att
and Ken Thomas.
Ohio State Univers
Wyatt, a native
of California law
attorney in San F
in 1962, and he c
cedure. Neither def-
  The all-white jur
  The prosecution
lins, the investigat
Cartwright, Russell
  Collins and Ca
husky, olive-skinne
Because of the utt
had, in the course
been unable to
who had witness
days after the selec
teered in a casual
proach the car.
  On the stand he
and hold the shotg
tion" just prior to
see the car's driver,
within the car.
  The blast from th
Ludlow off his feet,
He had seemed to h
onto his back. To
real that his first re
ing off and playing a
  Lauer was the fina
old with light brow
his face, he has a su
background was stri
had attended Fullerto

[18] Two of the fourte

year-old graduate of Loyola University of Los Angeles. A
stocky, serious, bespectacled man, he has spent his entire legal
career in public service.

The defense attorneys, both Negroes, were Benjamin Wyatt
and Ken Thomas. Thomas, a tall, light-skinned graduate of
Ohio State University, handled the interrogation of witnesses.
Wyatt, a native Californian and graduate of the University
of California law school, had himself been a deputy district
attorney in San Francisco prior to entering private practice
in 1962, and he concentrated on questions of law and procedure. Neither defense attorney was being paid.

The all-white jury consisted of nine men and five women.[18]

The prosecution presented four witnesses: Sgt. Roy E. Collins, the investigating officer; and Deputy Sheriffs Robert
Cartwright, Russell D. Owens, and William B. Lauer.

Collins and Cartwright could contribute little. Owens,
husky, olive-skinned, with black hair, was a surprise witness.
Because of the utter confusion at the scene, the prosecution
had, in the course of the many months from August to April,
been unable to come up with a single deputy, besides Lauer,
who had witnessed what happened at the car. Then, two
days after the selection of the jury had begun, Owens volunteered in a casual conversation that he had seen Lauer approach the car.

On the stand he testified that he "saw him lean backward
and hold the shotgun in a backward, swinging-to-left motion" just prior to its discharge. He had not been able to
see the car's driver, but had noted an arm coming out from
within the car.

The blast from the shotgun, Owens testified, had knocked
Ludlow off his feet, his legs going straight up into the air.
He had seemed to hang there for a moment, then fallen flat
onto his back. To Owens the movement had seemed so un-
real that his first reaction had been "that Ludlow was goof-
ing off and playing around—like in a slapstick comedy."

Lauer was the final prosecution witness. Twenty-eight years
old with light brown hair and premature lines etched into
his face, he has a superficial likeness to Richard Nixon. His
background was strikingly similar to Ludlow's. Married, he
had attended Fullerton Junior College as a chemistry major,

[18] Two of the fourteen were alternates.

392   THE LEGACY

and had held several jobs—construction laborer, aircraft
worker, finance company collection agent—before joining the
sheriff's force in 1962.

Several deputies were shouting at the driver of the black-
and-yellow 1957 Ford to move on when he stopped short of
the intersection, Lauer testified. He said that he did not think
the occupants of the car had posed any danger to the officers, and that he himself, as he approached, did not say anything to the driver until he was one foot from the door.
Then he had shouted, "Get the hell out of here!"

As Lauer had started for the car, he had been holding the
shotgun at port arms. As he neared the auto, however, he
had shifted the gun to a "combat" position, pointing more
or less directly at the driver. When he came directly up to
the side of the car, Lauer said, Brooks's left hand had
reached for the top of the side mechanism. It was at this
moment that, as Lauer had jerked backward on the gun, it
had discharged.

In his cross-examination, Thomas brought out that, after
the shotgun had discharged and Lauer had seen Ludlow fall,
he had dropped the gun right by the door of the car, where
it would have been easy for one of the occupants to reach
and pick up. This was an important point, as it tended to
show that Lauer had not been concerned about violent or
aggressive action on the part of the people in the car.

It was during this portion of the trial that a tall, slender
Negro entered the courtroom and took a seat in the front
row. He was clad in a bright, Kelly-green suit and was wearing miniature, rectangular, Ben Franklin type glasses tinted
a dark green. He looked like an incarnation of the Jolly
Green Giant, and for 20 minutes after his appearance some
of the jurors seemed more interested in him than in Thomas's
questioning.

"My God!" groaned the attorney afterward. "I wish these
people would stay away."

The first defense witness was Harold Potts, Noranyce Allen's boyfriend. The record player, he testified, had been going full blast. At the intersection of Wilmington and Imperial,
he had observed officers pointing shotguns approaching the
car from both directions. Since, he said, he and the others
didn't know what they had done, and since, with several persons shouting at them and the record player drowning out the

complicated by the fact that, on the last day of testimony at the trial, the district attorney had released the voluminous, four-volume report of his own investigation of the actions of the highway patrol, and concluded—not having had the benefit of Officer Wilson's testimony—that no undue force had been used. The conclusions of that investigation had been prominently reported by the press and on radio and television, and had been seen or heard by at least some of the jurors.

The jury deliberated a little over three hours before bringing in a verdict of guilty. Judge Dell fined Mrs. Frye $250, and placed her on probation.

The defense appealed, on the grounds that the combination of the release of the district attorney's report plus Fountain's linking of Mrs. Frye's actions to the ensuing riot, had unduly influenced the jurors. The appellate court, agreeing that there was an "unfortunate 'totality of circumstances' climaxed by the prejudicially improper prosecution argument," reversed the conviction in July of 1966.[11]

*   *   *

In the matter of Joyce Ann Gaines, Dist. Atty. Younger believed that "the act [of someone spitting] might have been ignored under the circumstances," and that, in any case, "I don't think they got the woman who did the spitting." Charges against Miss Gaines were dismissed, and she was never brought to trial.

*   *   *

Not until April, 1966, after spending almost seven months in jail, was Philip Brooks brought to trial on a charge of second-degree murder in the death of Deputy Sheriff Ronald Ernest Ludlow.[12] His two companions, Joseph Levine and Harold Potts, similarily charged, had had the indictments against them dismissed by the California Supreme Court in December. They, too, had spent the months between August and December in custody.

The prosecutor was Deputy Dist. Atty. McCormick, a 45-

---

[11] Rather than go through another lengthy trial, Mrs. Frye's attorneys agreed to submit the case to Judge Dell on the basis of the transcript. He found her guilty once more, and reimposed the $250 fine.
[12] See pages 250–52.

On Monday, November 1, when the attorneys met with Judge Dell in his chambers to discuss instructions to be given to the jury, Fountain acknowledged: "If the police had beaten that boy and had used unreasonable force, the mother had every right to interfere, and the police officers would be in serious trouble. . . ."

Said Wirin, "The whole question is whether or not the officers used reasonable force, and if they used excessive force . . . resistance by that person or by a member of the family is not illegal."

Judge Dell summed up his impressions: ". . . There is evidence from which the jury could find that there was use of excessive force on Ronald. . . . I think you can properly agree that all the jury is to be concerned with is whether excessive force was used on Marquette. . . . I hate to put something special in that last instruction which would have perhaps the effect among other things of my almost telling the jury that there was excessive force used on the person of Ronald. . . ."

It was, perhaps, the feeling that he was on the verge of losing the case, that led Fountain to bring up the matter of the riot in his closing argument: "Because of Mrs. Frye's actions, taking the law into her own hands . . . we have 30 or 40 people dead, and we have millions of dollars worth of destruction, and we have a blight on our city's history that is going to take 50 or 100 years to erase!"

This was, of course, not only a gross rationalization, but entirely unfair to a woman who had pleaded at the Athens Park meeting for calm and order. Judge Dell's instructions to the jury were: "If you feel Officer Wilson or other officers acted in a manner that was not discreet or even that Officer Wilson may himself have been guilty of violation of some law, this is not a matter with which you are concerned.

"As far as the matter of the Watts riots, we cannot try a case in a vacuum. [But] you are not to speculate on this. . . . Counsel for the people made a remark which I think was perhaps unwise. . . . I don't agree with it and I don't think it should have been made. . . . I want you to, if you can, banish it from your mind completely."

It appeared, however, from some of the juror's listless attention as the long set of instructions was given, that some probably already had made up their minds. The issue was voices, they could not hear what was being said, they had all put up their hands to indicate they were offering no resistance.

In his cross-examination of Potts, as well as subsequent witnesses, McCormick hammered at three points: 1) Why were the three of them there in the first place? 2) Did they really have the record player on—did that make any sense driving through the riot area? 3) Why, if they intended to buy food, did they not go east to Lynwood, instead of west through the riot area?

The first point was important to the prosecution because it was McCormick's contention that the three of them were out joy riding, and were in the process of disobeying the deputies when Ludlow was killed. On point two, it would appear irrational to have a record player turned on in the middle of a riot—and of course it was. But here again it was not the middle-class Anglo-Saxon culture that McCormick was dealing with, but a less complex one in which each action is not thought through to all of its possible consequences.

On point number three McCormick displayed a Caucasian naïveté that would have been unremarkable except for the fact that he was an eight-year veteran of the district attorney's office. He apparently had never heard of the "Berlin Wall," and, as Negroes in the audience snickered, kept pounding at the Lynwood question—what sense did it make to travel five miles to the west, when there were stores open in Lynwood just across the railroad tracks?

"We was scared to go to Lynwood!" Potts answered him succinctly. In fact, he had never been to Lynwood in his life.[14]

Parked at the gas station on the corner had been attorney Rayfield Lundy, a Negro, and his 17-year-old son, William Lloyd Lundy III. They had been out sightseeing for an hour and a half before witnessing the action on Imperial.

William Lundy, articulate, intelligent, made an excellent witness. He said he had seen no struggle, nor any hands coming out of the window of the car. Under cross-examination by McCormick, who attempted to establish—and succeeded to some extent—that Lundy's angle of vision had been such that the body of the car might have blocked his seeing hands extended from the window, he was calm and explicit.

[14] See page 203.

As all eyes in the courtroom were focused on Lundy, a heavy-set, squat Caucasian suddenly appeared in the aisle. "I was just nearly shot by a police officer in the hall!" he shouted. "I testified to the McCone Commission about the police. I can see you're trying to disqualify this boy. . . . I'm an unreliable witness! You can print that!"

The guards invited him to leave. Rayfield Lundy took the stand. A well-known attorney, it was expected he would make an excellent witness. Instead, he turned out to be like a runaway bull—one question would send him butting this way and snorting that, rambling on and on. He had first become involved, he said, because, in their original reports, newspapers and broadcasting stations had made it appear that the deputy sheriff had been killed by a shot from within the car, and he had called a television station to correct this impression. In court, however, he floundered hopelessly, and finally declared rather plaintively, "We're trying to reconstruct [the scene] for the court—but Billy is a little sharper than his old man, so I'm asking him!"

This was pathetically comic, coming, as it did, from an attorney. In fact, it pointed up the differences in the generations: William Lundy, sophisticated, self-confident, fully able to hold his own in the competition with Caucasians; Rayfield Lundy, despite being a successful attorney, unable to entirely overcome his unequal beginning, his feet entangled in the undergrowth of Negro culture and perspectives.

Every day, as the trial progressed, sitting as inconspicuously as possible in one of the back rows, was a petite young hazel-eyed blonde, so attractive one could not help noticing her. Spectators, seeing her take notes, assumed she was covering the trial for some publication.

In actuality, she was Carole Thomas, the wife of defense Atty. Ken Thomas. A divorcee of Scotch-Swedish descent she has two children by her prior marriage to a Caucasian. She had met Thomas when she had filed suit against her Glendale landlord for evicting her because she had had Negroes as guests in her house. For fear of prejudicing the jurors should they discover that Thomas was married to her, she would not talk to him in the corridor or even ride on the same elevator with him. Considering the fact that most polls show that approximately 90 per cent of white Americans still consider miscegenation unacceptable, it was, perhaps, a wise decision.

The final witness was Brooks himself. Married, with four children, he was 23 years old, a high school graduate who had served honorably in the navy from 1960 to 1962, and was employed as an automobile paint shader.

He declared that, after halting the car at the intersection, he had heard several shouts, including, "Halt!" and "Get out of there!" He said he hadn't known what to do, and, when the officer approached with the shotgun, "was shook up . . . I can't hardly explain it!" He had put up his hands, he asserted, and a moment later had felt the butt of the shotgun hit his elbow, which was resting on the door frame. Simultaneously, the gun had discharged.

After that, Brooks said, he and the others had been pulled out of the car by deputies. Levine was taken around to the back, the other two to the front. Their heads were pushed against the side of the car and bloodied. At the station they were made to sit on their hands, and one deputy ripped a scab off Brooks's face with his fingernail.

"If counsel wants to resort to this type of questioning," McCormick was incensed, "I'm not going to object!" In cross-examination he asked, sarcastically, "It was police brutality—is that what you're telling us?"

In his closing argument, McCormick declared it was the State's theory that Brooks was resisting an officer. "They went down there either sightseeing or looking for trouble, and they got a little carried away!"

He then took the remarkable step of impeaching his own witness, Deputy Owens, telling the jury, "Only two people could know what really went on: Lauer and Brooks." It was, he said, a question of which of the two the jury believed.

The jury, after three days deliberation, responded that they believed Brooks. They found him not guilty.

The incident embodied two tragedies. One was the death of Ludlow. The other the compulsion to try to pin the blame on someone, to establish everything as either black or white, refusing to acknowledge that some things happen because of a combination of circumstances over which no one has control. Even had Brooks pushed at the shotgun as it was pointed at him through the window, it was evident that this could only have been a reflex action, without malice, and to convict a man of murder under such circumstances can hardly be to the benefit of society. Yet, in the acquittal of Brooks, Lauer was, by implication, found guilty of contribu-

tory negligence in the death of Ludlow, because, as Mc-
Cormick said, "The deputy sheriff got too close to the car—
that was a mistake." And to hang this albatross around
Lauer's neck is just as gross an injustice as a conviction of
Brooks would have been.

53   The Inquests

Coroner's inquests were scheduled to investigate the cause
and responsibility in the other deaths that occurred during
the riot. Beginning on Sept. 14, they were held two a day
on Tuesdays, Wednesdays, and Thursdays, and concluded on
October 21. Of the 32 deaths investigated, 26 were held to
be justifiable; one accidental (Leon Posey, Jr.[1]); one homicidal, with no determination (Theophile Albert O'Neal[1]); and
four criminal (Deputy Sheriff Richard Raymond Lefebre,
Fireman Warren Earl Tilson, Rita Rena Johnson, and George
Adams, Jr.[1]). The inquest into the death of Eugene Shimatsu
was canceled at the request of the family.

The coroner's inquest is a curious procedure. Having its
basis in English common law, it exists outside the framework
of the courts, and therefore contains none of the legal safeguards to assure a fair procedure. Its *raison d'être* in California, as in many other states, is to establish a cause of
death and whether death was occasioned by criminal means,
in cases in which the district attorney's office believes a public hearing would best serve the purpose. The California
statutes are so loosely written that local jurisdictions have
considerable autonomy in the manner of conducting an inquest, and the Los Angeles County procedure differs from
that in most of the remainder of the state.

The presiding officer was Charles G. Langhauser, the coroner's chief inquest deputy, a dour man whose principal in-

---

[1] See pages 245, 280, 350, 266, 261, and 256, in that order.

terest, at times, appeared to be in getting through each inquest with the least possible fuss. The district attorney's office was represented by Deputy Dist. Atty. Patrick McCormick. With his lack of comprehension of the Negro ethos, and his orientation toward the law enforcement point of view, he was ill prepared to act as an impartial interrogating officer.

When it was decided to hold the inquests there was a fear that, with hordes of spectators, the hearings would become arenas of chaos in which law enforcement officers would come under attack for their roles in the suppression of the riot. It was, therefore, decided to circumscribe the interrogation of witnesses as stringently as practicable.

Said Langhauser in his opening statement at each of the inquests after the first two or three, when the matter became a point of contention between him and attorneys representing the families of the deceased, "The only agency which is specifically authorized by law to be present at the inquest is the office of the district attorney. Attorneys may be present to advise a witness as to his rights; otherwise, the coroner has the right to exclude persons. . . . As far as attorneys taking part in the inquest by interrogating witnesses is concerned, we would say that the same is wholly unauthorized."

In his report to the McCone Commission, Dist. Atty. Younger voiced his opinion: "The purpose of a coroner's hearing is to provide a proper public forum for the preliminary determination of the cause of death from a medical and legal standpoint. The coroner's inquest procedure is designed to secure, in as expeditious a manner as feasible, the testimony of witnesses to the facts surrounding the death. . . ."

It is the district attorney's prerogative, Younger said, not to call an inquest, but to make unilateral conclusions. Further, the district attorney still has the ultimate decision in determining whether criminal proceedings should be instituted. In other words, since the jury's findings are advisory in nature only, the district attorney may seek an indictment even if the jury's verdict is that the homicide was justifiable; or, vice versa, he may decide not to file charges albeit the jury has brought in a verdict of criminal homicide.

Cross-examination was not permitted, the district attorney's report said, "Because of the utter confusion that could result." For example, "What if each member of the family had a different lawyer?"

Atty. James N. Adler, of the firm of Munger, Tolls & Hills, was charged by the McCone Commission with writing an impartial critique of the inquest procedure. "The conduct of the inquests and the verdicts themselves raise serious, and interrelated, statutory and constitutional problems," he wrote. "The county counsel's office [Irvin Taplin] advised the Coroner that he did have discretion to permit such participation [of attorneys] or to preclude it." Although cross-examination is never permitted, in cases in the past the Coroner had permitted counsel representing families or other interested persons to ask "material" questions. Referring to the riot inquests, Adler said, it "is clear that the Coroner does not desire and did not permit attorney representation."

Each jury, consisting of nine persons chosen from the regular Superior Court panel, heard two cases. Most had one Negro member, but, since verdicts need be by majority only, he did not have, as would be in the case of a regular jury, a veto power. Prior to June, 1960, members of coroner's juries had been, literally, picked up off the street. This procedure was changed after such a jury, containing several minority group members, found an officer "guilty of criminal responsibility" in the shooting of an unarmed 16-year-old Negro, Leon Carter.

(The district attorney refused to accept the verdict, and the case was taken before the Grand Jury, which ruled the homicide justifiable.)

The location of the inquests was Room 501 of the old Hall of Records, a large, dark, windowless chamber intersected with gilded pillars, its walls decorated with WPA murals. Done in the style of the jut-jawed, rectangular school, these depict such nonrelated events as the "Butterfield Overland Stage"; "Czar Issues Russian-American Charter, 1799"; "Granting Magna Charta, 1215"; Landing of Cabrillo, 1542"; "Constitution of the United States, 1787"; "Dana at San Pedro, 1835." Across the front of the room, in large letters, is the legend: "This Country Is Founded on Enterprise— Cherish and Help Preserve It."

There were no crowds. There were never more than two dozen persons in attendance at any one inquest. Of these, four or five would be witnesses, and an equal number would be plainclothes deputy sheriffs there to protect the witnesses from possible acts of revenge by members of the family or friends of the deceased. Most newspapers never bothered to send a reporter. In fact, the reaction of the community, both white and Negro, was one of such indifference that it may be said to have contributed significantly to the pat celerity with which the inquests were conducted, few lasting more than an hour from the time Langhauser began his lengthy opening statement to the jury's returning of a verdict.

Trained in the adversary system, McCormick could not break himself of the habit of accepting each law enforcement officer's statement as if it were issued from the Mount, while, in effect, cross-examining those witnesses whose testimony differed from that of the "official" version.

As a result, Negro witnesses, already leery of appearing in the "white man's" courts, were persuaded that not only were they not wanted, but that to testify would be futile. Attorneys, unable to question their own witnesses or to provide the usual legal safeguards, were reluctant to put witnesses for the families on the stand, and on several occasions advised them against testifying. Much potential testimony, therefore, was never heard, a curious situation in what was supposed to be a complete investigatory process.

The distinct lack of enthusiasm for probing into and challenging the statements of the "official" witnesses not only resulted in some half-baked presentation of evidence, but also in some plain, if inadvertent, distortions.

In the inquest into the death of Charles Patrick Smalley, Lt. Col. Thomas Haykin [2] was on the stand.

Col. Haykin: "Shortly after we took over the Watts area and some 260 policemen had been relieved, a Cadillac with four men came into the area and shot directly into my command post. . . ."

McCormick: "Now, after that, did you again then go around and contact the various locations where you had deployed your men?"

Col. Haykin: "That is correct, sir. I checked each of my guard outposts, and the roadblocks, and told them to allow no one to enter that area. This was after the curfew. The curfew was 8 o'clock, and this happened about, oh, I would say about 8:15, the Cadillac incident."

McCormick: "All right. Prior to 9 p.m., you had recontacted your men."

Haykin: "This is correct."

[2] See pages 273, 276, 328–30, and 348.

There is rampant confusion of times and dates here. Smalley was shot on Saturday night. The Cadillac incident happened on Friday night, around midnight. On Friday night there was, as yet, no curfew. There was close to a 24-hour interval between the time Col. Haykin and the troops moved into Watts and the time Smalley was shot at the roadblock.

The fact that Col. Haykin made an entirely honest mistake, having, under the pressure and confusion of the riot jumbled the chronology of events in his mind, is not at issue. Neither is the fact that this chronological jumbling was, probably, not significant in the rendering of the ultimate verdict. What is at issue is that, under the system, it could go unchallenged, and that, thereby, the jury could be presented a distorted picture. The question becomes: though the errant testimony was not significant in this case, could, or would, it have been in another?

It was this point that Atty. Albert Jones made in the inquests into the deaths of Leon Cauley and Miller Chester Burroughs.[8]

Jones: "Your honor, if this witness's statements are not cross-examined by me, the entire proceedings here is a sham. If his testimony cannot be cross-examined, then we do not have any idea at all as to the strength of that statement, quality of that statement—"

Langhauser: "You may not cross-examine."

Jones: "If the witness's statements cannot withstand cross-examination, then the witness's statement is not to be believed."

Langhauser: "Any more outbursts, you will be excluded from this inquest."

Jones: "I am just trying to make a point, your honor."

Langhauser: "You may be excluded. Exclude this witness!"

Some counsels attempted to lay ground rules when they placed their witnesses on the stand. Such was the case when Leroy Simon was called to testify at the Leon Posey inquest. Simon, said his attorney William G. Smith, would be "willing to testify under two conditions: the first condition being that he be allowed to tell a complete version and account of the events which occurred—"

[8] See pages 290–92.

McCormick: "There will be no conditions. The man is either going to testify or assert the fifth amendment."

Leroy Simon did not testify.

Neither did Harry Clay, who apparently was a witness to the shooting of Theophile Albert O'Neal.[4] Because of the inhibitory effect the manner of conducting the inquests had on Negro witnesses, the district attorney's office was, therefore, forced to list the death as homicidal, with no determination.

Many times, an answer to a question was left hanging like an innuendo.

In the death of Neita Love,[5] Lt. Robert J. Geary of the National Guard responded to a McCormick question regarding the condition of Claude Love with: "The gentleman was intoxicated, his speech was incoherent, and he had a wound in one of his legs."

There was no amplification. The jury was left with the impression that Claude Love was staggeringly drunk. In actuality, there was no evidence to show that he had had anything to drink whatsoever. What was fact was that, at the time, he had just suffered close-range .30-caliber gunshot wounds in both his arm and his leg, and that, under the circumstances, with a dead wife by his side, a man much younger than his 77 years might well have been incoherent.

There were some particularly edifying exchanges in the Fentroy Morrison George inquest.[6] Harold Battle was on the stand when this one took place.

McCormick: "Did you witness the shooting?"

Battle: "No. I was there when he was shot."

Langhauser: "Will you remove whatever you are chewing, sir."

Battle: "I don't have anything."

McCormick: "Now you were arrested and charged. Is that correct?"

Langhauser: "Is that clear?"

Battle: "That is clear."

McCormick: "But you don't know what you were charged with?"

Battle: "No. Not clear. I know at first I was charged with murder. This is all I understood, while I was going to court, and stuff, even when I was in jail."

---

[4] See page 280.
[5] See page 351.
[6] See pages 292–94.

McCormick: "Who told you you were charged with murder?"

Battle: "The detective that arrested me."

McCormick: "Who?"

Battle: "The detective. The homicide detective."

McCormick: "You went to court?"

Langhauser: "And the judge told you—"

Battle: "He dropped this case. My attorney—"

McCormick: "Just a minute."

Langhauser: "Answer the question."

McCormick: "When you went to court, the judge told you what you were charged with and asked you how you pleaded, didn't he?"

Battle: "No."

McCormick: "All right. I don't have any other questions."

Harold Battle's account of the Fentroy George shooting having thus been deeply delved into, the next witness was Donald Lewis of 337 W. 61st St. Lewis, who lived cater-corner from the Hudson Department Store, testified he saw the incident from a telephone booth on Broadway, directly across from the store.

"When Harold [Battle] went upstairs," Lewis said, "the news car stopped two tow trucks and ordered them to tear up the car, wreck the car. . . . The newsman stopped the police just behind the car.

"He told them something was going on in the building. The police called, shouted 'Halt' over behind the news car, which was a panel truck. When George came back out of the building the second time and got in his car, he noticed the police car over at an angle. So he got out of his car and started walking, because of the police behind the car with big guns on him."

Lewis stated that he was in the public phone booth in order to place a call to New Orleans. McCormick then produced a bill from the telephone company listing a call placed from the booth, and charged to Lewis's phone, at 1:49 a.m. on Saturday, the 14th; the inference being, since George was shot at 5:15 a.m., that Lewis had been in the telephone booth some three hours earlier than he claimed, and had, therefore, not witnessed the incident. Showing Lewis the bill, McCormick asked him to read the itemization.

Lewis: "895-4706—public phone booth. That is one, but not the one on the 14th. The time is different."

Langhauser: "Well, now, this witness is confused. Are there any further questions, Mr. McCormick?"

McCormick: "I will ask you this question. One of them was the time. It lists one at 1:49 a.m. Isn't that right?"

Lewis: "One time, yeah."

McCormick: "No other questions."

The jury was not shown the bill in dispute.

Robert Fawcett, of 1736 N. Alameda St., the tow truck operator, took the stand.

McCormick: "Did you see the firemen put a ladder up to the second floor?"

Fawcett: "I'm not sure whether he put a ladder up or not."

Langhauser: "Just answer the question. Did you see them put a ladder up to the second story?"

Having already said he didn't know, the witness was understandably confused as to what question he was supposed to "just answer."

Houston Hall, the NBC news cameraman, was unavailable for the inquest, but his deposition was read into the record.

". . . The two tow trucks pulled up beside us, and I hollered to them that the building was being looted. One of the wreckers proceeded to ram the parked car in an attempt to disable it. . . .

"After filming the dying Negro, the smoldering fire burst into flames, and I proceeded to film firemen arriving on the scene and their fighting fire. . . ."

Harold Battle claimed he and George had started running because, suddenly, without any warning that they were aware of, shots had started to be fired at them. The key question, then, was: had Battle [7] and George been looting the department store, or had George been shot because of tragic errors of assumption and judgment all the way around?

Douglas L. Bentley, a homicide detective, said that on August 24 he checked the Corvair, which had been impounded and parked on a lot, and found in the front luggage compartment six separate items of juvenile apparel with price tags that the manager of Hudson's identified as having been received in a shipment on August 12, which had not, *in its entirety,* been placed on sale. George's wife Janice, when shown the clothing, said she had never seen it before.

[7] At his trial, Battle was found guilty of trespassing, fined $300, and placed on three years probation.

August 24 was 10 days after the killing, and Stanley Malone, the family's attorney, pointed out that in those 10 days any of a number of persons possibly interested in establishing that George was looting could have placed the clothing in the car.

There are, in any event, a couple of interesting questions about the George case.

If it was George's intent to loot the department store, why did he have Battle drive the Corvair around to the street where everyone could see them loading the car, instead of leaving it parked in the rear of the building, where the probability was no one would have seen them?

With most of his household goods and personal possessions, including the television set, still in the apartment of a building that was on fire, why would George concentrate on stealing a motley assortment of children's clothes, worth at most $20?

These questions were not posed for the jury to ponder.

The film that Houston Hall shot might, perhaps, have contributed to clarification, but it was revealed that somehow it had been ruined in the process of being developed.

The Negro view was fairly representatively stated at the inquest into Joseph Glenwood Wallace's death.[8] The jury was told that Wallace had been arrested and served time for burglary and grand larceny from 1952 until 1955; that he had been rearrested on a charge of burglary in 1957, and had spent the next six years in prison.

"If they're gonna talk about that, why don't they tell the truth, instead of making him look like a hardened criminal?" his brother asked.

"I'm from Texas," the dead man's pregnant girlfriend sobbed, "but I'm just as black as the Mississippi. They do a lot of talking out here about Mississippi justice, but I don't see no difference."

It is many months since these two have returned to the Negro community and taken their bitterness with them, spreading and amplifying it among tens and hundreds of others.

And one cannot help but wonder the impression that the

[8] See page 341.

widow of Juan Puentes took with her from the inquest into his death.[6]

The jury was presented with the circumstances that had led Officers Young and Wagner to Puentes, and resulted in his being shot. They were told that Puentes had .29 per cent alcohol in his blood, and that he had had one prior arrest for theft.

They were not told that 1) no stolen articles or weapons of any kind were found by the body; 2) that the shotgun was fired from such close range as to leave powder burns; and 3) that the bushes behind which Puentes was standing were *within 50 feet of his home!*

Considering the circumstances one could not, in any way —presuming that they were telling the truth—blame the officers for the shooting. They undoubtedly felt in fear of their lives. Puentes might, even, have been one of the men they spotted fleeing from the hardware store.

On the other hand, there is no evidence to indicate that he was. It is equally probable that, drunk, he had simply stepped out of the house, and happened to be standing in the bushes when the officers appeared. As such, he was a victim of circumstance, and it is difficult to see what purpose can be served by leaving the impression to posterity that he was gunned down during the commission of a crime.

The same point may be raised even more strongly in the case of Andrew Houston, Jr., who was killed on the balcony of the Villa Maria Hotel under the mistaken assumption that he was a sniper.

First of all, it would have been virtually impossible for anyone to fire from the front of the hotel into the front of the police station unless he had invented a rifle firing a bullet with a curving trajectory. It was, in fact, never claimed that the police station was being fired into directly. The bullets were striking on the opposite side of the street. It was the ricochets that were bouncing into the station, and it would have taken a truly diabolical sniper to attempt to knock off a few law enforcement officers via bank shots.

McCormick's questioning of Pfc. Mercer, the soldier who had shot Houston, closed in the following manner:

McCormick: "What did you do?"

[9] See page 336.

Mercer: "I shot him."

As a result of the shot, Houston had flopped over backward onto the floor.

McCormick: "Now, after you had fired that shot and saw a man fall, was there any more sniper firing?"

Mercer: "No."

McCormick: "I have nothing further."

Lt. William C. Johnston, Jr., of Headquarters Company, First Battalion, 160th Infantry, was called to the stand.

McCormick: "Were you detailed to go into that hotel?"

Lt. Johnston: "Yes, sir."

McCormick: "And did you search for fire arms?"

Lt. Johnston: "Yes, sir."

McCormick: "Did you find any?"

Lt. Johnston: "Yes, sir."

McCormick: "What did you find?"

Lt. Johnston: "Found a fully loaded, .22 rifle, with a sawed-off stock, and a .22 automatic revolver, fully loaded."

McCormick: "Did you take those into your possession at that time?"

Lt. Johnston: "Yes, sir, and they were turned over to the Los Angeles Police Department."

McCormick: "I have no further questions."

This was the end of the presentation, taking little more than 15 minutes. The jury was charged, and sent out to bring in a verdict.

The jury, however, balked. Twenty minutes after being sent out it returned, wanting the answers to several questions, which were handed to Mr. McCormick.

McCormick: "I might state for the record and for the jury, that as far as the first question goes, nobody can answer that."

(And, presumably, nobody will ever know what the question was, since Mr. McCormick did not see fit to state it, and it was not incorporated into the record.)

Langhauser: "That is your decision, Mr. McCormick."

Lt. Johnston was recalled to the stand. In response to the jury's questions, he testified that other police and National Guard personnel went into the hotel, but no other guns were recovered. The .22 rifle and revolver he had discovered were found in the manager's apartment, on the first floor. In addition to Houston, Lt. Johnston said, there were several other persons in the building at the time.

(It was clear, then, that the guns had no connection with Houston. The fact that they had not been fired recently was never pointed out to the jury.)

Pfc. Mercer was recalled. He stated that all he could see was the white T-shirt the man was wearing. He had not been able to see whether he held anything in his hand. He could not say whether or not he had had a gun.

Langhauser (to jury): "Does that answer your question?"

Foreman: "That answers the question."

Juror: "Almost."

Langhauser: "Well, you will have to base your verdict on the testimony that you hear."

Juror: "Well, okay."

Langhauser: "Any further questions?"

Juror: "Did they trace the gun to anyone in particular?"

Earl J. Cludy, a detective in the homicide division of the LAPD, was called to the stand. Mr. Cludy was the investigator in all of the deaths occurring at the hand of the National Guard.

Cludy: "The ownership [of the guns] was never ascertained."

Langhauser: "Does that answer your question?"

Juror: "Yes."

McCormick: "Let me ask you a couple of questions, Mr. Cludy. Do you have to own a gun to use it?"

Cludy: "No, sir."

McCormick: "And whoever owned the gun, that still would be immaterial, would it not?"

Cludy: "Yes, sir."

McCormick: "That is not the standard condition of a rifle?"

Cludy: "No, sir. The rifle had a sawed-off stock."

Langhauser: "What would the purpose be for sawing the stock off a rifle?"

Cludy: "Concealment, sir."

Langhauser: "Concealment?"

Cludy: "Yes, sir."

Langhauser: "Thank you, you may be excused."

The reader, of course, knows that a gun in Watts is about as unusual as an egg in a hen house. The jury, however, was not necessarily privy to that information. Once more sent out to deliberate, it brought in a verdict of justifiable homicide.

Attorneys who had to sit silently through such exchanges in the spectator section of the court room, having, if they wanted to have a question asked of a witness, to write it on a slip of paper and run it up to the bailiff, who would then transmit it to McCormick, blew their tops.

Albert W. Jones called it "a farcical imitation of justice and a kangaroo court."

Leo Branton asserted, "The whole hearing is designed as a whitewash. It is not being held for the purpose of detecting the truth."

Stanley Malone, president of the Langston Law Club, averred, "The coroner's inquest is completely inequitable and an obsolete way of determining the facts. It makes a mockery of just process of law."

The district attorney's office shot back that "People who have labeled as a 'whitewash' the coroner's inquest . . . either fail to understand the true function . . . or they are deliberately trying to undermine confidence in governmental agencies.

"It is apparent that certain of those persons who are now attacking the coroner's inquest would never be satisfied unless the procedure as adopted led to a prosecution of some police officers."

A dispassionate person would be inclined to agree with the district attorney when he said, "[One] must take into consideration the atmosphere which prevailed at the time the killings occurred. You must not forget that these young men in law enforcement and National Guard were operating under conditions which compared to a war zone in a foreign land. Violence was occurring all about them. . . . The total picture was not conducive to that calm and reflective judgment which hindsight might now suggest."

However, the same person might begin to squirm when this continues as: "The morality of the actions . . . may be the subject of academic discussion . . . but are not germane to the question of whether legally the actions of an individual involved constitute a prosecutable criminal offense."

And he would ask the district attorney to look at the other side of the coin, as it was presented to the McCone Commission by Atty. James N. Adler, who must certainly be considered a disinterested and objective analyst.

"A finding of justifiable homicide is very likely as a practical matter to blacken the name of the deceased," especially when, as in the typical verdict, it was coupled with: ". . . died of gunshot wounds . . . while under the influence of alcohol, and was shot by known police officers while committing a felony.

"That the deceased died 'while committing a felony,' " Adler wrote, "goes completely beyond the authority of the coroner's jury which is to a) determine cause of death, and b) concern itself with the *criminality of the actor who causes death.* . . .

". . . The procedures of the coroner's inquest do not provide the essential elements of fair play and due process which would be required were the coroner's jury to be permitted to make a determination concerning the guilt of the deceased.

"The Constitution therefore requires that a choice be made. Either the deceased must be afforded, as an absolute right, a fair trial with opportunity to participate fully, or no determination of his guilt should be attempted."

Dist. Atty. Younger himself, as he told the McCone Commission, had his suspicions and was far from satisfied. "I think we have to conclude that all along the line there are questions of judgment involved in every one of these shooting cases. . . . A couple of them where I think bad judgment was used. . . . We are taking a further look at these despite the coroner's hearing."

A look, however, was all. It took two more major incidents to demonstrate that, provided with intelligent leadership, the community could avoid a second explosion of the magnitude of the Watts riot.

54   The Ides of March

Hardly had the riot been contained than police began receiving reports that new outbursts were planned. The Labor Day weekend, Halloween—these and others approached with dire forebodings. However, although there continued to be the usual clashes between residents and police, it was not until mid-March of 1966 that the next challenge to the city's equilibrium occurred. As in August, the circumstance was unpredictable, the ignition unplanned.

On Monday night, the 14th of March, 16-year-old Dwayne Graves, a Negro, of 9609 Evers St., and 26-year-old Joe Garcia, a Mexican-American, of 11354 Foster Road, Norwalk, became involved in a scuffle at a liquor store near the intersection of Grape and 103rd St.[1]

A short time after the scuffle, Garcia, together with two younger brothers, Robert, 20, and Carlos, 19, allegedly returned and fired several shotgun blasts toward the store, wounding Graves and another Negro, George Sanders. Shortly thereafter rumors began to circulate that there was going to be a march against Mexican-Americans, comprising 5 to 10 per cent of the community's population. (And owning a considerably larger percentage of the property from the days of their coeval occupancy of the area.)

Tension continued to build all Tuesday morning, especially along the half dozen blocks on 103rd St. between Grape St. and Jordan High School, where the unemployed youths hang out. When, at 3 o'clock, school was dismissed, these youths began a desultory attack on cars being driven through, almost precisely in the same manner as on Avalon Blvd. in August.

A Caucasian teacher, whose automobile was hit, called police. The police, when they came, chased Thomas Lee Galloway, 21, into a barbershop. When they attempted to arrest him for throwing rocks, he began raising howls of "police brutality."

Immediately a crowd of 200 to 300 persons was galvanized. The only new store to have opened in Watts since August was looted. A truck was overturned. Caucasians were attacked.

Thirty-five-year-old Larry Gomez, a Mexican-American deeply involved in the civil rights struggle, and the Sparkletts Drinking Water Corp.'s "Man of the Year" in 1965, was making a delivery in the Jordan Downs Housing Project two blocks away. Suddenly he found himself surrounded by several teenagers who shouted, "Let's get the water man!"

---

[1] The same location at which a riot had nearly started in the summer of 1964 as a result of the shot bandit, and also the spot where Ramon Hermosillo was killed.

It is quite probable that the incident would not have grown into serious proportions had it not been for 17-year-old Sam Lewis Fulton. Fulton, at 6 feet 5 inches and 150 pounds, an almost incredible beanstalk, had been raised near Tallulah, La., by his sharecropping grandparents, his parents having separated before his birth. Fulton's mother lived in the Jordan Downs Housing Project, and, in January of 1965, he had arrived in Los Angeles.

He attempted to enter high school, but his rural Louisiana education proved hopelessly inadequate. In this limbo, without any skills, lacking an education yet unable to go to school, he began gambling, hustling, and playing pool. He slept wherever a bed was available, and on the nights of March 13 and 14 he stayed in the apartment of Dan Doyle, a 23-year-old he had known in Louisiana.

Doyle had been given a .22 Colt derringer by a friend. Fulton testified that the two of them had been planning to use the gun in a robbery, but that they chickened out. (Doyle was, in fact, later convicted of robbery in an unrelated incident.) On March 15, Fulton, apparently without Doyle's knowledge, was carrying the gun.

When he came upon the teenagers surrounding Gomez, he saw his chance "to be the big man." Without a word he walked up to Gomez, placed the pistol to his body, and pulled the trigger. Gomez, the father of five, toppled over, killed instantly.

Within the hour, as the special "Code 77" brought all available police manpower rushing to the scene, 100 officers faced the crowd along 103rd St. As the officers advanced, a sniper began firing. One of the officers shot over the head of the people. Other officers joined in, and police fired an estimated 40 shots in all. A Negro bystander, Joseph Lee Crawford, 28, was, like several other persons, caught in the exchange. He was struck in the head and killed by a 9-mm. bullet, apparently fired by the sniper, since police were using only .38's and shotguns.

If the cast of characters was much the same as it had been in August, it quickly became apparent that the circumstances were not. The police response was one of immediate and impressive strength. A reorganization of the department made possible the assembly of many Negro officers, including a Negro lieutenant appointed since August. Plainclothes officers immediately began circulating, and the gathering of intelligence was vastly improved. Police cars and fire engines, going out on calls—most of which were false alarms—glided silently through the streets without using their sirens, so as not to attract crowds.

Most important, by far, was that the police, instead of sneering at workers from the probation department, neighborhood groups, and civil rights organizations, worked actively with them to stop the spread of rumors and to calm the situation.

By 11 o'clock Tuesday evening Watts had grown so quiet that newsmen on the scene were yawning, desperately chasing will-o'-the-wisps in the hope that something would happen. Nothing did.

Nothing, that is, until May 7, when the clash between Negro and Caucasian cultures erupted in the Deadwyler incident.

*   *   *

Leonard and Barbara Deadwyler, both 25, had arrived in Los Angeles from Georgia 11 months before. They did not own a car. They already had several children, and on May 7 Mrs. Deadwyler was several months pregnant. (She was not quite certain as to the exact number.) Both she and her husband had been drinking—Leonard had a blood alcohol count of .35 per cent, double the amount legally considered intoxicating—and in late afternoon she began experiencing cramps. Stomach cramps are part of the life of the ghetto; they often result from the high incidence of food poisoning and kidney infections.[2] Leonard, however, thought that his wife was going into labor, as she had a history of giving birth quickly. In the South they had never lived more than a few blocks from the hospital; this time the hospital, Los Angeles County General, was 10 miles away.

It was a Saturday and the day before, Gamalyel Ferguson, a friend, had been sold an old clunker of a Buick by a used-car dealer. (There seems to be a mysterious attraction between ghetto Negroes and second-hand Buicks.) Neither Ferguson nor Deadwyler had a driver's license, but, in the emergency, Ferguson agreed to lend Leonard the car. Since he was not used to driving, it did not occur to Leonard to go the several blocks out of the way that would have been

[2] See, for example, page 240.

necessary to reach the Harbor Freeway. Instead, with the Buick emitting smoke like a turn-of-the-century coal burner, he set sail up Avalon Blvd. To indicate that it was an emergency, he had tied a white handkerchief to the car's antenna. This, in Georgia, is apparently an accepted folk custom. In Los Angeles it had no meaning whatever.

Leonard traveled at flank speed, somewhere in the vicinity of 60 miles an hour. Next to him in the front seat was Barbara. In the back seat, holding the Deadwylers' 2-year-old boy, who was munching from a bag of potato chips, was Ferguson.

The first police car to spot the racing Buick did so after Deadwyler had gone only 10 or 15 blocks. With siren and red light it began the pursuit.

Deadwyler accelerated. He assumed the police, having noticed the white handkerchief, were providing him with an escort, that they were as interested in getting his wife to the hospital as he was. The faster the police pursued, the faster he drove. Through red lights, across the double line to go around cars waiting for signals at intersections—he was really moving.

As the chase continued, the police became convinced that they were either dealing with a madman, or someone fleeing the crime of the century. Two other patrol cars joined the pursuit. Not until after a distance of three miles, when one of the patrol cars was able to pull alongside, and an officer pointed a revolver out of the car's window, did Deadwyler apparently begin to think the police were not just interested in providing him an escort. He slowed down and pulled to the curb at 60th St.

Officer Jerold Bova, 23, with a little over a year's service on the force, was the first policeman to run up to the Deadwyler car. He stuck his head in through the window on the passenger side, leaning across Mrs. Deadwyler. As he did, the cocked .38 in his hand pointed directly at Leonard. Police officials did not argue the point that, in putting the upper portion of his body inside the car, Bova was imprudent.

When Leonard saw Bova, he leaned toward him to tell him that he was taking his wife to the hospital. In that moment his foot apparently slipped off the brake, and the car lurched forward several feet. The sudden motion jerked Bova off his feet, and the gun in his hand went off.

The bullet struck Leonard Deadwyler in the chest. He slumped across his wife's lap, fatally wounded.

*   *   *

"Wanted for the Murder of Leonard Deadwyler, a member of the concentration camp—Bova the Cop, a guard in the concentration camp," militant Black Nationalists waved placards as they appeared at the courthouse for the inquest 12 days later. Not since the Birmingham incidents of 1963 had there been such fever pitch unanimity of feeling in the Negro community. Feeling generated by the belief that the inquest, like the inquests into the riot deaths, would be stacked against an impartial investigation; that it would serve only to whitewash the police.

The National Guard was placed on alert, and, had Dist. Atty. Younger taken one misstep, a repeat of August would have been not at all improbable.

Well aware of this, Younger took every precaution to make the inquest a model of judicial fairness. As the representative of the district attorney's office, McCormick was replaced by another deputy, John Provenzano, not so committed to a specific point of view. The Deadwyler family attorney, Johnnie L. Cochran, Jr., was seated next to Provenzano at the counsel table. While, in order to preserve the *pro forma* appearance of nonparticipation, Cochran was not permitted to ask questions of a witness directly, all he had to do was whisper in Provenzano's ear, and Provenzano would ask the question. In essence, therefore, not only was Cochran permitted to ask "material" questions, but also to cross-examine. He and Provenzano worked together harmoniously, and Cochran placed a score of Negro witnesses on the stand. Although the procedure of Cochran's having to use Provenzano as his voice was cumbersome, it was completely fair, and Cochran termed himself fully satisfied.

When, on the first morning of the inquest, 500 Negroes, shoving and shouting, tried to force their way into a courtroom that could hold no more than a fourth of them, loudspeakers were set up in the courthouse plaza to broadcast the proceedings. Younger then prevailed upon station KTLA to telecast the entire hearings live from the courtroom the next day and each day for the week thereafter. By so publicizing the inquest, he choked off the rumors that would, most surely, otherwise have sprouted in the ghetto. The verdict that Deadwyler's death was accidental was, with a few exceptions, received with equanimity.

The question, then, whether justifiable homicide was an equitable verdict in such deaths as those of Aubrey Griffin, Andrew Houston, and Neita Love, remains sharper than ever.

55   The McCone Commission—An End or a Beginning?

Even as the National Guard was withdrawing from Los Angeles, Gov. Brown appointed a commission to investigate the causes of the riot. Consisting of seven members of diverse backgrounds and views, it was an independent investigative body comparable in American annals only to the Warren Commission.

Named chairman of the commission was John McCone, former director of the CIA. Vice-chairman was Warren M. Christopher, an attorney. Politically the members ranged from conservative Asa V. Call, chairman of the board of Pacific Mutual Life Insurance Co., to the liberal Rev. James Edward Jones, a Negro and a member of the city board of education. Other members were Sherman M. Mellinkoff, dean of the medical school at UCLA; Mrs. Robert G. Neumann, former president of the League of Women Voters; The Very Rev. Charles S. Casassa, president of Loyola University; and Judge Earl C. Broady, of the State Superior Court, a Negro.

The fact that the Commission, *in toto,* pleased no one may be the best indication of its nonpartisan makeup. Liberals were not enchanted with the appointments of McCone and Call; Mayor Yorty criticized the selection of the Rev. Jones.

When, after three months of hearings, the commission's report appeared in December, it was criticized for being superficial, dealing in generalities, lacking incisiveness, and certainly not being worth the almost $300,000 that was spent on it.[1]

Much of this criticism was not valid. Some of it was. A good deal, over-all, was the fault of the manner in which the final report was composed.

There was, first of all, the pressure of time. Gov. Brown had promised that the report would be out during the first part of December, and the commission was determined to meet the deadline, even though, realistically, several more months would have been needed to assimilate all of the material. In fact, even as the final report was in preparation, witnesses were still being interrogated by staff investigators.

Second, in the reaching of a consensus of divergent viewpoints, there must always be a muting of sharp opinions, and a blunting of impact. Some aspects which should have been taken up were not, because of their controversial nature and because portions of the population—not to speak of the panel itself!—might have taken offense.

Third, staff investigators tended to sit on their haunches and wait for witnesses to come to them, rather than actively go out and dig for information. Not until several weeks into the hearings did it become apparent to the staff that poverty area Negroes were not going to come flocking to the commission offices in the State Building downtown, since they considered the commission to be simply another extension of the long arm of the Whips. Even after this realization, when offices were opened in the southeast area, staff investigators continued to act, principally, in the role of receptionists. As a result, certain elements of the riot were never delved into.

Fourth, the report was couched in language that had all the sparkle of a corporation report. It was necessary to husk every paragraph to get at the kernels inside.

Fifth, and most important, the report failed to present the hard and often harsh facts and figures on which the recommendations were based. Thus, when the commission declared that ". . . we believe news media may be able to find a

---

[1] Commented the California State Advisory Committee to the U.S. Commission on Civil Rights: "The report is elementary, superficial, unorganized and unimaginative . . . [exhibiting] a marked and surprising lack of understanding of the civil rights movement. . . . The McCone Commssion failed totally to make any findings concerning the existence or nonexistence of police malpractices. . . ."

voluntary basis for exercising restraint and prudence in reporting inflammatory incidents," this is a generality with little meaning, unless one is aware of the incidents that the commission was referring to.[2] Commission members knew what these were, but readers of the report were left in the dark.

Similarly, the statement: ". . . little has been done in recent years to encourage the Negro youth's support of the police, or to implant in the youth's mind the true value of the Police Department," seems a blatant truism, unless one is apprised of the nature of the demise of the Deputy Auxiliary Police program,[3] and the philosophy of Chief Parker. By this kind of tip-toeing around the people and organizations being criticized, the commission did itself a serious disservice.

It did itself a disservice because the 18 volumes and almost two million words of testimony it collected contain much information of value. Had some of this been presented as background for the recommendations, the latter would likely have received a great deal more attention and, perhaps, have carried more weight.

Following are the commission's principal recommendations, and what has happened in the nine months since they were made.

THE POLICE DEPARTMENT

"We propose more intensive in-service human relations training programs for officer personnel; youth programs such as the Deputy Auxiliary Police programs; periodic open forums and workshops in which the police and residents of the minority communities will engage in discussions of law enforcement; and frequent contact between the police and the students in junior and senior high schools.

"Such programs are a basic responsibility of the police department. They serve to prevent crime, and, in the opinion of this commission, crime prevention is a responsibility of the police department, equal in importance to law enforcement."

[2] See, for example, pages 51 and 154.
[3] See page 114.

Even as they made these recommendations, commission members must have known that, since they went against the grain of Chief Parker's philosophy, they were not likely to be implemented by him. Seriously ill with heart and artery disease, he knew just how ill he was, and those who dealt with him during these months found him irascible, short-tempered, and sometimes unreasonable. What had once been opinions, had become obsessions. Making off-the-cuff statements, he would blow up when challenged on them. He called a city council investigation of the riot an "inquisition"; appearing before the McCone Commission, he took its members aback by snapping, "The thing that irritates me about all of this proceeding is that you have all laid back there with bits of information . . . and ask questions on them as if you were cross-examining a defendant in a criminal action. . . . I resent having to deal this way."

Even when he bowed to the commission's recommendation "that an 'Inspector General' should be established [to remove] the impression, widespread, that complaints by civilians go unnoticed, that police officers are free to conduct themselves as they will, and that the manner in which they handle the public is of little concern to higher authorities," he gave the office no support, and it began to atrophy from the day it was set up. In August, 1966, a follow-up report by the commission declared the Inspector General's office to be "not in operation."

Perhaps the greatest misfortune was that there were in the top echelon of the police department men who disagreed with the Chief, and saw the necessity of changing some of the department's ways. But, while Chief Parker continued to be the official spokesman, their voices remained muted. Simply knowing they existed might have done much to soothe the ruffled feelings of the Negro community. The McCone Commission, however, did nothing to dispel the impression—among both Negroes and Caucasians—that the Chief stood above criticism; that anyone who questioned his policies must —according to his dicta—be bent on the destruction of the police department.

Said Deputy Chief Thomas Reddin [4] to the McCone Com-

[4] Reddin and Fisk were two of the three top finishers in civil service examinations to find a successor to Chief Parker. In February, 1967, Reddin was appointed the new chief of police, and Fisk was named his deputy.

mission, "If the answer is that the Negro population feels that they are mistreated by the majority society and they vent their resentment on the only omnipresent symbol of that society, the police, this is a general problem of minority versus majority society. It can only be solved by an attack on all real and imagined social ills that plague the Negro community."

Insp. James Fisk [4] elaborated. "The community needs to tell us it's not going to evaluate us purely in terms of crime statistics. . . . We measure our services now . . . in terms of how many crimes we have, how many arrests we make.

"Our culture makes it very difficult for a Negro to feel any sense of self-esteem. My personal feeling about Watts was that we were dealing with a people demoralized by society."

Added Deputy Chief Richard Simon, "Negro-police problems exist everywhere that migration has taken place because . . . the policemen [in Southern states] have been 100 per cent vigorous in upholding white supremacy at all costs. . . . The policeman is not regarded as a friend of the Negro at all . . . and you can't expect them [the Negroes] not to have this carryover of this feeling. . . .

"That indicates the problem when groups of people do not communicate. . . . Cries of police brutality have militated against the solution of the problems which are very real."

Since such honest and altruistic statements never reached the general public, the key question in the operation of the department was never posed, or answered: Can any city afford a police chief, no matter how administratively competent, who, by his public statements, antagonizes not only large portions of the population, but even some of his own colleagues? [5]

---

[5] A month after Parker's death, Acting Police Chief Thad Brown had breakfast with Negro community leaders at a church on Avalon Blvd. near Watts. Said he, "I assure all residents of this community my complete cooperation and my hope to make this a better community, and make the police department a better police department."

His visit immediately created a surge of optimism among Negroes that a new era of police-community relations was dawning. The day after this meeting, Chief Brown met with Sheriff Peter Pitchess to establish closer relations between the police and sheriff's departments.

UNEMPLOYMENT AND WELFARE

It was the commission's opinion "that both willful and un-witting discrimination in employment have existed and continue to exist within our community. There is an opinion among many employers that the lack of skill and motivation on the part of many Negroes makes them undependable employees, and thus preference is given to those of other ethnic backgrounds. In addition, in many labor unions, past practices result in discrimination against the Negroes. . . ."

In order to eliminate such discrimination, the commission advocated legislation to empower the California FEPC to require labor unions and all firms with more than 250 workers to file annual reports listing the ethnic breakdown of members and employees.

In most training programs, the commission said, " 'attitudinal training' to help the candidate develop the necessary motivation" is missing, and "there is an apparent lack of coordination between many of the training programs and the job opportunities. All too often a youth in the south-central area goes through training, acquires the necessary skill to fill a job only to find that no job awaits him. The results are disastrous. . . .

". . . When a man's efforts to find a job come to naught, inevitably there is despair and a deep resentment of a society which he feels has turned its back upon him. Welfare does not change this. It provides the necessities of life, but adds nothing to a man's stature, nor relieves the frustrations that grow. In short, the price for public assistance is loss of human dignity.

"The welfare program that provides for his children is administered so that it injures his position as the head of his household. . . . The unemployed . . . neither serves as a worthy example to his children nor does he actively motivate them to go to school and study. Thus, chain reaction takes place. The despair and disillusionment of the unemployed parent is passed down to the children. The example of failure is vividly present and the parent's frustrations and habits become the children's."

It is in the field of employment that the only really tangible improvement has come since the riot, and much of this is due to one man: H. C. "Chad" McClellan.

McClellan, an industrialist and director of various corporations, is a past president of both the Chamber of Commerce and the NAM, and in 1959 organized the American National Exhibition in Russia. Following the riot, the Los Angeles Chamber of Commerce asked him to head its Management Council for Merit Employment and Research, the task of which is to find jobs for people in the riot area.

The first step was to provide a link between industry and the unemployed. Industry did not recognize there was a pool of labor available, and the people did not realize there were jobs they could get. McClellan prevailed upon many of the companies to relax their hiring standards, especially in regard to persons with police records, and the experiences of the companies, so far, has been uniformly good. As of March, 1966, McClellan had succeeded in enlisting 267 major employers in the program. A survey showed that 90 of these had hired 4,751 previously unemployed workers, or worker-trainees.

There are, however, still thousands and perhaps tens of thousands of men, who, for one reason or another, have been unable to find employment. McClellan believes that the principal problem is one of attitude: the willingness by Negroes to overcome their resentment at what has happened during the course of the last 100 years. Equally pressing is the problem of literacy. Like others, McClellan has found the level of verbal skills in the poverty area appalling.

Comprehensive training programs for people in the area are in their infancy, and have, as yet, had little effect. With 1,000 or more newcomers, most of them with few or no skills, arriving in southeast Los Angeles every month, and the schools ejecting 3,000 young people into the labor market every year, unemployment continues high.[6] The precise number is open to debate. The standard means of determination have a tendency to place the figure far too low in minority areas, because many of the unemployed never come into contact with State Employment Services, lacking even the encouragement to go looking for a job, as well as the education to know how. In mid-1966 the California FEPC's figures showed that purchasing power in the minority areas had decreased by almost $400 since 1961, with male unemployment standing at 31 per cent. In Watts itself male un-

---

[6] While there are 180,000 new jobs being created in California each year, 800,000 persons are looking for work.

employment reached 41 per cent. As a result, in the 18 months following the riot, welfare cases increased by 20 per cent, and, in January, 1967, almost 31 of every 100 persons in southeast Los Angeles were on relief.

EDUCATION

The McCone Commission concluded that "the average student in the fifth grade in schools in the disadvantaged areas is unable to read and understand his textbook materials, to read and understand a daily newspaper, or to make use of reading and writing for ordinary purposes in his daily life. . . . Essentially, the reading and writing level of students in the disadvantaged areas is far too low for them either to advance in school or to function effectively in society. . . .

"Children in disadvantaged areas are often deprived in their preschool years of the necessary foundations for learning. . . . Their behavior, their vocabulary, their verbal abilities, their experience with ideas, their view of adults, of society, of books, of learning, of schools, and of teachers are such as to have a negative impact on their school experience. Thus, the disadvantaged child enters school with a serious educational handicap, and because he gets a poor start in school, he drops further behind as he continues through the grades."

The commission's recommendations in the educational field were, probably, the most important of all.

"We propose that the programs for the schools in disadvantaged areas be vastly reorganized and strengthened so as to strike at the heart of low achievement and break the cycle of failure. We advocate a new, massive, expensive, and frankly experimental onslaught on the problem of illiteracy. We propose that it be attacked at the time and place where there is an exciting prospect of success. . . .

"First, school services in disadvantaged areas must be extended down to the ages of three and four, in order to give these children the background and reinforcements, particularly in language skills, that they have not received in their 'informal' education prior to school. These programs for disadvantaged three- and four-year-old children must be provided throughout the regular school year and they must be permanently maintained. . . .

"Second, class size must be significantly reduced for children now in elementary and junior high schools in disadvantaged areas. In order to maximize opportunity for effective teaching, class size in these schools should be reduced to a maximum of 22. . . .

"It is our belief that raising the level of scholastic achievement will lessen the trend toward *de facto* segregation in the schools in the areas into which the Negroes are expanding and, indeed, will tend to reduce all *de facto* segregation. . . . In turn, school segregation apparently contributes importantly to all *de facto* segregation. We reason, therefore, that raising the scholastic achievement might reverse the entire trend of *de facto* segregation. . . ."

The commission recommended that, in order to implement this program, schools in disadvantaged areas should be designated as "Emergency Schools," and that the cost would be at least $250 per year per student in addition to normal expenditures.

The recommendations have been ignored. This is due, perhaps, to their very extensiveness, and the expense that would be involved. Other factors, however, are apathy, political pressures, and a system so bureaucratically encumbered that it takes two and a half years simply to change the standard-issue pencil from round to hexagonal so that it will not chronically roll off pupils' desks.[7]

The city has made no effort to alleviate the situation developing from its lack of a free-lunch program, and some children still go without a midday meal.

Although Head Start is one of the more enthusiastically accepted of the antipoverty programs, only a minor fraction of preschool children are, as yet, able to participate, and diminishing Federal contributions were necessitating a reduction in the program at a time when it should have been expanding.

THE DISADVANTAGED CONSUMER

"We deplore the tactics of some merchants and lenders who help induce low-income persons to become heavily debt-

---

[7] The suggestion for the changes was submitted by a school principal, Jack E. Perry, in November, 1963, and the change was finally adopted by the Board of Education in the spring of 1966.

burdened," the commission asserted. "Still another problem
for the Negro consumer is the lack of an adequate remedy
when he feels he has been unfairly treated. Public and private
agencies exist to help the consumer in such a situation, but
while manned by able and conscientious professionals, these
agencies are generally understaffed, underfinanced, and over-
burdened. Often the consumer does not even know of the
agency's existence."

One of the first, and practically the only, burned-out business to reopen on 103rd St. in Watts was a pawnshop.

THE NEED FOR LEADERSHIP

The commission summarized its findings by admonishing,
"No longer can the leaders of business discharge their responsibility by merely approving a broadly worded executive
order establishing a policy of nondiscrimination and equality
of opportunity as a basic directive to their managers and personnel departments. They must insist that these policies are
carried out and they must keep records to see that they are.
. . . In labor, as in business, pronouncements of policy,
however well intended, are not enough. Unless a union con-
ducts its affairs on a basis of absolute equality of opportunity and nondiscrimination, we believe there is reason to
question its eligibility to represent employees at the bargain-
ing table. . . .

"We are convinced the Negro can no longer exist, as he
has, with the disadvantages which separate him from the rest
of society, deprive him of employment, and cause him to drift
aimlessly through life.

"This, we feel, represents a crisis in our country."

*   *   *

The commission's report is one that no objective citizen,
cognizant of the conditions, can quarrel with. Unfortunately,
there is one vital area that was not dealt with at all, apparently because of its sensitive nature.

This is the several-sided problem of chaotic family conditions, illegitimacy, and birth control. It is, in many ways, the
key link in the chain of despair, and to omit it is like leaving out one of the elements in a complex chemical equation
—the entire structure is changed, and becomes disjointed and
incomprehensible.

56   The Land of Milk and Honey

Los Angeles, like other cities before and since, exploded into riot because Negroes were fed up and whites were fed pap. The Caucasian community did not know the score, and had no motivation for learning it. If one is permitted to generalize —and it is a generalization supported by polls—the middle-class white will back the Negro's drive for statutory equality: the right to vote, the right to access to all public accommodations, the right to equal education, the right to equal job opportunity, the right to equal treatment in the courts. He will support, or at least not oppose, legislation to these ends. Without thinking about it much, he assumes that once such legislation is on the books the goal has been accomplished. That there is then no reason, unless it be his own deficiencies, for the Negro not to work himself up to a par with the Caucasian American.

To the Negro—at least the lower-class Negro—who cares not a whit about the ideal, whose only concern is his daily encounter with the end results of white attitudes, the policy of the Whips amounts to sheer hypocrisy. Psychologically he was able to deal far better with acknowledged prejudice than with a situation in which he keeps being told that he is equal, but finds himself less and less equal in the competition for jobs, and more and more segregated. Convinced that the *de jure* prohibitions had been removed only for the sake of looks, and that the whites were not about to lift the *de facto* ones, he considered he had nothing to lose by rebelling.

Hopefully, the explosion might have led the middle-class white to an attempt at comprehending the ghetto; but it quickly became apparent that he was more interested in explaining away the riot than in understanding it. Sen. Thomas Dodd of Connecticut declared that "organized extremist groups under Havana and Peking influence" appeared to have been a factor, because "such violence runs counter to the entire tradition of the American Negro and counter to the teachings of the legitimate civil rights movement." [1]

Sen. George Murphy of California contended that "the looting was so expert that there are grounds for belief that there may have been 'rehearsals' for the incident. . . . It was done by a small vicious group of trained troublemakers who should be treated for exactly what they are—criminals who have been pampered and pardoned and turned loose time and again by society to create havoc and mischief." [2]

Columnist James J. Kilpatrick pondered: "For the first time, really, a great many Americans are reflecting upon the initiative, ambition, and industry of such law-abiding minorities as the Irish, the Chinese, and the Jews, and the hard question is being asked: What's so different about the Negro?"

Columnist George Todt's answer in the Los Angeles *Herald-Examiner* was "The riot . . . was caused by weak character traits in uncivilized human beings who yielded to their savage emotions in a barbaric display of ill will and hate. . . .

"Too many Negroes have been inflamed unhappily with passion and emotion in recent years by hateful demagogues, subversives and corrupt leaders. . . ."

William F. Buckley, Jr., perhaps the most rational Conservative spokesman, thought that "The notion that the Negroes in Los Angeles expressed the frustration of the larger community at the intransigence of American white society is hardly plausible. . . . The best way to guarantee that what happened at Los Angeles shall happen again is to moon over the affair and yap about injustices by whites to Negroes, the guilt of the white slave trader, and the rest of it." [3]

The Christian Anti-Communism Crusade blamed the outbreak on "an unholy alliance between communists and black muslims . . . for the purpose of promoting a racial war within the United States. . . . A contributing factor to the riots was the breakdown in family life. This is due to individual self-indulgence and sin on the part of the parents and not to prevailing economic conditions or the pattern of discrimination." [4]

According to an analysis in *American Opinion,*[5] the organ

[1] Associated Press dispatch, Sept. 3, 1965.
[2] Los Angeles *Times,* Aug. 16, 1965.
[3] Los Angeles *Times,* August 20, 1965.
[4] News letters of Aug. 24, 1965, and Jan. 10, 1966.
[5] September, 1965.

of the John Birch Society, the riot "had to be planned. . . .
It is right out of Ché Guevára and Mao Tse-tung." It had
to be deliberately fomented because "Los Angeles has one of
the best records of racial tolerance of any city in the world.
For generations we have had no segregated schools, businesses, buses, washrooms, beaches or public facilities.

"People of all races are hired out here for their *ability,*
and that is that. No barriers are artificaly created that would
in any way hamper the industrious. . . .

"If the Welfare State is the land of milk and honey, as
'Liberals' maintain, then California is Paradise and Watts is
its crowning glory. . . ."

A moderate, commentator M. B. Jackson, believed that:
". . . The Negro leaders . . . must say to their own people: we have fought hard for laws which will insure to us a
fair shake, and we are on the threshold of a new day. Now
it is up to us to make the most of the opportunity this
gives us. It's time to roll up your sleeves, spit on your hands
and go to work: Keep your children in school; reeducate
yourselves, keep your homes together; learn to know your
community and learn to know its police and other peace officers—they're not bad types at all when you get to know them.
. . . Don't let yourself be suckered into the temptation or
the luxury of claiming that every setback or disappointment
is the fault of some white man or some brutal cop. It may
seem comforting to tell yourself that, but it's a phony com-
fort and one that will betray you. If you want decent things
—good housing, good jobs, good education, then work for
them—put out. The opportunities are there, but the job is
up to you. . . .

"Respect cannot be demanded or given; it has to be *earned;*
it has to be merited."

Laudatory and lucid as Jackson's words might seem to the
middle-class white community and the Negro intellectual,
they were hooted at by the ghetto Negro because they were
not congruent with his own, concrete experiences. The gap
in communications between the lower-class Negro and the
middle-class white remained as great as if they were speaking
different languages.

To a considerable extent, the media of mass communications must bear the blame for the lack of understanding
among white Americans as to what happened in the riot, and
why it happened at all. Television concentrated on the im-

mediate and the dramatic, but its presentations, as exemplified by that of the Athens Park meeting, were often distorted; and in relaying every bit of raw, unverified information it was hardly acting in the public interest.[6]

Metropolitan newspapers were handicapped in their coverage by a lack of Negro reporters. Not until the Los Angeles *Times* fortuitously discovered an able writer in the guise of Robert Richardson, a trainee in the advertising department, was any paper able to present its viewers with an account of what was occurring, "behind the lines" in the Negro community. Accounts of the action were mostly heat-of-deadline first impressions, with no follow-ups. Thus, for two days the Los Angeles *Herald-Examiner* continued to carry accounts of a gun battle that had never happened, a fact that a careful reporter could have discovered for himself within hours of the purported occurrence.[7]

One national news magazine,[8] whose over-all account of the riot was far better than most, reported: ". . . Another of the Negro victims killed had incredibly taken up a post on a rooftop overlooking Watts's 77th St. precinct station. As he directed sniper fire at police and soldiers below, a Guardsman wheeled, drilled him cleanly through the head with a rifle bullet.[9]

"But the war-weary police were still doing most of the yeomen work. They shot four looters dead in stores they were sacking, fought a pitched gun battle with several others holed up in a garage; the rioters emerged carrying a wounded woman and waving a white flag." [10]

If inaccuracies are an inevitable adjunct to deadline publication, no such plea can be made for the lack of reportorial enterprise after the riots.

With the exception of an outstanding series of articles probing the problems of the Negro community by Los Angeles *Times* reporter Jack Jones, newspapers did little to help bring the riot into focus. Coverage of the inquests was cursory. Coverage of the trials was, for all practical purposes, nonexistent. Apparently no reporter was curious enough to find

[6] See Chief Parker's comment, page 244.
[7] See page 246.
[8] *Time,* Aug. 20, 1965.
[9] See page 279.
[10] See page 246.

out what had happened to all those persons charged with
sniping, arson, murder and the like.[11]

As a result, the reportorial distortions of the riots tended
to be perpetuated. In mid-autumn, 1965, CBS-TV did a special on the riots that reran the same slanted, out-of-context
film clip of the Athens Park meeting, again representing it
as an accurate recounting. As late as July, 1966, writers were
accepting unquestioningly Chief Parker's account of this meeting and using spot newspaper stories—instead of the many
original records and documents by then available—to piece
together a supposedly factual account of the riot; which
would be like writing the history of the Battle of Britain
from the stories, appearing at the time, in the London *Times*
or the *Berliner Tageblatt*.

Said the McCone Commission in criticizing the press: "It
is understandably easy to report the dramatic and ignore the
constructive; yet the highest tradition of a free press involves
responsibility as well as drama."

                              *   *   *

To the Caucasian, with his perspective of the "good life,"
the riot made little sense. Much of what he saw in the press
and on television during and after the violence only muddied
already murky waters. The declarations of Chief Parker that
"Los Angeles has been the most progressive city in the country in eliminating racial friction," [12] and Mayor Yorty that
"The cry of 'police brutality' had been shouted in cities all
over the world by Communists, dupes and demagogues irre-
spective of the facts," [13] enabled him to rationalize that the
riot certainly did not reflect any malady in American society.
The ever more strident expostulations of Negro Nationalists
—ranging from Stokely Carmichael to LeRoi Jones—reinforced his belief that the explosion was plotted, and provided
material for his argument that these were not fires of discontent; that they could not have ignited spontaneously with such
fury.

[11] See page 381.
[12] July 9, 1963.
[13] The mayor, once a fiery liberal, has, of late, seen standing
behind every critic or opponent of his a Communist. Said he in his
unsuccessful campaign for the Democratic nomination for governor
in 1966: "Of course he [Governor Brown] has the support of the
Communist Party against me in the primary because I'm anti-Communist."

Yet, had there been organization, the $35 million worth of damage could have been multiplied a hundredfold. Not only were there, within the confines of the riot area, scores of industrial concerns, but some of them were literally arsenals: a warehouse containing $100,000 worth of ammunition; a processing plant for magnesium (a highly inflammable material); a factory producing napalm bombs. Combining such materials with the mobility provided by the automobile, the city could have been set ablaze from one end to the other.

It remained for a publication viewing the holocaust from a distance to provide the most lucid assessment. Said *The Economist,* a British weekly, "It is not just an American tragedy. . . . What happened in Los Angeles is pretty certainly going to happen in many other countries, both capitalist and communist, as the conditions that caused it spread to them. This was an American phenomenon only in the sense that the United States is half a generation ahead of the rest of the world in the development of an industrial urban society with the special problems that brings. It has the first taste of both the pleasures and the terrors of this new sort of life. . . . It was an insurrection of anarchy, an outburst against any kind of system by the people left at the bottom."

Who are these people? What is the history of the man left at the bottom?

IV.   The Black Print of the Negro

57   The Glass Door

Consider Willy Brown. Willy Brown is the archetype of the Negro born in the Black Belt in the early 1920's. He lived in an unpainted shack with a leaky roof, blistering hot in summer and freezing cold in winter, and infested with insects. Water was hand-drawn from a well. His mother cooked on a wood-burning stove. Electricity was one of the marvels of the city. He had a half dozen brothers and sisters, and they all worked in the fields. School was an uncertain thing that would begin in October after the cotton had been picked and end in March when the fields had to be prepared for planting, interrupted every so often in between by heavy rains that made impassable the road to the one-room schoolhouse, presided over by a half-educated teacher. Willy Brown went to school for eight years, but he never learned more than to read a label on a box or to scrawl his name. His social life centered about the church, but with the church's fundamentalist prohibition on cards, dancing, and the like, social life wasn't synonymous with entertainment. A lot of the girls would get pregnant, but the boys, unless they ran away, would usually marry them. As long as the family stayed on the farm there was a good chance it would remain as a unit. Once a man decided to try his luck in the city, however, the probability was strong that it would begin breaking up.

At the time of Willy Brown's birth, the country was just entering the automobile age. Radio programming was unknown. Electrical appliances were primitive and expensive. Airplanes were a county fair novelty.

A few miles from the shack in which a midwife delivered Willy Brown, a country doctor came to oversee the birth of Tom Smith. Although it was slightly sounder in construction than the Brown shack, in other ways the Smith house was not much different: it had no electricity, no hot running water, no indoor plumbing. The principal difference between Tom Smith and Willy Brown was not in their economic standing, but in their castes. Tom Smith was white. Being white, his education, his medical care, his food, his clothing—though inferior by middle-class standards—were vastly superior to those of Willy Brown.

By the time Willy Brown reached manhood, in 1941, every middle-class home had a radio, and the radio was bringing on-the-spot accounts of events all over the world to its listeners. In the same home, electricity was perking the coffee, making the toast, and running the vacuum cleaner. It was possible to drive across the country in three days, and in an airplane you could fly in one. Motion pictures were bringing the most exotic locations—however distorted—into neighborhood theaters.

All this bypassed Willy Brown. He had no electricity, so he had no radio. He couldn't read a newspaper, so he knew nothing except what his neighbors, most of them as uninformed as he, told him. He saw automobiles and airplanes but, as far as his ability to relate to them was concerned, they might as well have been battleships. While the progress of the world was continuously accelerating, nothing had changed for him since his birth, and, with some minor exceptions, nothing had changed for his father, or his grandfather before that. Only when Willy's selective service board ordered him to report, and then promptly rejected him—for not only was he, like great numbers of his Negro neighbors, a functional illiterate but he was already suffering from a variety of physical ailments, having never in his life been seen by a doctor—was he stirred briefly from his isolation.

Willy Brown married, and, like his father, he became a sharecropper. The land company that provided him with the shack in which he lived staked him to his first crop of cotton, furnishing him with the necessities of life, from seed to salt pork, and he mortgaged the crop to them in return. Thus began the cycle that would go on year after year. The company paid the rock bottom price for the cotton, and if the market price of cotton rose, which it frequently did, it was the company that benefited, not Willy. He was encouraged to live on credit, so as to remain in the company's servitude. He seldom saw more than $25 in cash in an entire year.

By the time Willy's son was born in 1945 the atomic bomb had exploded over Hiroshima. If Willy heard of it at all, it was only to the extent that a big bomb had ended the war

—a war about which he really didn't know anything, and cared very little.

Television, jet propulsion, and a myriad other developments passed by Willy's shack, leaving no impression upon him or his growing family. The fertile mind of man began to supplement that mind with computers, and to build instruments that, with their electronic cunning, eliminated the need for human labor. Willy Brown, although he didn't know it, was becoming obsolete. If he had been a machine, he would have been scrapped.

Since he knew nothing of government, he did not know that the government subsidies, intended to help him, were, instead, going to the land company; which, being paid not to produce cotton, cared less and less about retaining his labor. What he did know was that the earth was crumbling about him. That the machines that were threshing across the land were making it impossible for him to exist even on the most primitive level. With his position continuously deteriorating, going from terrible to impossible, he had no choice. About the time that men began orbiting the earth in satellites, he decided to pull up stakes and move to one of the cities in the north or west about which he had heard a hundred rumors.

When he arrived, he might as well have been a man dropped into his new environment from the 16th century.

So 35-year-old Willy Brown, who had been no match for the machine in tilling the land, came to the city to compete in the shrinking unskilled jobs market. He didn't know how to go about finding a job. He couldn't express himself. He had no knowledge of the value of money, or how to handle it. The law was incomprehensible; the restraints and restrictions of city living a welter of confusion. Some of the services supposedly tailored to his needs were denied to him because he did not know they existed. Utterly naïve, he was prey to every trickster and sharpster, both Negro and white. Hardly able to count, he had no concept of interest; hardly able to write, he did not comprehend the meaning of placing his signature on a piece of paper. For information and help, he was dependent on his neighbors, and how he fared often was in direct proportion to their intelligence and honesty.

If he were able to get a job at all, it was of the most menial and usually transitory nature, providing not even the benefit of unemployment insurance. Left to grub desperately for a living, he and his family were always but one step ahead of hunger—and sometimes overtaken by it. Without hope of improving his position, he grew ever more despondent and frustrated. In due time he learned that the nation, while considering him a bum, would, with its social conscience, not let his wife and children starve.

So he gave up on a responsibility that seemed hopeless, and deeded his wife and family to the nation.

During the somnolent 1930's, the life of Tom Smith had continued to parallel that of Willy Brown, albeit on a higher level. Although Tom's teachers at the rural elementary school and small-town high school left much to be desired, the facilities were adequate, there was a free milk-for-lunch program, and Tom was checked by a doctor at least once a year. The school year was nine months long, and by the time he graduated at the age of 19, he had a better education than either his mother or father.

Two years later he was drafted into the army. Three-fourths of the next three years he spent in Europe. When he returned, the G.I. Bill enabled him to enroll in college. He majored in pharmacy and, though not particularly brilliant, managed to pull through. By the time Willy Brown gave up and decided to move to the city, the Smith farm, also, had withered away, but Tom Smith was the proprietor of a small drug store which netted him $12,000 a year. He lived in a three-bedroom house with two television sets, and two cars in the garage. His children—who, in the seventh grade, were in many ways more sophisticated than he had been in the eleventh—were receiving an education that put his own to shame.

Willy Brown's children could have received an equal education in the city, except for the fact that they were utterly unprepared for it. They were like hungry people summoned to a mountain of flour and told to help themselves. The offer of the flour only increased their bitterness and frustration, for they lacked any kind of bag or basket in which to carry it, and had no oven in which to bake it into bread at home.

Willy's eldest son was 15 when the family came to the city. At the age of 15 his education wasn't much better than his father's had been—at the age of 15 his father had been through with school, and was working on the farm. Willy's son for all practical purposes was through with school also, for, from a scholastic standpoint, he belonged in the third grade, and schools don't enroll 15-year-olds in the third grade.

The ninth grade, in which he was put, was beyond his comprehension, so he was soon getting his education on the streets. On the streets it didn't take him long to pick up a rudimentary sophistication—he learned about the cops, and how one could make a fast buck, and how there weren't any rules when it came to Mr. Charley, because Mr. Charley had been waging war on the soul folk for hundreds of years. When he was 18 years old he got a girl pregnant, and if he had been living on the farm that meant they would have gotten married. But in the city, without a job, you'd have to be stupid to take on that kind of responsibility—he'd learned from his father what happens to a man when he tries—so he decided to let the BPA take care of the child.

Weaned on television, the children of the Willy Browns are bombarded with admonitions to enjoy the material goods of an affluent society. By the time they reach puberty the realization is forced upon them that those admonitions are not directed at the people among whom they live. At the threshold of adulthood they begin to view television as a glass door. Through it they can see white America, but for them the door will never open. Every day they are tantalized. Every day they become more frustrated.

At the threshold of adulthood they are thoroughly embittered. Isolated from contact with white Americans, their bias against the Caucasian becomes as thoroughly ingrained —and sometimes more venomous—then the Southern redneck's against them.[1] As the principal manifestation of their oppressor, the white police officer becomes their logical target.

In the rural Black Belt, Willy Brown's anger was kept damped by a mantle of fear, but in the urban Black Reservation Willy Brown's son derives a sense of power from living in an all-Negro community, and from the militant Nationalist psychology that black is good and white is evil. He sees no reason why he must continue to abide by or to obey the white man's laws.

*   *   *

Today's migration to the cities is as massive a movement of people as was the immigration from Europe to America in

[1] Mrs. Helen Floyd, vice-president of a tenants organization in St. Louis, told D. J. R. Bruckner, a Los Angeles *Times* staff writer: "I grew up integrated. But my children are now growing without ever knowing a white person." (L. A. *Times*, Feb. 2, 1967.)

the 19th century. And those who like to make comparisons between the immigrant then and the Negro today rhetorically ask the question: What is the difference?

The differences are both numerous and staggering.

The immigrant arrived in the midst of the greatest industrial expansion in history, in a country in which the land was so vast and cheap it could be used as fodder for industry. The immigrant, upon arrival, was not only virtually assured of being able to make a living in the Eastern industrial belt, but for many years would be wooed by railroads as a settler on the Western lands that the roads were giving away in order to build up their traffic.

The immigrant needed no skills, and he did not even need to be able to speak—much less to read or write—the language, for first- and second-generation machines of the industrial revolution were creating a multitude of unskilled and semiskilled jobs. The immigrant was exploited, but he was seldom frozen out of a job. He usually brought with him strong family ties, and, in a larger sense, ties of nationality, and this clannishness carried him over the first years of hardship and discrimination. Perhaps most important of all he had immense motivation—success stories were being written all about him, and as his children became Americanized the bars to their advancement melted away. It was easier for the son of an immigrant to become a member of the upper class in America than for the son of an English laborer to become a member of the "establishment" in England.

Despite his long residence in America, however, the Negro, like the Indian, remained officially a lower caste. He was for all practical purposes barred from participating in the country's great expansion. Upward mobility within his caste was permitted him. But the lateral mobility that has made America the great melting pot was, and still is, denied to him—the story of the hard-working immigrant boy marrying the boss's daughter long ago became a cliché; but the story of a hard-working Negro boy marrying the white boss's daughter would create shock waves of large proportions even in the latter half of the 20th century.

Unlike the immigrant, whose European culture tended to be similar to that he found in the United States, the Negro had had the bridge to his culture and historical ethos destroyed by the years of slavery. In many ways that culture had been incompatible with the European to begin with.

Because the plantation economy of the Americas, both North and South, created the need for masses of cheap labor, the first three centuries' history of this continent is inextricably linked to that of the slave trade. In order to give a moral pretext to the trade in human chattel, the European rationalized that the Negro was a subhuman savage being *rescued* from darkest Africa, and that, by having his soul saved, this savage was being liberated from an eternity in hell.

In truth, while Africa lagged 1,000 or more years behind Europe in the development of tools and industry, many of the varied African civilizations were highly developed in their agriculture and ethos. The emphasis was on familial and communal loyalties, and there was little private ownership of property. Individual excellence was not considered a particular virtue. The Bantus, for example, had such an egalitarian society that it was necessary for them to devise an explanation as to why some men were superior to others. This was the "shave," a wandering spirit that would bestow its special gift upon a man and remain with him as long as he took pains to please it.

When the African was enslaved and brought to America, he was, literally, beheaded from his culture. While in South America the Catholic Church interested itself in the salvation of his soul, and thus acknowledged his humanity, in North America the pragmatic plantation owner considered him as but another draft animal, incapable of being educated. The difference in attitudes toward the slave in the different halves of the continent made the stigma attached to slavery much less in South America than in North, and South America never had the restrictive laws against free Negroes that North America did.

In North America, not only were Negroes considered uneducable, but several states passed laws making it a capital crime to teach a slave to read or write. The Baptist and Methodist missionaries sent to baptize the slaves were, for many years, frowned on by the plantation owners, and suspected of being abolitionists in disguise. This attitude hardened after Nat Turner, a Negro preacher, led a slave revolt in Virginia in 1831.

Despite variations in the market price of slaves—as in that of any other commodity—many a plantation owner's principal asset was his slaves. Since he could increase his wealth by increasing the number of slaves he owned, he encouraged fecundity, selling his surplus in the flourishing domestic slave trade. If there were a marriage ceremony at all, it took the form of "jumping the broom"—a broom would be held across the doorway of a hut, and the boy and girl would step across it. The ceremony was meaningless, for many planters had no compunctions about breaking up families; a Negro man never knew when he might be sold away from his wife, a mother when she might be parted from her children. The effect on the Negro psyche was devastating, for if a man has no control over his own fate, he loses interest in the future. If he cannot profit from his own labors, he loses ambition. And if he is beaten back in every attempt to improve himself, he loses hope.

A slave's only hope, then, was to ingratiate himself with his master. The qualities of servility and sycophancy merited the highest praise—qualities that were translated into "knowing one's place" following abolition.

While the Civil War had, for a relatively short period of time, a major effect on the political structure of the South, it never greatly altered the sociological or psychological ones. In fact, after the accommodation reached between the Democrats and Republicans as a result of the disputed election of 1876, leading, in turn, to the end of Reconstruction, the Supreme Court's ruling of the era's Civil Rights laws as unconstitutional, and the passage of the Jim Crow laws, the Negro's social position in the South declined below what it had been prior to the Civil War.

In the antebellum days, a considerable class of Negro freedmen had grown up in the cities. They were largely an artisan class, and while they did not have social equality with the whites they did, by and large, have their respect, and tended to identify with them. Like the whites they owned slaves, and anyone who has doubts regarding the contempt in which many of them held the "niggers" is referred to such works as *The Barber of Natchez*, the diary of William Johnson, a Negro freedman.

Despite the fact that the post-Reconstruction period in the South tended to wipe out distinctions between the genteel Negro and the nonacceptable *nigger*, the Negro middle-class —which had developed from the freedmen—usually disassociated itself from the lower-class Negro as emphatically as had the freedman from the slave. More and more—often in

the form of a son sent to college in the North and not returning—it migrated to the cities in the North.

Here then, is another key distinction between the 19th-cen-
tury European immigrant and the 20th-century Negro migrant. The immigrant could expect to receive help from his
compatriot who had arrived earlier and begun to climb the
economic ladder; the migrant has been largely ignored by his
own people. The Negro who has *made it* and adopted white
values does not want, by associating himself with lower caste
members of his race, to be reminded of his Negroness.[2]

Sociologists have noted that certain traits and characteristics of a people tend to be passed on as part of the cultural
heritage. The son, patterning himself after the father, sets the
example for his own son. The Anglo-Saxon virtues of thrift,
ambition, individual enterprise, sexual (largely mythical) con-
tinence, and the like, were not bestowed upon the white American like manna from heaven.

The only traditions the Negro has had in America are
those of slavery, repression, and turmoil. If he lives, today,
with little thought for the future, it is because he has never
had any future, and there is no point in saving and preparing for what may not, for him, exist. If he spends recklessly
and gets himself head over heels in debt, this is precisely
what his forebears were encouraged to do at the plantation
store.

If he has no concept of the ability of thrift to create capital, and capital wealth, it is because—as a generality—he
has never owned property. If he lacks ambition, it is not only
because ambition in his circumscribed surroundings in the
South was futile, but because aggressiveness in a Negro immediately brought him under suspicion. The Southern Negro
with thrift and ambition who began to move up in the world
brought the envy of his white neighbors upon him, and exposed himself to danger. If he were an "uppity nigger," he
had little choice but to move North. Only if, despite his success, he acknowledged his *inferiority* and took pains to ingratiate himself with the local Whips—which usually meant,
among other things, helping to keep the *niggers* in line—
would he be accepted and left alone.

[2] This attitude is beginning to change, especially among middle-
class Negroes with political ambition.

If the Negro does not understand that education has monetary value, it is because in his experience he has never witnessed the power of education.

If the Negro male appears irresponsible in regard to his family, it is because he was emasculated on the plantation, where he had neither control nor responsibility over his wife and children. The hundred years since—in which he was barred from commingling with whites while his wife and daughter were welcomed into their homes as domestic servants, achieving, in white eyes, a position of worth above him —could hardly have served to instil that responsibility. Nor could the knowledge and fear that he was, for all practical purposes, helpless should a white man decide to bestow his favors upon a female member of his family have had a beneficial effect. The attitude of the Negro man that he didn't *care*, that he *wouldn't* accept responsibility, freed him from the impossible position of being a protector, and so provided him with a psychological defense.

If the Negro's rate of reproduction is higher than the white's (whose own birth control practices are of recent vintage) it is because fecundity—from the days in Africa when the newborn underwent various rites to insure his adult fertility, through the time of slavery when each child had its pecuniary value, down to sharecropper days when every fieldhand could be put to work—was always a virtue. And if there is no particular stigma attached to out-of-wedlock births it is because the Negro's experience on the plantation convinced him that marriage was an easily dissoluble, *pro forma* sham.

The Negro who has been exposed to the majority values and been in an economic and social position in which he could see the benefit of conforming to them, has done so with a vengeance. The middle-class Negro, in fact, is often accused of having *overconformed*.

*   *   *

The problems of the cities in the latter half of the 20th century are not new. They are the problems that have been nurtured in the bosom of the South for the last 100 years, and which the nation chose to ignore. What is new is that they are being transported, *en masse*, from the back shed, where they were out of sight, out of mind, into the parlor, where they are becoming horrifyingly visible.

Contrary to the generally held opinion, there has been no

startling rise in the Negro illegitimacy rate. In 1940, 16.8 per cent of the births were illegitimate (and because of the difficulty of gathering statistics in the boondocks, the number might well have been higher), and by 1963 the figure had risen to 23.6 per cent. While this is a cumulative increase of 43 per cent, it does not match the rise of the white illegitimacy rate, which increased 55 per cent, from 2 per cent to 3.1 per cent.

Nor has there been a significant increase in the birth rate among Negroes. The fact that today almost three Negro babies are being born to every two white is probably due to two factors: the greater use of birth control measures by the white population; and, in comparison to the rural areas, the availability of more and better hospital facilities for Negroes in the cities.

Births Per 1,000 Women [3]

Year	White	Nonwhite
1920	115.4	137.5
1963	104.3	149.3

Neither is the instability of the Negro family a new development. Even on the farm, in 11.2 per cent of Southern Negro families the father is missing. In the rural, nonfarm South, 20 per cent of Negro families lack a father, a rate nearly equal that of urban areas. That there is a significant correlation between rising illegitimacy rates in the cities and the growing Negro urban population appears, therefore, to be clearly a cultural phenomenon, not one stemming simply from the migration—though this, undoubtedly, is an aggravating factor.

Poor and uneducated whites arriving in the cities from such areas as Appalachia face, basically, the same problems as the Negroes. Puerto Ricans and Mexican-Americans, who must not only overcome prejudice but the language barrier, tend to be worse off than the Negroes.

This is demonstrated in California, which has 1.5 million persons of Mexican descent, of which a third reside in Los Angeles, making it, after Mexico City, the second largest Mexican community in the world. The Negro and Mexican-American populations of the city are roughly equal in num-

[3] *Vital Statistics of the United States, 1962.*

ber, and, with 44,000 legal emigrants arriving in the United States from Mexico yearly and a majority of these coming to California, the Mexican community may be growing at an even faster rate than the Negro.

The average Mexican-American family is larger than the Negro, having 4.6 members against 4.2. The Mexican-American's education is less: an average 8.7 years against the Negro's 9.5. And his income falls far short, the Mexican-American annual family median income being $4,361 as against the Negro's $5,163.

Like the Negro community, the Mexican-American has a high crime rate. The same problems with the police are encountered, and the same charges of "police brutality" made. In the schools, the children have often met with the same stultifying attitudes on the part of the teachers. Cong. Edward Roybal, who wanted to take a college preparatory course, was told by his counselor, "You're good at mathematics. Become an electrician."

Ralph Guzman, assistant director of UCLA's Mexican-American Study Project, was told by his counselor when he indicated he wanted to go to college, "Ralph, your mother is on relief, and you don't have any way of paying for college, so how can you go? Really, you don't want to go into places where you're not wanted. I'm looking out for your psyche. You don't want to be hurt."

Housing in the Mexican-American section is, over-all, worse than in the Negro. Job discrimination is as great. Pitted against each other for the dregs of available employment, each tending to consider himself superior to the other, the Mexican-American and the Negro constantly rub each other the wrong way, bringing on such explosions as the second Watts riot.

If the Mexican-American community has not been as assertive as the Negro, it is because it is still in an earlier stage of political development. Less than 50 per cent of the people are registered voters, and for those who have not yet been naturalized, not to speak of those who may be residing in America illegally, there is the fear that, if they foment trouble, they may be returned to Mexico.

Nevertheless, Eduardo Quevedo, president of the Mexican-American Political Association, told the McCone Commission that his community is "ripe for a riot similar to Watts."

Puerto Rican, Mexican-American, rural Negro—all are in

the same barrel. The electronics-computer revolution, plus, ironically, the advances made by labor, are working together to make their economic position vis-à-vis the white community a deteriorating one. While economists express surprise that the age of the computer has not resulted in the threatened unemployment, but has, in fact, seemingly created a shortage of labor, the nonwhite minorities are wallowing in unemployment as great or greater than that of the depression. The fact is that the electronics-computer revolution has had the precise effect predicted for it in the unskilled labor market. But because laborers seem to melt away with the jobs— or simply were unable to find jobs when they arrived from rural areas—and never went on the unemployment rolls, this fact has not been recognized.

Thus, the Negro unemployment rate, officially, in 1966, 8.2 per cent compared to the Caucasian 3.4 per cent, in actuality is probably considerably higher.[4] The base from which 1950-1960 unemployment statistics were compiled tends to corroborate this conclusion.

According to the U.S. Census Bureau, the white male population over 14 years of age in 1960 was 78,367,149, of whom 45,686,330 were considered in the labor force. This was 58 per cent of the total. The Negro male population over 14 years of age in 1960 was 9,964,345, of whom 4,371,-786 were considered in the labor force. This was 44 per cent of the total.

Why the difference? The most logical hypothesis would seem to be that the missing 14 per cent did not make themselves available to be counted through normal channels. And, if this is true, then there were a million and a quarter Negro males beyond the *official* figure who were unemployed.

Not only is the Negro's unemployment rate higher than the white's in every occupational category, but he is overrepresented in those occupations in which the unemployment rate is highest, and underrepresented in those in which it is lowest. For example, he makes up only 3.5 per cent of professional and technical people, where the unemployment rate is less than 2 per cent. But he constitutes 26 per cent of unskilled laborers, among whom unemployment is 12 per cent or higher.

---

[4] Among teenagers, unemployment was 27 per cent among Negroes as compared to 12 per cent among whites.

He is virtually frozen out of apprentice training programs, in which he makes up only 3.1 per cent of the total.

Unemployment hits hardest at the young Negro, precisely in those years in which he should be receiving training and building up experience and seniority. Male Negro unemployment in the under-35 age bracket is roughly twice the percentage for all Negroes, going as high as one-third of the work force.

Since the Negro urban population has almost tripled since 1930, growing from some 5,350,000 to 14,840,000, the cities are awash with unemployed Negro youth.

*   *   *

While liberal whites compare the Negro's present position with that of 30 years ago and find the gains encouraging, the Negro compares his position today with that of the whites today, and finds the gap appalling. The meretricious tricks statistics can be made to play may be demonstrated by a comparison of white and Negro income.

Between 1950 and 1960 Negro median income increased 59 per cent, compared to 47 per cent for whites. What this meant in actual cash was:

MEDIAN INCOME

	1950	1960
White	$2,053	$3,027
Negro	$ 952	$1,519

Not only did the Negro's comparative position not improve, but between 1950 and 1960 the white's advantage in income *increased* from $1,101 to $1,508!

Similarly, while the median number of years of school completed by Negroes rose from 6.9 years in 1950 to 8.2 in 1960, the increase for whites was almost precisely the same, from 9.7 years to 10.9. Whites continued to hold an educational advantage of almost three years over Negroes.

In September of 1965 the Gallup Poll reported that 64 per cent of Negroes were dissatisfied with their income, 66 per cent with their housing, 38 per cent with their work, and 46 per cent with their education. (For whites, the respective figures were 28, 20, 9, and 19 per cent.)

[5] See page 100.

Such progress as is being made often sticks in the throat of the Negro, who sees it not as an example of his increasing stature and acceptance, but as a reluctant and exceptional granting of basic rights that have been denied to him for 100 years.

Is it progress, he asks, when it was not until 1966 that the House of Representatives of the U.S.—years after passing a variety of civil rights bills and presumably putting itself on record in favor of equality—desegregated its barbershop?

Is it progress when a Negro is appointed judge of the Superior Court of the State of California, but his wife is refused admittance to a fashion show in Beverly Hills? Is it progress when on college athletic fields all over the nation the Negro is Saturday's hero, but remains a social pariah on the campus, fraternities and sororities faithfully reflecting the mores of the segregated suburbs? Is it progress when a Negro is appointed director of the U.S. Information Agency, but is shown to the servants' entrance when he goes to the White House?

The Negro generation represented by Thurgood Marshall and Roy Wilkins, born into a time when Negro gains were dependent on the oscillating mood of the white liberal community, might be willing to accept that it is. The generation of Stokely Carmichael, which has heard all its life from Washington that it is equal, but knows that in Cleveland, Kansas City, and Kokomo it could not be more unequal, will not. And when the legions of Milton S. Olives return from Vietnam, the old platitudes are no longer going to be enough to protect the way of life of white suburbia.

With the Negro population of even such still-growing cities as Los Angeles increasing three times as rapidly as the white, and a majority of this population belonging to the militant generation, if Caucasians continue to counter the demand for "Full Equality Now" with no more than "What's your hurry? Slow up!" the collision between black and white is as inevitable as it will be internecine.

58   A Ladder Standing on Quicksand

While there is an imperative need for untrammeled Negro-white dialogue, everywhere the specter of hypocrisy effectively prevents the making of honest appraisals that might lead to honest solutions.

A simple but basic example is the opinion held, according to the Louis Harris poll, by a considerable majority [1] of the white population, that Negroes "smell different." The sociologist's reply is "stereotype," the Negro's the cry of "Prejudice!" Neither is going to have any effect whatever on the belief of the whites.

The honest and thoughtful reply is to acknowledge that a great number of Negroes *have*, in the past, smelled different. They have smelled different from acceptable middle-class standards because they have worked at the dirtiest, sweatiest jobs and have lived in shacks and slums without bathrooms. They have smelled precisely the same as the white man working and living under the same conditions. The only reason that the "different smell" has seemed to be a Negro characteristic is because the proportion of Negroes forced to live under these conditions has been infinitely greater than the proportion of whites.

Such a reply might provoke thought. While it would do nothing to change the *belief*, it might do a great deal to change the *attitude* of those persons holding that belief.

The white resists residential integration with all his might on the argument that integration leads to an increase in crime and is the first step toward the creation of a slum. Again the Negro cries: "Prejudice!" In a tangle of shouts the opposing advocates become ever more disputatious. Civil rights groups stage marches, and are met by a defiant "Never!" [2]

[1] 61 per cent of the lower classes, and 52 per cent over-all.
[2] The California State Poll recently found that 72 per cent of the population believed a property owner should not be forced to sell or rent to a person against his will.

The honest and thoughtful argument would admit that, in fact, a deteriorating neighborhood often is the end result of residential integration. But it is the end result not of Negro action, but of white. Of the continuing practice of *de facto* discrimination in educational opportunities and jobs; and of *de facto* segregation.

Unskilled and basically unemployable, migrants crowd together into the districts to which Negroes are restricted. Already overloaded with children, and lacking both the sophistication and the will to practice birth control, they beget more children. Into the space where one year five persons were crowded, the next year it is six, and the year after that seven. Unable to get jobs of any decency or permanence, the migrants find themselves utterly incapable of improving their position. In fact, with the combined pressures of their own prolific reproduction and the continuing influx from rural areas, they see that position becoming worse and worse. It is impossible for them to return to the farms. It is impossible for them to live decently where they are.

Abandoning hope, the men abandon their families. Lacking parental supervision, virtually undisciplinable in the schools, bored and frustrated youngsters roam the area, hastening its deterioration. Middle-class Negroes, as well as whites, flee in horror, leaving it to the police to quarantine the diseased portion of the city.

Middle-class Negroes thus create pressure on the white community for housing in a previously white area. Despite white anguish, along the edge of the ghetto another few blocks are "busted." Once two or three Negroes have moved in, it becomes impossible to sell a house to a white person. The area begins to change color through a process of attrition.

Like an avalanche, this is a movement that, once started, no one has yet been able to reverse. The Negro middle class replaces the whites. The employed blue-collar Negro replaces the middle-class Negro. The migrant replaces the blue-collar Negro. It is the classic pattern of the new arrival entering at the bottom and being funneled upward—only for the Negro the flue is so narrow that few can get through.

Yet it is not only the Negro that the ghetto traps. Those of other races who lingered too long during the period of his infiltration drown with him.

The small shopkeeper is the classic victim. Caught in the maelstrom of increasing crime, rising insurance rates and taxes, and changing marketing practices, he must raise prices in order to make a living. Negroes, who have never known the area as anything but a ghetto, damn him as an alien exploiter. The comfortable white suburbanite echoes the damnation, and by such projection eases his own conscience.

The property owner who did not see the light in time is likely to get similarly stuck. The more valuable the property, the greater the difficulty he will have disposing of it. If it is a large house, he will probably become convinced that the only solution is to cut it up into apartments. If it is a modest, older home, a promoter may talk him into tearing it down and erecting a cheap apartment building in its place. If it is already an apartment house, he will try to make up in the quantity of tenants for whatever the decline in their economic status. If he has 10 apartments, but can expect, on the average, three of the tenants to renege on their rent, he will increase the rent from $60 to $85. To the tenants this is exploitation, and, since they have no property interests, they make little effort to keep the area from going to pot.

*   *   *

The American cities are being consumed by a cancer. In another quarter century, unless immediate and drastic remedial measures are taken, virtually every major urban area will have a solid black core, and be crumbling as a result. Even though the fact of what is happening has been recognized for several years, the statistics are shocking.

Baltimore's Negro population increased from 23.8 per cent to 35.0 per cent in the 10 years between 1950 and 1960; Chicago's from 14.1 to 23.6 per cent; Cleveland's from 16.3 to 28.9 per cent; Detroit's from 16.4 to 29.2 per cent;[3] Philadelphia's from 18.3 to 26.7 per cent; St. Louis's from 18.0 to 28.8 per cent; Washington's from 35.4 to 54.8 per cent. Despite the tremendous influx of Negroes, more than half of the major cities are decreasing in population, because of the white population's flight to the suburbs. In the flight to the suburbs the whites effectively, if perhaps temporarily, found refuge from the Negro encroachment. In the decade that saw him begin to take over the cities, the Negro's representation in the suburbs declined.

According to an estimate by the Department of Health,

[3] In 1967, the Negro population was estimated at 37 per cent.

Education, and Welfare,[4] every one of the above cities already has a majority of Negro pupils in the elementary schools. In Baltimore it is 64 per cent; Chicago 56 per cent; Cleveland 53 per cent; Detroit 57 per cent; Philadelphia 60 per cent; and St. Louis 64 per cent. It has previously been pointed out that the tipping of the school population to more than a third Negro almost always presages the resegregation of an area—white parents taking their children out of the integrated schools before they themselves give up and move.

That the city is in deep trouble almost everyone agrees. Just how deep, however, may not yet be fully recognized. To acknowledge that this trouble is a direct result of the nation's complicity in the South's racial policies for the past 100 years, and of continuing *de facto* discrimination everywhere, may be so agonizing for the white majority that it will do so only with the greatest reluctance. Only when the alternative, continuing in the established behavior patterns, becomes even more painful and, in fact, unbearable. It is postulated that this point is rapidly being reached.

In Los Angeles property owners are on the verge of open rebellion. The property tax rate has skyrocketed, until it is now approximately 2.5 per cent of the actual value of the property. On a $40,000 house—which, in Los Angeles, with its inflated land values is not exceptional—the yearly tax comes to $1,000.

Why the explosion in the tax rate? Because, on the one hand, the cost of city services—from police protection to welfare—increases wherever the ghetto is bred. And because, on the other, the ghetto, where the people are underemployed and the economy is underproductive, produces far less in tax revenue than a comparable middle-class area. Thus the middle class must subsidize the ghetto. It must pay in hard cash in order to continue the policy of discrimination.

The ghettoizing of a city is an accelerating process. The larger the ghetto becomes, the greater the tax burden on the middle-class whites. The greater the tax burden, the more middle-class whites move out. The more whites move out, the larger the ghetto becomes.[5]

At some point, then, the Negro minority becomes a ma-

---

[4] As reported by columnist Joseph Alsop, July 14, 1966.
[5] For example, the assessed valuation of property in Detroit decreased from more than $5 billion in 1958, to less than $4.4 billion in 1967.

jority in the city.[6] Within a few years of becoming a majority, they may be expected to take over the reins of government. Once this occurs, the pattern in the entire city is likely to take on that of an *integrated* area. White residents will depart *en masse*. Since it is inconceivable that the Negro residents then would continue to put up with the manifestations of white power, the police, the fire department, and other public services will become predominantly Negro. The tables will be turned, and it will be the white who, coming to work in the city, will give voice to the cry of "police brutality" and "verbal abuse."

Inevitably, whites will be more and more reluctant to come into the cities at all. Industry will have to bear the tax burden underemployed Negro residents are unable to. Soon industry will take the logical step of following the white residents out of the cities. The end result will be a black city with a white city adjacent or surrounding, and a separation of the races as complete as any Black Muslim or white Ku Klux Klanner could wish.

Black Power is, in fact, no longer a matter of academic discussion. Within 10 years it will become a fact of life in major cities throughout the U.S. And political power without concomitant education, social status, or economic power is a historic avenue to chaos and revolution.

To the white American of the latter part of the 20th century the cry of "Black Power!" is both frightening and shocking. He has been weaned on the propaganda that, though the Negro may be of somewhat lower intelligence than the white, and, as an individual, is likely to present a threat to white womanhood, as a people he is almost superhumanly passive and gentle, and when he flares into violence it is because someone agitated him against his true nature.

The truth is that "black power" was bruited about the South 100 years ago. After the Civil War, when Negroes were being elected lieutenant governors of states and U.S. senators, Alfred Gray, a Negro, stood before a crowd in Uniontown, Ala., and orated in favor of the passage of the state's Reconstruction constitution as follows: "The constitution, I came here to talk for it. . . . Am I afraid to fight

<hr />

[6] In Los Angeles a situation now exists in which, if the 99 per cent white San Fernando Valley, which really has no geographic links to the city, decided to secede, the city would in one swoop become more than 50 per cent Negro and Mexican-American.

the white man for his rights? No. I may go to hell, my home is hell, but the white man shall go there with me. . . .

"Boys, now I want you to hear. . . . Bring your gun and stand up for your rights! . . . We'll fight until we die, and go to hell together. . . ."

It is hardly likely that in the 20th century the measures applied by the Southern whites to reassert their dominance and remove the threat of black power in the *19th* could be repeated. But it should be remembered that it was a political accommodation between the Republicans of the North and the Democrats of the South that enabled the South to throw off the onus of Reconstruction, and that all the noble sentiments voiced about the Negro by Northern politicians did not prevent them from sacrificing him when it was to their own self-interest to do so.

One of the basic errors of Reconstruction was not only to put the cart before the horse, but then to take a cavalier attitude toward that horse, as if it did not really matter. Political power, it was said, was the ladder leading to equality. The Negroes were handed political power; but the Southern whites retained insuperable advantages in education and economic power. And it soon became evident that political power without anything to support it—except the guns of the U.S. Army—was a ladder standing on quicksand.

If civil rights cannot be achieved except by the force of arms of U.S. marshals and the National Guard, the Negroes' political power today is hardly more secure than it was 100 years ago. Pushed to a certain point, the whites of the cities, like the whites of the South, may refuse to abandon their economic interests. Unlike 100 years ago when the whites had such overwhelming force that the Negroes were able to offer only scattered and ineffective resistance, a direct Negro-white confrontation for control of the cities could well turn into a struggle of apocalyptic fury. Should that happen, the rivers of blood and years of darkness of the past century will pale before those of the next.

59   The City's Not for Burning

Los Angeles in the summer of 1965 was the scene of the opening skirmish. That is the reason why the August riot has importance and implication far beyond the turmoil of a few days.

It was a rebellion by the Negroes against the economic power the whites retain in the ghetto—in essence, the Negro city. Once the motif of the rebellion became established it was not upon the white person that violence was committed, but upon white property—and only in the ghetto! Although, at first, it may not seem so, it was an exercise of political power by the Negro—in this particular case political power in raw, physical terms. Twenty years from now the youths who threw rocks and burned will have learned more sophisticated use of such power. What they failed to do in 1965 with the torch they will succeed in doing in 1985 with the vote.[1]

They will succeed unless white reaction is even more aggressive than Negro action. In 1965 the reaction came in the form of the National Guard. By 1985 it may be in the form of a full-blown White Backlash, with all its attendant perils.

That there is already a white backlash can hardly be doubted by anyone analyzing political trends, or sampling the opinion of the groups that feel most threatened by the Negro —the small property owner and the middle-class white whose income and education straddle or are below the median.

[1] It is clear that the incidents which are sparking the riots in the cities are so insignificant as to give credence to the white contention they are "senseless." In Chicago, in the summer of 1966, the riot began over the refusal of the fire department to let Negro kids turn on fire hydrants on a hot day. In Cleveland, over an altercation between Negroes and a white bar owner regarding a funeral collection. Only when one realizes there is a single *theme*—that of rebellion against white authority and control over the Negro's life—does a pattern emerge.

While the Negro and white at the top of the ladder are in many respects working to reduce the separation that exists between them, there is a growing polarization of the races and hardening of existing prejudices at the bottom.

It is almost impossible for the white to comprehend the alienation the Negro feels in American society. When, as happened recently, a Negro contends he is not subject to the draft because service in the armed forces is the duty of a citizen, and he has been denied the rights of citizenship; and another claims that U.S. courts lack jurisdiction over him because, as the descendant of persons brought to this country against their will, he is an involuntary resident, the general white reaction is to laugh at what seem utterly specious arguments. But to many a Negro they are not specious, and certainly no laughing matter.

A Negro signing himself *C.M.A.* wrote an eloquent letter to the Los Angeles *Times* following that newspaper's series on Watts.

"As an American Negro I must say to someone who has shown basic understanding, that the present attitude of the white community—newspaper columnists, radio commentators, reporters and ordinary citizens—toward all Negroes is creating a bitterness and resentment which is becoming overwhelming.

"I do not know the answers. I was reporter and editor of Negro newspapers in the affected communities for 10 years and served with the information office of a government agency for two years, during which time I became conversant with a few of the problems. Even I was unprepared for the revolution.

"I have never harbored hatred, because I have always believed that it is an emotion more harmful to the hater than to the hated. I have always abhorred violence; yet in the past two weeks the kinds of comment to which I have been subjected have brought me to the point where I actually resent being included among 'our fine, responsible Negro (colored) citizens who make up the vast majority of our population.'

"Such condescending phrases make me gag.

"I feel a deep sense of responsibility for what happened. I feel that somehow I should be able to do something—what, I don't know—to alleviate the situation. But generally speaking, there seems to be very little real desire on anyone's part to understand that down through the ages when men have been oppressed and denied the simple necessities enjoyed by other men, they have revolted.

"Whether such revolts are justified has no bearing on the fact that they have occurred and will continue to occur. They are inevitable.

"For 300 years the black man in America has tried desperately to adjust to the white man's society. Until two weeks ago I thought, like hundreds of thousands of other Negroes, that I had done so. Now, it seems that there is no hope of my ever becoming a full-fledged American citizen, because every act committed by any Negro becomes the responsibility of all Negroes.

"Yet the white man accepts little responsibility for the acts of other white men and anyone who expected him to do so completely would be considered a stupid oaf.

"I am afraid that . . . if politicians pursue their present course of denying facts which every Negro knows but cannot prove in court, and if recriminations go on much longer with no attempt to seek solutions, the result will be a greater or complete separation of the Negro and white communities. This would be a disaster.

"I view this not as a Negro riot, but as a revolution of men and women who are tired of too few jobs, too little food and no hope for the future.

"Even if, for the sake of argument, it is granted that many Negroes are incapable of pulling their full share of the load in this great white society, some effort must be made to help the weaklings make some adjustment.

"After all, if one-tenth of the money spent for foreign aid, one-tenth of the money spent to free the Vietnamese, one-tenth of the money spent to explore the outer reaches of space, had been spent on a constructive program to help train these American citizens to live in our complicated society, the revolution would not have been attempted.

"As an individual who has managed to exist on the fringes of your society, support his family, educate his two sons and abide by the rules you have set up—which I had little if any part in making—I am becoming desperate.

"I have always considered myself an American, although it was quite obvious that I am an American Negro—one can never quite forget that—but if the present attacks on my race as a whole continue, I'm going to have to become a NEGRO, with little identification with the total American community.

"If the present trend continues, those of us who believed that we had made a beginning, but now find ourselves a part of an isolated, condemned group, must adapt ourselves to the attitude of the group to which we have been arbitrarily assigned. We won't like it, but all of us will be forced to defend the actions of any of us."

* * *

Only if honesty replaces hypocrisy; only if expediency gives way to enlightenment; only if policy is made paramount to politics, may a genuine beginning be made to solving the interwoven racial and economic problems of America. And the problems must be solved, for they present a threat to the very survival of this nation on the concepts upon which it was founded.

When a politician cries "Communist!" every time he is embarrassed by Negro violence, the principal danger is not that he is adding a few persons to the ranks of those convinced of the ubiquitous Communist menace; nor that he is inflating the egos of a few generally ineffective agitators, giving them stature among the disaffected that they did not have before; but that by thus "solving" a complex problem with a simple panacea—*get rid of the Communists*—he is like a police chief pinning the murder on the first person who comes up and cries "Guilty!" Thus preventing the bringing of the real culprit before the bar of justice.

When political delicacies prevent a McCone Commission from coming to grips with the fact of prolific and indiscriminate procreation, the tragedy is not that this is a dereliction of the assigned analytical task; but that in avoiding the issue the commission prevented its inclusion in the problems to be solved.

When the citizens of a nation, both individually and collectively, would rather subsidize despair and pay billions of dollars as tribute in order to maintain order than to acknowledge that there is a sickness in the body, they are like a man who uses alcohol to escape the reality of a tumor. And the end result will be just as fatal.

It is not necessary to convince the white American that he must *love* the Negro in order to make him realize that he has a stake in raising the Negro's standard of living to a comparable level with his own. It is in fact folly to attempt to do so—the folly of one piece of legislation after another carrying a pseudo-altruistic ring, so that it seems the Negro suddenly has come into special favor, and is being granted that favor as a result of the pressure exerted by the civil rights movement.

Americans did not *love* the Germans and the Japanese after the end of World War II. They had, in fact, been taught for years to hate them. Yet within a very short period of time Americans became reconciled to the fact that they must pay taxes to help the erstwhile enemy. They accepted it not because they had suddenly been brainwashed to *love* the perpetrators of Pearl Harbor and mass murder, but because they were convinced that it was essential to American *self-interest* to help pull the enemy back to their feet. Self-interest must replace love and other abstract concepts as the motivating reason in the drive for full equality for the Negro.

It is, most assuredly, to the self-interest of the property owner not to have the property he owns turn into a ghetto, and then into a slum. It is to the self-interest of the suburbanites not to have the cities in which they work became bastions of black hatred. It is to the self-interest of the police to eliminate the hives of crime. It is to the self-interest of every city's civil servants to have reasonable racial balance maintained in the central city. It is to the self-interest of the metropolitan newspapers to have a literate population. It is to the self-interest of business to add millions of persons to the ranks of customers. And it is to the self-interest of every American tax payer, no matter what his race or occupation, to convert the millions of underemployed and unproductive into self-sustaining, positively contributing elements of the population.

To attempt to do this by fiat alone is as futile in the 20th century as it was in the 19th. If, after the white American becomes convinced that it is to his self-interest to have Negro children attending school with his own, he finds that the Negro children bring with them a deterioration of the standards of the school and have a pernicious effect on his own children, the human reaction will be for him to say "to hell with it!" If, after the white home owner has been convinced it is to his self-interest not to set up bars to a Negro's moving into the area, the result is, nevertheless, that the area de-

THE BLACK PRINT OF THE NEGRO

teriorates, he will be of the opinion that he has been conned. If, after industry has been convinced of the benefits of an open hiring policy, the Negro who is hired is unable to compete with the white, both industry and the Negro will be disillusioned—the Negro rationalizing that the reason he is unable to keep up is because he is discriminated against, the white reaffirmed in the stereotyped belief that the Negro is of a lower mental capability.

If Negroes and whites are to mix successfully, their standards will have to be approximately equal. Where such equality exists, integration tends to work. Where it does not, the measures to achieve integration by law usually turn out to be a perverse hoax. For an underprivileged minority to impose its concepts upon a nation's power-holding majority, against the will of that majority, is a practical impossibility.

To raise the standards of the poverty classes will take an effort as intense, massive, and integrated (in the generic, not the racial, sense) as any in the history of this country. It will have to be a true war, not simply a *war* of semantics. The U.S. has shown its capability to wage such a war. The space race is one brilliant example. Another is a 20-year-old project that has been unqualifiedly successful, and which might well serve as a pilot study.

The contributing role the G.I. Bill of Rights has played in the unprecedented prosperity of the postwar era is deserving of a separate study. But there can be no question that it enabled millions of ex-servicemen to purchase homes, thereby stimulating the boom in the construction industry. That hundreds of thousands of men who, otherwise, would not have been able to obtain a higher education, became college graduates. These college graduates became the base material for the electronics revolution. Their purchasing power is high. They have provided the impetus that has raised the standard of living of the U.S. far above that of any other country. They are raising children better fed, better housed, better educated than any previous generation in history.

Yet the G.I. Bill of Rights, quite inadvertently, turned out to be a measure that grievously discriminated against the Negro.

It discriminated against him because his educational level —as well as physical condition—was so low that the armed forces would not take him in the first place. In the South, where by far the greater number of Negroes still lived 20 years ago, two thirds were rejected by the armed forces because they failed the mental test, a passing grade on which is the equivalent of a seventh- or eighth-grade education. This was four times the rate of white failures.

That this is a result of educational failure and not of innate ability is demonstrated by the fact that in the Western states the Negro failure rate of 31 per cent—although still two and a half times that of the white—was less than half that in the South. And, in fact, came very close to the white failure rate of 26 per cent in the Northeastern states.

It may now be better understood why white median income increased by $407 more than Negro in the decade between 1950 and 1960.

*   *   *

The government of the U.S. would do well to consider enactment of an economic bill of rights for the poverty classes —whether Negro, Mexican, or white. This should not, and must not, be viewed as a welfare or a giveaway program, but a capital investment in human resources that may be expected to repay, ultimately, many times the initial investment.

Such a program should embody, and be planned for, both short-term and long-term goals. If it does not view all of the problems as a unit, but attempts to solve them by a piecemeal approach it is very likely to fail. For to protect a population from smallpox is not the same as insuring its health.

The short-term program must aim for the alleviation of immediate pressures. Perhaps the most difficult, yet essential, task will be to provide jobs for people who, basically, lag a generation behind the economy of this country.

Dead-end make-work programs are not the answer. Neither is a training program in simple skills that are already obsolescent. The only real hope, though one encompassing great difficulties, is to launch a massive effort to raise the people to the level required by modern-day technology. This can only be done with the full participation of American industry. Just as the government has, in the past, subsidized certain industries, such as airplane manufacturers and airlines—not to speak of agriculture—which provide essential services, and has granted special tax incentives for capital investment, so it should now subsidize and provide incentives for industries participating in long-term training programs for previously unskilled workers. A small start has been made in this direction. But it is only a small start.

A major stumbling block to the inception of such a program is the fact that large proportions of the unskilled are functional illiterates. Industry should not be asked to cope with persons who cannot fill out orders or understand written instructions. (Often they cannot even understand *spoken* instructions, because of their lack of verbal skills.) It is ironic that the world's greatest industrial nation, which has sponsored literacy programs in underdeveloped countries everywhere, should exhibit such little concern for the illiterates in its own back yard.

It is essential, therefore, that the government initiate a program of adult literacy education whose theoretical aim is to bring every person in the U.S. up to at least a seventh- or eighth-grade reading and writing level.

A study should be made of the police practice of keeping permanent records of every arrest, no matter what the disposition. However theoretically innocent such a practice may be, the practical effect is the conviction of persons without a trial. It is, in truth, inimical to the operation of the police itself, since every person who, as a result, finds it difficult or impossible to obtain a job becomes a potential police problem. If the police deem it essential that arrest records be retained, and the courts support the police, then the records should be classified and made available to no one except the police authorities themselves.

Legal and consumer counseling offices should be established by the government where they are easily accessible to everyone in the poverty areas. Laws should be passed placing additional restraints on the rate of interest that may be charged, and on sales practices that, if not strictly illegal, are morally reprehensible.

Whereas the doctrine of *caveat emptor* may be one that can be lived with by the middle class, which has learned to protect itself to some degree against sharp business practices, it is too much to expect a semieducated, virtually illiterate lower-class person to do so, and there should be a reduction of an individual's responsibility to protect himself. In fact, the experience of such suburbs as Larkdale, near Chicago, where 40 per cent of the residents went bankrupt in recent years—as a result of such follies as buying food freezers, worth an estimated $250, for $700 under a contract calling for an additional $500 in interest charges over a period of five years—seems to indicate that the middle class is almost as much in need of protective legislation as the poverty class.

Consumer counseling should be directed toward teaching the people the essentials of comparative shopping, how to tell a good bargain from a bad, and how to resist the pitches of unscrupulous salesmen.

The aftermath of the Los Angeles riot revealed that people in the poverty areas have all kinds of legal problems they are incapable of solving for themselves, and that, as a result, they fail to obtain the protection that the law presumably provides for all. Other problems stem from the expense of legal advice and court procedures. A woman may be "living in sin" for no other reason than that the $500 to $700 required for a divorce is more money than she has ever had all at once in her life. And, if she did have it, she would want to spend it for something of more material benefit to her than a divorce decree.

Welfare codes should be revised to stimulate rather than stifle individual incentive, and to induce the exercise of individual responsibility in the practice of birth control. While complex and difficult issues are involved, it is believed that it would have a salutary effect to permit women on welfare who go to work a total income considerably higher than those who do not. Consideration should be given to raising the bare-necessities-of-life allowance—which, in actuality, does not even suffice to provide the bare necessities—but sharply reducing the amount of money granted for each additional child born after a woman goes on welfare. While in theory this might have the effect of "punishing the children," in actuality, since each additional child would reduce a woman's standard of living (and there must be no doubt that she understands this), it is quite likely to have a profound effect on the attitude of "what's the difference if I have another one or not?"

These should be the short-term programs. Some of the long-term programs are of a parallel nature, but they will be vastly more difficult and expensive to achieve.

Since it is elementary that one cannot build a dam in the midst of a flood, one of the first long-range programs that will have to be tackled is that of bringing some discipline to the conception of children. With 30 million Americans in the poverty classification reproducing at a rate only slightly lower than that found in some countries of the Far East, it is evident that a program, if it is to succeed, cannot be of a half-hearted or piecemeal nature, hamstrung by the kind of specious morality that has prevented the Office of Economic Opportunity's birth control attempts from being effective. (OEO was prohibited from actively promoting birth control, and from providing contraceptive devices to unmarried women, who, of course, are the principal problem in the ghetto.) That the program will come under severe attack—from Catholic conservatives, on religious grounds, on the one hand, and Negro Nationalists, on the argument that it is a white scheme to exterminate the Negro, on the other—is inevitable. But every program of preventive medicine aimed at social improvement—from smallpox vaccination to the fluoridation of water—has faced such opposition in the past.

Since nothing is being done to lift the children out of the morass of the ghetto, the troubles of the parents are more than likely to become the troubles of the child. The scope of the problem may be understood when it is realized that it is not beyond the realm of possibility for an unmarried woman having six children to be responsible for 36 illegitimate grandchildren.

The only real hope for the children of the ghetto is education. To raise the standards of their education to the level enjoyed by middle-class children will take money and effort unprecedented in the educational field. It is not enough, as the McCone Commission suggests, to increase the intensity of academic education in poverty area schools by such measures as decreasing class size, and the like. The schools must be operated under the concept—entirely new on a mass basis—that they are responsible for every phase of a child's life. They must take over the functions the parents are either incapable of, or derelict in, performing.

This means that they will have to operate on a schedule of 12 or more hours a day, providing not only basic education, but a continuing program of sports and cultural activities, as well as study halls. They must take responsibility for the children's health and nutrition, and must provide the intensive counseling—not confined to educational matters—in those cases where the parents appear incapable of doing so themselves.

Clearly this will involve massive outlays of money that only the Federal government is capable of providing. To those who balk at the expense, one can give a simple answer. *Whether* or no the money is going to be spent is not in dispute, only *where* and *when*. If it is not spent in the schools, then it will be spent in the correctional institutions—at a cost of $4,000 per person per year—and for the support of uneducated people who are unable to support themselves.

Scholarship programs for higher education should be expanded so that college is not denied any person mentally capable of a college education, but they should be done so on a *quid pro quo* basis. If the government is to pay for four years of college, then the graduates should be committed to serve the government for an equal period of time—a policy that has been in effect in the service academies. Thus the skills acquired could be channeled back to aid in raising the standards of the poverty areas.

The government must undertake a large-scale program of property renewal in the deteriorating areas. It is incongruous that the poorest people should have to pay the highest prices for the essentials of life because, under the profit system, it does not pay large-scale firms to locate in these areas.

Industrialist H. C. "Chad" McClellan believes the government should, and will have to, provide insurance and financing for industries, supermarkets, and the like, since private rates are prohibitive. A study should be made of the advisability of creating tax incentives similar to those that have worked well in inducing industry to build in Puerto Rico, a previously underdeveloped area in many ways alike to the ghetto districts of the cities.

To stimulate the purchase of homes by people living in the ghetto, the government should provide home-loan insurance to the same extent it has done for ex-servicemen, since, again, the risks are too high for the setting of reasonable rates by private companies.

Finally, the government should put the weight of its prestige behind a reeducation of the American public regarding racial myths. The forms such a program may take are varied. They range from revision of textbooks to present a more balanced view of the Negro's place in history, to the encouragement of greater recognition by the media of mass communications that the Negro represents 10 per cent or more of the American population.

(It is ironic that the American sense of fair play insists on equal time on the air waves for political candidates, but has had no concern for the proportional representation of its minority people.)

*   *   *

Studies reported by Gordon W. Allport in *The Nature of Prejudice* have shown that prejudice tends not to be so much specifically directed as a general attitude; that the prejudiced person tends to be biased against any *number* of races, religions, cultures, or customs—anything that seems foreign. Yet it has been similarly demonstrated that prejudice may be tempered by education. That, in fact, there is an inverse correlation between education and prejudice—the higher the education, the less the prejudice.

*   *   *

In a way, Bob Bailey, a Negro member of CORE, summed it all up when he described his emotions during the riot.

"When I saw the police, and they were standing off—way off and wouldn't come down—I felt free for the first time in my life. I felt like I was really part of America, and America was part of me. And that if this is what the white people have been feeling all these years, what a wonderful thing it must be!

"I'd participated in the civil rights movement, but I'd never felt that way before. And it seemed to me that that was what America was all about. I felt like I had the Constitution in my brain and that my body and soul were part of the land— that I owned it and wanted to plant flowers and make it green and beautiful. And I ran in the park with the kids and shouted Hallelujah! Hallelujah!"

Methodology

Much has been written about the Los Angeles riot. Most of it has been fragmented, or presented from a specific viewpoint. It was the author's goal to compile a complete historical account.

Clearly, such an account could not be written before the records gathered by various agencies became available. The author was fortunate in being the first person granted access to many of these.

It was equally clear that, amidst the confusion and violence, a witness to an incident often saw, or was cognizant of, only one particular phase of it, and, as a result, had a mistaken impression of what had occurred. Only by piecing together impressions from various sources could such an incident be reconstructed in its entirety.

Between August of 1965 and May of 1966 the author devoted himself exclusively to research into the riot, assembling material that eventually filled an entire filing cabinet. This represented, in addition to information culled from documents compiled by various agencies, interviews and discussions of varying length with nearly 1,000 persons, and the written accounts of occurrences, as well as personal opinions, of some 500 more.

The author had become familiar with the south-central area a considerable period of time before the riot, and, by exercising prudence, was able to move about the area even while the riot was still in progress, thus observing some of the happenings firsthand.

The Los Angeles County District Attorney's office made available the four volumes, totaling more than 1,300 pages, of its investigation into the arrests of Marquette, Ronald, and Rena Frye, and Joyce Ann Gaines. Later, the office provided invaluable help in determining the disposition of the cases of those persons arrested during the riot, permitting the author to study the master sheet of felony case dispositions.

The cooperation of the California National Guard was outstanding. The author was given complete access to all documents pertaining to Guard action during the riot. These included the Guard's own unpublished historical account, logs and reports of the participating units, and 16 hours of taped interviews with officers and men who were on the scene. The author wishes to express his especial appreciation to Col. Robert L. Quick, assistant adjutant general.

Additional information regarding the actions of the National Guard, as well as developments leading to the Guard's mobilization, were furnished by the California Attorney General's office.

The Los Angeles Fire Department gave the author virtual carte blanche in examining its records in regard to the riot. These included, in addition to the written historical account, reports of various units, and the comments of the fire captains and battalion chiefs on the scene. Talks were held by the author with more than 60 firemen who participated in the action.

The Los Angeles Police Department permitted the author to examine fully and without restriction the log of the Emergency Control Center which listed every call received during the riot. This, together with the *Riot Capsule,* and the chronological account compiled by the McCone Commission, furnished an excellent outline to all the action that took place during the riot.

While Police Department policy does not permit other than department personnel to examine original reports, the author received a full and honest answer to every question asked regarding a specific action, and was thereby aided in clearing up many ambiguities. The author talked to numerous officers personally involved, and wishes, specifically, to thank Capt. Thomas King, Lt. Frank Beeson, Lt. Elbert W. Mead, and Sgt. Richard Rankin for the recounting of their impressions.

The author attended more than half of the coroner's inquests held to determine the circumstances surrounding the deaths of those persons killed during the riot, and read all of the 32 transcripts. Many persons, including officers on the scene and members of the families, were interviewed.

The L.A. County Probation Department provided data on the characteristics of persons arrested during the riot, and aided the author in interviewing some of the arrestees. Department memoranda and other documents provided much valuable background information.

The Bureau of Public Assistance made available, on a confidential basis, the case histories of persons receiving aid. The author examined some three dozen of these, in several instances following up with personal interviews of the recipients. The California Fair Employment Practices Commission provided the author with a score of case histories.

The complete transcript of the McCone Commission hearings, consisting of 18 volumes with some two million words of testimony, was read in its entirety by the author at the University of Southern California library, the depository for one of the eight copies of this document extant.

The records of some 200 felony trials—approximately 10 per cent of those that took place—were examined in detail by the author. In addition to documents secured from official sources, much information, including court transcripts, was obtained from private attorneys. The author personally attended 10 of the more important trials, including those of Rena Frye and Philip Brooks, the latter the only person to be brought to trial on a charge of murder.

The L.A. County Human Relations Commission was a valuable source of information regarding minority-majority relations, not only in Southern California but throughout the nation.

One hundred and fifty sworn statements—collected by various civil rights agencies—of personal experiences by area residents during the course of the riot were examined by the author. The author himself interviewed hundreds of other residents, including many who admitted participation in the riot. In several of these cases the people refused to furnish the author with their names, and in others they gave the information only with the proviso that the source would be kept confidential.

Hence, in several instances pseudonyms have been used to protect the identity of persons involved. All names of persons obtained from the confidential files of public agencies, such as the Bureau of Public Assistance, have been changed. The chapter-by-chapter record of sources at the end of the book provides a full list of pseudonyms.

In order to coordinate and cross-reference material from the many diverse sources with the actions that occurred during the riot—in some cases the author discovered that his files contained a half dozen or more descriptions of what proved to be a single incident—the author began an hour-by-hour plotting of the riot. This graph, 2 feet wide, ultimately grew to 25 feet in length. Among other things, it enabled the author to discover an apparent witness to one of the riot deaths recorded by the district attorney's office as a homicide by person or persons unknown. (See page 280.)

It is impossible to thank, individually, all of the persons who were helpful to the author. With one or two exceptions, all of the agencies who had personnel involved in the riot displayed a commendable frankness and honesty. As Deputy Chief Richard Simon of the LAPD told the McCone Commission: "We feel it's better to tell the truth. Even if the truth is not good, it's better than rumors, which are generally horrible."

Sources and References

Wherever personal or family histories that are not public record have been presented, names have been changed in order to protect the privacy of the persons involved. In some cases, such as those of youths—and their families—who were involved in the riot, certain additional details have been altered to preclude identification.

Wherever there is reference to "National Guard Records," the following material is indicated: the unpublished National Guard history, entitled "Military Support of Law Enforcement During Civil Disturbances"; 16 hours of tape recordings of interviews of officers and men made by Col. Robert L. Quick during and shortly after the riot; reports of officers on the scene; logs and records of the units involved.

Wherever there is reference to "Fire Department Records," the following material is indicated: the statistical and narrative histories compiled by the department; the written commentary and analyses of some 40 battalion chiefs and captains; various maps and charts; the author's interviews of approximately 60 members of the department employed in fighting fires in the riot area.

CHAPTER 1

The history of the Frye family was drawn by the author from a number of conversations with Marquette, Rena, and Ronald Frye, the records of Marquette Frye's earlier arrests, the transcript of the Frye family's conversation with Mayor Sam Yorty, and the author's talk with a friend of the family, Eva Gibson.

The scene on Avalon Blvd. Wednesday night was recreated by the author from the following material:

The Los Angeles County District Attorney's records of his investigation into the arrests, consisting of four volumes including statements of virtually every police officer, and many civilians, on the scene. The transcript of the trial of Rena Frye in Municipal Court, Los Angeles, October, 1965. The author's discussions with California Highway Patrol officers Bob Lewis, Lee Minikus, and Veale J. Fondville. A brief talk with Joyce Ann Gaines, and her father, Walter Gaines. The statement of, and the author's interview with, Sgt. Richard Rankin. Informal talks with various residents who averred that they were present.

The names of Gabriel Pope and Lada Young are pseudonyms, since, for obvious reasons, their real names cannot be revealed. The author first met Pope on the Wednesday of the week following the outbreak of the riot, and subsequently had two other conversations with him. While there is no real way to corroborate the account of his actions during the riot, they appear to jibe, essentially, with the facts as they are known. The same may be said of his family history, where some corroboration was possible. Miss Young agreed with Pope on most of the points.

The references to Communist Michael Lasky are corroborated by various of his writings in the author's possession, by the author's brief personal contact with him, and by the experiences of various Jordan High School students approached by him.

CHAPTER 2

The notes of, and the author's conversations with Sgt. Richard Rankin, Lt. Elbert W. Mead, and Lt. Frank Beeson are the sources for the description of the police action. The civilians' perspective is represented by various recountings, including those of Trixie Russell and Timothy O'Seyre (pseudonyms), the latter of whom the author was brought into contact with through his brother, Warner. (See Chapter 11.) The Los Angeles Police Department's Statistical Digest for 1964 provided the statistics quoted. The author met Frank Pinter (a pseudonym) during the course of the preliminary hearings into the riot cases.

CHAPTER 3

The history of the Williams family was derived from the records of the Bureau of Public Assistance, and the author's interview of family members. All names, and certain facts, have been changed to protect the identity of persons involved.

CHAPTER 4

Lt. Beeson, Deputy Chief Roger Murdock's declaration to the McCone Commission, the accounts of newspaper reporters, and the statements of various civilians are drawn on for the picture of the continuing action on the scene. The author met the youths to whom the pseudonyms Garban Tivoli Godrick and Pancho Pedrally (see Chapter 9) are ascribed, in Watts on August 17, 1965, and talked to them and two others for several hours.

CHAPTER 5

John Buggs, Leon Smith, Herbert Carter, Lt. Beeson, Robert Hall, Timothy O'Seyre, Atty. Morgan Moten, Tom Owan of the South Central Welfare Planning Council, and the accounts of Nicholas Beck and other newspaper reporters, provided the information on which the first part of the chapter is based.

The latter portion is based on talks with Dandy and Bill Briggs (pseudonyms), plus records of the Bureau of Public Assistance. Dandy first claimed, then denied, setting the car on fire, but remarked, "Anyway, I felt like it!" The author decided to use the incident because Dandy's state of mind, and the events that created it, are valid reflections of the psychological conditioning many Negro youths undergo.

CHAPTER 6

Supervisor Kenneth Hahn's experience was described by him to members of the Board of Supervisors and to the McCone Commission. Other descriptions come from Lt. Beeson and Sgt. Rankin. Statistics regarding Jordan High School were derived from its principal, William J. Settle. Lada Young's story was told by her to the author. Records of the California FEPC Commission, and Wesley Brazier's testimony to the McCone Commission regarding the problems of Negroes in the trucking industry back up elements of her story. Dave, the college student, recounted his experiences to the author. The incidents involving Cleo and Avan Ticey are drawn from court records, and from the District Attorney's investigation. Additional information was provided by Timothy O'Seyre and other civilian eye-witnesses.

CHAPTER 7

For the history of the Williams family, see Chapter 3.

Information on the Beverly Tate case comes from the District Attorney, police records, and newspaper accounts. Attorneys, welfare workers, the Better Business Bureau, the Public Defender's and District Attorney's offices, and others have recorded the many shady business practices prevalent in the ghetto. Several sources provided the author with descriptions of the customs in the housing projects. References to Johnnie Lee Tillmon and *Mothers Anonymous* are derived from the author's conversation with Mrs. Tillmon and from her testimony to the McCone Commission.

CHAPTER 8

A number of facts have been altered in the story of Barney Wateridge in order to disguise his identity. However, the essentials of his experiences, including the encounter with the police officer, the years of his roaming about the country, his arrest for marijuana peddling, and the making of a new life for himself are true.

CHAPTER 9

The description of the party in the garage is that given by Godrick, Pedrally, and another youth (see Chapter 4). The history of Pedrally was drawn, additionally, from talks with his mother, as well as from the records of the Bureau of

Public Assistance. The figures on disease are derived from an unpublished U.S. government study, "Hard-Core Unemployment and Poverty in Los Angeles."

CHAPTER 10

The incident of the two police officers aiding in the birth of a baby—not an uncommon occurrence in the poverty areas—was recorded by Lt. Beeson.

The experiences of the California Advisory Committee to the U.S. Civil Rights Commission, and the circumstances surrounding its hearing in Los Angeles, were drawn from the records of the committee, its "Report on California: Police-Minority Group Relations," and from records of the Los Angeles County Human Relations Commission.

A copy of the original memorandum written by California Asst. Atty. Gen. Howard H. Jewel was placed in the author's hands.

Several interviews were conducted by the author with John Buggs in order to obtain the report of his actions, as well as biographical data. Additional information was culled from various of his writings, and from his testimony to the McCone Commission.

Comparative statistics quoted are from the following sources:

"The Urban Reality," and "Minority Groups in Los Angeles County," studies published by the Los Angeles County Human Relations Commission; from "Hard-Core Poverty and Unemployment in Los Angeles," a U.S. government study; from "Economic Aspects of the Los Angeles Riots," a paper prepared for the McCone Commission by Jeffrey B. Nugent and Michael E. DePrano; from the McCone Commission testimonies of Dr. Paul Bullock and Prof. Walter Fogel of UCLA, and from an article by Los Angeles *Times* Labor Editor Harry Bernstein on March 28, 1966.

Special Order No. 33 is quoted from "Report and Recommendations of the Special Citizens Law Enforcement Committee," Jan. 6, 1964.

The incident involving Philip Wing was related by him to the McCone Commission.

References to police-minority group altercations and to circumstances surrounding the campaign to pass Proposition

14 are from records of the L.A. County Human Relations Commission.

The advertisement by the "Committee of One Million Caucasians" was carried by a Glendale newspaper in April, 1964.

The Harris Poll has periodically checked on white attitudes toward Negroes. The "different smell" question has drawn a 50 to 60 per cent positive response.

The result of the Edward Ramsford study is part of the record of the McCone Commission.

The reference to the experience of the blind girl in Orange County is from the records of the Southern California Community Relations Conference.

Quotations ascribed to Chief Parker in the latter portion of the chapter are from the Los Angeles *Herald-Examiner*.

CHAPTER 11

The names of Warner O'Seyre, a teacher at Jordan High School, his wife Marian, and his brother Timothy (see Chapter 2) are pseudonyms. The experience of Marian O'Seyre in attempting to obtain employment is factual, and is backed up by numerous case histories in the files of the California FEPC.

Figures on residential segregation and the discriminatory practices of realtors are from the records of the L.A. County Human Relations Commission, and the California Real Estate Commission.

Crenshaw Neighbors Association, as well as similar neighborhood organizations, have collected material on the problems of integrated neighborhoods.

Experiences of members of the Catholic Human Relations Council were described to the author by a number of persons, and testified to at the McCone Commission hearings by Miss Sue Welch.

Information pertaining to the area's health and hospital facilities was presented to the McCone Commission by Paul Ward, director of the California Health and Welfare Agency, and by Dr. Milton I. Roemer, professor of public health at UCLA.

Unscrupulous business practices were detailed by Helen Nelson, California State Consumer Counsel, to the McCone Commission. Additional information was derived by the author from the Los Angeles Public Defender's office, area so-

cial workers such as Tom Owan of the South Central Welfare
Planning Council, and conversations with residents.

The mood of the area on Thursday morning was drawn by
the author from his own observations, as well as the observations of various members of the L.A. County Human Relations Commission.

CHAPTER 12

The author was permitted access to several interoffice memoranda regarding the controversy between the police and probation departments. A three-hour discussion with Ralph Reese
resulted in the material attributed to him. Other information
came from Ralph Merola, president of Local 685 of the L.A.
County Probation Officers union, from Jim Burks of the
Group Guidance Unit, and from the Rev. Casper Glenn's testimony to the McCone Commission.

CHAPTER 13

The appraisal of the Los Angeles Police Department, prepared at the University of Southern California Youth Studies
Center by Prof. John Piffner, M. Oslund, and C. R. Guthrie,
was furnished to the author by Ralph Merola. Other information was derived from the LAPD Statistical Digest for
1964.

CHAPTER 14

The author is indebted to John Pannitch, director of the Bureau of Public Assistance, for authorizing the cooperation of
the bureau's social workers which made possible the compilation of the case histories of the two families to whom the
names of Williams and Pedrally have been ascribed. After in-
specting some 30 files and interviewing members of 12 families, the author believes that, with minor variations, the two
histories may be duplicated by the thousands.

Also included is information derived by the author from
conversations with social workers, and material furnished to

the McCone Commission by Ellis P. Murphy, the former director of the BPA.

The name of Anita Greyson is a pseudonym. Her experiences during the riot, including the receipt of the card from the Nazis after being injured, were related by her to the author. (See Chapter 20.)

CHAPTER 15

The following persons provided information pertaining to the Athens Park meeting: John Buggs, executive director of the County Human Relations Commission; Anthony Serrato, Jim Burks, and other members of the Group Guidance Unit; Curt Moody of the Southern California Community Relations Conference; Sgt. Vivian Strange of the LAPD; Rev. Joe Hardwicke of the Praisers of Zion Baptist Church; Rev. H. H. Brookins of the United Civil Rights Committee; Councilman John Gibson; Ralph Reese; and Supervisor Kenneth Hahn, and Insp. James Fisk and Deputy Chief Thomas Reddin of LAPD, in their testimonies to the McCone Commission.

References to LAPD practices and problems are derived from the 1964 edition of the Statistical Digest of the department, Atty. Hugh R. Manes's monograph, "A Report on Law Enforcement and the Negro Citizen in Los Angeles," and Chief Parker's appearances before the McCone Commission and a Los Angeles City Council committee.

Information relating to events occurring on the Frye family's ride to the police station was obtained from the District Attorney's investigation of the California Highway Patrol.

CHAPTER 16

Sources for the chapter are the Riot Chronology supplied by the McCone Commission; Lt. Gen. Roderick Hill and Col. Robert L. Quick of the California National Guard; Ralph Reese; and John Buggs and Leon Smith of the County Human Relations Commission.

Quotes attributed to Chief Parker were derived from his testimony to the McCone Commission, various statements to the press, and a booklet, "Police Chief William H. Parker

Speaks," prepared by the Southern California Community Relations Conference.

CHAPTER 17

Conditions in the 77th division were described to the author by sheriff's deputies, by Thomas King, police captain in charge of the division, by Lt. Frank Beeson, who headed the vice detail for some time, and by the undercover police investigator to whom the name Mac Benton has been given as a pseudonym. On occasions the author accompanied vice squad members on their rounds.

James C. Williams, executive director of the Los Angeles World Trade Center Authority, testified to the McCone Commission regarding his experiences with the police.

CHAPTER 18

The scene and conversations at the 77th division police station were re-created by the author from discussions with John Buggs, and from the testimonies of Buggs, Deputy Chief Roger Murdock, and the Rev. H. H. Brookins to the McCone Commission.

CHAPTER 19

Errol Lawrence—a fictitious person—is the prototype of a certain kind of police officer described to the author by past and present members of the LAPD, including one who is now professor of police science at a state university.

Statements attributed to Fi-Po were excerpted from the "Newsletter of the Fire and Police Research Association of Los Angeles," which claims a circulation of 2,000, and has as its motto: "What you believe depends largely upon what you believe in."

The statement attributed to the John Birch Society was contained in a full page advertisement in the Los Angeles *Herald-Examiner* entitled: "What's Wrong With Civil Rights?"

Court and police department records provided information on the actions of Offs. Price and Samaniego.

The police department trial of Off. Michael Hannon is described from the records of the case.

CHAPTER 20

The log of the Emergency Control Center, listing every incident reported during the riot, was made available to the author by the Los Angeles Police Department Bureau of Administration.

The incident between the Muslim and the police officers was witnessed by the author.

The statement by Officer "Wild Bill" Davis was made to District Attorney's investigators.

The statement by Deputy Chief Murdock was made before the McCone Commission.

Others contributing material to the chapter were Lt. Beeson, the Revs. Casper Glenn and Joe Hardwicke, Ralph Reese, Timothy O'Seyre, and Mac Benton. The incident at the service station was described by the attendant.

Additional information on the history of the Briggs family (see Chapter 5) was obtained from BPA records.

CHAPTER 21

Sources for the chapter were Los Angeles Fire Department and Police Department records, and newspaper accounts. Individual histories were recounted to the author by Mac Benton and Newlyn Brunton. The incident involving Raul Milera was derived from his sworn statement, and court records. Court records were also the source for the description of the action involving Harry L. Atkins. The experiences of Assemblyman Mervyn Dymally were recounted by him to the McCone Commission.

CHAPTER 22

For information in compiling this chapter the author relied on the ECC Log, on conversations with Sgt. Richard Rankin, Mac Benton, Col. Robert L. Quick, Pancho Pedrally, and various residents of the Jordan Downs Housing Project, as

well as on testimony to the McCone Commission by Col.
Quick, Deputy Chief Murdock, Lt. Gov. Glenn Anderson,
and John Billett. Police Department records provided the material on Leon LaCour.

In reference to Gabriel Pope and Lada Young, see Chapter 1.

CHAPTER 23

The testimonies of Chief Parker and Col. Quick before the
McCone Commission, and the author's conversations with
John Buggs and the Rev. Joe Hardwicke are the sources for
the chapter. The quote attributed to Mayor Sam Yorty was
taken from a statement by him to the press.

CHAPTER 24

The experiences of Wendell Collins and Harvey Claybrook
were related by them to the McCone Commission.

Descriptions of the early history of Watts are derived from
Carey McWilliams's *Southern California Country*.

Population density figures are from the Los Angeles County
Human Relations Commission's study, "The Urban Reality."

Watts on Friday morning was described to the author by
Atty. Morgan Moten, whose office is on 103rd St.; by Drs.
Francis Hobson and Christopher Taylor; by Carl Margolis;
and by Richard Townsend and Bill Armstead, who also contributed a variety of other material. Several teachers at Jordan
High School were helpful to the author. Quotes of high-school
students were excerpted by the author from a tape-recorded
discussion held by the students among themselves.

Statistics on the comparative standings of students in priv-
ileged and minority areas were presented to the McCone
Commission by Dr. Kenneth A. Martyn.

CHAPTER 25

The McCone Commission testimonies of Winslow Christian,
Chief Parker, Col. Quick, Gen. Hill, Lt. Gov. Anderson,

Richard Kline, and Sherill Luke were drawn on for the compilation of the chapter. Memoranda on the 1963 and 1964
meetings between National Guard and LAPD officers were
furnished the author by the California National Guard.

CHAPTER 26

Basic sources for the chapter were the ECC Log, and Fire
Department and National Guard records.

The author held a number of discussions and interviews
with Dr. Harold Jones.

Capt. Thomas King described his experiences in Watts to
the author, and an eye witness provided information on the
incident at the V and F Market.

Other material was drawn from testimony to the McCone
Commission by Wendell Collins and Atty. Gen. Thomas
Lynch.

In reference to Pancho Pedrally, see Chapters 4 and 14.

CHAPTER 27

The history and actions of Flip Borrago (a pseudonym) were
recounted by him to the author while he was in custody. Descriptions of the incident at South Park and subsequent events
were provided by Borrago; by Winston Slaughter, a college
student and former member of the Businessmen; by Dr. James
R. Silber of the Southeast Mental Health Clinic; by a number
of probation officers; and by Lt. Charles Rees of the police
department.

CHAPTER 28

The ECC Log, National Guard records, and the McCone
Commission testimony of Chief Parker, Maj. Gen. Charles
Ott, Col. Quick, Thomas Neusom, John Ferraro, Lt. Gov.
Anderson, Hale Champion, Sheriff Peter Pitchess, Undersher-
iff James Downey, and Deputy Chief Thomas Reddin were
the sources for the chapter.

CHAPTER 29

Fire Department, Police, National Guard, and court records were consulted in the compiling of the chapter.

Police officers contributing material were Lt. Elbert Mead, Sgt. Rankin, Mac Benton, and a number of others.

Court records provided information on the actions of Jimmie Hoffman, Robert Jackson, Norman Martin, and George Oliver Carter.

The deaths of Leon Posey, Jr., and Calvin Jones, Jr., are described from inquest testimony and additional statements by police officers and other witnesses.

The trial of Mardis Dorton, and a conversation with Sgt. Morris Yedwalski provided the material for the description of the action at the White Front Store.

Police Department records, Edward Jones, and the Los Angeles *Herald-Examiner* are responsible for the description of the occurrence at the McCray residence.

Mrs. Gladys Mozetti, a member of the hospital staff, described the scene at Oak Park Hospital to the author.

Information pertaining to the circumstances surrounding the death of Deputy Sheriff Ronald Ernest Ludlow was derived from the trial of Philip Brooks, and the author's conversations with Mac Benton and other persons who witnessed portions of the incident.

CHAPTER 30

Sources for the chapter are Fire Department and National Guard records, and the inquest into the death of Homer Ellis.

CHAPTER 31

Fire Department records, the inquests into the deaths of George Adams, Jr., Charles Shortridge, Rita Rena Johnson, and Warren Tilson, and the record of the trial of Willie Cobb, Willie Tom Little, and Errol Drew provided the nucleus of material. Sgt. Rankin related to the author descriptions of the events in which he was involved.

The controversy regarding the integration of the L.A. Fire Department is recounted from the accounts and records supplied by Atty. Arnett Hartsfield, Jr., from newspaper stories, and from the booklet, *The Mayor and the Fire Chief,* published by the University of Alabama Press.

CHAPTER 32

Sources for the chapter are the inquests into the deaths of Thomas Ezra Owens, Montague Whitmore, and Carlton Elliott; the trials of Julius Riggins, John E. Kirk, and Don Lockhart, and the sworn statement of the latter; the preliminary hearing in the case of Allen Arnett Browning; and the statement of Milton S. Ackerman.

CHAPTER 33

National Guard records, and the inquests into the deaths of Albert Flores, Sr., and Andrew Houston, Jr., were consulted in the writing of the chapter.

The description of the running down of Sgt. Wayne Stewart is based, in addition to National Guard records, on the court and probation records of Charlie Edward Rhone and Brooks Berry, and on the account of the incident by Marvin Goldsmith, a member of the California Attorney General's staff.

A description of the incident involving Ben Bennie Steel was obtained from court records.

CHAPTER 34

The death of Theophile Albert O'Neal is reported according to the inquest records and the statement of Harry Clay.

Court records are the source for the history and actions of Elvin Wharton.

In reference to Baby Doe Simmons and Cotter Williams, see Chapter 3; for Flip Borrago, see Chapter 27.

The acts ascribed to Errol Lawrence were, according to several police officers who related them to the author, committed by a number of officers during the riot. Other persons involved, such as National Guard and Fire Department personnel, and residents of the area, verified their authenticity in principle.

The statement of Capt. Richard W. Baer is contained in National Guard records.

The story of the experience of Betty Pleasant and Brad Pye was published in the Los Angeles *Sentinel*, and expatiated upon by Miss Pleasant in conversation with the author.

Police and Fire Department records, and the author's conversations with various officers are the source for the description of the changes in tactics.

Court records and a sworn statement were used in describing the experience of Shyrlee Williams.

CHAPTER 35

The trials of Freeman Waterhouse and James Allen provided information used in the first portion of the chapter.

The incident in which Miller Chester Burroughs and Leon Cauley were killed was re-created from inquest records and the trials of Louis Curtis Wharry, Calvin Joe Jones, and Lawrence Jacques.

Inquest records, the trial of Harold Battle, and conversations with Battle, Janice George, and attorney Stanley Malone provided the information on the death of Fentroy Morrison George.

Court records and a conversation with attorney Abraham Gorenfeld were used in the description of the incident involving Hurlbut Hardy, a pseudonym.

CHAPTER 36

The author became acquainted with Nathan Finckel, a pseudonym, at the site of his former store, and learned from him the circumstances surrounding its destruction. The shady practices of some poverty area merchants have been documented by social and welfare agencies.

Material relating to the Los Angeles *Herald-Dispatch* was culled from three years of issues of the newspaper, and from the author's conversations with Mrs. Pat Alexander.

CHAPTER 37

The description of the death of William Vernon King is based

on testimony at the inquest, and the author's conversation
with family members.

CHAPTER 38

The contents of the chapter are based on the author's interview of Rev. Seely James, a pseudonym. The minister expressed fears for his safety should his real name be used.

CHAPTER 39

The chapter is based on Fire Department and National Guard
records, the ECC Log, the author's personal observations, and
his conversations with Chief Ken Long, Lt. Raymond Wrenn,
and Marvin Goldsmith.

CHAPTER 40

The ECC Log, and the record of the trial of William Henry
Shufflebotham, Jr., and Grover Lee Talley were used in the
compilation of the chapter.

CHAPTER 41

In reference to Barney Wateridge, see Chapter 8.
    Other material used in the chapter was derived from the
following sources:
    National Guard and Police Department records; the au-
thor's personal observation of the area on Saturday, and his
conversations with residents; talks on two separate occasions
with "Dale"; and the court record of the trial of the latter.
The scene inside the jail was described to the author by various arrestees and a number of attorneys, and by Arnett
Hartsfield, Jr., and Mrs. Abraham Gorenfeld, who worked
with sheriff's deputies in an effort to process and provide bail
for the prisoners.

CHAPTER 42

The scene at Gold's has been re-created from the records of
the trials of various persons arrested there, and from the inquest into the death of Curtis Lee Gaines. The inquest into
the death of Willie Curtis Hawkins was the source of information on him. In reference to Dandy Briggs, see Chapter 5.

CHAPTER 43

National Guard, Police Department, and Sheriff's Department
records, and the inquest records into the deaths of Ramon
Luis Hermosillo and Charles Patrick Smalley were consulted
in writing "The Roadblocks of Watts." Additionally, the author talked to members of the Smalley family, and listened
to a tape recording made by Sgt. John Sutherland shortly after
the incident involving Smalley. The intelligence units of both
the Police and Sheriff's Departments reported they could find
no evidence that there were ever any groups of men using red
armbands. The reference to the experience of Sammy Davis,
Jr., is taken from his book, *Yes, I Can.*

CHAPTER 44

The history and death of Joe Nelson Bridgett are described
from testimony at the inquest, and from court and Probation
Department records.
    Circumstances surrounding the death of Juan Puentes are
described from inquest records and the author's own investigation.
    Fire Department, Police Department, and court records are
the source for the description of the actions of Robert Ernest
Pegues.
    The scene in the 4600 block of S. Broadway has been syn-
thesized from National Guard and Fire Department records,
from the author's conversations with Chief Ken Long and
with Sgt. Charles Buckland and other officers of the Police
Department, from the preliminary hearing in the cases of
Ann Randolph and Neal Minor, and from a sworn statement
by James Sanders, Jr.
    Other information was derived from the inquests into the

deaths of Joseph Glenwood Wallace and Frederick Maurice Hendricks, and from Police Department records of the cases of Eugene Shimatsu, Bobbie Cannon, and Bruce and Garland Moore.

CHAPTER 45

National Guard records, and the inquests into the deaths of Paul Edgar Harbin and Lonnye Lee Cook were the sources for the chapter.

CHAPTER 46

National Guard and Police Department records, the ECC Log, and Chief Parker's public statements are the sources.

CHAPTER 47

National Guard and Police Department records, the ECC Log, and inquest records into the deaths of Richard Raymond Lefebre, Neita Love, Aubrey Gene Griffin, and Joseph Irving Maiman, plus conversations with family members of the deceased, provided the nucleus of information.

The particulars of the incident involving Willie Walker are taken from his sworn statement, and from court records.

CHAPTER 48

Shortly after the riot, the author was able to listen in on a bull session of a group of youths who had participated in it. The material in the first part of the chapter was derived therefrom.

In reference to Gabriel Pope, see Chapter 1.

CHAPTER 49

National Guard, Police Department, and court records were consulted in the writing of the chapter. The author's personal observations are responsible for the description of the Joe Pyne television program, Martin Luther King's visit to Watts, and the meeting at Westminster between area residents and representatives of Gov. Brown. Attorney Roscoe Carroll, who headed the legal aid office in Watts, familiarized the author with legal problems stemming from the riot.

Capt. Thomas King described the visit of the German journalist to the 77th police station, and Lt. Robitaille the incident at the roadblock.

Insurance and business problems of the area are described from a series of articles in the Los Angeles *Times* by Paul Beck, and the McCone Commission testimonies of D. Gene Meyers, P. O. Corbett, Sadie Rubenstein, and Leon Beck.

CHAPTER 50

National Guard and Police Department records and the ECC Log provided information for the first part of the chapter. The incident at the Muslim Mosque is described from testimony by Deputy Chief Thomas Reddin to the McCone Commission, from Fire Department records, and from eye-witness reports of various police and National Guard officers.

CHAPTER 51

Sources are the inquest into the death of Carlos Cavitt, Jr., National Guard records, the testimony of Chief Parker and Deputy Chief Murdock to the McCone Commission, and Mayor Yorty's public statements as reported in the press.

CHAPTER 52

Sources for the chapter are the testimony of William McFaden, presiding judge of the Los Angeles Juvenile Court, and of Betty M. Edmundson, a psychiatric social worker, to the McCone Commission; the master disposition sheet and other records of the District Attorney's office; an in-depth study of juveniles arrested, by the L.A. County Probation Department; the police and sheriff's departments records of arrests; the records of the Fire Department arson squad; court and attorneys' records; statistics compiled by the American Civil Liberties Union; the transcript of the Rena Frye trial; and the author's personal observations at the trials of Mrs. Frye and Philip Brooks.

CHAPTER 53

The description of the inquests is based on the transcripts, and the author's personal observations; and, in the case of Juan Puentes, by the author's own investigation. The analyses of the inquests by Atty. James N. Adler and Harold Solomon, associate professor of law at USC, were at the behest of the McCone Commission. Dist. Atty. Evelle J. Younger is quoted from a statement released by him, and from his testimony to the McCone Commission.

CHAPTER 54

The history of the second Watts riot has been written from the author's personal observations, from the accounts of various members of the L.A. County Human Relations Commission, from police department records, from newspaper reports, and from the trial and probation records of Sam Lewis Fulton and Thomas Lee Galloway.

The inquest into the death of Leonard Deadwyler provided the information on which the latter part of the chapter is based.

CHAPTER 55

The chapter is based on the McCone Commission report, a follow-up report in August of 1966 by the Commission, the testimony of Chief Parker and other indicated police officers, the author's interview with H. C. "Chad" McClellan, and the author's conversation with various commission staff members.

CHAPTER 56

Sources are indicated as they appear.

CHAPTERS 57-59

Statistics used were derived from the *Census of Population, Characteristics of the Population,* Vols. 1 and 2, U.S. Department of Commerce, 1950 and 1960, as well as other volumes dealing with individual cities; and from the U.S. Department of Labor Publication, *The Negro Family,* edited by Daniel Patrick Moynihan.

Sociological and historical references to the Negro in the South are based on publications listed in the Bibliography, and on six years of the author's observations in Alabama, Louisiana, and Mississippi.

References to "Black Power" are from a series of articles under that title by Lerone Bennet, Jr., in *Ebony* magazine.

The reference to Carl Rowan's being reflexively shown to the service entrance at the White House is from an article by him in *Ebony.*

The passage on the comparative status of Mexican-Americans has been composed from testimony to the McCone Commission and from the records of the L.A. County Human Relations Commission.

Karl Key was the person claiming to be not subject to the draft; Fred Clark the person contending he was not subject to U.S. law, since he was being held "illegally in bondage" in the U.S.

The reference to the Chicago suburb of Larkdale is from the Los Angeles *Times* editions of Feb. 10 and March 11, 1966.

Other material was derived by the author from conversations with H. C. McClellan, Roscoe Carroll, Arnett Hartsfield, Jr., and Bob Bailey.

Bibliography

AFRICA

Davidson, Basil. *Black Mother*. Boston: Little, Brown & Co., 1961.
Murdock, George Peter. *Africa—Its People and Their Cultural History*. New York: McGraw-Hill, 1959.
Oliver, Roland A. & Fage, J. D. *A Short History of Africa*. Baltimore: Penguin Books, 1962.
Rayner, William. *The Tribe and Its Successors*. New York: Frederick A. Praeger, Inc., 1962.

HISTORY

Davis, Edwin A. & Hogan, William R. *The Barber of Natchez*. Baton Rouge: Louisiana State University Press, 1954.
Douglass, Frederick. *Narrative of the Life of Frederick Douglass*. Garden City, New York: Dolphin Books, 1963.
DuBois, W. E. Burghardt. *The Souls of Black Folk*. New York: Fawcett Publications, 1961.
Franklin, John Hope. *From Slavery to Freedom*. New York: Alfred A. Knopf, Inc., 1947.
Higginson, Thomas W. *Army Life in A Black Regiment*. Boston: Beacon Press, 1962.
Meier, August, & Rudwick, Elliott M. *From Plantation to Ghetto*. New York: Hill & Wang, 1966.
Ottley, Roi. *Black Odyssey*. New York: Charles Scribner's Sons, 1948.
Phillips, Ulrich B. *American Negro Slavery*. New York: D. Appleton & Co., 1918.
Starkey, Marion Lena. *Striving to Make It My Home*. New York: W. W. Norton & Co., 1964.
Tannenbaum, Frank. *Slave and Citizen*. New York: Alfred A. Knopf, Inc., 1946.
Washington, Booker T. *Up From Slavery*. New York: Bantam Books, Inc., 1956.

Woodward, Comer Vann. *The Strange Career of Jim Crow*. New York: Oxford University Press, 1957.

SOCIOLOGY

Bardolph, Richard. *The Negro Vanguard*. New York: Vintage Books, 1961.

Clark, Kenneth. *Dark Ghetto: Dilemmas of Social Power*. New York: Harper & Row, 1965.

Conrad, Earl. *Jim Crow America*. New York: Duell, Sloan & Pearce, 1947.

Drake, St. Clair & Clayton, Horace R. *Black Metropolis*. New York: Harcourt, Brace & Co., 1945.

Frazier, E. Franklin. *Black Bourgeoisie*. New York: Collier Books, 1962.

Johnson, Charles S. *Growing Up in the Black Belt*. Washington, D.C.: American Council on Education, 1941.

Kardiner, Abraham. *The Mark of Oppression*. New York: W. W. Norton & Co., 1951.

Karon, Bertram F. *The Negro Personality*. New York: Springer Publishing Co., 1958.

Lincoln, C. Eric. *The Black Muslims in America*. Boston: Beacon Press, 1963.

Lomax, Louis E. *The Negro Revolt*. New York: Harper & Row, 1962.

Thorpe, Earl E. *The Mind of the Negro*. Baton Rouge: Ortlieb Press, 1961.

STRIVING FOR EQUALITY

Baldwin, James. *Another Country*. New York: The Dial Press, 1960. *The Fire Next Time*. New York: The Dial Press, 1962. *Nobody Knows My Name*. New York: The Dial Press, 1961. *Notes of a Native Son*. Boston: Beacon Press, 1955.

Furnas, J. C. *Goodby to Uncle Tom*. New York: Sloane, 1956.

Handlin, Oscar. *Fire Bell in the Night: The Crisis in Civil Rights*. Boston: Little, Brown & Co., 1964.

Hentoff, Nat. *The New Equality*. New York: The Viking Press, 1964.

King, Martin Luther. *Stride Towards Freedom*. New York: Harper & Bros., 1958.

Mitchell, Glenford E. *The Angry Black South*. New York: Corinth Books, 1962.

Nichols, Lee. *Breakthrough on the Color Front*. New York: Random House, 1954.

Peck, James. *Freedom Ride*. New York: Simon & Schuster, Inc., 1962.

Proudfoot, Merrill. *Diary of a Sit-In*. Chapel Hill: University of North Carolina Press, 1962.

Redding, J. Saunders. *On Being Negro in America*. Indianapolis and New York: Bobbs-Merrill Co., 1951.

Wright, Richard. *Black Boy*. New York: Harper & Row, 1937.

MISCELLANEOUS

Allport, Gordon W. *The Nature of Prejudice*. Reading, Massachusetts: Addison-Wesley Publishing Co., 1954.

Bagdikian, Ben H. *In the Midst of Plenty*. Boston: Beacon Press, 1964.

Bibby, Cyril. *Race, Prejudice & Education*. New York: Frederick A. Praeger, Inc., 1960.

Blausten, Albert P. & Ferguson, Clarence C., Jr. *Desegregation and the Law*. Rutgers, New Jersey: Rutgers University Press, 1957.

Cash, W. J. *The Mind of the South*. New York: Alfred A. Knopf, Inc., 1941.

Collins, Winfield H. *The Truth About Lynching and the Negro in the South*. New York: Neale Pub. Co., 1918.

Dollard, John. *Caste and Class in a Southern Town*. New York: Harper & Bros., 1949.

Friedman, Leon (Ed.). *Southern Justice*. New York: Pantheon Books, 1965.

Haas, Ben. *KKK*. Evanston, Illinois: Regency Books, 1963.

Handlin, Oscar. *Race and Nationality in American Life*. Boston: Little, Brown & Co., 1950.

Key, V. O. Jr. *Southern Politics*. New York: Alfred A. Knopf, Inc., 1949.

McWilliams, Carey. *Southern California Country*. New York: Duell, Sloan & Pearce, 1946.

Rowan, Carl T. *Go South to Sorrow*. New York: Random House, 1957. *South of Freedom*. New York: Alfred A. Knopf, Inc., 1952.

Silberman, Charles E. *Crisis in Black and White*. New York: Random House, 1964.

Silver, James W. *Mississippi: The Closed Society*. New York: Harcourt, Brace & World, 1964.

Smith, Lillian E. *Killers of the Dream*. New York: W. W. Norton & Co., 1961.

Stringfellow, William. *My People Is the Enemy.* New York: Holt, Rinehart & Winston, 1964.

BOOKLETS

————. *Californians of Spanish Surname.* State of California, Division of Fair Employment Practices, May, 1964.

————. *FEPC Report.* 1961 & 1962, and Jan. 1, 1963—June 30, 1964.

————. *Hard Core Unemployment and Poverty in Los Angeles.* United States Government Study (unpublished).

Manes, Hugh R. *A Report on Law Enforcement and the Negro Citizen in Los Angeles.* (Privately published) July, 1963.

————. *Military Support of Law Enforcement During Civil Disturbances.* Military Department, State of California. (Draft Copy, unpublished).

————. *Negro Californians.* State of California, Division of Fair Employment Practices, June, 1963.

————. *The Negro Family.* U.S. Department of Labor.

————. *Report on California: Police-Minority Group Relations.* California Advisory Committee to the U.S. Commission on Civil Rights, August, 1963.

————. *Riot Participant Study.* Los Angeles County Probation Department, November, 1965.

Rowe, Arthur J. *Profiles of Delinquency.* Los Angeles County Department of Community Services, 1962.

Sherwood, Frank P. & Markey, Beatrice. *The Mayor and the Fire Chief.* University of Alabama Press, 1959.

————. *Special Citizens' Law Enforcement Committee: Report and Recommendations.* Los Angeles County Human Relations Commission, Jan. 6, 1964.

————. *Statistical Digest.* Los Angeles Police Department, 1964.

————. *The Urban Reality.* Los Angeles County Human Relations Commission, June, 1965.

————. *Violence in the City—An End or a Beginning?* Governor's Commission, December, 1965.

PAMPHLETS AND PAPERS

Buggs, John. *The Negro Mood—A Synthesis from Baldwin to Podhorotz. Police-Community Relations—A Critique on Issues That Tend to Divide Us. The Social Dynamics of Relations Between Minority and Majority Group Members. It Can Happen Here: The Shape of Things to Come.*

———. *Log,* Emergency Control Center.

Jackson, M. B. *The Second Civil War.*

Jewel, Howard H. *Memo* to: Atty. Gen. Stanley Mosk, May 25, 1964.

Lohman, Dr. Joseph D. *Significant Changes in Our Society.* L.A. County Dept. of Community Services.

———. *Minority Groups in Los Angeles County.* L.A. County Human Relations Commission, October, 1964.

———. *Population and Housing in Los Angeles County—A Study in the Growth of Residential Segregation.* L.A. County Human Relations Commission, March, 1963.

———. *Proposals for the Improvement of Human Relations in the Los Angeles Metropolitan Area.* L.A. County Human Relations Commission, November, 1965.

———. *Report and Recommendations Concerning Recent Incidents Involving Police and Minority Groups.* L.A. County Human Relations Commission.

———. *Riot Capsule.* Los Angeles Police Department.

———. *Task Force Committee for the Reduction of Community Tension and Prevention of Riots.* South Central Welfare Planning Council.

———. *Youth Problems and Needs in the South Central Area.* South Central Welfare Planning Council.

SPECIAL

———. *Transcripts* of Testimony. Governor's Commission on the Los Angeles riot. Volumes I through XVIII.

ABOUT THE AUTHOR

A graduate of Stanford University, ROBERT CONOT has been a newspaper reporter, an editor and a television writer. Before moving to California, he lived and attended schools in Louisiana, Mississippi and Alabama for six years. *Rivers of Blood, Years of Darkness* is his second published book.

TWO DOCUMENTS OF MAJOR INTEREST
TO ALL AMERICANS

On November 29, 1963 President Lyndon B. Johnson appointed a special committee of distinguished Americans under Chief Justice Earl Warren to search for the truth behind the most shocking crime of the century. Here are the two monumental documents based upon The Warren Report. Now, as discussion continues to center around the conclusions of this report, every American should read these essential books.

☐ **PZ2935 REPORT OF THE WARREN COMMISSION ON** ($1.00) **THE ASSASSINATION OF PRESIDENT KENNEDY,** edited by *The New York Times*. Here are the complete and official conclusions reached after more than six months of interrogation and investigation—the long awaited answers to questions the world had been asking. In addition to the Report itself, the Bantam edition contains exclusive material prepared by the staff of the world's great newspaper, *The New York Times*, including 32 pages of exhibits and evidence, an introduction by Harrison Salisbury as well as background articles by Tom Wicker, Anthony Lewis and James Reston.

☐ **PZ2966 THE WITNESSES: HIGHLIGHTS OF THE HEAR-** ($1.00) **INGS BEFORE THE WARREN COMMISSION ON THE ASSASSINATION OF PRESIDENT KENNEDY,** selected and edited by *The New York Times*. This 626-page book contains about 300,000 words of the key testimony of important witnesses—in their own words—plus 64 pages of significant exhibits. Here in one volume are the highlights from the full twenty-six volumes of testimony and exhibits presented in hearings before the Warren Commission. Also included are the official prefaces discussing the full contents of the twenty-six volumes and an introduction by Anthony Lewis. An invaluable companion volume to REPORT OF THE WARREN COMMISSION.

Buy these Bantam Books wherever paperbacks are sold, or write—

THE
COMPLETE
TEXT

U.S. RIOT COMMISSION REPORT
WHAT HAPPENED?
WHY DID IT HAPPEN?
WHAT CAN BE DONE?

REPORT OF THE NATIONAL ADVISORY COMMISSION ON CIVIL DISORDERS

SPECIAL INTRODUCTION BY TOM WICKER OF
The New York Times

WITH 32 PAGES OF SELECTED PHOTOGRAPHS

A Bantam Book/ $1.25/ Where paperbacks are sold

40-200